"In *On the Edge of Human Imagination*, Thys unfolds the thesis that it is precisely in its limits that the essence of the human comes into its own par excellence. Using examples from psychoanalytic practice, art and literature, and linking these to ideas from philosophy, Thys gives language to situations in which the linguistic is under pressure. The flowery treatises exemplify the author's broad background. From ingredients of all his worlds, he makes new creations. Thys is a true word artist. The book is 'food for thought' and is very suitable for joint reading in, for instance, intervision groups; it provides new language for sharing experiences."

Esther Spuijbroek in *Tijdschrift voor Psychoanalyse en haar toepassingen* [*Journal of Psychonalysis and its applications*]

"In *On the Edge of Human Imagination*, Thys arrives at a coherent theory of fascination and the 'inhuman'. His lucid exploration of the limits of the human is marked by a deep engagement with several thinkers and disciplines and provides a framework to better understand certain experiences, such as trauma. Thys' clear use of language also makes the book a good introduction to various currents within philosophy and psychoanalysis. He deftly manages to draw the reader into his reflections and thought processes. The diversity of vignettes makes the reading itself a fascinating experience."

Kasper Essers in *Filosofie en Psychiatrie* [*Philosophy and Psychiatry*]

I0130810

On the Edge of Human Imagination

In this fascinating book, Michel Thys explores the limitations of human imagination and symbolization, showing the potentially destructive result of a mind that cannot confront reality. His wide-ranging research takes us into the domain of the unimaginable, unthinkable and unspeakable.

Divided into four parts, *On the Edge of Human Imagination* sees Thys adopt a phenomenological perspective to move through experiences encountered in the analyst's room, from depression and psychosis to PTSD. Through a dialogue with philosophers such as Jean-Paul Sartre, Maurice Blanchot and Emmanuel Levinas, Thys investigates the relationship between fascination, identification, socio-cultural phenomena and aesthetic pleasure. Throughout, he uses the paintings of Edward Hopper, Sophocles' *Antigone*, Mary Shelley's *Frankenstein*, Franz Kafka's *Metamorphosis* and Charlie Chaplin's *Modern Times* to support his ideas. Integrating Freudian, Kleinian and Bionian theories, he shows the psychic impact of humanity's attempt to balance fear and passion on the edge of the imaginable and the liminality of the search for meaning. The book brings together psychoanalytic theory and practice and philosophical anthropology, confronting, in the end, Freud's ideas of the death drive with Sartre's understanding of the desire for being as the main driving force in human existence.

This book offers an illuminating evaluation of what it means to be human, making it an important read for psychoanalysts, psychologists and psychotherapists, as well as philosophers interested in the intersection between psychoanalytic, philosophical and phenomenological thought.

Michel Thys is a clinical psychologist, psychotherapist, psychoanalyst and doctor of philosophy. He is a member of the Flemish Association of Psychoanalytic Therapy and the Belgian School of Psychoanalysis. He is the former editor-in-chief of the Dutch-Flemish journal *Tijdschrift voor Psychoanalyse*. He works in private practice in Antwerp, Belgium.

On the Edge of
Human Imagination

Philosophical-Psychoanalytic Perspectives

Michel Thys

Routledge
Taylor & Francis Group

LONDON AND NEW YORK

Designed cover image: Berlinde De Bruyckere, Aanéén-genaaid [Sewn-together], 2000, watercolor and pencil on paper, 48 x 32 cm, Collection De Pont Museum Tilburg, copyright Peter Cox

First published 2025
by Routledge
4 Park Square, Milton Park, Abingdon, Oxon OX14 4RN

and by Routledge
605 Third Avenue, New York, NY 10158

Routledge is an imprint of the Taylor & Francis Group, an informa business

British Library Cataloguing-in-Publication Data
A catalogue record for this book is available from the British Library

ISBN: 978-1-032-84988-1 (hbk)
ISBN: 978-1-032-80212-1 (pbk)
ISBN: 978-1-003-51598-2 (ebk)

DOI: 10.4324/9781003515982

Typeset in Times New Roman
by Apex CoVantage, LLC

To my grandsons Hektor, Odin and Idris,
for long lives full of imagination.

Contents

Onset and setup

The limits of representation, imagination and meaning

Man is a creature of imagination. Spinoza, among others, sometimes called a fore-runner of psychoanalysis, leaves no doubt about this in his *Ethics*. By 'representation', Spinoza understands a perception that is not determined by the confrontation with a present object, which distinguishes it from sensation. It is an independent action of the thinking mind. What is the operation of the human mind other than envisaging, imagining and putting in one's mind what is not plainly given? Desiring, coveting, fantasizing, thinking about something, remembering, indulging in dreams of the future, contemplating possible actions, cherishing feelings – all involve imagination. Every 'soul-affair' is accompanied by a representation or image (*imaginatio*) of the thing at which it is directed. 'Man thinks' is one of Spinoza's foundational propositions (Spinoza 1979, pp. 63–64). Sadness, for example, is to imagine that something one loves is to be destroyed. To imagine, however, that something that one hates, perishes, will rejoi. The basis of all representations and, therefore, the primordial to the being of the mind, according to Spinoza, is the representation of one's own body.

We also find this latter idea, albeit in a different coloration, in psychoanalysis. The Austrian-English psychoanalyst Melanie Klein worked out – in the wake of Freud's drive theory – a whole vision of how the baby's first representations arise from a kind of primary 'interpretations' of bodily sensations. Our earliest representations are still very bodily, but by their representational nature, they already take some distance from that bodily. The sensation is their source; they lean closely to it, but they no longer coincide with it. Of course, a biological substrate is needed for thinking, and of course, the physical world of experience remains a lifelong source of inspiration, but at the same time, all thinking is inevitably also a distancing from the purely organic. By desiring, imagining, remembering, using language and so on, we already no longer coincide with that substrate without question. It is part of man's 'nature' not to be completely absorbed in (his) nature.

This paradoxical positioning of what is typically human is found in both philosophy and psychoanalysis. The many different views and not always reconcilable points of discussion and emphasis within both disciplines are transcended by that one fact: Man is an imaginary being. The German philosopher Martin Heidegger, continuing from his predecessors, formulates a distinction between being and

DOI: 10.4324/9781003515982-1

thinking. Although thinking, which he too understands as envisaging and imagining, is not separate from being, just by thinking man does not coincide with being as such. And with Sartre, man is not a being himself, but from his empty consciousness, is involved in the being of the world. Things are, man as a creature of consciousness is not(hing). For Sartre, imagination is an essential structure of consciousness, which can never be only a perception of reality. In this, he concurs with Spinoza's definition of representation. Precisely because consciousness can imagine, it can distance itself from the natural world. In this imagining or propositional consciousness, human freedom finds its origin.

Meanwhile, Sigmund Freud has shown that the pure drive can only tilt to a psychic level via representations and how our entire psychic household derives from thing representations and word representations. Thinking, which develops from initial representations, is a suspension of motor drain and is a trial-and-error, 'internal' action which includes, for example, fantasizing and daydreaming. The whole theory of thought of the English psychoanalyst Wilfred Bion, who combines his strong influence of Klein with a distinctly Kantian slant, is a commentary and further elaboration on this: man is a thinking being through which the thing-in-itself becomes inaccessible.

So much for a few bucks within and between psychoanalysis and philosophy. I present them to reflect roughly how imbued we are with the image of man as an imaginary being who does not naturally coincide with but is intensely involved in things, in reality. The human mind, human functioning, interpersonal relations and forms of coexistence, the whole spectrum from small everyday actions and experiences to grand cultural achievements, are expressions and productions of this immeasurable imagination.

This forms the starting point of and impetus for the present book. However, it is not its focus. The aim of the book precisely concerns the *limits* of the self-evidence of this starting point. That man is an imaginary being is so obvious, so intertwined with our idea of man, that we carelessly ignore its limits. Man's capacity for imagination may seem inexhaustible – something can be as crazy or bizarre as we imagine it – yet this capacity is not endless. To reinforce the extraordinary impact of an event or phenomenon, we say, 'this defies all imagination' or 'reality surpasses imagination'. We then end up in the realm of what we call the unimaginable or the unthinkable. As soon as we make statements about it, think about it or write about it, we naturally bring it back into our imaginary world anyway. Nevertheless, this never quite works and there is a sense of a zone at the limit of our experiential potential in which things do not allow themselves to be imagined or depicted in the usual sense of the word. More strangely, our thinking and imagining are also involved in, or perhaps are attracted to, that boundary because we are not satisfied with its limitation.

Throughout or hidden behind our usually comfortable sojourn in our familiar linguistic space of representations, there also plays a dimension of being intrigued by its dark margins. At the perilous edge of our humanity, the unfathomable abyss exerts a lurid attraction on us, the abyss into which words and thoughts threaten to disappear, but in which we also hope to gain new experiences, experiences beyond imagination, where words and thoughts are superfluous or inadequate. Eager as we are, we also want to be able to imagine the unimaginable; we also want to be able to say the unsayable. There is a fascination with 'unimaginable representations', representations that undermine or compromise their representational character as such because there is too much reality and too little distance. Because it is precisely because of this that functioning as human beings is compromised, this fascination is not free of anxiety. With the French psychoanalyst Jacques Lacan, we can say that human desire, the dynamics of which is precisely kept going by an unattachable deficit, is directed at the Thing as such, at *la Chose,* but precisely to be able to continue to function as desire, it must also keep its distance from that same Thing.

We cannot actively turn off our insatiable 'urge to imagine' ourselves. If we imagine something unimaginable, it is no longer unimaginable, for it has already nestled itself in our imagination. The unimaginable-as-unimaginable can only surprise us unexpectedly and can only suddenly appear before it can even be called an imagination. Perhaps the unimaginable belongs to an elusive in-between area between perception and sensation. We cannot prepare for the confrontation with the dark margins of the imaginable; it can only bewilder us. We are thrown into it despite and beyond ourselves. Spinoza (1979, p. 196) defines bewilderment as the fear that makes man so dumbfounded that he cannot avert some evil. His desire to avert evil is hindered by astonishment.

Probing these margins of the human realm of imagination is the focus of this book. It is about the whole field of tension in which phenomena take place that challenge the limits of the imagination, that baffle us, put our functioning as a subject under pressure or freeze its dynamics, render us speechless and immobilize our thinking, that affect language and the symbolic, but that can also inspire or enrapture us in an overwhelming and unforeseeable way. The very act of letting go of the familiar regions of the human also opens up unsuspected new horizons. It seems that this zone at the edge of human experience can also precisely produce very intense experiences, 'experiences' that hardly deserve that designation anymore because, at their peak, they undermine or transcend our personal involvement in them. Precisely in their uncommon intensity, they deprive us of any personal position: we undergo the event more than it is something 'ours'. These phenomena on the edge of the phenomenal, that is, peripheral phenomena, can take a variety of forms, but each time, they are experiences that take us – usually briefly, but therefore not without long-lasting effects – out of our ordinary, suspend our human functioning or threaten to do so. These are both, in a 'negative' sense, traumatic experiences or confrontations with the catastrophic, as well as in a 'positive' sense, mysteriously encountering previously unthinkable completely new things that can also throw the subject into total confusion. The celestial or infernal of such experiences are not always easily distinguishable, their revelatory and killing scope sometimes running into each other. Then, the person (or the group) is overwhelmed by something that he cannot immediately bring home, cannot connect with anything and, thus, does not connect with the familiar chain of representations. It, therefore, initially presents itself as unimaginable.

Because the whole domain of representation, imagination, is so closely linked to meaning and sense, this will also be a focus of attention. The notions of sense and meaning, as well as truth, are brought into existence precisely by imagining. By not being the thing itself or coinciding with it, we can only imagine it, envisage it and give signs to it. Due to our 'lack of being', we signify things, making them mean this or that. Language, this collection of signs, refers to things but can never replace them. Our linguistic wealth is always deficient in this sense, but it does establish a field of meaning and symbolization. Every human child is born into an already existing field of meaning, a generous supply in which it can seek its way and its place. Within this collective field of support, this place will also be co-colored by individual drives and phantasmatic baggage and thus never exclusively determined by that field in itself. Every dynamic of symbolization and assignment of meaning, like identity development, is the result of the body and others.

To say that man is a being of representation or an imagining being is to say that he is a symbolizing being. And symbols always refer to something else, mean something. They can evoke the symbolized very powerfully; yes, their eloquence almost makes it present, but they can never coincide with it because then they would no longer be symbols, and all meaning would be lost. Inherent in the connecting dynamics of reference inherent to symbolization is thus also the preservation of distance: without distance, no reference and thus no creation of meaning is possible. It is precisely the tension between the two that makes a meaningful human reality appear.

A collective term that in philosophical anthropology and psychoanalysis brings together all phenomena related to imagining, signifying, representing and symbolizing is *the representational*: processes that relate to something or represent something and thereby distance themselves from its pure *presence* in reality. Representation refers to a possible reality and thus, by definition, does not coincide with it. How closely can representations approach the thing itself without meaning ceasing to exist entirely? Where does representation pass into presence and vice versa? Can we describe phenomena whose representational character is under pressure or in which the movement from presence to representation is prevented? Again, we are on the fringes of being human, as mentioned previously. Imagination and meaning, their possible rise and fall, go hand in hand. My research focuses on the limits of both the capacity of imagination and the capacity for assigning meaning, on experiences on its margins, experiences that put pressure on the representational and thus on the linguistic as such but at the same time (and because of this) bring its essential characteristics all the more forcefully to the fore.

Phenomena on the edge of meaning, on the edge of representation and imagination, on the edge of the symbolic, these are all typically human categories so that we can speak overarchingly of 'marginal or epiphenomena of the human' where man encounters his limits and that which makes him so typically human is cornered. But is this self-subversion not precisely what man is essentially directed toward, not as a conscious personal desire but as an inevitable tendency that accompanies his whole being? Does man perhaps show his true face precisely where he abandons himself? Just as it is precisely when we say goodbye to a dear person that the meaning or 'essence' he has for us becomes extra prominent and more intensely perceptible than ever, that is, precisely on the verge of his disappearance, so the human appears most strongly and impressively when it is about to disappear, when it falters or becomes uncertain. It is precisely in this almost-not-more-human, precisely on the edge of it, that the human appears most strongly. Then, the aforementioned peripheral phenomena are not incidental but, on the contrary, belong to the essence of being human. Man is as much a seeker of boundaries as he is a seeker of meaning. Precisely, as a seeker of meaning, he is also necessarily a seeker of limits. The edge shows the core. It is about experiences that leave an impression, impressive experiences. This book wants to give some impressions of them.

The successive chapters form a thematic whole and cover, as it were, the entire tension between *self-realization* in the most intense experiences and how those very same experiences bring about *self-subversion*. The 12 chapters, divided into four sections, each treat a different angle that illustrates in different tones the overarching theme based on a specific sub-theme. The reader will notice that some aspects recur in different ways in various chapters and complement each other. Frequently, philosophical-anthropological lines of thought are confronted with phenomena from psychoanalysis or, conversely, experiences from psychoanalytic practice give rise to philosophical reflections. Through its penetrating practice and theory, psychoanalysis also teaches – as a clinical anthropology – what it is to be human and how precisely on its margins the human presents itself pre-eminently. The chapters refer to each other and build on each other but can also be read separately.

The *first part* revolves around the border experience of so-called 'fascination', which in its radical form, in which the subject is quasi-absorbed into an exclusive object pole, implies a loss of self that is as frightening as it is attractive.

With fascination, the starting point of the entire investigation, we are immediately in the middle of the issue the book seeks to present. Fascination is a prototypical experience of the limits of the familiar human, which I will broaden further in the book to related states and phenomena. Starting from experiences in psychoanalytic practice, the first chapter discusses a phenomenology of fascination in dialogue with Sartre, who wrote interesting things about it.

Building on this, the second chapter zooms in on how fascination can occur in the psychoanalytic clinic, and I present a 'metapsychology' that brings a clinical complement and clarification to the phenomenology described earlier. Central to this is the process of 'excessive projective identification', in which the subject becomes almost completely absorbed in the other, resulting in a solidified metamorphosis consisting of rejected parts of the self.

In the third chapter, I try to show that in severe trauma, as in war trauma, torture or early childhood sexual abuse, there is often a dimension of fascination. Trauma in itself is something from which a certain fascination emanates, and the traumatized subject himself, in a state of fascination, often finds it difficult to detach himself from what has imposed itself as so self-destructive. Injury and wonder are intertwined bizarrely. The idea that fascination and trauma evoke something of what the 'desire-for-being' is directed toward brings us back to Sartre and completes the circle.

The experience of impending self-loss puts pressure on the subject's identity. It no longer knows who or what it is or desperately seeks a possible identity in the fascinating object to which it is so 'attached'. The *second part* focuses on this problem of identity and broadens it to different areas of life. The underlying question is whether our so-called identity is not an illusion anyway, which comes to light, especially in experiences 'in the periphery' and threatens to be disproven.

The fourth chapter explores this at the level of the body. What I call the body of 'disincarnation' is the body insofar as it escapes precisely from the purely organic but does not yet participate fully in psychological-cultural processes, the body between the organic and the intersubjective, between flesh and soul. It is an 'in-between body', between the real and the represented, where the distinction between the physical and the psychic is unclear. It wavers between the order of pure flesh and the order of words, and it still has a shaky meaning between being a body and having a body.

In Chapter 5, this issue shifts to how we want to shape and display our identity in public space, but also protect and insulate ourselves from it. Here, the tension is between discretion and self-disclosure. Without a relationship with the other, any identity remains empty and speechless, but on the other hand, our dominant culture of transparency, voyeurism and exhibitionism restricts our personal freedom in this regard. I mean nothing without the other, but an excess of culturally claimed confessions threatens to expropriate my very identity. What does psychoanalysis teach us about this tension between meaning and confession? Don't we – all transparency notwithstanding – inevitably remain a stranger to ourselves?

The second part culminates in the conception of human identity as something both inescapable and elusive, which I elaborate on in the sixth chapter. Identity is something we cannot do without; that is beyond question, but at the same time, it eludes us and is always outside ourselves. Between the poles of feeling oneself as nothing, as in melancholy, and imagining oneself as everything, as in megalomania, stretches the whole spectrum of human identity problems as they are also addressed in psychoanalytic practice.

The *third part* brings together the themes of fascination and identity from the previous sections and illustrates the common problem of the margins of representation and meaning through some narrative creations from visual art and literature. In each of the three chapters, the starting point is an artistic creation that evokes the experience of dwelling on the edge of the human, where our imagination and perception of meaning are cornered. The three creations are powerful narratives that succeed in giving shape to the subversion of narrative and, thus, of the human. Curiously, the corpse, as a metaphor for the limit of the human, emerges in all three.

Chapter 7 explores how Edward Hopper's paintings present a 'frozen subjectivity', so to speak, with figures who seem to stand outside of time and the world, hesitant to join humanity or not. Through dialogue with Emmanuel Levinas and others, I explore the relationship between fascination, identification and aesthetic pleasure.

In Sophocles' famous tragedy *Antigone*, the subject of Chapter 8, everything revolves around the corpse of Antigone's brother Polynices. Whether or not it is buried according to human symbolic rituals determines whether or not Polynices is human. The drama of the play draws its power from the constant balancing between those two positions and keeps the outcome undecided. I raise the idea that it is precisely the evocation of that confusing intermediate position that has sustained the tragedy for millennia.

The third illustration, in Chapter 9, is Mary Shelley's *The Monster of Frankenstein*. Using the excessive projective identification from Chapter 2, I show that the monster is a *sample of* Frankenstein himself. The entire novel can be understood as Frankenstein's self-destructive struggle with the inhuman, the monstrous, within himself.

By the concept of the 'inhuman', I designate those phenomena and experiences on the edge of the human in which the distinction between the human and the non-human becomes blurred. This theme, which was already the thread and background in the previous sections, comes to the fore in the *fourth section*. The boundaries of what is human exert an attraction that we simultaneously resist. We are intrigued by what we find difficult to integrate into our symbolic systems. But, culture also tries to incorporate and master that zone as well.

Culturally based 'disaster tourism' is the subject of Chapter 10. The border zone of the inhuman compromises our hold on familiar meanings and orders. In this chapter, I bring together several objects, phenomena and situations that lend themselves pre-eminently to land people in that border zone. As 'fascinated witnesses', they are sucked into it. It also raises the question of what strategies cultures have at their disposal to bring their members into contact with this intriguing area in a non-destructive way. I illustrate this with examples of religious, transitional and other rituals, as well as from literature and the visual arts.

In Chapter 11, I explore the margins of symbolization – inspired in part by Freud and philosophers such as Ludwig Wittgenstein, Henri Bergson, Gilles Deleuze and Giorgio Agamben – in a comparative phenomenology of the infantile and the traumatic. In both, language and meaning are at stake. The bizarre tendency of man emerges to transform himself into a mechanical automaton, but without wanting to reveal his hermeneutic essence in the process. In a certain sense, we can say that this dynamic is also operative and even encouraged in free association in psychoanalysis. On the edge of the human, man appears as a grotesque being.

All in all, I conclude in the recapitulating twelfth chapter that there is a dimension in man which, in his pursuit of self-realization, is paradoxically directed toward his own subversion. This 'eschatological' track, which brings us back to the desire-for-being and also to the Freudian death drive, is inherent in the subject as such. I use the metaphor of the ruin: in its true nature, the subject lies shattered. Precisely where man is not a beautiful whole, where his crumbling is visible – in his excesses or pathology, his impropriety and his strangeness – man reveals himself. At the same time, this crumbling revelation of truth on the edge of the human shows exactly man as he is as a whole. For, automatically, the ruin evokes the representation of the reunion of the fragments. Automatically, the crumbling merges into an illusory unity and the shabby fragments are stitched together into a triumphant but always questionable monumentality.

Similarly, through the successive 'fragments' of the individual chapters, connecting lines develop, the recurring seams or joints of the book: the unimaginable, the metamorphosis motif, fascination, the *Unheimliche*, the human remnant, the wanting to be 'in one piece', the shaky distinction between the psychic and the physical, between subject and thing, the desire-for-being, self-loss, trauma, the impairment of the linguistic, of the symbolic, of narrative coherence.

Part I

From fascination to the desire-for-being

Phenomenology of fascination

A dialogue with Sartre

Impending self-loss

When we say that something fascinates us or that we are fascinated by something, we usually have in view an intense experience in which we, as a subject, are fully and actively involved in an object that captivates and attracts us to an extreme degree. We are full of that which fascinates us, and we do not want to let go of it. For example, we may be fascinated by ancient Egyptian architecture, Middle Dutch literature, the horror of World War I, the Belgian soccer league or our neighbor. I seek out these objects, which can count on my utmost interest, myself. In this use of the term, allowing oneself to be absorbed in the fascination is understood as emanating from the subject itself. The subject does get driven and carried away by the fascinating object, but in this conception, the subject remains the center and driving point of the event. It is the subject that develops intense involvement in a hobby or profession, for example. But even a one-time experience that lies completely outside my habitual sphere of interest can overwhelm me and stay with me to such an extent that I cannot refrain later from telling everyone who wants to hear how 'fascinating' this or that encounter, reading or trip was. Even a sudden frightening situation that overwhelms us from the outside is afterward narratively transformed into an account, not devoid of pride, of a 'fascinating' experience in which the frightened person promotes himself to hero.

But can we ascribe the characterization of fascination to all such experiences? Rather, don't they refer to a much more fundamental experience in which the subject is seized by an object to such an extent that it does not master the situation? We could reserve the designation 'fascination' for those experiences in which a (momentary) threat of self-loss occurs as a result of being radically sucked in by an all-dominant object pole. Are not the previously mentioned experiences an extension of such fascination in the narrow sense? Can we suppose, more precisely, that these uses of the term obscure the experience of self-loss, restore the endangered and belabored subject to its rightful place and bolster its undercut self-determination? What is then called fascination is already a defense against and a dilution of a much more absolutist grasping and being disabled as a person by a terrorizing objectality. What threatens to expropriate us is quickly appropriated by

DOI: 10.4324/9781003515982-3

us. Should we not, in other words, distinguish between the day-to-day 'inflationary' use of the term fascination on the one hand and what we might call actual 'core fascination' on the other?

It is the latter that I want to elaborate on phenomenologically in this chapter. The neglect of this distinction, I believe, deprives us of a very specific experience at the edge of human subjectivity. What we, understandably, as poor mortals, want to escape (in the inflation mentioned previously), we should not let slip away as the subject of phenomenological inquiry. So, I am looking for a phenomenological specification of the fascination from which we seem to want to escape in ordinary language. This specificity is lost in the everyday use of the term. For example, what is still the difference between fascination and a strong drive, between being fascinated and being passionate? In a broader sense, the concept seems to be invoked as a power term to denote any kind of intense experience. But even if we do not follow the hypothesis of defensive inflation, I think it remains relevant to separate a phenomenology of fascination in the strict sense from related but different states.

As a starting point, I take a clinical example from psychoanalytic practice. Such a starting point is unusual in phenomenological research. However, it concerns a phenomenon that I do not consider specific to the psychoanalytic setting or whose occurrence is limited to it but which may just as well take place outside it. Nevertheless, the psychoanalytic attitude lends itself pre-eminently to approaching clinical phenomena phenomenologically. Indeed, the psychoanalyst may be expected to consider the material brought spontaneously by the patient in his free association as open-mindedly as possible. In this sense, we can characterize him as a 'clinical phenomenologist' (Thys 2010). Therefore, my clinical starting point can be a springboard to a further phenomenological elaboration of fascination. Sartre seems to me a privileged interlocutor here. After all, he writes – in *L'être et le néant* – about fascination, shaping on a general human level what I encountered in a clinical situation. Moreover, his examples resemble my example from psychoanalytic practice.

To begin, I will confront my clinical example with a situation described by Sartre in *La nausée*. Then, in my further elaboration of the dialogue with Sartre, I will take two paths: perception and affect, precisely because the combination of their fates, in my opinion, gives fascination its specific status. I will examine fascination from these two different perspectives. Regarding the former, I will also refer briefly to Merleau-Ponty's phenomenology of perception, which was developed in constant dialogue with Sartre. In both areas, perception and affect, I will bring out the specificity of fascination. This will bring me to some questions about the position of the ego in fascination. In Sartre's description of fascination in *L'être et le néant,* the ego is not discussed at all, and fascination is approached purely from his phenomenology of consciousness. In *La transcendence de l'ego,* however, Sartre developed a theory of the relationship between the ego (the psychic) and consciousness. In my analysis of fascination, I will show that this theory is of enduring importance to understanding fascination. The entire chapter culminates in the question of whether we can understand fascination as an experience that evokes something of a 'metamorphosis of the ego'.

The bathroom lady and the tree root

In the course of her psychoanalytic psychotherapy process, a woman reluctantly reports an experience she just had during the session. As she talks about it, she is still very confused. During the experience itself, she now says, she could not utter a word. Nor was there anything in her that even tried or could try to do so. There was just no linguistics left. At this quiet moment, she was in a strange state for a while, giving the impression of being absent while her face turned pale. Just before the experience in question, she recounted some events of the past few days. In her story, it came up – almost in passing – that she saw a white wall tiled with shiny bathroom tiles in the room where she was going to do her new job. She hates such tiles; they give such a grim bathroom feeling. She doesn't like bathrooms. Then she pauses in her speaking. It is silent. Then she stammered,

> Suddenly, there was the image of a bathtub, a green bathtub with those green tiles around it, that very specific green. There is also a water faucet with one of those lifting knobs, not a dial. The water flows into the bathtub. There is a hand on the faucet, and next to the tub, a piece of leg. I see everything from a frog's perspective, from bottom to top. The tub is abnormally narrow and short, but the depth is that of an ordinary bathtub. I could not go into it now, as an adult. I see the jet of water from the faucet to the tub, but it does not move, nor does it make a sound. Nor do the hand and leg move. The image as a whole is remarkably static and sharply defined. Beyond that, there is nothing. There was nothing beyond that image and myself. Even I was not there, there was only that image. I feel empty in my head now and nauseous; my bowels, I could vomit. I feel that now, just now, that too was not there. I didn't feel anything. I wasn't breathing. There was nothing to say. I was gone, or rather, *I was that image.* Now I feel distressed, some breathing space is already returning and I can take some distance. What does this mean? It's so absurd. I'm not well.

In this example (which I will explore further in the next chapter), the patient is momentarily so captivated by a particular object, the bathroom tableau, that she can barely distance herself from it and the rest of the world disappears for her. This is not merely a being sucked in strongly by something, but a much more radical state, in which the whole category of language, symbolization and meaning is fundamentally affected. All subjectivity seems to be absorbed by a bizarre object pole. Are we dealing here with a state of fascination? What is happening in this example in terms of perception and affect?

The clinical example reminds me strongly of a situation Sartre describes in *La nausée* (Sartre 1999). In the novel, Sartre shows how the first-person narrator, Roquentin, is disgusted by the excess of pure existence, which invades his eyes and ears and from which he can no longer distance himself. He characterizes the experience of the I-figure, sitting on a park bench and completely captivated by the root of the chestnut tree in front of him, as fascination.

> The root of the chestnut tree dug itself into the earth, right under the bench on which I was sitting. I no longer knew it was a root. The words had disappeared and, with them, the meaning of things. . . . Gnarled, bulky, nameless, it fascinated me, I was short of eyes and it constantly reminded me of its existence. And whether I kept repeating to myself, 'That thing over there is a tree root,' words no longer had a hold on it. . . . It was a miraculous moment. There I sat, motionless and petrified, prey to a shuddering ecstasy. . . . I had wanted to tear myself away from that horrifying rapture, but it didn't even occur to me that that would be possible; I was in the middle of it, the black stump *went no further*, it stuck in my eyes, like an oversized lump stuck right in your throat. I couldn't say no and yes to it. . . . Existence is not something that can be thought of from afar: it must overwhelm you unexpectedly, clinging to you, you must feel it resting heavily on your heart like a great motionless beast. . . . How long did I sit like that, captivated by what I saw? I *was* the root of the chestnut tree. Or rather, I was nothing but awareness of its existence. Still, I was separate from it – after all, I was aware of it – and yet I had merged into the root, I was only the root.
> (p. 201–209)

I will elaborate on some interesting aspects of the position of the ego in this example in what follows.

I was the bathroom tableau, says the woman from the clinical example. I was the root, says Roquentin. In both situations, the subject's distance from the object falls away, it sticks to it, so to speak, or the subject shifts to or disappears into the object pole, as it were. What is also mentioned in both situations is the disappearance of language and meaning and the striking immobility. Let us now distance ourselves for a moment from both examples and sketch a broader framework into which we can incorporate them again.

The subject-minimum and the exclusive object

The least we can say, with Sartre, of fascination is that it is a state of consciousness (see Sartre 2003, p. 258, 479). There is a fascinating object of which the subject is aware, just as the woman is aware of the bathroom and Roquentin is aware of the root. The notions 'subject' and 'consciousness' refer to different things: consciousness I use in a Sartrian sense, by the subject I designate the agency to which consciousness is attributed (the bathroom woman, Roquentin; see the later section on the relationship between the ego and consciousness). Something cannot fascinate us if we are not aware of its existence and perceive it in some way. Insofar as consciousness is also perceptual consciousness, we can approach fascination, besides as an affect, within the framework of a perceptual phenomenology. Sartre calls the non-thetic consciousness 'perceptual consciousness': 'The [non-thetic consciousness] thus immediately defines itself as perceptual consciousness as well as perception'. (2003, p. 38). Since Sartre further characterizes fascination as a non-thetical consciousness, the approach to fascination as perceptual consciousness is, in my view, legitimized, at least within a Sartrian phenomenology. Also for Merleau-Ponty (1997, pp. 69–71), for that matter, consciousness is perception, and perceptual consciousness lies at the basis of any relation to the world. First of all, I start from the intuition that fascination is not an ordinary, everyday form of perception but a perception accompanied by an extreme intensity of attention. We can situate the fascinated attention as a special mode of perception in an attentional continuum ranging from minimal attention in indifference to an extreme intensity of attention concerning an exclusive objectality. I distinguish the following segments in this continuum.

The attention continuum

In *indifference,* the object almost completely escapes my attention. It is characterized by an absolute externality: it is completely outside me, it does not enter in any way and it does not 'animate' me. In its indifference, the object does not exercise any power over me. All – albeit passive – domination lies on the side of the subject. The subject disregards the object without question. Indifference is passivity without attention or inattentive passivity. We could call indifference the phenomenological freezing point. The subject does not allow itself to be warmed by the object, which can only bounce off it without affecting the subject.

In the next segment, *neutrality*, there is attention, but it is fleeting and superficial and not accompanied by an active orientation of the subject. The attention is purely functional and of a referential nature. The shoes I put on in the morning do not interest me per se but only in function of the movement I am preparing to make. Neutral objects lie somewhat recessed in the background of my field of attention. I handle them mechanically; they have nothing of interest and I do not feel personally addressed by them. Even though I have an inkling of their existence, they remain trivial.

In the *interested openness* thereafter, my attention takes on a more active character. If, in my haste, I do not find my shoes, the longer their untrace ability lasts, the more those damned shoes will push themselves to the forefront of my attention. I feel more personally addressed by them, so to speak; they hide themselves *from me*. As a result, they rise above their purely functional and referential nature. The object takes on a certain dominance or singularity. The shoes I want to put on don't care about my impatience. In the interested openness, my active orientation does not primarily emanate from myself; it is only provoked by an intrusive quality of the object, for example, the unexpected absence of the shoes in their familiar place to me. The openness of my interest quickly closes as soon as the (finally found) object sinks back into its ordinary functionality.

In the segment of *curiosity*, however, I actively pursue the object, an activity that also involves more of myself. My attention here is accompanied by an increasing personal drive. The value of the object is less referential and more intrinsic. I am not simply interested in the fact that something is hanging on my wall; even that it is a painting does not suffice; no, my perception is specifically focused on the work of Edward Hopper. It must be a Hopper. In curiosity, a tilt from subject to object dominance takes place. I do pursue it, but it is still more Hopper that haunts *me*. He demands my attention. On the other hand, curiosity implies that I eagerly allow myself to be sucked in and claimed by the object. At the same time, this actively driven perception is accompanied by decreased mobility. The object, too, moves less freely in the world and isolates itself somewhat from the other objects, although the links with them (other modern painters) remain readily available.

In *obsession*, the next segment in the continuum, the subject is even more seized by the object. It is slavishly subjected to it. The functional referentiality here is reversed from that of neutrality: in obsession, it is the other objects that, from the background, merely refer to the obsessing object in the foreground. The world and I shrivel up and are taken in by the object. I am full of the object, and the rest of the world is empty. The object, which stands out sharply and obtrusively in the foreground of my field of perception, is not exclusive but absorbs virtually all other objects. I, along with the object, become very isolated from the world. Obsessional attention starts from one fixed point, from which I am entirely focused on the object. Every movement of the subject is channeled into this one vector from the subject to the object, while both have barely any room to move 'in width'.

Finally, *exclusivity* is a radicalization of obsessed attention. There is only one – hence 'exclusive' – object left for the subject. All references have fallen away; there is no other object. There are no paintings other than Hopper's, or taken even further: there is only that one painting by Hopper. All existence, all objectality, is limited to that one overwhelming object. The object is existence itself. It has complete control over me. I no longer have any possibility of movement; I am paralyzed. The object holds all the strings and manipulates me like a puppet. All activity emanates from the object. The extremely driven attention that is rampant here is no longer of the subject and has, as it were, been taken over by the object.

Now, I want to zoom in even further and situate the *fascination* in the extremes of exclusivity. We saw that, in exclusivity, there is only movement emanating from the object. In fascination, in my opinion, all movement falls away, including that at the pole of the object. Fascination is a state of absolute immobility. In exclusivity in the broad sense, the object still goes after the subject; in fascination, the object gets hold of the subject. There is no more space between the subject and the object; the subject clings to the object. Yet there is no fusion between the two because there must still be a subject position to be fascinated. However, this subject position is reduced to a minimum. While in indifference, we can speak of an existence minimum of the object, fascination is characterized by a *subject-minimum*. Fascination is the bizarre state of an *extreme intensity of attention in which, however, virtually all personal involvement is abolished*. In its excessive, fascinated intensity, attention detaches itself from the person. In this representation, the subject-minimum is far from being a consciousness-minimum. On the contrary, in fascination, consciousness, in the form of extreme attention, is prominent. Phenomenologically, fascination constitutes the maximum intensity in the encounter with an object in which the subject has not yet disappeared or dissolved. Fascination is, so to speak, the attention boiling point, where subjectivity is about to evaporate or go up in smoke. Unlike in indifference, we must now situate volatility on the side of the subject.

A field of perception?

I would now like to briefly confront the rather bizarre capacity that perception acquires in this view of fascination with an element from Merleau-Ponty's phenomenology of perception. While in the framework of object exclusivity outlined previously, any space around the fascinating object falls away, Merleau-Ponty argues that every perception necessarily presupposes a field within which the observed is located: 'The 'something' of perception is always embedded in something else, it is part of a 'field'' (Merleau-Ponty 1997, p. 46). And: 'An isolated fact of perception is if we possess at least the mental experience of its perception, incomprehensible' (Merleau-Ponty 1997, p. 46). In fascination, then, can we still speak of a perception? Or does precisely fascination challenge this law of perception? Because of the disappearance of distance in relation to the object, fascination indeed seems to be a perception that no longer sees anything. The object is a colossal close-up that no longer represents anything because of its puffiness. At the same time, fascination seems to be a perception of an object that I *cannot* not see (cf. Visker 2005, p. 90) since the very object fills the entire field.

One might suggest that in the clinical example is a clearly differentiated field of perception within which the woman distinguishes between the bathtub, the tiles, the faucet, the hand and so on. According to her own account of her experience, however, these are subsequently made distinctions. At the very moment of fascination, the tableau overwhelms her as in one piece, as a perceptual object characterized by an absolute density beyond which there is nothing else. While in ordinary perception, the bathroom could be the field within which, for example, the faucet can be distinguished as an object, in fascinated perception, the 'field' itself becomes the exclusive object that only disintegrates into mutually separable objects when the fascination is broken.

In Sartre's example, too, the fascinated protagonist sees the root; he is even short of eyes, while for a moment, the rest of the world falls away. Only in the next moment does the tree reappear in its entirety, the park, a black pool of water in the sand next to the root.

Thus, we seem to have to characterize fascination phenomenologically as a *marginal state of perception*. It is still, at the last minute, a perception, just as the perceiving subject is also minimized. It is a perception devoid of any mental activity and, therefore, as the examples indicate, the subject or what remains of it appears absurd. It is, to refer back to the higher quote of Merleau-Ponty, a perception whose subject 'does not possess the mental experience'. With the words, all meaning falls away because the perceived object, the fascinating object, is disconnected from any other object with which it could enter into a relationship that generates difference and, thus, meaning. At the moment of fascination itself, all differentiations fall away, while the perception, as it were, according to the law of inertia, remains intact for a while. However, this can never last long, and soon, the object, then no longer fascinating, reappears in the background of a field or disintegrates into a field itself. In a broader time frame, the absurdity of the fascinating object can become absorbed into an as-yet-emerging context of meaning, as the further course of the woman's psychoanalytic process demonstrates (see Chapter 2). For the same reason, one could also say that there must still be a minimal field somewhere for the perception to acquire meaning in any case. That field may be so small that the subject caught in fascination does not perceive it. Both the woman and Roquentin are daunted.

Sartre on fascination in *L'Être et le néant*

Back to Sartre. Compared to the inflationary use of the term fascination, there is not much left of the subject in actual core fascination. Do we find this subject-minimum, combined with the exclusivity of the object, in Sartre's vision of fascination? Let us see what place fascination is given in his phenomenology of consciousness. Sartre characterizes consciousness as pure negativity; it is not something; it is only pure relation to what it is not itself (Sartre 2003, p. 35ff.). Consciousness is absolute transparency; it has no content or comprehensiveness itself. Being, the world, that of which consciousness is aware, lies outside consciousness and is 'transcendent' to consciousness. The world *is*; consciousness is *not*. Etre and *néant*. Consciousness, therefore, is a deficiency of being, a *manque d'être* (Sartre 2003, p. 696). This distinction between world and consciousness recurs in terms of *en-soi* or in-itself and *pour-soi* or for-itself. Being in-itself of things in the world is a being that coincides completely with itself, develops no negation and has no relation to anything it is not. The in-itself is entirely positivity and knows no alterity; it is simply what it is (Sartre 2003, pp. 52–53). Opposed to this is the for-itself of consciousness, which by definition does not coincide with itself. While the being-in-itself of things is infinite 'compression-of-being', consciousness is '*de*compression-of-being' (Sartre 2003, p. 142). The in-itself is just what it is; the for-itself is what it is not and is not what it is (Sartre 2003, pp. 52–53).

In Sartre's description of man as a creature of consciousness in terms of lack of being, negation is fundamental. In this regard, Sartre distinguishes between internal and external negation (Sartre 2003, pp. 255–257). The external negation concerns the notion of the difference between two beings in the world and thus presupposes the perception of at least two objects. For example, 'the computer screen is not the keyboard' or 'fascination is not passion'. The internal negation, on the other hand, indicates the absence of a capacity from within; for example, 'the keyboard is not black' or 'I am not fascinated'. Any form of negation implies the for-itself of consciousness; after all, the in-itself of things in the world knows no alterity (a keyboard cannot relate to itself or anything else, let alone determine what color it is not). We should mention one final distinction, which Sartre made earlier. Non-thetic or non-positional consciousness is consciousness of consciousness; it is (prereflexive) self-consciousness. Consciousness is consciousness of itself, thus does not coincide with itself, but yet is not object to itself. Thetic or positional consciousness, on the other hand, is consciousness of an object in the world transcendent to consciousness (Sartre 1988, p. 48).

Now we can the various descriptions that Sartre gives of fascination in *L'être et le néant* and the context within which he does so summarize in two formulas, which approach fascination from consciousness and the world, respectively: 1. fascination is the non-thetic consciousness of being nothingness in the presence of being (Sartre 2003, p. 479), 2. in fascination there is nothing but a giant object in an empty world (Sartre 2003, p. 258). What does this mean? Fascination as non-thetical consciousness, according to Sartre, is a consciousness that has consciousness of itself without having this consciousness as an object for itself, for consciousness is pure transparency and is not itself a thing in the world. It is a consciousness *not* to be. But, now we come to the second part of the first formula, this 'in the presence of being'. The concept of presence takes on a specific meaning with Sartre, which we can best clarify based on what he calls the 'original negation'. This he characterizes as an internal negation that is the foundation of every experience (Sartre 2003, p. 254). It is in an initial being present to an object that it is not; consciousness emerges as non-being. This fundamental negation is also what Sartre calls 'knowledge' (Sartre 2003, p. 253): knowing an object is not to be the object itself. Knowledge *realizes* the knowing (consciousness) and the known (the world). This internal and realizing negation is transcendence as such (Sartre 2003, p. 261).

In this original differentiation between and thus the constitution of consciousness and the world, Sartre situates fascination. Fascination is this pure negation that is knowing (see Sartre 2003, p. 257ff.). The only qualification the knowing can possess is not to be a fascinating object. All there is is the being-there of the known, a presence that simply is. But this presence of the known is a presence to nothing since knowing is pure reflection of a non-being. This presence, then, must be understood as an *absolute presence, without any distance* of the for-itself from the in-itself. The for-itself is flattened on what it denies. The non-being of the knowing is not outside the known. Nay, the for-itself appears there, in and upon the being that it is not, to itself as not being what it is not. It is a relation of pure negation, of merely denied identity. Precisely because knowledge is not absence but presence, there is nothing that separates the knowing from the known. This immediate presence implies the absence of any mediator. Sartre emphasizes, however, that fascination is *not a fusion* with the object. Indeed, otherwise, the negation would be dissolved and the for-itself would become rigid in an in-itself, which would immediately make the world (the in-itself as presence) disappear as well.

Sartre thus characterizes fascination as the consciousness of this fundamental internal negation. This consciousness is a non-thetical consciousness in which it constitutes itself as non-being, which is only possible in the presence of a being that it realizes at the same moment. Further on in *L'être et le néant*, therefore, Sartre will characterize fascination succinctly as transcendence as such: 'Fascination does not posit the fascinating object as the ultimate final term of transcendence; it is transcendence' (Sartre 2003, p. 482).

In the whole of this vision, do we not recognize what I called the subject-minimum in the context of perception and attention? *At the subject pole, almost only consciousness remains.* The subject position is reduced to mere non-being, to mere consciousness, without any more elaborate mental activities involved or anything that we might call differentiated psychic functioning. The subject merely undergoes being overwhelmed by a pole of objects against which there is no distance, what Sartre calls 'absolute presence'. To characterize fascination as transcendence as such and not as its result, I understand it as a first moment, an initial impetus to creating an objectality without already being able to speak of a world in the usual sense of the word. Fascination is transcendence *in statu nascendi*.

To give a place to the impassivity – the motionlessness we saw in both examples – I think we should add that this 'hesitant' transcendence falters for a moment. The fascination then occurs at the moment when this first impetus to a presence in consciousness comes to a halt, as it were, for a moment. Can we not then characterize fascination even more precisely as the faltering or freezing of a movement that is *on its way to* full objectality, to transcendent negation? The fascinating object, then, is a 'near-object', an object-in-the-making. Without observing this aspect of the cessation of transcendence, we would be constantly (with each new perception) fascinated, which is not the case. What fascinates, as it were, is always a *precarious* objectality. What overwhelms me is the fact that there is such a thing as an object, and this in such a surprising way that I am drawn into it and, for a moment, I do not yet or no longer allow the object to detach itself from me *as* an object.

Because, in fascination, we cannot speak of an object in the ordinary sense, we end up with the second formula: in fascination, there is nothing but a giant object in an empty world. This emptiness is precisely the knowing or pure transparency of consciousness. All there is is the fascinating object. In this formula, we easily recognize the exclusivity of the object. Indeed, that object is always huge (*objet géant*) because it is exclusive. After all, it is the field of perception itself, filling my entire field of vision to burst. Therefore, and not because of their nature (a bathroom or a root), fascinating objects are impressive and imposing. Fascination turns a mosquito into an elephant. This exclusivity is closely linked to the absence of any distance, which brings us back to Sartre's absolute presence. Indeed, this leaves no extensiveness beyond the fascinating object and no room for other objects. Here again, the characteristic of motionlessness or paralysis emerges: without extensiveness, no movement or displacement is possible. The only spatiality that remains – and there must be space to speak of an object and perception in a minimal sense – is that of the fascinating object itself. Therefore, without Sartre himself explicitly saying so, we can characterize fascination as the *absence of external negation.* In fascination, there is only (an impetus for) internal negation. As soon as external negation appears, which presupposes the perception of at least two objects, the actual fascination is abolished. Other objects begin to surround the previously fascinating object, as in the example of the root, or the fascinating object itself disintegrates into mutually distinguishable objects, as in the case of the bathroom tableau.

The eye of the storm: fascination and affect

In terms of perception, we had to label fascination as a marginal state, which has everything to do with subject-minimum and object-exclusivity. The second angle from which I will now examine fascination is affect. What is the affective status of fascination? Can we call fascination an affective state? Can we separate perception and attention from affect? Isn't every relation to the world and isn't every consciousness automatically also an affective involvement? Phenomenology teaches us that, indeed, any attentiveness to an object is, by definition, also an affective relation. To be attentive to an object *is* to be already affectively moved by it. Thus, Sartre argues that any consciousness is always simultaneously all-knowing and all-affectivity; he speaks of '*une conscience cognitive-affective*'. In his study of the imaginary, Sartre (1986, p. 143) states, '[Une conscience] doit donc être, à la fois, tout entière savoir et tout entière affectivité'. Merleau-Ponty (1997, pp. 69–73) also emphasizes the connection between attention and affect. He accuses both empiricism and intellectualism of turning attention into something sterile. In terms of its status as an affect as well, I think fascination occupies a special position. Does the subject-minimum, as I described previously, leave room for affectivity? Isn't the mobility of the affective in conflict with the fascinated impassivity? And doesn't affectivity already immediately imply a distance to the object?

Disgust: an excess-of-being

Let's take the attention continuum as a starting point. Going from indifference to fascination, this continuum is characterized by an increasing intensity of attention. Now, it seems very plausible to equate the increase in attention intensity with the degree of affective involvement. The more an object concerns me, the more attentive I will be to it and the stronger I will feel affectively attached to it. If I say that a person means a lot to me affectively, whether in my fear, hate or love, he or she will be able to count on a similar amount of attention from me. Those who are indifferent to me will evoke little or no affect from me. We can indeed suggest that the degree of affective involvement increases directly proportional to the increasing intensity of attention. My obsession or passion for Egyptian architecture is not purely intellectual involvement but rather is fueled by a more than average affective attachment. I 'have' something with the subject, which goes beyond wanting to gain rational knowledge.

I situated fascination in the regions of extreme attentional intensity. Now, we are spontaneously inclined to characterize fascination as a very intense experience also in terms of affectivity. But is this correct? The intensity of the actual fascination, as I have elaborated in the foregoing, in my opinion, concerns purely the attention and not the affect. In my view, fascination emerges as a pure intensity of attention, an admittedly radical involvement but one in which any affectivity is suspended. The equalization of attention and affect throughout the continuum breaks at the level of fascination. In this sense, we can understand fascination as *the fundamental break between attention and affect:* attention is maximal, but affectivity falls back to its zero point. In terms of attention, indifference and fascination are each other's opposites, but in terms of affectivity, they are each other's equals. This is precisely the bizarre thing about fascination: I am most intensely involved in an object pole that, at the same time, leaves me affectively cold. Indeed, we can call fascinated attention a sterile attention. Let us test this for a moment with the clinical example.

While being fascinated, at the moment when the bathroom tableau paralyzes and disables her as a subject, *while consciousness remains intact,* the woman feels nothing. She was not there as a person to feel, want or say anything. The elimination of affect goes along with the higher-mentioned suspension of any mental experience. It is only when the fascination is dissolved that affectively a lightning-fast catch-up seems to occur, as if the affectivity objectified during the fascination explodes in the next moment and overwhelms the subject. The affective intensity with which we associate fascination is that which surrounds fascination but, strictly speaking, is not part of it. Immediately after the fascination, the woman is all affected. The affective freezing point and the affective boiling point are right next to each other. The silent immobility of fascination is the eye of the affective storm. The most striking sensations the woman has once the fascination is broken are *mental emptiness* and *physical disgust.* She feels mentally empty and physically full, too full. Just a moment ago, she was frozen and now she is already boiling over. The feeling of mental emptiness indicates that the space of movement lost in fascination is suddenly returning but mentally still unexplored. The subject still lies fallow. Physically, the woman feels nauseous. Being overfilled is a purely physical matter. She is mesmerized. Aren't the vomiting tendencies, which were not there at all during the fascination itself, already a first impetus to the reintroduction of distance, to begin with, between the vomiter and the vomit?

Sartre also gives a fascination example of the root in the context of disgust, the disgust resulting from the intrusion of being. Being presses on Roquentin in such a way and invades his body in such a way that it becomes an *excess* (1999, pp. 202–203). The I-figure is disgusted by the excess of pure existence from which he can no longer distance himself. Nevertheless, I think we should specify here and distinguish between the disgust and the fascination *strictu sensu.* At the moment of fascination, there is certainly an excess of being, but the disgust seems to me to fall right outside the actual fascination. Even if we read closely the pages of Sartre around the example of the root, we see that his reflections on disgust emerge about the various objects (the trees, the trunk, the bark, the fountain in the park and so on) that surround the root. The excess, which occurs most extremely at the moment of fascination itself, only makes itself felt affective, in the form of disgust, at the very moment when exclusivity has already been impaired, 'affected'. It is a retroactive disgust. Sartre's descriptions are remarkably similar to those of the woman immediately after the fascination. The feeling of disgust, she says, was not there during the fascination. The disgust and the stammering of words are already a severing of the fascination; they are already a movement. The fascinating object is vomited, as it were. The disgust is the breaking of the fascination.

Affect implosion

In fascination, the distinction between the mental and the physical virtually falls away. In other words, the too little mental emptiness and the too much physical overcrowding are, so to speak, 'in the same place'. Or: the mental space is overwhelmed and occupied by a physical intrusion. It seems that with the disappearance of any distance to the object, there is also no longer any place for any affectivity. The equalization of attention and affect intensity is true insofar as there is still distance between the subject and the object. Where this distance disappears, as in fascination, any possible affectivity is 'compressed', as it were. Where fascination appears, passion disappears, says Baudrillard (2002b, p. 104). Being comes so close that it threatens to suffocate the for-itself and *desubjectivation* takes place (the subject-minimum). We can speak of an 'affect implosion' at the point where attention is at its most extreme. Exactly at that point, where affectivity also peaks, it collapses. Let's take a closer look at this.

The distinction between mental emptiness and physical fullness falls away in fascination but flourishes 'around' fascination. The disgust at the breaking of the fascination is a clear reaction of repulsion (with vomiting as a physical form of it): full of disgust, the subject brings the repulsive object back at a distance. In both examples, however, we see that, at the same time, a strong suction force emanates from that same object that wants to dissolve the distance again. The mental emptiness generates, like a black hole, an enormous attraction toward that exclusive being. Consciousness finds itself, as it were, in a *hopeless impasse in the face of being*: on the one hand, it is suffocated and crushed by being and anxiously wants to tear itself away from it in order not to be absorbed by it; on the other hand, it passionately clings to it because the exclusive object is still the only being with which it can maintain itself. So, this extreme affective ambivalence between attraction and repulsion has everything to do with the exclusivity of the object, which brings the entire subjectivity to the brink of its existence.

The logic behind this is that the arsenal of objects over which the affective poles of attraction and repulsion can spread continually shrinks throughout the continuum of attention until, in exclusivity, they have no choice but to get in each other's way about that one remaining object. And it is here – in the affective storm surrounding fascination – that Sartre's expression of the 'horrible delight' fits, which I believe implodes during fascination proper. In fascination, the distinction between horror and delight falls away because, in the fascinated paralysis, any struggle and move-ment between affects also fall silent. Fascination is the break with ambivalence at the point where it is most extreme, where extreme attraction and extreme repulsion feel each other's hot breath on the neck. In fascination proper, their distinction falls away and thus affectivity as such. In the implosion, both affect poles are so immeas-urably close together that they block each other in extreme density *as* affect. Every affective differentiation, and thus every ambivalence, is already a breaking open of absolute exclusivity and consequently already an escape from fascination.

Thus, in this view, fascination is located near the very states with which it forms the rupture. As a radically affectless state, fascination is enclosed by the most extreme affectivity. That we confuse fascination primarily with its opposite of extreme affect-laden states may seem surprising at first glance, but on closer inspection, it is not surprising because it is precisely these poles of extreme repul-sion and extreme attraction that are closest to it. If we confuse fascination with anything, it is with fear and passion, with which I conveniently refer to the extreme affect poles of repulsion and attraction. In this sense, as we saw, the term fasci-nation lends itself to designating any extremely intense affective experience as a power term where fear as the prototype of ultimate repulsion and passion as the prototype of ultimate attraction is never far away. For example, we are 'paralyzed with fear', and we are quick to say we are fascinated, whereas 'passionate' would be more strictly accurate. Even if we must situate passion and fear in the zone of exclusivity, they are distinguished from fascination because the space around the object has not completely disappeared. In passion as reaching for and fear as recoiling from, the affective drive – to reduce or increase the little distance to the object – reigns supreme.

Unlike in fascination, the object status as such of that which impassions or fright-ens me is not compromised. What distinguishes the object from me is precisely the affect. The intermediate space lost in fascination *is* affectivity. In the top-driven ambivalence in object exclusivity, passion and fear are intimately intertwined. In their whirling mutual dialectic, they necessarily evoke each other. After all, an absolute zooming in on the object (reaching out) from passion and an absolute zooming out (recoiling) from fear would make the world and the subject disappear. At the last moment, fear turns into passion moving toward the object, only to want to flee the object again and passion turns into fear moving away from the object, only to drive desire again immediately. Within this yo-yo movement of extreme affective ambivalence, the object remains unattainable and, thus, *as* object avail-able. The condition in which this movement solidifies into a frozen affective block is fascination. In this absolute presence, the unreachability of the object is now out of reach and its availability as an object is no longer available.

In *L'être et le néant*, Sartre describes the desire-for-being as the orienta-tion of the for-itself toward the in-itself: the for-itself, which is non-being, also wants to be. The for-itself, which can be described ontologically as *lack-of-being*, wants to be in-itself but then ás for-itself; it thus wants to paradoxically become in-itself-for-itself (2003, pp. 696–698). This is an impossible goal to realize.

One cannot be a thing without any inwardness and, at the same time, not reveal the consciousness of it and of oneself anyway. Therefore, this desire-for-being, in its extremities, is stranded on *fear-of-being*: consciousness cannot let itself be absorbed into a thing. Conversely, an unbridled fear-of-being ultimately turns into a desire-for-being: consciousness, after all, needs a thing to be conscious of it. We can, therefore, understand the extreme ambivalence described previously as a *struggle brought to a head between fear-of-being and desire-for-being,* in which conscious- ness is entangled. In my opinion, we can characterize fascination, where this entire affective struggle is already at a standstill but consciousness remains intact, as the *closest possible approach to this impossible realization of being.* This is in contrast to fainting, which Sartre describes as the ultimate escape from an imminent danger, which we can apply here to the danger of merging into an in-itself. I lift this danger to consciousness by lifting consciousness itself (see Sartre 1981, pp. 94–95). This fainting can also be a reaction to a disinhibited passion, as the ultimate attempt to escape self-loss, which, incidentally, illustrates how closely fear and passion are related. We could say that fainting is the ultimate way to escape fascination, where consciousness, in the threat of merging with the in-itself, does still stand. In fasci- nation, there is a lack of lack-of-being; there is an excess-of-being. Just before the impossible point where for-itself and in-itself would merge, the storm of fear and passion solidifies into an affectless coagulation. Fascination is the limit of what is still possible in a rapprochement with being without relinquishing consciousness. I will return to this in Chapters 3 and 12.

Towards a metamorphosis of the ego

My analysis so far, in dialogue with Sartre, allows me to understand fascination as a state of consciousness in the context of an 'excess-of-being'. This excess takes the form of a monumentally exclusive object that I cannot keep at bay and that 'flattens' me to a subject-minimum. This is accompanied by a rupture with affectiv- ity, with perceptual consciousness remaining intact. We can understand the latter because there is no fusion with the object. Therefore, Sartre can say that fascination is the consciousness of not being in the immediate presence of being. But how can we reconcile this with his depiction of the relation to the root, which he also calls a fascinating object? I repeat the quote already given: 'I was the root of the chestnut tree. Or rather, I was nothing but consciousness of its existence. Still, I was separate from it – after all, I was conscious of it – and yet I had merged into the root, I was only root' (Sartre 1999, p. 208). Similarly, the woman in the clinical example says she was the bathroom tableau. The part 'I am not the root because I am aware of it' refers to the first formula, which concerns non-being. But there is more; namely, there is also the statement 'I definitely was the root', which refers to the second formula, that of being. Sartre's explication of this distinction suggests that it is not without meaning for him either.

But how can we understand the simultaneity of both? May we not, after all, exclude the possibility of being a thing without any interiority and, at the same

time, not revealing the consciousness of it and of itself? How can we give fascination a place in the 'original negation' while still allowing the fascinated subject to
bear witness to the experience of being the object? Does it suffice to say, as Sartre
does, that fascination is transcendence as such? In that case, it would suffice to have
Roquentin simply say something like 'however much he presses and intrudes on
me, I am not the root'. Does not the empiricism of being fascinated necessitate a
closer look at the experience of being, which is also part of fascination and marks
it precisely in its bizarre way? How should we understand the position of the ego
in statements like 'I was the root' and 'I was the tableau'? Even if we cannot completely equate fascination with an ego metamorphosis, it seems to me worthwhile
to consider how to understand an intrusion of an experience that seems to go in that
direction. In the context of this line of questioning, is not what Sartre says in *La
transcendance de l'Ego* about the relationship between the ego and consciousness
of enduring importance for an accurate understanding of fascination? Let us briefly
examine the status of the ego, according to Sartre.

The intimacy of the ego

Consciousness, the for-itself, is pure transparency, a pure relationship to what it
is not. It is not something. The in-itself of things in the world is transcendent to
consciousness, is pure positivity and is plainly what it is. Similarly, the ego is a
transcendent object: it is not in consciousness but outside it; it is a being in the
world (1988, p. 41). For consciousness, the ego is something other than itself. Here,
Sartre refers to Rimbaud's famous phrase: *Je est un autre* (1988, p. 92). 'Thus the
Ego appears to consciousness as a transcendent in-itself, as something existing of
the human world, not as *something of* consciousness' (2003, p. 176). The ego is the
ongoing virtual unity of the 'psychic', which Sartre calls 'the transcendent object of
reflexive consciousness'. The ego lies on the side of the psychic (1988, pp. 71–72).
According to Sartre, the psychic has the status of the reflected (2003, p. 243), in
the in-itself hypostasized (2003, p. 244) or objectified (2003, p. 246) for-itself. The
ego and the psychic that synthesizes it exist only in the reflection on the for-itself.
Through reflection, consciousness makes itself 'personal'. The ego is consciousness in its 'fundamental selfhood' (2003, pp. 176–177). It gives the for-itself a *form*,
as it were. The ego may be a thing in the world; it may appear to consciousness
through reflection as an in-itself and exhibit the 'inertia' typical of it (2003, p. 244),
yet it has a special status in comparison with the other things in the world.

The ego is, so to speak, 'closer' to consciousness than the rest of the world. It is
an object to consciousness, but I cannot walk around it as is possible concerning the
non-psychic things in the world. It is infinitely close. Sartre, therefore, characterizes the ego as *intimate to consciousness* (1988, pp. 82–83, 97). We should distinguish the ego from consciousness, but it cannot be separated from it. I cannot 'step
out of my consciousness' since my ego presupposes consciousness. This intimate
connection between ego and consciousness takes shape as the degradation of the
transparency of self-consciousness. Sartre calls the ego a 'synthesis of interiority

and transcendence' (1988, p. 81); 'The ego is interior *to itself*, not *to* consciousness (1988, p. 82). The ego may be a thing in the world, but it possesses an 'interiority'.

According to Sartre, however, the ego as a transcendent object appears only through reflection, in which consciousness takes itself as an object and thus becomes a thetic consciousness. The ego is the transcendent object of the reflexive act (1988, p. 51, 57). Now, Sartre describes states of consciousness without reflection: states of consciousness 'without ego', that is, non-thetical. Sartre gives the example (1988, p. 53) of reading a book. I can remember being aware of the book and the characters of the novel, but the ego did not 'inhabit' consciousness; nowhere was the ego the object of consciousness. Only in reflection do I become aware that it is *I* who is reading. Any 'egological' consciousness implies such reflection. The same can happen when I look at my watch, walk quickly to catch the streetcar or sink into a painting. There is only awareness of the-tram-that-must-be-caught and non-thetical awareness of consciousness, but I, I am gone, I am undone (1988, p. 54).

Sartre's definition of fascination as the non-thetical consciousness not(hing) to be in the presence of being is very similar to the way he describes these states of consciousness without an ego. It seems that we should also characterize fascination as consciousness without an ego. Yet walking-to-catch-the-tram is not fascination. I can be completely absorbed in the running-to-catch-the-tram and say afterward, 'I *was* the running-to-catch-the-streetcar'. However, this is nothing more than a synthesis of the consciousness of an action I performed, as we perform hundreds of them every day. Nothing is fascinating about that. The absence of egological reflection is not a sufficient condition to speak of fascination, otherwise we would be constantly fascinated, which is not the case.

Let us return to the example of the root, which – with Sartre – we can call fascination. The fascination is not in being absorbed in the looking-at-the-root, which allows me to say afterward, 'I was the looking-at-the-root', but in the *being-the-root*: I was the root. The fascination is not in being absorbed in the act (walking, looking) directed at an object (tram, root) but in being absorbed in the object itself. The action (like the affect) still clearly implies movement and distance concerning the object – I am walking *towards* the tram, I am looking *at* the root – which have disappeared in fascination. We also see this distinction when we shift the perceptual position to that of an external witness: seeing someone completely absorbed in looking at a root has nothing fascinating, seeing that someone is a root all the more so. The same goes for the clinical example: not being absorbed in seeing the bathroom tableau but *being* the tableau is fascinating. Sartre calls actions, along with states and properties, an aspect of the ego (1988, pp. 69–70). Thus, walking or looking are not egodystonic, and they belong to the psychic. They are part of the synthesis of my interiority. A mere transcendent object in the world, such as a root or a bathroom, an in-itself without any innerness, is egodystonic.

Now, is it not typical of fascination that *an egodystonic object tends to take the place of the ego*? In fascination, the thing, which unlike the ego, does not possess an interiority, nevertheless acquires, as it were, an ego-status. *L'autre est un je*. Of course, the woman does not become a bathroom tableau, and Roquentin does not become a root, but both seem to bear witness to a bizarre experience that goes in that direction. In that alienating experience, the root or the bathroom tableau tends to become that special thing that consciousness cannot avoid. The synthesis of interiority and transcendence that characterizes the ego now passes to the thing: the root is inner to myself, not to consciousness. Shamelessly, *the thing enters the intimate place that belongs to the ego*. The ego-thing is, therefore, misplaced. The fascinating object is the embodiment of a misplaced intimacy. Elsewhere, I discussed this bizarre misplaced intimacy in the context of the fascination with incest (Thys 1995b).

With Sartre, we can argue that in fascination there is no fusion between consciousness and object (2003, p. 258). But should we not add that *a fusion does occur between the ego and the object*? It is precisely this impending – but not occurring – fusion that makes the object fascinating. A root has nothing fascinating in itself; it becomes so only as it threatens to take the place of the ego. It is purely about an 'intimacy (fusion) of place', not of content. So, in my opinion, it is not enough to characterize fascination as transcendence as such, as merely not being the object, but we must add the tendency to fuse the ego with the object. This emergence of an experience of fusion gives fascination a semblance of being since the 'objectification of the for-itself', as Sartre characterizes the ego (2003, p. 246), among other things, now occurs at the level of an in-itself without any interiority. Consciousness is so close to being, which, as we saw, has everything to do with object-exclusivity, that the normal 'degradation of transparency' belonging to the ego almost bumps through into a 'form-of-being'. The ego gets too much 'weight-of-being'; it holds itself more on the side of being than of consciousness. The ego has not simply disappeared but now holds itself up at the level of the object pole, which is why we cannot, strictly speaking, characterize fascination as a state without an ego.

This situation gives the subject *the experience of metamorphosing*: at the place where, for consciousness, my ego normally is, there is now, as it were, a root. In the other states of consciousness without ego, the ego also 'disappears' because of the suspension of reflection, but this is not accompanied by a feeling of changing into something else (a tram, for example) that takes the place of my familiar self. Because of this thorough internalization of the ego, the fascinated desubjectivation also cannot be equated with depersonalization of itself, where the self-alienation is purely negative and is not accompanied by the imminent appearance of the ego in another form (see also Chapter 2). This near coincidence of the ego-position with a non-psychic in-itself means that during fascination itself, I cannot say 'I *am* the image'. In fascination, the subject is speechless and falls – like all roots and bathrooms – outside language. With the recovery of reflection, which breaks the fascination, linguistics (the reflection par excellence) reappears: I *was* the tableau. This statement immediately introduces a minimal differentiation, for it articulates the distinction between 'I' and 'tableau' grammatically. The threat of fusion between the ego and the object has been lifted, but the subject is not yet well from it: the heaviness of being inert still reverberates.

Kafka and viscosity

It seems to me that this description of fascination as a quasi-being experience, as the bizarre experience of a looming metamorphosis, leans heavily on Sartre's complex analysis of viscosity or the syrupy at the end of *L'être et le néant*. Indeed, within the framework of viscosity, Sartre brings together the fascination and the 'specter of a metamorphosis' (2003, pp. 736–753). I retain only a few elements from the passage in question. In contrast to the liquid and the solid, both modes of being the pure in-itself (2003, p. 737), the viscous does not easily allow itself to be separated from me. By touching the viscous, the for-itself threatens to be absorbed by the in-itself. It clings to me like a leech; it is the gentle death of the for-itself. *At the same time, the viscous is myself* (2003, p. 747, my italics). The viscous evokes something of a mutual appropriation: the viscous substance is an extension of myself and I am an extension of the viscous. Sartre speaks of 'a touchable *fascination of the viscous*' (2003, p. 746, my italics). And: 'In the comprehension of the viscous . . . there is something like the specter of a *metamorphosis*' (2003, p. 747, Sartre's italics).

Now, it occurs to me that how the viscous obscures the otherwise clear distinction between the in-itself and the for-itself is indeed contained in the entire preceding analysis of fascination. A solid object I hold in my hands I can easily let go again. There is nothing to suggest that it would not allow itself to be separated from me, that I could not put it down in another place. The fluid, too, although now in its remarkable fleetingness, is easily demarcated materially. If it touches me, it drips right off me again or I can easily remove it. The viscous, like pitch or honey, on the other hand, is 'unreliable' (2003, p. 744). It is 'a liquid with an anomaly' (2003) or a solid that softens. In either case, the pure being-in-itself of things is affected, and its beingness allows itself to be less isolated from me. It *sticks* to me and makes stains. 'The viscous appears as the *impetus for a fusion of the world with me*', says Sartre (2003, p. 743, my italics).

In this sense, can we not also describe the fascinating objects described previously as viscous objects par excellence? After all, fascinating objects have me in their power and threaten to engulf me; I cannot detach myself from them. What Sartre says of the viscous seems to me to be eminently valid for the fascinating: 'At the moment when I think I possess the viscous, it possesses, by a curious reversal, me'. There, its essential characteristic appears: 'its softness acts like a suction cup' (2003, p. 745). The subject has no power over this capricious appropriation process, in which the possessing and the possessed fight each other's place. In fascination, there is no fusion with the object, but I urge it to merge with it ('impetus of a fusion'). The alienating experience of fascination is characterized by a pronounced 'elasticity' between the positions of myself and the object. Both the bathroom tableau and the root have a high viscosity. Through their malignant stickiness, fascinating objects threaten to encapsulate and take over the 'fundamental selfhood' that the ego (the psychic) confers on consciousness (2003, pp. 176–177).

As Sartre says of the viscous (2003, p. 743, 748–749), we could characterize the fascinating as that beingness that tends to *transcend the opposition between the psychic and the physical.* The bathroom tableau and the root, of course, have nothing psychic in themselves; they are unwieldy physical, material things in the world, but in their capacity as fascinating objects, they tend to behave in the subject's experience as something psychic (taking the place of the ego). In this sense, we can rightly refer to fascinating objects as ghosts of a metamorphosis. Not all that is sticking is also fascinating, but in the phenomenology of human experience, there is nothing more sticking than the fascinating.

The confusion of speech between the ego and consciousness makes fascination in some respects lean strongly toward the *Unheimliche*, in which there is confusion between the strange and the familiar. Applied to fascination: what is familiar to the ego is strange to consciousness. The fascinating object is at once strange and familiar. It is the familiar that we experience as strange: in the familiar place of the ego, there is suddenly something else and strange (which does not belong there) or something familiar like a tree root suddenly finds itself in a strange relation to myself (namely *as* myself). Conversely, it is the strange or heterogeneous that suddenly becomes one's own and familiar. So this swift back-and-forth between strange and familiar does not concern the object as such, but the place it respectively occupies for the ego and consciousness.

The motif of metamorphosis, of people taking on non-human forms, is as old as humanity itself. Just think of Ovid's influential *Metamorphoses*, in which gods, mortals, animals and things take on each other's forms. And there are the werewolf stories, for example. Metamorphoses hold a strong fascination. A very recent example from literature is the novel *Kafka is Dead* by Feuth (2020), in which the main character transforms into his deceased dog, Kafka. I think the reason why this story comes across as less fascinating, however, is because the change there is very gradual; for example, the person in question already feels a bit like a dog while still having a normal human body, and even when he has finally morphologically become a dog, he continues to reflect and philosophize 'as a human being' about this bizarre state. This story seems instead an extreme illustration of Freud's view of mourning, in which the subject incorporates the lost object into his ego (Freud 1916–1917). More powerful is the wonderful novel *My Fox, My Woman . . .* by Garnett (1967, originally 1922), in which the female main character suddenly and for no reason at all turns completely into a fox and the disappearance of her inner humanity soon follows.

The best-known and most powerful modern example of the *uncanny* nature of the break between ego and consciousness in fascination is found in Kafka's 'Die Verwandlung' (Kafka 1980, originally 1915). In it, the main character sees himself – suddenly and without any announcement – transformed into a dung beetle upon awakening.

When Gregor Samsa awoke one morning from restless dreams, he discovered that in his bed he had turned into a monstrous vermin. He lay on his armored back and, lifting his head slightly, could see his curved brown belly, divided by arched articulations, on which the blanket, about to slide down, could barely find hold. All his, compared to his other size, pitifully thin legs flickered help-lessly before his eyes.

(p. 840)

These are the opening sentences of a bizarre, typically Kafkaesque story in which the state of fascination takes on a grotesque form. Transcending any antici-patory representation, this is a completely unexpected form of an objectality that the character can no longer distinguish from himself.

To the absurd, this story draws out the idea of how drastically a person can suddenly change. This takes shape primarily through the literal change of form but relatedly also in the change of character. Kafka describes Gregor as a virtue who strictly follows the rules and wants all the good for his parents and sister; he is actually a somewhat dull but adored young man. And suddenly, he turns into a selfish, not above animal lusts and needs beast that can no longer be counted on. The masterful thing about Kafka now is that he simultaneously accompanies this total break and discontinuity between the two figures with a continuity in which the former Gregor, despite the metamorphosis, still shines through. Discontinuity occurs at the level of the ego: Gregor is a dung beetle and behaves entirely by this identity (crawls on the ceiling and eats stinking garbage). Continuity occurs at the level of consciousness: Gregor does not know how to get that ungainly body out of bed and dressed to catch his train as a commercial traveler and avoid falling into disgrace with his superior.

The split between ego and consciousness is clear. Seen from the ego, Gregor is without question a dung beetle, and at no point does he question that identity – he cannot avoid it. The dung beetle has taken the place of the ego. But seen from the consciousness, the life of before continues, albeit now hampered by the strange anatomy. However, the consciousness of not being the dung beetle is disconnected from the ego-Gregor. It is no longer the egological consciousness 'of' Gregor. Yet now, the dung beetle is the thing that consciousness cannot avoid. What I want to say is, for Gregor, the dung beetle is a fascinating object. For his ego, he is the dung beetle, while for consciousness, it remains a heterogeneous object. The paralysis and exclusivity lie in the fact that Gregor cannot change his position vis-à-vis the dung beetle and cannot move. No matter what he does or tries, the ego and the dung beetle occupy the same place.

I will return to this story of Kafka and the uncanny later. The whole motif of metamorphosis also ties in with the issue of identity, which I discuss in Chapter 6.

2

Fear of self-destruction

Fascinating metamorphoses and solidified truth

Precarious objects

As we saw in the previous chapter, I understand fascination in its basic meaning as a paralyzed state of self-loss in a radical seizure by an all-pervading object from which the subject is barely separated. Thus conceived, fascination has a desubjectifying effect; it undermines the subject. The subject is not full but 'away' from it or appears in an egodystonic form. All attention goes to the colossally exclusive object, and the powerless, subjugated subject itself is reduced to a 'subject-minimum' with a global impoverishment of mental and affective functioning. Attention is extremely intense but stripped of any personal affective investment. It is a sterile, disarming attention. The implosion of the ambivalence between extreme attraction and equally extreme repulsion described previously leaves the subject atrophied and unmoved.

In this sense, fascination is akin to several other forms of object relations described in the psychoanalytic literature, but it has its specific character. Throughout its history, psychoanalysis has described various kinds of 'precarious objects': objects that it is far from clear are experienced by the subject as entities separate from him. I refer, for example, to primary narcissism (Freud 1914a), primary identification (Freud 1923b), confusion between internal and external reality in excessive projective identification (Klein 1957), transitional objects (Winnicott 1951), bizarre objects (Bion 1956), mirror objects (Lacan 1966a), the Thing (Lacan 1986), self-objects (Kohut 1971), adhesive objects (Tustin 1980), the autistic-contiguous position (Ogden 1994) and the equivalence mode (Fonagy et al. 2006). Although we find such mental states, in which the distinction between subject and object is strained, mainly in psychopathology, they are latent in everyone and can become manifest in each of us in vulnerable circumstances. Thus conceived, they constitute invariants in the human psychic condition, making them significant in a general anthropological sense. I see fascination, with its specific color, as belonging to this family of precarious object relations.

Following the phenomenological description of fascination in the previous chapter, I now attempt to present a psychoanalytic and, more specifically, metapsychological elaboration of it. So-called 'metapsychology' is the field of unconscious

DOI: 10.4324/9781003515982-4

processes that help clarify and explain mental states and dynamics. What happens unconsciously when a person is in a state of fascination? To picture the metapsychological substructure of fascination, I draw on Melanie Klein's theory of excessive projective identification and the bizarre objects associated with it, as described by Wilfred Bion. By speaking of 'confusion' and 'perplexed states of mind' in the same breath, one could say that Klein (1957, p. 221) was the first to bring the problem of fascination – without mentioning the term – to psychoanalytic attention.

I see fascination as a possible result of excessive projective identification and the fascinating object as a special form of a bizarre object. More specifically, fascination is characterized as the freezing of the dynamic processes described by Klein and Bion, and this, combined with the loss of any distance towards the object, isolates it from all other objects and consequently gives it an exclusive and all-dominant character. In addition, I want to relate the fascination to the fear of self-destruction, which Klein also links to excessive projective identification (see Thys 2017). Precisely because of the exclusive status of the object, the fascinated subject ends up in a paralyzing impasse: it experiences the object both as vital because it is largely 'accommodated' in it by projection and at the same time as life-threatening because it is in danger of losing itself completely in it. This metapsychological exercise helps me understand fascination as an ultimate defense against being sucked in by a sudden intrusion of unconscious material into consciousness, which the subject experiences as life-threatening. Further examination of the clinical vignettes I supply as illustrations leads me to conclude that the fascinating object is a condensed and persecutory figuration of an internal 'superego violence'. Thus, the phenomenon of fascination takes its place within the totality of the many forms that fear of self-destruction can take (for an overview, see Hurvich 2003).

Clinical vignettes

I now present two clinical examples from psychoanalytic psychotherapy practice. In doing so, my primary focus is on how the experience of fascination occurs in the psychoanalytic process itself.

At the beginning of his psychoanalysis, Jan is a 30-year-old single man. He complains that in the artistic sector in which he has been trained and is now working, he is unable to live up to his potential and is not receiving enough appreciation and recognition. Throughout the analysis, elaborate fantasies emerge of grand successes that evoke much admiration and adoration from a frenzied audience. In the enjoyment of this success, however, the threat that also emanates from it is never far away. These fantasies of greatness alternate and stand in sharp contrast to regularly recurring dreams in many variants in which he comes to no achievement, goes off ashamed and feels inferior and small. In reality, Jan is not doing so badly professionally and finds himself, shall we say, somewhere between the megalomaniacal inflated greatness of his fantasies and the melancholic destructive smallness of his dreams. Either way, he suffers – and this is his reason for seeking help – that he is an anxious and inhibited man, unable to realize his potential sufficiently. We also see this painful split at work in the analytic sessions: sometimes, he speaks very inhibited, expressing denigrating views of himself and fearing my dismissive thoughts; at other times, he rises in lofty reflections on his qualities, which I and others lose out and are objects of his biting sarcasm. He describes his mother as a domineering, controlling woman who leaves him no breathing space and from whom he finds it difficult to distance himself. His father, on the other hand, emerges as an insignificant, boring man who, in turn, remains too distant and has nothing to offer him. While his mother is too interested in him, he experiences his father as indifferent. Throughout the analysis, his anger toward both of them becomes increasingly highlighted, not infrequently followed by an anxious retreat again.

I now zoom in on a moment in a session somewhere in the fourth year of his analysis. After a silence, Jan tells me, with the dejection still in his voice, that just now, out of nowhere, he had the image of me suddenly turning into a huge monster vomiting a black gash that spreads out over him.

> That mush is as black as the monster itself; actually, the mush is the monster vomiting itself out over me and under which I am completely buried, or rather it is a huge black tube that sucks me up completely. I see the monster outside me, yet it is inside my head; it is my head. I *am* the monster. It is as if I am allowed to come alive for a moment and then sucked back out and cease to exist again.

As bizarre as this experience is, Jan's description of it does not come across as psychotic; we cannot speak of a hallucination here. A few sessions later, he returns to the image:

> You turn into a monster, and I get buried under it. It's going to suffocate me. I especially see the greatness of the monster: it is tremendously large, up to the ceiling. If it falls on me, I can never get out from under it, like if I were walking next to a skyscraper and it were to fall on me.

What is striking is the static nature of the image; everything is frozen, without any movement. Nor is the experience accompanied by any affect; he feels nothing. At this moment of fascination, there is only the image of the black monster into which the analyst has been transformed, the fascinating object; everything else has disappeared. Moreover, the fascinating object (partially) coincides with the subject: the dialectic of inside and outside solidifies into a quasi-coincidence of the two. The swift oscillation between the two positions and directions comes to a standstill so that their distinction almost disappears: the black mush covers Jan's body (the object takes the place of the subject) and the monster sucks him in (the subject takes the place of the object). Object and subject take each other's place quasi-simultaneously. This state of self-loss goes together with a quasi-simultaneity of appearance and disappearance, aptly expressed by the patient: 'It is as if I come to life for a moment and then cease to exist again'. Fascination shows itself here as the freezing and canceling of simultaneous attraction and repulsion: the fascinating object both sucks in and evokes tremendous fear at the same time, but in the very moment of fascination, all affective experience falls silent in a frozen and bizarre image. The affects are neutralized in fascination. We see this especially with fear, which is clearly present in the description of his experience: ceasing to exist, suffocating, being buried, yet Jan does not feel the fear as an affect during the fascinating moment itself. In this freezing, the distinction between subject and object is in question. All of this state occurs on a hushed island in the middle of a stormy sea and seems completely isolated and disconnected from the rest of the session.

My second illustration is Marie. I already brought her up in the previous chapter of my phenomenological analysis of fascination. Here, I elaborate on the vignette more in its clinical context. Marie, a 22-year-old woman, was referred from a psychiatric ward for personality disorders, where she had been hospitalized for a year as a result of self-mutilation, increasing passive withdrawal from social interactions and dissociative moments with loss of reality without a real psychotic breakdown. During the hospital stay, there were moments of paralysis when she could no longer step or move, and she regularly caught herself in random, compulsive-feeling lying. She could lock herself into relational fantasies and self-blame. She is very demanding of herself. She has had to discontinue an ongoing education because of all this while her partner relationship is holding up. Upon referral, the condition has improved, but there is a demand for further therapy as a precaution for relapse. Marie is intelligent and verbally strong. Her initial hesitation hides a solid motivation for therapy, as well as a stubborn willpower. She was raised sheltered. She describes her father as little emotionally involved, while the image of her mother is clearly idealized; her endless and selfless love has nothing to complain about. When the patient does catch herself thinking critically about her mother, she has to pay for it with painful guilt. Nevertheless, she recalls much-undefined sadness during her elementary school years and a slow emergence of the symptoms from puberty onward. In her psychotherapy, she speaks meticulously, concerned about whether she is expressing herself precisely enough and whether I would understand her correctly. She wants to make me, whom she sees as an ideal caring figure, as comfortable as possible. Furthermore, she keeps me quiet at a distance: 'It should not become too personal'.

Then there is the moment of fascination, which I have already described in the previous chapter, in which the woman is completely captivated by the bathroom tableau, which occupies all visual as well as mental space so that she, too, can hardly exist as a subject. By saying afterward, 'I *was* that image', she testifies that she has not yet disappeared into a total fusion with the fascinating object. In this example, the patient is briefly so captivated by a certain object, the bathroom tableau, that she can barely distance herself from it and the rest of the world disappears before her. This is not merely a momentary being sucked in by something, but a much more radical state, in which the whole category of language, symbolization and meaning is fundamentally affected. The entire subjectivity seems to be absorbed by a bizarre object pole. The subject's distance from the object falls away, it sticks to it, so to speak, or the subject shifts to or disappears into the object pole, and all this occurs in complete immobility. This image also functions as a fascinating object that makes the rest of the world disappear, with which the subject virtually coincides and which totally isolates itself from the analytical process.

While being fascinated, at the moment when the bathroom tableau paralyzes and disables her as a subject, Marie feels nothing and is absent as a person. It is only when the fascination is lifted that affective catch-up seems to occur, as if the affectivity obstructed during the fascination explodes in the next moment and overwhelms her. The affective intensity with which we usually associate fascination is that which surrounds the fascination but is, strictly speaking, not a part of it. The affective freezing point and the affective boiling point are right next to each other. The most striking sensations Marie has once the fascination is broken are mental emptiness, disgust and a frightening tightness. The suspension of mental functioning and inner space in the moment of fascination produces immediately afterward, retroactively, a fear of suffocation, a fear of death. At the same time, the sudden return of mental space results in a feeling of immense emptiness: this space, as it were, still lies fallow and has not yet been psychically exploited. Like a black hole, it generates an enormous suction force. The suspension of all mental functioning makes her reduced, so to speak, to a purely physical existence. Physically, then, she feels too full, it's disgusting. She feels vomiting: repulsion as opposed to suction. Also, in Jan's vignette, we see the fact of vomiting.

I have seen this affective confusing ambivalence contrasted with the fascinated impassivity happen in several patients. As we saw with Jan, Marie also tears the whole experience apart from what was said, thought or felt before and later in that session. She has no associations with it and does not want to relate it to anything. In Marie's case, too, the state of fascination is a freezing affective overwhelm, in which, in combination with an uncontrollable suction, a fear that is difficult to handle seems to play a role and in which the subject can barely distinguish itself from the object. Jan sees the black monster right in front of him, without distance, barely existing himself, and he says that at the same time, he himself is the monster. Similarly, Marie says that she is no longer there, that only the image is there, and then she says that she herself was the image. The fascinating object is thus for the subject *both an object and itself*; it is 'something else' and yet also 'myself'. *There is a quasi-simultaneity of disappearing into nothingness and coinciding with everything of the imposing fascinating object.* However precarious the distinction between subject and object positions, there is no fusion. Indeed, to be fascinated, there must still be a sufficient 'portion' of a subject position – what I call the 'subject-minimum'.

Later, we will see that the state of fascination can be seen as an ultimate defense against a possible fusion with the object, against a total loss of self. In fascination, there is unmistakably an element of depersonalization, but here, too, the condition is more specific: it does not stop at an experience of depersonalization pure and simple, but it is accompanied by adhesion to a quasi-object that completely occupies the subject's attention. The same applies to the relationship concerning dissociation: fascination has a clearly dissociative, even disconnected character – the subject loses connection with a large part of the world and of himself – but on the understanding that at the same time, there is a very strong attachment to the exclusive, fascinating object. All the potential for connection is concentrated precisely in the attention to that one object; everything else has disappeared. As the clinical vignettes show, this being captivated by an exclusive object can be a very momentary, transient state, but the disconnection concerning what is unconsciously at stake and the suspension of associations with a wider affective context can continue afterward in a more than average dissociative state, now, however, without being manifestly fascinated. The fascination is there suddenly and, in its extreme form, briefly, but its aftermath can be persistently long-lasting. With Jan and Marie, it took months before the undermining and constricting impact of fascination gave in and gave way to the inspiring effect that could finally emanate from it. With both examples in mind, which I will elaborate on later, let me now explore the condition of fascination further psychoanalytically.

Excessive projective identification

How can we understand fascination experiences in psychoanalytic terms? At the heart of my metapsychological design of fascination is the experiential fact that the distinction between ego and object threatens to fall away, more precisely that the place of the sole, exclusive object and the ego are indistinguishable, however, without a fusion of the two because there remains a minimal ego-position necessary to be fascinated. This subject-minimum is safeguarded precisely by the momentary halting or freezing of the frightening suction. The object itself, which at the last moment remains intact *as* an object, acquires, so to speak, an ego-status anyway – 'I am the monster', 'I am the image'. There is the simultaneity of having the object in front of oneself and being the object oneself. It is precisely this ambiguity combined with the exclusive nature of the object that I think typifies fascination. In search of a psychoanalytic clarification of fascination, I choose an angle that I believe lends itself pre-eminently to a clinical elucidation of the dynamics of fascination and, moreover, clarifies the role of the annihilation anxiety, without which fascination is difficult to understand. I mean the projective identification as described by Klein and then, more specifically, in its excessive form. I will thus clarify my view of fascination with the Kleinian excessive projective identification and the anxiety theory associated with it. In doing so, I will focus on the phantasmatic, evacuative and defensive nature of projective identification as Klein originally intended. I will leave aside the post-Kleinian and post-Bionian intersubjectivation of the concept as it developed later – especially under the impetus of Thomas Ogden (see Spillius & O'Shaughnessy 2012) and in which its original meaning in terms of the drive takes a back seat (Thys 2015a). I will now briefly describe Kleinian projective identification and its relation to the fear of annihilation, brought to attention by Klein.

As early as 1927, Klein describes a mechanism that, in retrospect, could pass for projective identification (Hinshelwood 1991, p. 179). There, Klein briefly reports on Gerald, a 4-year-old boy in his full oedipal years, who develops intense anxiety during analysis. One of his objects of fear is an animal, actually a man who acts like an animal, who appears to represent his father. What frightens Gerald so much is that, as Klein interprets it, his unconscious desire and fantasy to castrate and kill his father will be paid in equal measure by the vengeful beast. Gerald had a toy tiger for whom he felt great affection and who would protect him from the beast. Now in his imagination, he allowed this tiger to enter the room and carry out its aggression against the father: biting off the father's penis, boiling it and eating it. The primitive part of the personality, characterized by oral and anal-sadistic fixations, was represented in Gerald's case by the tiger, which, it turned out later, stood for Gerald himself or at least for a part of himself that he preferred not to realize in his name (Klein 1927, pp. 171–172). Unconsciously and in fantasy, Gerald projects a sadistic piece of himself into the toy tiger, who is thus identified with that piece.

In her well-known 1946 text 'Notes on some Schizoid Mechanisms', Klein describes the process, only to mention it by name in the 1952 edition. According to Klein, the source of the first fear is the baby's own death drive or destructive drive: the baby is afraid of being destroyed from within. In its primitive fantasy world, the baby experiences painful or frustrating bodily sensations as 'dangerous, haunting evil objects', which Klein says act as inner 'representatives of the death drive' (Klein 1948, p. 30). Part of the death drive is, therefore, transformed into aggression against an object, initially the breast and, by extension, the mother's body. In this context, Klein describes anal attacks, in which dangerous substances – excrements – are introduced from the self into the mother. Along with these harmful excrements, hated parts of the self are also expelled and projected onto the mother. These excrements are not only supposed to damage the object but also to control it and take possession of it. To the extent that the mother comes to contain the bad parts of the self, she is no longer experienced as a separated individual but as the bad self. Klein concludes, 'This leads to a particular form of identification which establishes the prototype of an aggressive object-relation. I suggest for these processes the term 'projective identification'' (Klein 1946, p. 8).

Projective identification is an unconscious, but in primitive mental functioning, very concretistic fantasy, which for the infant quasi coincides with bodily sensations and is, therefore, attributed a strong realism. Such projective fantasies are provoked by and are a defense against internally experienced evil, haunting objects that are bent on destroying the good internal objects and the self, as such. Projective identification, which belongs within the logic of the paranoid-schizoid position, is, first and foremost, a defense against annihilation anxiety. Referring to Freud's well-known case of Schreber, Klein (1946, p. 23) argues that the fear of the end of the world is a projection of the fear of the disintegration of the self, of internal catastrophe. For the ego, the object becomes, to a greater or lesser degree, '*an extension of the self, a representative of the ego*' (Klein 1952, p. 68, my italics). The source of danger and anxiety is thus externalized and accommodated in an object.

However, the clear object status of the object is compromised the more drastically this process of projective identification proceeds. Indeed, to the extent that the object in question is identified with parts of the ego, it stands more for the ego and consequently becomes less distinct from the ego in the subject's experience.

With this fact, namely that projective identification creates objects with an ego-status, objects with a high ego content, we come to the problem of fascination. In excessive projective identification (Klein 1946, 1957), the distinction between ego and object can become very unclear. In extremis, the object will pass for the subject. What is actually an object simultaneously presents itself to the subject as a bulge or metastasis of its ego. Not much remains at the subject pole; all ego is accommodated at the object pole. Hence, as we see in the clinical examples, the object is so imposing that the subject feels small towards it. Excessive projective identification is, therefore, a very suitable breeding ground for the emergence of fascination. However, it is not a sufficient condition; not every excessive use of projective identification necessarily leads to fascination. For the subject to enter a state of fascination, the projected material must be experienced as coming together in one object, the exclusive fascinating object. This concentration in one object also adds to the fact that the object appears to the subject as impressively grand. The object of excessive projective identification becomes fascinating insofar as it is for the subject the exclusive object pole in which it recognizes itself, albeit in a strange guise. Precisely, this conjunction of holding out as an object and yet having an ego-status at the same time makes the object fascinating. In fascination, the subject is extremely, almost outside of itself, intrigued by something of itself, a strange 'self form' that it cannot integrate nor relate to other objects.

Bion (1956, 1957, 1958) speaks of '*bizarre objects*' arising from excessive projective identification, objects that combine characteristics of external objects and projected parts of the personality. He always mentions them in the plural and describes them as circling the subject. He even speaks of 'planetary movements' (Bion 1956, p. 39). The fascinating object now we can characterize as one gigantic bizarre object to which the puny, almost emptied subject hangs rigidly. Any motion of multiple objects floating in space is reduced in the moment of fascination to one unmoved, all-space-occupying agglomerate in which self and object characteristics form one impenetrable whole. In fascination, the dispersion of self-particles projected into various objects retraces its steps and clumps together into one remaining object. In this sense, we can conceive of the fascinating object as a special form of a bizarre object, namely, a form in which its dynamic motion has ceased.

For both excessive projective identification and fascination, let us now look at the role of fear of annihilation. The crucial point here is that projective identification is both – in its start – a defense against mortal fear and – in its excessive form – becomes a source of mortal fear itself. This paradox can be understood in two interrelated ways, namely, on the one hand, concerning the status of the object and, on the other hand, the mental impoverishment of the subject. The more incisive the projective identification is, the more likely it is that the defensive effect of splitting and projection fails since the external character of the object into which it is projected diminishes. The object becomes again the ego, becoming more and more like the subject. This means that the source of anxiety that was initially external now increasingly comes to coincide with the self again. What was originally a safe object to harbor the danger and control it from a distance comes closer and closer, transforming itself like a boomerang into something that threatens to swallow the subject completely. Now, the previously safe object itself becomes life-threatening, an 'uncontrollable overpowering object' (Klein 1946, p. 4). The distance becomes so minute that the subject can no longer shake it off and can barely distinguish itself from it. The outwardly projected source of agony can no longer be escaped. Klein pointed out that projective identification is thus the source of pursuit anxiety and claustrophobia, the fear as a subject of being permanently buried in the object and never being able to escape it (Klein 1946, p. 12; 1955, p. 166). At the same time, despite this fear of annihilation, the subject cannot afford to distance itself from the object because, after all, it contains an essential part of itself. To distance oneself from the object is, therefore, to leave oneself behind, and that would imply signing one's death warrant. The object is thus both life-threatening and life-necessary.

This brings us to the paradoxical situation that the object stands for both the 'extremely bad self' and the 'ideal self'. In several places, Klein (1952, 1955, 1957) speaks of the close relationship between the need for idealization and the fear of persecution. While idealization is initially deployed as a defense against the threat of the evil persecuting object, resulting in a split between the two, when excessive projective identification occurs, the two again become confused with each other and even more difficult to keep apart (Klein 1963). Since only one object remains in fascination, the extremely good and the extremely bad can no longer be split into different objects. Fascination is precisely the paralysis of the subject in this hope-less impasse, in which the extreme ambivalence of desire (for the life-giving, ideal object) and fear (for the life-threatening, bad object) implodes into an exclusive coagulation. Again, we see that a situation conceived by Klein as dynamic, which keeps pushing the subject to 'invent' new solutions and escape routes, freezes in fascination.

On the other hand, the drastic projective identification impoverishes and weak-ens the subject to such an extent (cf. Klein 1946, p. 11; 1957, p. 192) that – if it even wanted to – it no longer has the strength to be able to regain its distance and breath. The subject has 'emptied' itself into the object to such an extent that only a pale shadow remains, a puny creature that still means little in the face of the imposing, fascinating object. Together with the exclusivity of the object, it is this same impoverishment that makes the subject unable to distinguish the good and the bad – more specifically, the ideal and the reprehensible – within the same object. In fascination as the result of an out-of-control projective identification, as it were, a psychic amputation takes place on the part of the subject. The psychic is completely 'dispossessed' and takes on the bizarre form of an impressive 'phantom psyche' in the object, filled to bursting point, which seems mysteriously overloaded with meaning. Precisely because of the radical shriveling of mental space, fascination can be distinguished – besides the specific adhesion to an exclusive object – from a 'psychic retreat' (Steiner 1993), a 'private self' (Modell 1993) or a 'secret cocoon' (Rudden 2011). In these states, too, there is an isolation from the world, but in each case, there is still a – albeit covert – psychic space in which the subject can safely retreat into a fantasy world that is difficult to access. In fascination, that space is missing and there is no longer such a thing as a private self in which the subject could withdraw. All space is occupied by the fascinating object.

It is clear from the foregoing that fascination can never be pure attraction or a state in which attraction predominates; otherwise, the subject would reproject the projected parts and try to regain control over them. Nor can fascination be pure fear or a state in which fear dominates; otherwise, the subject would place the object safely at a distance again. No, attraction and repulsion are so equally matched that they cancel each other's affective stirring. The result is the fascinated state of being unmoved by an exclusively all-encompassing object. This object is at once something to embrace and unite with because it embodies an essential truth of the subject and something to abhor and distance itself from because that very truth is experienced as life-threatening to the subject. In the confrontation with this projected revelation of a truth of oneself in a strange object, the fascination, this 'intimidating intimacy', is momentary freezing: just not quite disappearing into the object yet not distancing oneself from it. These contradictory tendencies are united in a defense against annihilation. Let us now take a closer look at how this state can be understood clinically in the context of the analytic process.

Fascination and fear of annihilation in the psychoanalytic process

In the patient's talking in the analytic process, the connection between the conscious and the unconscious usually comes alive. The unconscious looms up between the words in surprising turns of speech. Throughout talking, new material emerges that engages in the chain of associations and colors its further course. That new material generated in becoming conscious gets connected – sometimes laboriously – with the familiar, places it in a new light or changes the punctuation in what was previously thought, felt or said. It does not become isolated from it; on the contrary, becoming conscious has a connecting effect. The new material acquires a place in the narrative unfolding in the analytical process.

In moments of fascination, the exact opposite happens. Suddenly and in an overwhelming way, something appears to consciousness that, instead of flowing with the talking or making the talking flow with it, shuts down the talking. The patient is no longer among the words but falls outside of them. Suddenly, something appears: an image, a representation, a dream image, which isolates itself from everything else. It is also something new, which also reveals itself in some (not always so clear) way from the previous speech, but immediately – as the two vignettes illustrate – it is cut off from it, amputated, isolated. Instead of being part of it, the new material isolates itself from the narrative. At the same time, it demands all attention and pushes away all other possible representations. The suddenly all-consuming image – of the black mash or the bathroom tableau – terrorizes the entire field of experience. It sucks in every mental functioning with immeasurable gravity. There is no more dynamism; instead of connection, dissolution reigns, desubjectifying. The paralyzed subject falls out of the mental and, as we see in the examples, out of the linguistic. Both Jan and Marie were tongue-tied and there was no more room in their heads for thoughts. While ordinary consciousness is a linguistic process that, through free association, simultaneously generates new language, fascination silences the subject and degenerates language: what appears to consciousness is simultaneously disconnected from language, which at once undermines all imagination and all creation of meaning. In fascination, the meaning-generating function of the link with the unconscious is suspended. Yet the fascinating object seems to be heavily pregnant with a mysterious meaning that does not yet release itself. The subject's hands and feet are tied to it, but cannot make sense of it.

My hypothesis about what happens at such times is as follows. Out of nowhere, new material suddenly wells up. That material imposes itself as a penetrating truth of the subject from which it cannot distance itself. This truth, coalescing into an overwhelming image, was once the object of excessive projective identification and now returns to the subject with full force and in a strange guise. We can speak, in terms of Bion (1965), of an unannounced transformation in 'O' (which, for Bion, is the symbol of ultimate truth) emerging from an infinite undifferentiated zone that is of a different order from the making of narrative and insightful connections (cf. Vermote 2013, 2015). The subject cannot distance itself from it – it experiences the 'object' as something fundamental to itself – but neither does it refuse to identify with it because it simultaneously experiences it as life-threatening, the reason why it was split off and projected. That the material has not lost its destructive power for the subject suggests that its projection has never been adequately contained by another, let alone been able to be reprojected into 'release' and bearable form (cf. Bion 1962). The revelation of an essential, long-dormant truth of the subject thus fuels the enormous fear of annihilation.

I see the state of fascination as an ultimate defense against this unexpected annihilation threat. From an unmanageable fear of death, the subject retreats into a 'psychic coma', a mental holding for death so as not to die really, comparable to what Bion (1981, p. 648) refers to as 'subthalamic fear'. The subject stiffens in a mental *rigor mortis*. Quasi simultaneously with the revelation of the subjective truth, it immediately goes still in an imposing but frozen appearance that flattens all mental space in the subject. What at first reveals as an entrapment of defense immediately cramps and entrenches itself in an inaccessible and exclusively fascinating object. The confusing thing about fascination is that it both admits and rejects a fundamental truth at the drop of a hat. It may relate to a transformation in O, but this transformation is immediately frozen. The possible dynamics that could emerge from this revelation of O are nipped in the bud. Fascination is a contorted transformation in O that is overwhelming but sterile. The whole of this phenomenology and metapsychology makes it understandable that the fascinating object cuts itself off from the rest of the psychic material in the analytic process. The sterile fascination can only become fruitful and the frozen fascinating object can only thaw by bringing it out of its isolation and into connection with other materials. Only in this way can O move toward K (knowledge) (cf. Vermote 2015). This presupposes an enlargement of the psychic space shriveled in fascination and a decondensation of the extremely condensed experience of fascination. Increasing the psychic space is equivalent to decreasing fascination. In fascination, there is no longer *unsaturated space* (cf. Riolo in Ferro 2006, p. 92). With Bion, we can say that analysis must bring back into the dimension of 'infinity' (Bion 1965; Vermote 2011) to break open the fascinating oppressiveness. Let us look at how all this worked in the clinical vignettes and try to gain more insight into the specific nature of the split-off and now re-emerging psychic material.

Jan is suddenly overwhelmed by the space-filling image of the black mush, the monster, which stands for the analyst but equally for himself. The fascination occurs in silence, in a moment of speechlessness. Then he tries to put the experience into words after all, yet to report from his dejection. This can only be done sparingly because the fascination completely decontextualizes the object, and with it, the subject who is quasi-absorbed by it isolates it from everything and consequently blocks further associations. After the description of the fascination experience, Jan is left in a state of extremely anxious confusion and overwhelmed while the fascinating image continues to impose itself. The mesmerizing object and the entire state he is in remain bizarre to him, seemingly overloaded with meaning and, at the same time, devoid of any sense. Associations remain absent and silences predominate. It is only many sessions later that a cautious thaw occurs, speech gets going again and the fascinating object becomes linked to an unconscious dynamic that fascination had put a stop to initially. Gradually, it becomes clear that the state of fascination is a radical defense against extremely frightening encroaching unconscious material, which clumps together in an inert metamorphosis: the fascinating object. Liberation from fascination is very laborious and not without struggle. The gradual liquefaction of the solidified dynamics only occurs through another fascinating object, which – more than the black mush – nevertheless lends itself, albeit reluctantly, to associations.

This other fascinating form, which presents itself, among other things, as a dream image, consists of a colossal, large head that hangs just above him and fills the entire space. This suffocating image, in which there is initially no movement and which is not accompanied by any affect, laboriously gets out of its isolation in the further course of the analysis. Gradually, it gains context. At first, Jan associates the head with the elementary school teacher, who was an impressive figure for him as a small boy. Later, the head increasingly becomes his father and also his mother, who, for him, was always 'too close' to his skin and by whom he felt drained. Jan seems to be frantically trying to *give that impersonal thing a human identity*. The head also comes to represent 'the big people' against whom he feels so void and insignificant. At certain moments, the representation appears that the head bursts open into many different heads, which, however, immediately coalesce back into one, even more colossal head. We can see the bursting open of the head as a way to escape fascination. If the search for open space 'around' the fascinating object fails, the subject searches, it seems, for space 'inside' the object. To do so, its absolute density must be lifted, a necessary condition to make the distinction between good and bad possible again. Jan tries, as it were, to free the various projected particles from their clumping together. This breaking open is not done without violence. Confusion, however, continues to prevail.

Afterward, the head, named 'the monster', becomes 'something that terrifies me enormously but at the same time attracts me very strongly'. Here, we recognize the extreme ambivalence between fear and passion that surrounds the fascination as such, indicating that Jan is no longer caught in the fascination *strictu sensu*. This is accompanied by two remarkable, highly illustrative experiences. First, there is the physical sensation of being very large and rising far above the puny humans. 'I feel terribly big now; my legs seem to be two meters long. Now I myself am the monster'. Perhaps fascination is not far off here and this is a moment – in the oscillation between subject and object position – when the monster is incorporated. Another telling experience, which Jan incidentally welcomes very much, is the sensation of space and distance, of three-dimensionality. 'Things are more at a distance. Something that stands there – a chair, a table, a person – is part of a setting; there is space around it. I, too, seem to be a person now in an environment'. Another time, jubilantly, 'Before, everything was so packed together as one thing, like when that head was hanging so flat above me and I couldn't move. Now, I have depth perception, and things are more at a distance. I can walk through the world now'.

The relief this spatialization brings, however, makes Jan end up in the affective storm that had been suspended by fascination. The fascinating object becomes part of a meaningful and affectively charged context. Gradually, we get a picture of what frightens him so much. Between the weakening moments of fascination, more and more representations of destructive violence appear. This violence is increasingly situated in the transformative fantasy that his father, whom he always depicted as a dull, withdrawn man, would suddenly erupt in anger and destroy him in a relentless frenzy. The explosive power of that father-monster, whose immeasurable Goliath magnificence, in stark contrast to Jan's own David-ness, comes to the fore, frightens him, but, he says, also attracts him in a lurid way as if he had something essential of his own to seek there. He had a similar feeling, for example, when seeing on television a report about the violent rapes of women in Bosnia during the Balkan War: 'That strangely attracts me, as if I have something of myself to look for there'.

Sometimes, it is not clear to Jan where the destructiveness lurks, in his father or himself, whether he or his father is the monster; after all, the difference between the two locations is then minimal. The rigid projective identification of one's destructiveness seems to loosen. In the first movement, the fear of the relentlessly destructive violence is directed toward his monstrous father; in the second movement, the analysis tilts more and more toward an awareness of the aggression within himself:

'That big thing, that head, that is me. I might well erupt with rage myself. What I always imagined about my father and the teacher and many others was actually about myself'. The excessive, desubjectifying projective identification of his destructiveness returns to its stride, clearly accompanied by a decline in fascination. Jan starts articulating fantasies like, 'And now, I'm going to kill my mother' or 'Suddenly, I saw myself throwing that baby out the window'.

This colossal anger in him frightens him greatly. The reintegration of his own aggression is accompanied by the increasing and perceived self-destructive realization of an enormous sense of guilt. Jan begins to experience himself more and more as morally reprehensible. It becomes clear to me in the analysis that it is precisely this violence of a dictatorial superego that Jan had projected into the parent figures out of self-protection, which flattened him psychologically and impaired his creative potential. It was precisely against the impending awareness of that self-destructive superego-violence and the attendant fear of annihilation that the fascinating object of the black mash had to raise a dam. The moment of fascination in analysis was, as it were, a last, desperate attempt to block the reintegration initiated by the analytic process. Immediately, the associated transference dynamics were also halted, frozen in the fascinating image of the analyst as black mush. With the decline of fascination and before acknowledging the destructiveness within oneself, the transference became more alive: Jan experienced me as a tyrannical rejecting authority figure bent on making him small. The paradox of the whole state of affairs, of course, is that in the defensive maneuver of fascination, the destruction of the subject takes place all the more, albeit now in a painless, comatose way because of the suspension of imagination and affectivity. The remainder of the analysis shows how aggression and death anxiety in Jan gradually assume manageable proportions and become part of a more affectively differentiated personality. Reintegration occurs in sufficient measure to enrich his relational functioning and enliven his creativity.

Similar processes are found in Marie. The degree of separation of the fascinating bathroom tableau from the rest of the material is initially very pronounced and persistent. During the session following the one where the fascination occurred, she appears to remember nothing about it. When I take a quick pulse to see if she remembered a specific experience during the previous session, she doesn't know what I'm talking about. Then she thinks back – without remembering the fascinating object – to an incident in which her older sister and her child were in the bathroom in the parental home. She heard the toddler crying loudly and her sister yelling loudly. Without thinking about it, she decided to go to the bathroom as well. Only afterward, she remembers now, did the reflection 'it is better to have a third person there'. The scene evoked an atmosphere of danger, threat and violence. As she thinks back to the bathroom, she feels distressed and nauseated, but the image of the previous session does not return. When I remind her of the scene, she reacts startled and immediately remembers. The non-movement of the water jet and the static nature of it all come to mind.

Another link that seems to bring the fascinating object out of its absolute isolation, is the occasion of its appearance. This was when Marie spoke of the tile wall in her new workspace. Even this link does not resist fascination: the fascinating object immediately jerks away from it; fascination cuts through the association. The association with the previous sentence exists only for the external observer, not for herself, which means that, for the patient, the fascinating object is isolated. As we saw with Jan, here, too, fascination seems to be in the service of an ultimate repelling of an imminent undoing of the amputation of frightening unconscious material, the violent nature of which only later becomes clear. So, it is of no avail, even in the next session. The whole experience remains bizarre for Marie and she does not understand anything about it. Then she suddenly tells, rather excitedly, about the children she deals with professionally, who report to her that they are being treated harshly at home and where she suspects that abuse is involved. She wants to take those stories seriously to intervene, if necessary, to prevent worse. She finds it strange that she is saying this now after it was about that bathroom scene. 'Surely there is no connection'. When I suggest to her that there might be a link to her memory of calling her sister and her sister's child in the bathroom, she is startled and immediately says, as if to contain herself, 'But nothing happened, huh!' When I suggest that perhaps a third person should be there to prevent something from happening, the patient feels confused and doesn't know what to do about it all.

These links could open up a possible field of meaning for the fascinating scene, bringing it out of its isolation. Marie, however, does not want to know that they are links. Here, fascination shows itself as a radical form of 'attacks on linking', incidentally also associated by Bion (1959) with excessive projective identification. Neither the memory of her sister in the bathroom nor the children's stories evoke resistance in themselves. But there is no room for the idea that these things could somehow be related to the fascination. My tentative attempts to link the violence to the fascinating object meet with fierce resistance as if she 'knows' that the fascinating object is something of herself. This resistance already indicates a becoming less-absolute of the fascinated impassivity. Once more, fascination appears as the stilled eye of the storm of violence swirling around it. It is indeed remarkable how much these representations, clearly circling the fascinating object, have a strong, violent character and are affectively intensely charged. The theme of violence between parents and children is increasingly prominent. It is striking that several times, the bathroom tableau looms up and stops associating again precisely at moments when she speaks about it. In that image, the violence associated with it (as in her memory of the scene with her sister) is frozen, for example, in the no longer moving water jet.

Gradually, cracks appear in the rigid idealization of her parents, especially her mother, with whom, to her surprise, she now finds herself in explosive, unprecedented conflicts. Such conflicts evoke intense sadness and guilt in Marie. With no recollection of incidents that could substantiate this, but always in response to representations of violence between parents and children, Marie increasingly feels she is a morally reprehensible person. When violent scenes are brought up in which children are victims, often in sessions in which the fascination image is evoked, she becomes very nervous and gets the feeling of being 'bad' without being able to link this to anything about her own actions. She could say, 'I am afraid that one day people will discover that I am bad, morally bad, that there is a monster in me that must not come out'. She is then very confused and anxious and beset by perceptions of impending self-loss. Here, too, as with Jan, a reintegration of superego-violence and ditto fear of death seems to take place. Here, we can assume the operation of a violent and destructive superego in the service of the death drive, as described by Klein (1958).

When I mention, in a session related to a difficult situation with her mother, that her reaction seems to have something destructive about it, she suddenly falls silent, wants to end the session early, doesn't show up the next time and at several subsequent sessions lets me know how angry she is with me. She experiences me, this much is clear, as a rejecting figure who abuses his position of power to render her powerless and destroy her. She does not accept that I present the possibility that she has something destructive in her, thus confirming her fearful suspicion. It has taken months to restore some confidence. Her anger at me is at least a hopeful sign, but at the same time, I sense how delicate this ever-escalating trail of recognition of her own aggression is. The resistance may come alive and thaw the subject out of the fascinated hypothermia, but the fascination will not be outsmarted easily. As long as the confrontation with the unconscious is experienced as destructive to itself, the subject has every reason to maintain its amputation and hide in fascination. Nevertheless, in the further course of psychotherapy, there gradually becomes more room to see the bathroom tableau, which gradually appears less frequently, as a representation of a violent showdown in which one's own destructiveness is also accommodated. For Marie, taking a bath remains an exciting affair. Taking a quick shower, which implies a more active attitude and in which the water flows as if by itself, is easier. In any case, she no longer washes her hands in innocence.

The violence of truth

Looking back, the moment of fascination appears to have given a crucial turn to the progress of the analytical process for both Jan and Marie. However, this 'moment of truth' constitutes a real ordeal for both the patient and the analyst because the fascination equally solidifies the appearance of that same truth. We must realize that the rich associations that develop out of fascination and revel in the truth encapsulated in it take a long time and are very laborious to move. This has everything to do with the fear of annihilation evoked by the fascinating object, a fear that emerges in both vignettes as a fear of becoming conscious, which is less able to be escaped because of the decrease in defense through (self)idealization. According to both Freud (1926) and Klein (1948), albeit in different ways, death anxiety plays out primarily between ego and superego. The excessive and persistent nature of the projective identification, which ultimately provides the substance for the fascinating object, suggests that an extremely strict superego is involved. That the bizarre objects contain, among other things, a 'murderous conscience', as Bion (1958, p. 84) argues, is consistent with this. Fascination makes that truth hard – so hard that it can only be softened with difficulty. But with fascination, truth has, in any case, appeared, and it is up to the analytical couple not to let this appearance die out fruitlessly.

Using the two clinical illustrations, I have tried to show how the paralyzing state of fascination is indicative of the revelation of a fundamental subjective truth and, at the same time, constitutes the ultimate defense against this truth, which is experienced as violent. The fascinating object is the condensed form of frightening psychic material that was the object of excessive projective identification. By reflexively freezing the material in a clenched image, an exclusively bizarre object, the subject attempts to halt its undigested reintegration. This transformation in O is nipped in the bud and results in what I call a '*transformation in fascinosis*', analogous to the '*transformation in hallucinosis*' described by Bion (1959). 'Hallucinosis' denotes hallucinations in an otherwise normal mental state without psychosis. 'Fascinosis', which can be understood as a special form of hallucinosis, is accompanied by an extreme mental impoverishment that puts the subject into a kind of psychic coma. On closer examination, the fear of self-destruction seems to stem from primitive and tyrannical superego-violence, which I was able to observe in several patients with above-average 'fascinosis'. Not without effort, the analyst can try to break open the fascinating object – during the sometimes lengthy aftermath of its sudden appearance – and connect it to other material, thus embedding the frozen density in a dynamic that brings movement back into the whole process. If fascination is the eye of the storm, then there is no fascination without a storm. It is, therefore, not surprising that the patient and the analyst end up together in this storm of extreme ambivalence. To reinstall the dynamic between the conscious and the unconscious is, in itself, a violent infringement of the fascinated impassivity. This 'violence of psychoanalysis' demands caution but should not be evaded by the analyst.

3

I is a thing

On trauma and desire-for-being

The atrophied subject

While in the first chapter, the confusing condition of the precarious distinction between subject and object position – with fascination as its prototype – was approached mainly from the object pole, the fascinated object, with the further psychoanalytic exploration in the second chapter, the attention shifted more to the subject pole, the fascinated subject. In fascination, we are dealing with an exclusive object to which the whole world is reduced. In other words, the distinction between various objects disappears, all interspace falls away and they clump together into one 'mass of existence'. The fascinating object occupies the entire field of perception for the subject. He cannot avoid it, literally can't miss it, because there is no more space outside the object. So there is hardly any space left for the subject itself. Flattened against the almost all-space-occupying object, the subject loses its three-dimensionality, so to speak, and is reduced to a subject-minimum. While the fascinating object is hypertrophied into a colossal close-up that barely represents anything and threatens to swallow up the subject, hardly anything remains of the flattened subject. In this chapter, I want to bring the mental state of the fascinated, atrophied subject more into focus. I will do this based on a phenomenology of trauma. In my view, fascination plays a prominent role in traumatic states, especially when they are extreme. My premise is that there is a certain fascination that emanates from trauma, that trauma and fascination are related and viscous – they have something in common. I think the angle of fascination helps us clarify the phenomenology of trauma as an anthropological phenomenon lifted above its pathological guises. I do not want to reduce trauma to fascination; traumatic phenomena are too complex and varied to allow such reduction. However, I do want to develop the idea that fascination can be a significant and, in my opinion, not-so-exceptional element in trauma, especially as imminent self-loss plays a dominant role in it. I believe that a phenomenological investigation of the relationship between trauma and fascination can be of service to clinical psychoanalytic work with traumatized patients insofar as this investigation brings into sharper focus an understanding of the traumatic experience. However, psychotherapeutic practice will not be my focus, but it does come up sideways. The perspective

DOI: 10.4324/9781003515982-5

of fascination, among other things, helps to shed light on the particular temporal experience peculiar to the traumatized subject. What is the effect of the fascination state on memory and recall?

The question I want to pose is: Why are we so fascinated by trauma? What is so fascinating about trauma? In this regard, I will distinguish between the fascination in which the traumatized subject himself is trapped, on the one hand, and the fascination of others, the witnesses, for that traumatized subject, on the other. In my view, the connecting link between trauma and fascination is what I call the 'inhuman' on the edge of the familiar human. My transitive reasoning, which I want to present as a hypothesis, is simple: trauma is inhuman and the inhuman is fascinating, so trauma is fascinating. Put differently, trauma is fascinating insofar as it evokes something of the inhuman. But what can we understand by the inhuman? What I elaborate on at the end of the book already gets an initial start in this chapter.

In Chapter 1, I referred to Rimbaud's phrase 'Je est un autre', 'I is another', picked up by Sartre and subsequently by Lacan, by which Lacan refers to the imaginary nature of human identity and relations. In fascination, we get an even different situation, namely: 'I is a thing'. Not 'I is another, another person, another subject', but: 'I is, for example, a tree root', and even when it comes to another person, it takes on the character of a desubjectified thing. Lacanian speaking, we do not dwell in the usual imaginary register of 'I is the other' but on the border of the real. The I, the psychic, transforms into a thing. It undergoes a *'thingification'* and is de-psychized. It is then not simply a matter of the Sartrian view that the I is for consciousness a thing, an object, but that in the very experience of the subject, that I is an object without an interior, an in-itself. Nevertheless, because by sticking to consciousness (the subject-minimum) in this way and occupying the intimate place of the I, it has something ego-like, it comes to seem to consciousness that there, in that thing, is its 'personification'. 'I is a thing, but that thing is my ego'.

This bizarre mode of being, in which strangeness and familiarity combine, precisely marks the fascinating object and gives it an *uncanny* character. Nevertheless, in my opinion, the fascinating does not correspond in all respects to the *uncanny* as the return of the repressed (see Freud 1919). The fascinating does not necessarily relate to the repressed. In fascination, therefore, the aspect of strangeness in comparison with the 'old familiar that had to remain hidden' is more decisive: the familiar pole of the fascinating object is only topical, concerns the ego-own place it occupies for consciousness, while its content can be truly ego-strange material (for example, a tree root). It is a monstrous ego-thing, my ego but unrecognizable and incalculably transformed into a form alien to me. My subjectivity (my 'inside') is there, 'outside' me, but at the same time, it is so strange that I cannot bring it home. Here, among other things, we see the difference between fascination and delusion. In delusion, the consciousness joins the ego, 'saying' together in chorus, as it were, 'I am the root', whereas in fascination, the minimal distance concerning the object is maintained by the consciousness and the object seen from the consciousness is thus 'outside'. In this sense, the delusion, unlike the fascinated object, is indeed integrated. A delusional object can, of course, be fascinating, but one need not be psychotic to be fascinated (see Thys 2006b, p. 119, 247). The fascinated subject is intrigued by something it cannot integrate. The fascinated object is a demon that holds the subject hostage. In another context, the French writer and art philosopher Maurice Blanchot talks about the 'ghost image', saying, 'The intangible is that from which one cannot escape' (Blanchot 1997b, p. 62). I elaborate on this fact in Chapter 7 in the context of the broader issue of identity.

A triple eccentric

At the moment of fascination, mental life falls silent. One who is fascinated cannot think. There is no room for memory, desire or judgment because there is no distance or difference. It seems that the question of the mental world of the fascinated subject will soon be answered: after all, there is no mental functioning. Yet the fascinated subject is not an empty subject. Emptiness presupposes space filled with absence. A box can be empty, or a room, a café, a can or a conversation. An empty conversation, for example, is notable in how things are not said. An empty gaze is a gaze that does not see. Emptiness implies absence and negation and leaves room for the notion of a breast that is not there. Even a head can be empty, empty of thoughts. But while feeling empty, I can still be aware of the world around me in all its differentiation and mobility. So, mental emptiness has nothing to do with fascination. More to the point: any emptiness excludes fascination because it leaves room for negation and absence. Like the outer world, the inner world of the fascinated subject is not a *monde désert*.

Nor is the fascinated subject a full subject. Fullness also implies – even more imperatively than emptiness – the notion of space: a packed space that leaves no room for emptiness. Here, we recognize the difference with idealization. In idealization, I am full of the object; it fills me from head to toe. I absorb the object completely. In fascination, on the other hand, I am *away* from the object. I am completely absorbed in it. The object does not fill me; it is I who 'fill' the object. In idealization, the introjective pole of identification dominates, in fascination, the projective pole, as we saw in the previous chapter in the context of excessive projective identification.

Fascination is not a matter of being full or empty, both of which presuppose spatiality, but of the minimization of spatiality itself. We then say that mental space at the subject pole is reduced to a point, the minimal position from which the vacated subject can still be fascinated. The fascinated subject is not an empty head but a pointed head. It is imploded. While the subject pole is reduced to a point, all being is on the side of the object. The fascinated object represents the exclusive extensiveness of being as such. The peculiarity of fascination now is that all this does not mean that there is no subject, but all the more that the subject resides at the object pole. Exclusive being stands for the subject, but in a form foreign to the point-subject, namely an object-form, a form it is not, hence the confusion between familiarity and strangeness. This minimal onset of internal negation is the only thing that affects this presence in its absoluteness. For the fascinated subject, mental space is, as it were, thingified in an 'external' object that embodies all being, including and especially the being of the subject itself. Therefore, it does not let go of the subject.

I would characterize the fascinated subject as an *eccentric subject,* and this in three closely related meanings. First, precisely because the subject is completely absorbed in an object exclusive to him, it is completely isolated from everything else and all others. Entirely involved in the fascinating object, the subject is disconnected from the rest of the world, which is consequently non-existent for him. At the moment of fascination, it is an autistic, solipsistic being. The fascinated subject is, therefore, at the edge of any intersubjectivity. It is marginal in this respect. In this sense, too, we cannot strictly speak of a subject in fascination. Indeed, the subject, in the strict sense, as the various psychoanalytic models teach us, thrives only as internally divided and in a network in which it is connected to other subjects. I become a subject only thanks to the other and the dialectic of recognition and separation that plays out in relation to the other. The fascinated subject is a subject without context and, consequently, without text. It finds itself in an extra-verbal register. There is no room for processes of reflective functioning and mentalization. After all, these processes involve interpreting one's own and others' thoughts in terms of mental states (feelings, desires, fantasies, intentions and so on) and thus require an intersubjective field. Fascination is located beyond any intersubjective exchange of affectively-mental differentiated contents and meanings. The fascinated subject is a subject-in-itself, without others, an eccentric being thus.

I have described this first form of eccentricity, in which the subject falls outside the world, elsewhere in the context of the relationship between trauma and culture loss (Thys 2009, pp. 279–282). Without the other, without a world, without a symbolic order and thus also without culture in the sense of a collectively borne dynamic of meaning assignment and associated patterns of intercourse, psychic or mental functioning is almost impossible. (The importance of this in the context of identity problems is discussed in more detail in Chapter 6.) To the extent that such a state emerges, the problem of trauma is never far away. Extreme trauma provides us with poignant examples of the desubjectivation we see in fascination. Normally, the psychic and the cultural are hardly distinguishable; they are intertwined and flow into each other. One might say that culture 'covers' the singularity of the individual psychic, but then it is not a covering draped loosely over the psyche and that one can take off again without a scratch. Rather, culture forms the *skin* of our mental functioning. One does not take away a skin just like that. It not only holds the mental fabric together, it is fused with it. Whoever loses his cultural garment is poached. He who loses the hold of his cultural security is stripped of his skin and is completely exposed to an overwhelming inhospitality. An individual thus poached and stripped of every cultural garment finds himself at the edge of the human and is indeed stripped as a human being. This lack of culture or this culture-distancing, where the obviousness of cultural embedding is suspended, we find in severe forms of trauma.

Incest, for example, is traumatic insofar as it occurs in a culture with a pronounced prohibition on incest (Thys 1995b). In addition to the disruptive personal experience for the child undergoing the incest, it is as if it is simultaneously abandoned by culture. Even in larger-scale situations, such as (civil) wars, genocide or holocaust, the individual trauma is intertwined with the undermining of cultural support. The loss of familiar culture also plays a major role in migration and, to an even greater extent, forced flight. Gomperts rightly makes the distinction between social and psychological integration. Among migrants and refugees, social integration can be great, while psychological integration is under pressure (Gomperts 2006a, p. 31). This does not alter the fact that in the case of serious trauma within this group, problems in both areas can, however, reinforce each other and go hand in hand. Where even culture is unable to accommodate, abandons or even turns against the psychologically traumatized subject, the psyche is doubly compromised. The psyche is 'undocumented' and faces cultural homelessness. The cultural bearing or not of certain behaviors or manners is also of interest in relation to what is considered pathological. Zempleni (1984, cited in Juranville 2000, p. 26, see also Zempleni 1985) provides a good example of this by making the distinction between 'possession-maladie' and 'possession-rituelle'. The collective ritualization of possession forms in certain cultures protects the subject from its subversive, dehumanizing power. Possession that escapes cultural embedding, on the other hand, can be pathological and traumatizing and, on the contrary, make the subject fall outside the cultural.

It follows that the fascinated subject, secondly, is also an eccentric for the other. The other does not get in touch with it and does not get access to it. For the other, the subject is apparently not in the place where it is. Nor is it on another planet, but near itself. The subject is away but not far to seek, namely in the fascinating object. In Kafka's story 'The Metamorphosis', already mentioned in Chapter 1, Gregor's parents and sister do not manage to get in touch with the Gregor dung beetle. After some time, they realize that he has disappeared 'into' the dung beetle, but they cannot get hold of it. Thus, the subject has merged into a strange form in which it, as an intersubjective and mentally functioning being, cannot be reached. At the same time, this strange form is not necessarily not a subject. After all, it is there that the other thinks he has to look for the subject. Gregor's family members behave differently towards the dung beetle than they would if they were confronted with such an animal they would not associate with their beloved son and brother. Only when the beetle has completely 'consumed' Gregor do his family members treat him as nothing more than vermin to be liquidated. All it takes to get rid of Gregor, his sister tries to convince her parents, is to let go of the idea that it is Gregor.

This inaccessibility also applies to the subject itself. Even in this third, metapsychologically crucial sense, the fascinated subject is an eccentric subject. It is not only without the others and the others are not only without the subject; the subject is also without itself. The subject is disconnected from itself; it is lost in the all-encompassing fascinating object. The pointed subject is completely involved in the object, but this fascination produces nothing. It only makes his head more pointed and his mind loses all perspicacity. But don't we run into a problem here? After all, I argued earlier that fascination is absolute attainment and any distance is absent from it, at least to the extent that there is a subject at the very last moment. The fascinating object clings to the subject it cannot avoid. So, how can I claim that the fascinating object is inaccessible to the subject? The point is that absolute accessibility concerns the fascinating object as a thing. The dung beetle in itself is anything but inaccessible. What is inaccessible to Gregor is his humanity. The dung beetle is himself (has an ego-status), but as a mental instrument, he can do nothing with it. He can only crawl on the wall and eat garbage. The little lefto-ver Gregor, in the first stage after metamorphosis, does try to get ready to go to work and makes every effort to explain things to his parents, but these attempts remain a huge and ridiculous failure. It is as if the beetle is gradually consuming Gregor's mental functioning as stinking garbage. The inaccessibility thus concerns one's own mental functioning and imagination, which have become inaccessible precisely because fascination is absolute accessibility and presence, whereas any mental functioning or representation requires negation, difference and distance.

Precisely because the fascinating object is infinitely close, it is far from suitable as a mental container. We can only speak or think about what is not there in reality, we read in Nietzsche. 'On the contrary, we can think of nothing at all insofar as it is' (Nietzsche 1992, p. 49). What became unattainable in fascination is precisely that mental world of absence. To think, I must be able to imagine the breast in its absence. The absent breast gives a thrust to thinking (Thys 1995a, p. 29; see also Bion 1962, 1965). Imagination presupposes absence. In fascination, it is the unattainability itself that has become unattainable. Because the subject has lost its mental functioning, it can no longer recover its (inter)subjective being in the world. Indeed, such recuperation presupposes being able to distance itself precisely from itself and not coincide with itself because of the inner division. There is no room for this distance in fascination. Reduced to a point, the subject does not possess the capacity to think.

The eccentric subject is also *ex-centric*: in the three forms discussed previously, the subject is outside the very 'center' of intersubjectivity and itself and thus out-side human subjectivity as such. The little that remains of the fascinated subject ends up in the margin of human imagination. Fascination is, so to speak, a radical and bizarre form of what Lacan calls the 'decentred' subject as an anthropologi-cal fact.

The fascinated subject is caught in a most bizarre ambiguity. The object is eve-rything to the subject, but it serves it for nothing. The fascinating object means everything to the subject, namely the embodiment of its being, and at the same time, it has absorbed precisely every meaning. For the fascinated subject, the object is a cryptic object. As an inaccessible 'space', we can call the fascinated object a crypt. In addition, it is cryptic because it seems to harbor a hidden meaning even though it reveals itself as something completely absurd. The fascinated subject cannot say, if it could speak at all, that the object means much to him, let alone what it means, but it behaves toward it as if the object hides the existence of meaning as such behind its strange armor. With the evacuation of its mental functioning, the notion of meaning (which, after all, implies reference between terms and, therefore, movement and, therefore, negation and so on) is also expelled. Meaning has been transformed into a foul beast, a sticky monster. Yet an echo or a glimpse of some meaning does not seem to have disappeared altogether: the completely bizarre and unconnectable object must still hide a spark of meaning somewhere deep within itself. My meaning, more specifically, which I simultaneously push away from me as something repulsive. The fascinating object is both the womb and the grave of all meaning. The only thing that is there for me and is, therefore, the source of every possible meaning for me, even though, as an atrophied subject, I have no idea what meaning could mean, is precisely that which sucks up and nips in the bud every meaning.

Fascination seems inspiring but is – at least as long as the subject is trapped in it – rather mind-numbing. My only hold is that in which I lose my subjectivity. Thus, we understand that fascination is under enormous pressure from an extreme ambivalence. The subject needs it as the only remaining object to cling to, but at the same time, it risks its subjective existence in doing so. The fascinating object is both destructive and vital (Thys 1995b, p. 88). The subject is caught up in all this ambiguity of being and non-being and of meaning and meaninglessness (see also Chapter 11). The only thing that is indeed and irrefutably there is the intruding and the, as it were, rubbing itself against me, presence of something that I am not and in which I nevertheless find myself entirely because there is nothing else outside of it.

Fascination and trauma

Thus, we have arrived at an intrusive objectality that is reprehensible insofar as it affects symbolization and imagination but from which I cannot escape and to which I cling despite myself. Do we not see this reflected – albeit to varying degrees – in many traumatized persons? We are indeed in the midst of the problem of trauma here. Trauma and fascination are not the same thing, and not all trauma victims are equally fascinated, but I think the clinic overwhelmingly shows that traumatized persons are more susceptible to and more easily prey to states of fascination. Trauma and fascination have a privileged relationship with each other.

The connection between trauma and fascination was represented by Freud. In his examination of the traumatic neurosis, he argued that an unprepared and drastic breaking of the stimulus barrier brings about a gigantic 'anticathexis', 'in favor of which all the psychic systems are impoverished so that an extensive paralysis or lowering of the remaining psychic functioning is the result' (Freud 1920, p. 187). It seems to me that fascination is the most extreme form of what Freud describes here. In fascination the psychic impoverishment goes so far that hardly anything is left of the subject, what I call the 'subject-minimum'; only the 'giant anticathexis' of the colossal exclusive object remains. Many trauma victims testify that they were disabled as persons at the time, sometimes literally paralyzed, unable to move. Heavily traumatized persons may feel psychologically, mentally and affectively, dead and reduced to meaningless physicality. Sometimes we can no longer even speak of physicality – which still refers to subjectivity: it is someone's body – but there is only 'flesh'. The subject is 'mesmerized' and is reduced to a soulless thing. In this regard, Lacan and Žižek speak of the 'acephalic subject', the decapitated subject that gets too much into the sphere of influence of the real, of the Thing (De Kesel 2012a, p. 52ff.). Erik Porge argues that the Thing *is,* in a sense, the subject ('La Chose, c'est le sujet') and Lacan, somewhere in his (unpublished) Fourteenth Seminar, refers to the subject as 'chosique' (in De Kesel 2002, p. 116, note 25). The persistence of traumatization seems proportional to the extent to which such desubjectivation was accompanied by a helpless surrender to a fascinating object.

Victims of sexual abuse, for example, speak of a state of paralysis and affective stupor, combined with being overwhelmed by something that made the rest of the world, including themselves, disappear. The subsequent bewilderment of this 'experience' that hardly deserves that name, this being crushed under the fleshy weight of a great motionless beast, is an indicator of the degree of stickiness at the moment of the bare facts. However violent and moving the event looks from the outside, for the person involved, it can freeze into a still image in which there is no movement. Some body-oriented treatments are literally aimed at getting the body moving again, completing unfinished movements or 'action patterns' as yet (see, e.g., Ogden et al. 2006; Levine 2007). What I want to emphasize is that there is not only the in-trauma familiar *freezing* of the subject but that it is or can be accompanied by sticking to a fascinating object. Fascination is the sum of both: freezing *plus* an exclusive object. The traumatizing event, or an element of it, acquires the status of an exclusive object from which the victim cannot distance himself. Some cases allow us to argue that the victim is fascinated by the perpetrator. If, as we saw, we take into account how exactly the exclusive object comes to stand for the ego in the fascination, and thus the positions of perpetrator and victim are difficult to keep apart, we also understand the diffuse feelings of guilt that we observe so frequently in trauma victims. The victim appears here as an accomplice, a vanishing subject reduced to 'guilty omission'. Both perpetrator and victim are – in an obscene entanglement – in the same boat of 'thingification'. For example, Primo Levi, in describing the harrowing conditions in the Nazi extermination camps, says that dehumanization affected both perpetrators and victims (Levi 2007, p. 223).

Just as in Sartre's *La nausée,* the petrified Roquentin opposite the tree root falls prey to a 'lurid ecstasy' and cannot extricate himself from the 'horrifying rapture', so trauma can continue to exert a mesmerizing force, a destructive attraction for the subject. The trauma continues to intrusively impose itself as a lurid attraction. The literature usually emphasizes the anxiety that trauma patients experience, the fear of getting back into the trauma and the fear of re-experiencing it. This is, of course, a legitimate concern. But to this, I would like to add the importance of that bizarre attraction that the trauma also exerts and plagues the victim and which precisely makes intelligible the fear of something that is so far away. This pole of attraction refers to the fascination dimension present in the trauma. The combination of the two brings us back to the aforementioned extreme ambivalence between repulsion and attraction: these patients are indeed afraid, but despite themselves, they are also constantly drawn to it. Clinging to the fascinating object, despite its repulsive nature, can at the same time be an ultimate protection against the fear of total self-loss. The fascinating object is the last hold to protect against the *Endlösing*, the subject's 'final (dis)solution'. Some get caught again and again in the affective storm of traumatizing violence, while others push through, so to speak, to the stilled eye of it (see Thys 2008a). The affect can be excessive and overpowering or, on the contrary, paralyze into an affective catatonia, or we see an alternation of both.

How can we understand this fascinating suction reflex? We might say that the traumatized subject is at the mercy of the tendency to return to the place where it lost its subjectivity. Not only the criminal but also the victim – and in fascination, the distinction between the two is blurred – goes back to the crime scene. There, he hopes, as it were, to regain and redeem his mental capacity, to recover his lost humanity. That mental capacity concerns, among other things, or perhaps especially, the dynamic between conscious and unconscious, which has come to a standstill in fascination; the unconscious seems to be radically cut off. The only thing left 'at the subject's disposal' is a bizarre, thing-like physicality, but even this is dispossessed in the guise of the fascinating object. This makes the traumatizing object a necessary evil that the subject cannot let go of: the object of horror and soul-murder, that monstrous ego-thing, is the same as that in which lies buried the treasure of my subjectivity. There I must be, in that place of death, to come back to life.

To free itself from its fascination, to allow the gagged subject to return to its words, an act is needed, the force of which must necessarily be drawn from that one act par excellence, which – as Musil (1996) so powerfully expresses literarily in *The Man Without Qualities* – is a crime, an act that not only makes me shudder but shakes the whole symbolic order to its foundations. Such is the impasse of the fascinated subject: it can only return to speech by a risky detour past the place where it has lost all speech. Similarly, the psychoanalytic therapy of trauma can only be sufficiently decisive and 'much-talked-about' if it does not shun the fascinated actlessness and speechlessness.

Unforgettable loss of time

At the crime scene, the subject also hopes to set time in motion again. Being included in a time sequence of past, present and future is a characteristic of human beings. The subject can look back from the present to what was and look ahead to what is yet to come. In the traumatized subject, this experience of time is stagnant and frozen. We can understand this likewise from the pole of fascination in trauma. Insofar as the world has been reduced to the exclusive, fascinating object beyond which there is nothing, any idea of an earlier or a later has also disappeared. Indeed, because every differentiation and distance between multiple objects have been eliminated, every space, every possibility of movement and, consequently, every passage of time have been suspended. In fascination, every space is reduced to 'here' and every time to 'now' (Thys 2006b, p. 254).

Insofar as it is characterized by fascination, the trauma is outside time and the subject has lost time. The trauma is purely a waste of time. Therefore, trauma as a fascinating object is 'unforgettable' not because I can retain it so well in my memory as a powerful memory image, but precisely because it continues to impose itself – beyond any distinction between forgetting and remembering – as a hideous presence. The fascinating trauma is not something that has passed and that I can look back on, nor something that I know will soon be succeeded by something else. Like the thingification of the subject, time is also solidified into 'material time'. This makes trauma an invading presence that is not evoked by a (memory) image that drags a past presence behind it like a shadow, but a presence that is too real, too intrusive to sink into a bearable absence or 'pastness'.

The trauma as a fascinating object never becomes an image, for there is no representation or imagination and consequently no re-imagination. It is not something outside that I carry as an inner representation. It remains a persistent mental quasi-outside from which I cannot detach myself, which sticks to me. Consequently, the trauma does not become incorporated into a time sequence. It is an eternal here-and-now, which I can neither forget nor remember, which becomes neither historicized nor narrativized. The prefix 're' in the well-known 're-experiences' of traumatized persons is, strictly speaking, in the phenomenology of the subject's own experience, not correct: at the moment it occurs, the experience is pure actuality – it is happening now, each time as it were for the first time – without any reference to anything in the past. Consequently, we can also understand the fascinating aspiration reflex as a desperate attempt to recover lost time. Psychoanalytic therapy of trauma, then, is making time and reviving the solidified dynamic between forgetting and remembering.

I concretize this with an example from my therapeutic practice of a woman in her forties who, as a child, was sexually abused for years by her mother's extramarital partner. She cannot affectively characterize the sexual abuse itself; there was only 'that', and she felt nothing. All the years thereafter, until today, she lived in a kind of state of non-being. She did 'function', as it is called; she was married and had children, but she didn't feel present. Images, or rather presentiments of the abuse, kept haunting her. Nothing more could fit in her head, she said. She couldn't think or remember anything else. Her head had shriveled, as I put it earlier, as it were, to a vacuous point. Periodically, including during the period of psychotherapy, she would get into a motionless, almost catatonic state in which only one, equally motionless object filled the entire space: the perpetrator's head. This occurs especially at night, in the dark, when the objects of the outside world have retreated more sensually anyway. The woman tried to free herself from the fascination by watching certain motion pictures about sexual abuse as if searching for motion in her own frozen 'picture'. Again and again, usually in the dead of night, she watched the same two films, identifying with the fragile main character. In certain passages, even then, sometimes the fascination took over and the rest of the story, like her own life, passed her by. But gradually – it took years – she was able to mold the theme of the film into a narrative structure and, analogously, her own traumatizing experiences gained a place in her own life scenario instead of completely overrunning it. Such an impetus to narrativization, which can occur in very different forms, seems crucial in the struggle of subjectivation against fascination. Throughout therapy, this woman, in very subtle steps, brought her own life story back into motion and was able to regain her narrative gradually. With the development of a narrative, time and historicity are also reintroduced. Her rudimentary, self-destructive way of being in the world gave way to a more nuanced affectivity and increased intellectual capacities. The fascinating object moved more into the background, and if it demanded attention, the woman could link it more and more easily to other things and representations so that it no longer grabbed her as an exclusive object.

Desire-for-being and the inhuman

Of the miserable traumatized subject, then, we can say that it is at the mercy of and fascinated by trauma as the site of its lost humanity. Now, I want to zoom out from the traumatized subject itself to the question of why trauma fascinates people in general. The Nazis, and they not only, were fascinated by the Jews, whom they treated as dehumanized things. Many Jews imprisoned in the extermination camps became fascinated and captivated by their inhuman guards. For decades now, humanity, in turn, has been fascinated by the *Endlösung*. A fascinating power emanates from Auschwitz and the like. Oegema (2003) devoted an entire book to what he calls 'the public religion surrounding Auschwitz'. We may not be caught up in the traumatizing fascination of those who sojourned in the places where 'man is a thing to man', as Levi put it (Levi 2007, p. 200), but it is as if the fascination radiates at us, as witnesses. Man is a fascinated witness. Like accomplished disaster tourists, we all stand in the rubberneck traffic jams in order, in horror, with inescapable gaze, not to miss anything of the destruction that is taking place 'on the other side'. Social workers who specialize in working with traumatized patients may also be ennobled disaster tourists: they find it terrible what patients have to suffer, but they are also fascinated by them, they are intrigued by it – but now from a safe distance.

We see the distinction between the fascinated subject itself and the fascinated witness strongly depicted, for example, in Michaël Roskam's film, *Rundskop (Bullhead)*, which focuses on the trauma of the castration of the main character, Jacky. Both victim and witness are scarred by the trauma for the rest of their lives in intense yet different ways: Jacky is scarred by the total helplessness as the victim; his friend Diederik, who watched from a distance and in hiding, is scarred by the helplessness of the witness. In this scarred being, the two boys and later adults remain chained together for life in a fearful but inescapable way.

I want to approach the clinically relevant question of why we are so fascinated by trauma through and broaden to the anthropological question: What fascinates human beings? My answer is: What fascinates humans is the inhuman, which can manifest itself on the edge of the human. But what do I understand by the inhuman?

With Sartre, in the first chapter, I made the distinction between, on the one hand, man, who is divided into himself, who saddled with self-consciousness and with the capacity for negation and imagination, does not coincide with himself, is doomed to be involved with what he is not and, on the other hand, the pure being of things-in-itself, which coincides with itself and has no notion of alterity. Psychoanalysis and philosophical anthropology teach us that man 'ex-ist': he has a relation to himself and stands 'outside himself' at a distance from himself. This typically human, this rupture with a natural immediacy, is, at the same time, the tragedy of man. From this 'lack-of-being' (manque d'être), man is driven by what Sartre, as I touched on in Chapter 1, calls a 'desire-for-being' (désir d'être), to which Lacanian desire is so indebted. Man also wants, as it were, to be completely 'himself', to coincide with himself. He wants to be a thing-in-itself while maintaining his self-consciousness. In certain respects, the Sartrian desire-for-being corresponds to the Freudian death drive, which Freud (1920), after all, conceived as an orientation toward and return to an inorganic state. (I will return to this in Chapter 12.) Now, that cannot be. One cannot be a natural thing without any inner alterity and at the same time not reveal the consciousness of it. That 'self-realization' inevitably culminates in a loss of self as a human being. It is one or the other. Either you are a human being or you are something else.

Now, I think fascination puts phenomenological pressure on this obvious distinction between the human and the non-human. This intermediate zone or edge between what we can clearly attribute either to the human or the non-human is what I call the 'inhuman', the zone where the human and the non-human overlap and are confused with each other. In fascination, something similar happens, which expresses itself well in the formula 'I is a thing': the subject 'feels' itself being a thing but at the same time continues to possess its consciousness. It is this confusing and paralyzing state in which the fascinated subject is stuck, and it is this state in others that so fascinates us as witnesses. What fascinates us is this inhumanity, this peripherality of the human.

I want to distinguish the inhuman from the non-human clearly. Unlike the non-human, which by definition does not belong to the human, I conceive of the inhuman as typical of humans. Only humans can be inhuman. From his self-awareness, man is focused on what he is not, but that non-human, of course, remains, by definition, beyond his reach. The furthest he can go is the inhuman: that which he can only, with difficulty, reconcile with the obviously human but which is nevertheless not external to it either. It is precisely this simultaneity of the human and the non-human in one object, what I call the inhuman, that so fascinates us. We are intrigued by what we can no longer fully integrate into the human, but neither can we radically separate from it. The inhuman is that thing of the human that attacks and violates the familiar contours of the human, that thing that raises an image or suspicion of the destruction of the human. Hence, such a fascination with the apocalyptic and catastrophic, with the downfall of the world (see Zwart 2010). Crucially, in these edge representations or border experiences, the human continues to shine through; it is not completely dissolved. The 'ordinary' human simply will not fascinate us; it is always about matters where the familiar human is at risk, inclined to pass into strange metamorphoses. I work this out further in Chapter 10 and limit myself here to trauma.

Insofar as trauma, as we saw, desubjectivation also affects the common human; it will fascinate us (see also Thys 2024). The more the traumatized subject is 'thingificated', the more strongly it will fascinate us. And here again, the answer is: of course, this is a human being, more specifically, a human being whose humanity is seriously affected, mutilated. 'Destroying a human being is difficult, almost as difficult as creating one', said Levi (Thys 2024, p. 174). He was well-placed to realize how trauma can challenge this truth. Moreover, the traumatized subject – under the motto 'I is a thing' – is burdened with a being deficit: the typically human being deficit is compromised and pushed away by an excess-of-being. There is a lack of lack-of-being. As in Sartre's novel, the excess-of-being in trauma, like a great rudderless beast, heavy, disgusting and obscene, comes to weigh on the subject. As we have seen, this excess-of-being is reflected in the disappearance of the experience of time through which the trauma weighs down on the subject.

Now, this is precisely the state into which our unstoppable desire-for-being can lead us. Trauma, as a fascinating object, as one of the possible forms of the inhuman, is the ultimate mode to which the desire-for-being is directed without really leaving the domain of the human. This makes trauma, as that condition which in a human-destroying way most accommodates the so typically human desire-for-being, a most intriguing thing, one that simultaneously attracts and repels us. After all, the traumatized fellow human being embodies, in this sense, the human par excellence. I said that trauma attracts as a fascinating object because the *late subject* wants to recover his lost subjectivity and experience of time or, in other words, wants to shake off the weight of being, but at the same time, the opposite, the loss of being, could also play its role here. In this sense, the fascinating is miserable and blissful at the same time: it is both a disaster, a catastrophe and blissful, a beatific redemption from the caprices of being a subject.

The German philosopher Adorno (1955) raised the question of whether it was barbaric to write poetry after Auschwitz. This statement has often been barbarically taken out of context and ridiculed. Of course, after Auschwitz, more than ever, it is important to write poetry, that is, to turn the culture's hostile side of the inhuman into a, however lurid, inspirational force. This is – on a modest scale – also the challenge for psychoanalytic therapy. In its own way, perhaps psychoanalysis can also make room again for the imagination, which in the traumatized subject had become numb under the weight of the heavy, motionless beast of the excess-of-being. In this way, psychoanalysis can perhaps contribute to bringing the vacant subject back into culture with the understanding, however, that it does not lose sight of the inhumanity inherent in man. Along the lines of Blanchot (1997a), we might even say that the passage through the 'night' of trauma reveals the most powerful poetry. Perhaps, hopefully, mind-numbing fascination, even in its traumatic allure, can illuminate that same mind all the more powerfully and inspire renewed life.

Part II

From body to identity

4

Dysincarnation

The body on the edge of the symbolic

Between flesh and soul

In our dreams, the craziest, the most wonderful and the most terrible things happen to the body. Not infrequently, the forms in which the dreamed body appears are at odds with the prototypical human body. Newborn babies with teeth appear, women with enormous penises, the skin opening up into deep crevices as in a landscape, confusions between vaginal and anal orifices, the female sex organ as nothing more than a colossal black cavity, defecating in another person's mouth, being penetrated by a meters-long penis that turns out to be an umbilical cord, vermin crawling out of an abrasion, and so on. The anatomical sex difference is in question; the various orifices of the body are mixed up and show bizarre contents, the status of appendages gets tangled, the demarcations of the body blur, and so on. These grotesque dream bodies fascinate us insofar as the prototypical human body, the body of which we do not look up, as it were, is under pressure and loses its fixed contours. It is from such body dreams that I want to arrive at what we might call the 'psychoanalytic body'.

To make such a general and complex subject as 'the body in psychoanalysis' somewhat manageable, I choose a particular angle. This angle is my preliminary answer to the question of what is specific about the way psychoanalysis thematizes the body. Further on, it will appear that this thematization connects to the problem of the margins of the human, the body as a peripheral phenomenon. What body is psychoanalysis concerned with? What remains as specifically analytical if we put what psychoanalysis has in common with other psychological approaches in parentheses? To be more precise, in which view of the body does the specificity of psychoanalysis come into its own? I am not talking so much about psychoanalysis as a clinical stance or in its various therapeutic guises but primarily as an anthropology.

My answer, which I would like to submit for consideration, is as follows: the psychoanalytic body par excellence is the body insofar as it escapes precisely from the purely organic and does not already participate fully in psychological-cultural processes, the body between the organic and the intersubjective, between material substance and spirit, between flesh and soul if you want. It is the body in a state of faltering or wavering symbolization, where incentives to symbolization do not detach from the body as an organism but still stick to it. They are bodies,

DOI: 10.4324/9781003515982-7

as in the dream fragments, as entities functioning apart from a person. I place the psychoanalytic body in the tension between the real and the represented body, in the realm where the distinction between the physical and the psychic is unclear. This leans to Sartre's metaphor of the viscous in Chapter 1, where the opposition between the psychic and the physical is transcended. The psychic can be distinguished conceptually from the organic, but phenomenologically, in experience, it virtually coincides with it.

The psychoanalytic body is an intermediate body, a tension body, a body of ambiguity. We can describe it as the body of *dysincarnation*, a mode of existence wavering between the order of the flesh and the order of the word, between incarnation and non-incarnation. If incarnation is 'becoming flesh' of the soul or spirit or inner self, non-incarnation is the opposite: 'becoming soul' of the flesh. Dysincarnation lies in between, where the distinction between flesh and soul remains undecided. It is about 'the flesh of the soul', or 'the soul of the flesh'. This view later runs into the characterization of the psychoanalytic body between the body one is and the body one has, the body in the zone where the distinction between having and being is murky.

Now, one can rightly make two points. First, psychoanalysis also has much to say about man as a thoroughly symbolic-cultural being and how, in these supposedly 'high' regions of human existence, the body remains immutably significant. I believe, however, that psychoanalysis comes out strongest where it does not lose sight of the link with the ambiguous zone between flesh and word, in other words, where the symbolic is not disconnected from its adherence to the organic. Secondly, it can be said that psychoanalysis emphasizes and demonstrates more and more that the human body is intersubjective from the beginning and the other is present in it from the beginning; the human body is, by definition, relational and social, and, therefore, symbolic-cultural. However, this does not exclude, in my opinion, that this intersubjective body has its margins and that the anchoring of the other is not always convincing or obvious. The body is not reducible to the other.

My perspective focuses precisely on these margins and assumes – without seeking to isolate itself from a broader intersubjective approach – that it is there, where the phantasmatic link with the body as substance remains operative, that the psychoanalytic body is at its best. So it is not, to give just one example, about Dolto's (1984) 'unconscious body image', which is already abundantly linked to language, steeped in the symbolic and marked by relations with the other. The body of dysincarnation is about experiences of which human culture bears traces but, at the same time, does not allow themselves to be fully integrated into that culture, not fully absorbed into it. It is an unruly and subversive body. This line of thought fits with the view that psychoanalysis is necessarily at odds with culture and, by its very nature, remains in touch with what is socially incompatible or difficult to integrate (Thys 2009). Along the same lines, Moyaert (2012, 2014) writes that psychoanalysis does not take the side of social inclusion and, on the contrary, is interested in the individual insofar as it is always somewhat outside the framework of the community.

That the body can come to speak and the symbolic finds much of its ground in physicality does not mean that it is necessarily eloquent. I am talking about the stuttering, stammering body. Along the lines of Blanchot, we can also speak of the bodily 'murmur' or 'noise', something between speaking and silence, a speaking silence, in which no meaning is yet fixed (cf. Blanchot 1971, see also Schulte Nordholt 1997, 2012). Instead of the body inhabited by language, it is about the body where language cautiously knocks on the door, the body where the sounds echo from it, where the images that emerge from it and where the gestures that set it in motion move in all directions, do not yet allow themselves to be delineated by meaning although they seem to be looking for it, or at least we like to think so. It is about the proto-narrative body. As hospitable as the body may be, language does not yet live there, let alone feel at home. The body is ajar, and language is trying to get a foot in the door. (This theme also returns in Chapter 11.)

All of this twilight zone I represent with the formula: '(letting) dream the body'. The parentheses leave open whether the body is the subject or object of the dream process. If the body is the acting agency, then it is the body itself that dreams – the dream springs from the body; if the body is the object of the dream action, then the individual dreams (about) his body. With this perspective, I hope to do justice to the origin question characteristic of psychoanalysis with which the investigation of the psychic is always associated (cf. Van de Vijver 2010) without necessarily implying a developmental psychological focus. This niche is, in my opinion, the place where psychoanalysis, which is, of course, much more than that, expresses its *specificity* the most. Moreover, the very theme of the body shows where the various analytic currents differ from one another. Does not each current derive its uniqueness precisely from, among other things, the place it assigns to the body? In this twilight zone, in my opinion, the uniqueness of psychoanalysis is most expressed. Of course, I cannot elaborate on this in detail here; there are many authors and models I must leave unmentioned. I limit myself to some reflections from Freud, Klein (with a little Bion) and Lacan to bring all this together afterward in an overarching approach.

A trilogy of corporeality

The respective concept duos in my characterization of the psychoanalytic body are Freud's drift and body-ego, Klein's unconscious fantasy and internal objects, and Lacan's object a and *jouissance*.

The drive and the bodily unconscious

Freud always conceived of the psychic as anchored in the body, beginning as early as the *Entwurf* (1950c [1895]) and the hysterical conversion in the *Studien über Hysterie (*1893a and 1895d). He saw the first representations as arising from experiences of one's own body (Freud 1950 [1895], p. 365, 385). All of his work is full of references to somatic processes and constitutional factors. The bridge concept par excellence is the drive, which Freud situates in the borderland of the psychic and the somatic, whose source lies in the interior of the body and which, on the way to its goal, is simultaneously represented in the life of the soul (Freud 1915c, pp. 27–29). The *Three Essays on the Theory of Sexuality* discusses how both the lip area and the anal area lend themselves to an attunement of sexuality to vital bodily functions (Freud 1905b, p. 61, a 1915 addition). In his case study on Dora, Freud argues that every hysterical symptom is of both somatic and psychological origin. The somatic accommodation establishes a connection between the symptomatic expression and the unconscious thought content and provides the unconscious psychic processes an outlet to the somatic. (Freud 1905c, pp. 154–155) Similar reasoning is employed by Freud, for example, in his analysis of psychogenic visual disorder: the somatic 'contribution' of organs as the constitutional component of the disposition for psychogenic and neurotic disorders (Freud 1910d, p. 319).

Freud emphasizes that psychoanalysis does not advocate a purely psychological conception of psychological processes and recognizes the influence of organic factors on the psychic apparatus (Freud 1913b, p. 264). At the end of his life, he distanced himself from the so-called 'psychophysical parallelism' (Freud 1940b, p. 508). Freud was not a 'parallelist' but an interactionist. In *Outlines of Psychoanalysis* (Freud 1940a), he had already put it succinctly: 'The somatic processes, which are generally agreed to accompany the – conscious – psychic processes, but which are not entirely parallel to them, come to be paramount in psychoanalysis'. More to the point: 'It calls the supposedly accompanying somatic processes the actual psychic, leaving aside for the moment the quality of 'consciousness'' (Freud 1940a, p. 458). In psychoanalysis, therefore, the actual psychic unconscious concerns somatic processes. In this sense, Freud (1915d) suggested that the question of whether one should regard the latent states of soul life as unconscious psychic or as physical states threatens to end up in an unresolvable war of words. The psychic and the somatic are originally intertwined.

This Freudian view of the specific status of the body, which is first and foremost a pleasure body, comes together in the well-known concept of the 'body-ego', which Freud introduces in *The Ego and the Id* (Freud 1923b). The ego, arising from internal and external perceptions of the body, is, above all, something physical, not only a body-surface entity but is itself the projection of a surface (Freud 1923b, p. 392). In an original 1927 English note, Freud adds,

> The ego is thus derived in the last instance from bodily sensations, principally from those which have their source in the surface of the body. Apart from representing, as we saw, the surface of the psychic apparatus, it can therefore also be regarded as a psychic projection of the surface of the body.
>
> (Freud 1923b)

Here, a reference is in order to Anzieu's (1974) later 'moi-peau'. The unconscious ego is, above all, a body-ego (Freud 1923b, p. 393). It is apt that we read almost the same thing with the well-known contemporary neurologist Oliver Sacks:

'The ego is largely a body ego' (Sacks 2000, p. 70). So, at the heart of Freudian thought, we find the idea that the actually psychic, the unconscious, is bodily. With this, we have the Freudian formula to underwrite the specificity of what I call the 'psychoanalytic body'. The object of investigation of psychoanalysis is eminently characterized by the psychic insofar as it is embedded in the physical.

Unconscious fantasy and internal objects

While Freud focused primarily on the surface of the body, Melanie Klein delves into its deep inside. Central concepts in her theory and clinic are the 'unconscious fantasy' (see, e.g., Cambien 1988) and the 'internal object'. For Klein, object relations, the totality of relationships to 'objects', exist from birth and are primarily physical as well as fantasmatic. Klein is, therefore, at the basis of the later 'object relation theory'; she is the first representative of it, but at the same time, the object relation theory has moved away from the strong drive and bodily character that essentially characterizes object relations in her view. This near coincidence of body and fantasy so typical in her work brings us to our subject. The unconscious fantasy is a kind of animistic 'interpretation' by the baby of bodily sensations. The sensation of persistent hunger, for example, is, for the baby, equivalent to an evil object operating in the body that causes bodily pain. The salutary sensation of warm milk filling the body, in turn, flows from the presence of a good, benevolent object, as does, for example, the pleasurable relief of bowel movement that removes the pain in the abdomen.

Klein goes on to 'deepen' the Freudian body-ego into an internal bodily world in which good and bad objects interact in the unconscious fantasy world. These objects are objects of phantasmatic projective and introjective processes, which makes their internal or external nature not always clear. The mother's breast, for example, is fantasmatically incorporated as part of one's own body, but internal objects are also inversely excorporated and accommodated in the mother's body. Through this outward projection, as it were, the baby tries to make the good object escape the threat of the internal bad objects that want to destroy it. Consider the dream image mentioned at the beginning of this chapter in which another serves as a container for the dreamer's bowel movements. Also, out of envy, the baby may want to destroy the good objects in the mother's body (milk, feces, children, penises), upon which may follow the fear that these will turn on the baby in revenge and invade its body to destroy it. The Kleinian fantasy world is a battleground of scenarios essentially tied to bodily sensations in which the good and the evil, the creative and the destructive, are constantly at loggerheads with each other, in which one's own and the mother's body (see, e.g., Klein 1936, 1945, 1963) can merge into each other. What is interesting now is precisely the ambiguous nature of the unconscious fantasy and the internal object.

Isaacs (1952) specified the concept of unconscious fantasy as the mental correlate of the drive. Every drive appeal is experienced as an unconscious fantasy, which distinguishes Klein from fantasies that go back to repressed representations. They precede actual symbolization in which the object is represented in absence (e.g., Klein 1959, p. 251). Strictly speaking, they are not mental representations but concretist proto-fantasies in which the corporeal and the mental are undifferentiated. In some ways, this basic layer of experience is analogous to what Bion (1961, pp. 101–102) called the 'protomental system', where there is no differentiation (yet) between the physical and the psychic. It is a transitional zone between or rather an area of overlap of body and mind, something very corporeal that at the same time carries a mental connotation which, however, has not yet been psychologically processed. While Spinoza, as we saw, makes a clear distinction between sensation and perception, from a Kleinian vertex, there is room for a transitional zone between the two.

Van Haute points out that in the archaic experiences Klein describes, feeling and meaning are indistinguishable. The bodily experience there is immediately meaningful and/or meaning-building (Van Haute 2005, p. 66). The unconscious fantasy is a first step in what Kristeva (2001, p. 148) describes as the 'anamorphosis of the body into the mind', a distorted representation of the corporeal, which thus does not correspond to that corporeal as such but at the same time is indistinguishable from it. I think here of a patient in whom the fear of not being able to control her emotions takes the form of the fear that substances will spill out of all the body orifices and stain the divan and the analyst. Emotions are like bodily substances.

For Bion (1962), dream thoughts are the first mental product of any experience arising from raw sensory sensations. For Meltzer (1983), dream and unconscious fantasy are synonymous, and they are the representation of internal space where new meanings are generated (Meltzer 1981, see also Hebbrecht 2010). Could we say that it is the body itself that produces the dreams? The body dreams?

The internal objects are both imaginary and organic-sensory. Therefore, we cannot call the unconscious fantasies imaginative narratives in the full symbolic sense. Insofar as the subject *is* the internal objects, I would rather speak of proto-narrative drive figurations (cf. Stern's 1993 'prenarrative envelope'). This brings us to another aspect of ambiguity: internal objects are – the word says it – both internal, my own, of myself, and object and thus not-me. For internal objects, it remains undecided whether they are foreign or owned. In this sense, the internal object has an *unheimlich* character; however, it is not in the sense of the *Unheimliche* as the return of the repressed, as Freud (1919) describes, but beyond any repression. I think of a sex scene in a dream told by a patient where it is unclear to whom the penis belongs, or the woman who in her dream discovers another appendage in herself and very aptly articulates the ambiguity: 'a genital of my own that is foreign to me'. With this wondrous status of the internal object, we anticipate the tension between being the body and having the body, which I will discuss later.

To conclude this Kleinian line of thought, let me say a few words about Bion's contribution. Although he is strongly influenced by Klein and can certainly be labeled without question as a Kleinian at first, I believe that, through the evolution of his thinking, he moves increasingly away from Klein's view of the crucial role of the body in the psychic. Whereas with Klein, the body and the unconscious

fantasies interwoven with it continue to play a fundamental role in psychic functioning throughout life, Bion increasingly separates the psychic and mental from
and places them in opposition to the sensorial. 'There are no sense-data directly
related to psychic quality', says Bion (1962, p. 53). From the sensory 'beta elements', thoughts may arise via alpha function, but they are purely sensory and
belong to another order than the mental. To understand the psychic, he says, we
must, on the contrary, distance ourselves from the sensory; they are two totally different spheres (Bion 1974, p. 42; López-Corvo 2003, p. 267). With the Symingtons,
we can speak of 'the contrast between psychic and sensory reality' in Bion's work
(Symington & Symington 1996, p. 85). Ferrari (2004) calls the body a 'great silent
protagonist' in Bion's work (see Leysen 2013).

Where in Klein, we see entanglement and continuity in Bion, separation and
caesura stand out. In this respect, we are far removed from Klein's 'body thinking',
this twilight zone between the physical and the psychic, which in Klein is even
more acute than in Freud, which we never definitively leave behind and which
represents an inexhaustible source of inspiration for the psychic. Bion's formula 'a
thought for a breast' implies that the elimination of the sensorial experience at the
object is a prerequisite for thinking, whereas in Klein's thinking, starting with the
unconscious fantasy, is already set in motion precisely in contact with the sensorial.
In Klein, unconscious fantasy accompanies every experience of reality, not only
those in which the presence of the gratification object is suspended, and thinking
is already contained in corporeality as such. In Klein, it is rather, 'a thought with
a breast'. While the platonic Bion says 'suck *or* fantasize', as it were, the vitalist
Klein says: 'suck *and* fantasize' or 'suck fantasizing'.

Those familiar with Bion's later work, especially his reflections on the caesura (Bion 1977, 1987), may find that some nuance is appropriate here. There,
he develops interesting thoughts about a possible proto-mental functioning of the
fetus and speaks of a 'physical anticipation' of later mental functioning. Such and
related reflections indeed give rise to a certain relativization of my representation
of Bion's thought but do not, in my view, detract from its main tone. Indeed, even
in that later work, he continues to speak of how difficult it is to break the caesura or
'barrier', penetrate, bridge and translate physical phenomena into mental ones and
vice versa. His thinking, I think, assumes less continuity than Klein's.

Object a and jouissance

Also, concerning Jacques Lacan's work, I limit myself to pointing out some
aspects that illuminate my perspective. Whereas in Klein, the body is essentially
kinesthetic and the visual is a subordinate or secondary element to it (Isaacs 1952,
pp. 104–105), in Lacan, it is and remains primarily of the order of the image and
the gaze. From this, Lacan returns to the outside of the body, whereas Klein had
led us into the body as internal space. All later developments in Lacan's work after
the mirror stage (Lacan 1966a) notwithstanding, he maintained that man is fundamentally gripped by the image of his body and that it is through the gaze that the

body gains its weight (Lacan 1985). The Lacanian imaginary is of a different order than the Kleinian fantasmatic, though. In it, in my opinion – even more than with Freud – the body is looked at from the outside, and this in two ways: not only in the imaginary body of the alienating mirror experience but also in the symbolic body, where any conferral of meaning comes 'from outside', namely through the word of the other (Lacan 1985).

It is in the body's encounter with language and the Other that something emerges for the human being that generates meaning, according to Lacan (Lacan 1985). The human body is primarily a body discussed by the Other. It is stressed again and again that this body of language, this discussed and speaking body, implies an inevitable loss of that same body as a 'real' organism, a rupture with its immediate presence. On this point, Lacan and Bion are related: 'a thought for a breast' here becomes 'the symbolic for the real'. The signifier has a distancing effect concerning the body: we only get to see it 'from the outside'. The spoken body is essentially *hors corps* (Libbrecht 2001, p. 36). The real body is essentially separated from the body as a human-symbolic entity. Unlike Klein and more in line with Bion, there is more rupture and caesura in this Lacanian body than continuity and connection. The body, therefore, is something we are not but something we have, as Lacan keeps repeating (e.g., Lacan 1978, 2001; see also, e.g., Miller 2009, p. 52; Vanheule 2013, p. 150).

However, while this Lacan of language (Lacan 1966b) places the corporeal as such at a distance, there is also the later Lacan who turns his attention to the limits of the symbolic order (Vanheule 2013, p. 8) and who wants to bridge the installed distance again, as it were. This is the Lacan of the *objet a* and *jouissance*. The real body that at first was merely residual, pure 'waste', which falls off when entering the symbolic, is picked up again and re-established. The rest is restored, and the real body is now given an honorable place in the dynamics of the subject. In my opinion, however, it is questionable whether this catching-up abolishes the former dichotomy between body and subject. In this regard, Miller (2009, pp. 132–138) makes the distinction between *signifiantisation* and *corporisation*. In the aforementioned accession to language, the organism, which offers its materiality for processing, is elevated from thing to signifier. Afterward, Lacan adds the objects 'little a' as corporeal elements, which he situates at the level of the orifices of the body as erogenous zones, the places where the body opens and closes. They are the objects that are 'left behind' as bodily complements – 'the remains of the body' – after entering the symbolic order (Lacan 1973).

It is characteristic of how Lacan – in his 'Subversion du sujet' (Lacan 1966d) and in the Tenth Seminar (Lacan 2004) – also links object a to the gaze again: it is the non-mirrorable residual object of the body that holds the image together, gives the mirror image it's covering (Geldhof 2014, p. 140). From the introduction of object a, says Miller, the reverse movement comes into view, that of corporization: the body is not elevated to the signifier, but the signifier now, inversely, enters the body and becomes itself materialized. Knowing is now 'incorporated' and touches the body. This 'body event' refers to affect as a bodily effect of the signifier, not a semantic effect but an effect of delight, *jouissance*, which goes beyond the pleasure principle and the mental experience of pleasure (see Lacan 1975). Vanheule (2013, p. 176) puts it this way, 'Words are also bodily invested elements, they also embody an affect value'.

In addition to the Freudian body-ego and the Kleinian unconscious fantasy, the Lacanian object a, as a bodily entity and the *jouissance* attached to it on the verge of symbolization, are also given a place in the psychoanalytic body. The status of this object a also remains dubious. On the one hand, more than a transitional object embodying the continuity between the physical and the psychic like Klein's internal objects, it is placed radically outside the symbolic and is not a tentative announcement or proto-version of it. As components of flesh and blood, the objects remain inert to the signifier (Vanheule 2013, p. 153); as 'lumps of flesh', they remain excluded from the signifier's chain (Lysy 2009, p. 196). Lacan places the 'subject of the signifier' against the 'subject of *jouissance*', language against corporeality. All corporealization notwithstanding, the body remains a radical outside. On the other hand, the bodily event of the symptom does leave traces in the body as enjoying substance, which, in addition to being the subject of the signifier, is also a dimension of being a subject. So, is the dichotomy not so absolute after all? According to Miller (2009, p. 116), the speaking being for Lacan is precisely the union of subject and substance, signifier and body. Association, then again, that sounds like the other extreme. It becomes more interesting for my characterization of the psychoanalytic body where he speaks of a 'wavering mixture of the lack-of-being that works and moves the individual' (Miller 2009) – a wavering between being and lack-of-being, between being and having?

I recapitulate briefly. In Freud's body-ego, the psychic and the physical are originally intertwined, but his interactionist view is characterized by a mutually distant positioning of the two. With Klein's unconscious fantasy, this distancing falls away; body and representation cannot be separated. This continuity between the two is again compromised by Bion through his polarization of the mental versus the sensorial. Lacan makes the reverse move: after first distancing corporeality in favor of the signifier, he returns with the object a and *jouissance* to the body that the signifier now incorporates. This turn to the body, however, remains a detour via the Other and the signifier. After all, this is the – secondary – corporealization of the signifier, which is something other than an original presymbolic mixture. Reference can be made here to Aulagnier (1981), who, in her study of psychosis and from a Lacanian background, introduces a concept that is closely related to the Kleinian internal object, namely the 'pictograms', a first form of representations in which the distinction between object and organ, the complementary sensory zone, is difficult to make. How such proto-representations can break through into the analytic session, resulting in a suspension of the distance between body and object, she calls 'signes blancs'. These bear some affinity to my description of the fascinating object. Regarding my positioning of the psychoanalytic body between organism and subject, the respective models each occupy their own position, but all thematize a zone of 'dysincarnation', a zone in which the psychic and the physical are intimately intertwined, where neither incarnation nor non-incarnation yet fully persists.

Psychoanalysis and phenomenology: the body between having and being

In its way, psychoanalysis struggles with the age-old debate about the relationship between body and soul, body and mind, and more specifically with Western so-called 'Cartesian dualism'. This same Descartes emphasized the intrinsic connection between body and mind, at least if one is to be a real human being, *un vrai homme* (Descartes 2002, p. 81). Even if the recognition of their phenomenological connection did not prevent him from studying them ontologically-conceptually as aspects to be distinguished, one has made Descartes much more dualistic than he was. In addition to connectedness, Descartes even speaks of the 'unity' of body and soul (Descartes 2002). Psychoanalysis has clinically examined and theorized the connectedness of body and mind. What I want to emphasize, above all, is that this connectedness is one of tension and not unity: in their interconnectedness, the physical and the psychic remain at odds with each other. Compare with Blanchot the term 'neutrum', in the sense of 'ne-utrum': both 'neither the one nor the other' and 'both the one and the other', to be distinguished from two forms of unity in which, on the contrary, the opposites are dissolved: the mediated unity of the Hegelian synthesis, and the immediate, mystical unity (Blanchot 1969, see also Schulte Nordholt 2012). On the contrary, the psychoanalytic body escapes the mere being of organic substance, nor is it absorbed into the mere existence of the subject.

Even in psychoanalysis, the dialectic between body and soul is not overcome or transcended, as has been said, nor is the speaking being the 'union' of subject and substance, as Miller (2009, p. 116) briefly suggests. Even in such neuropsychoanalytic formulations as 'signifiers in the brain tissue' (Bazan 2010), 'a physiology of the unconscious' (Bazan 2010), 'fMRI of the soul' (Kinet 2010) or 'signifiers of flesh and blood' (Van Gael 2012), the very tension of ambiguity remains audible. In recent research of so-called 'neuroplasticity', one arrives at the notion of an internal reality that is both 'psychic' and 'somatic', and in which even the idea of 'interaction' between the two poles disappears (Ansarmet & Magistretti 2007, in Verhaeghe 2010). But even if we abandon interactionism à la Freud, the phenomenology of experience, in my opinion, prevents us from speaking of a real integration or unity. The BMI of psychoanalysis, its body-mind index (Thys 2015b), can be reduced neither to a 'biology of the mind' nor to a 'hermeneutics of the body', but must respect precisely the tension between the two in its investigation of the human being.

An interesting examination of dualism in psychoanalysis, in dialogue with the work of Laplanche and Anzieu, is found by Diamond (2013, especially pp. 61–89), who, however, portrays Freud and certainly Klein as more dualistic than I think they are. In her view, the psychoanalytic notion of 'anaclisis' confirms the dualism between the 'vital order' and the 'psychic order' rather than bridging the gap between them. She argues for broadening the view of the vital order common in psychoanalysis as a static biological system to an open system whose vitality unfolds only through the action of the other and that the other, therefore, does not have to be added to it but is inherently part of it. In my opinion, it is exactly that which Klein was already trying to thematize without the implication that any relationship of tension between the two registers would be removed.

We find a similar field of tension in Merleau-Ponty's phenomenology. His approach seems to me especially very much akin to Klein, for example, where he speaks of the 'body-subject' and of corporeality as an 'original level of meaning' (Merleau-Ponty 1997). Merleau-Ponty's synthesization of object and subject is very reminiscent of Klein's internal object. I cannot elaborate on a mutual confrontation of both their approaches to the relationship between the bodily and the psychic here; I limit myself to a few hints. It is immediately noticeable how far Bion, considered the quintessential Kleinian, is removed from Merleau-Ponty. However, the analytic attitude that Bion advocates in the clinical situation, namely the suspension of memory and desire concerning the analysand, can be characterized as distinctly phenomenological (see Thys 2010).

Let me briefly point out Lacan's critique of Merleau-Ponty, more specifically where, according to Lacan, the latter attempts to restore the co-naturalism of man and world and aims at a point of unity of body and world (see, e.g., Miller 2009, p. 53; Lysy 2009, p. 197). Indeed, this unity, according to Lacan, is always already and definitively lost because of the accession to the symbolic order. Indeed, Merleau-Ponty thematizes what he calls *la chair*, the flesh: the fabric out of which both body and world exist or at the level at which body and surrounding world interact. The term 'flesh' can cause conceptual confusion: whereas in psychoanalytic debate, 'flesh', as the purely organic, is sharply distinguished from human, symbolically drawn corporeality, with Merleau-Ponty, the same term refers precisely to the corporeality that man shares with his surrounding world.

In defiance of Lacan, I think there is something to be said for including the flesh as conceived by Merleau-Ponty in analytic discourse. The dream image in which the skin opens up like a gap in a landscape is an apt illustration of this. We can understand this Kleinian as the unconscious fantasy, inspired in part by the earliest object experiences, but still looming at the level of the body, which cannot be distinguished from the mother's body, which for the infant is the surrounding world, but does not simply coincide with it either. This 'reversibility' between body and world, which Merleau-Ponty refers to as the basic characteristic of the flesh (Merleau-Ponty 1993, p. 189; see also Baeyens 2004, p. 39), I recognize in the continuous back-and-forth of fantasmatic introjective and projective processes as Klein describes between one's own and one's mother's body. Quite appropriately, Merleau-Ponty calls the body 'the cast of things and things the cast of my body' (Merleau-Ponty 1993, p. 173). The body is the mold of meaning; here lies the germ of subjectivity (Baeyens 2004, pp. 54–55).

When one starts from the signifier and the Other, there remains little room to think of this original entanglement. What both Klein and Merleau-Ponty aptly portray is something like 'animated flesh' – a minute animated organism that transcends the animal but has barely outgrown it 'organically'. I am also thinking of Lyotard's 'anima minima', who also speaks of *la pensée-corps* and 'the secret conformity of the soul to the sensuous' (Lyotard 2013). That the nerve in itself cannot be the basis of meaning, as Sartre (2003, p. 690) argues, does not take away from the fact that the first hesitant assignations of meaning lean very close to the corporeal.

From this fleeting confrontation of Merleau-Ponty with Klein, I want my reflections to culminate in the tension between having and being, which in human beings are intimately intertwined but can never merge. If they did, both consciousness and the unconscious would become unthinkable. We must also situate this field of tension in the zone of dysincarnation. It is impossible to *have* a body without more, as a foreign thing that does not intrinsically belong to us. Besides, what instance would that be that 'has' the body? The ego? But we saw that the ego cannot be separated from the body. One patient put it very pointedly, 'The ego is scar tissue'. A glimpse of the experience of that body-thing, we see, for example, in depersonalization states, where there is a split between the body as a foreign thing and the experiencing ego (Nicolai 1997). Also, in severe trauma, we sometimes see a kind of mental and affective coma, and the victim may be inclined to sink into a purely bodily, desubjectified or 'numbized' state, as we saw in the previous chapter. Automutilation may have the function of re-appropriating that foreign body, experiencing it as one's own. So, if the body were purely a matter of having, without interweaving with subjectivity, it would lose its humanity. So, a dimension of being must also come into play. At the other pole, the same is true. If we were only a body, completely coinciding with it and any distancing from it removed, we would be reduced to an organism without more and dehumanized equally. So, there must also be a dimension of having and thus of some distance. The psychoanalytic body constantly moves between appropriation and expropriation.

Both aspects are necessarily present simultaneously: there is the body that I have and which appears to me as a thing, which Husserl designates as *Körper*, and there is the body that I am and experience as 'me', the *Leib* (Husserl 1952 [original 1912]; see also Slatman 2007). I dream the body I have *and* the body I am dreams me. The unconscious may be structured like a language, but it is certainly also structured like a body. Intersubjectivity is primarily inter- or better 'co-corporeality'. As De Preester and Slatman (2010) cleverly describe, there is an intrinsic entanglement of ownness and strangeness that produces an 'identification with the strangeness of one's own body', also referred to as the 'ambiguity of a *Leibkörper*' (De Preester & Slatman 2010, pp. 204–205). See also Ramachandran and Blakeslee (1999, p. 58, cited in Diamond 2013, p. 129): 'Your own body is a phantom'. It is this specifically human ambiguity between thing and subject that I believe is most strongly expressed in the 'psychoanalytic body'. All this tension between strangeness and ownness, between ego- and object-position and also between the physical and the psychic that is found in the phenomenology of fascination and related experiences of self-loss described previously. It is precisely this intermediate or peripheral position that, in my view, provides an important psychoanalytic-anthropological ground for human existence.

Mind the body!

We know the endless warning 'Mind the gap' from the London underground. Entering and leaving a subway car can be dangerous. In Hertmans' play of the same name (2000), Antigone, Klytaemnestra and Medea dramatically shape human existence, which in a way is one big gap, with the image of the body itself as one big body opening. This evokes the aforementioned dream image of the immeasurable depth of the vulva, this gaping intimacy. But, a gaping also has edges that can give hold and implies a passable surface of which the gaping is precisely the interruption. These edges immediately prove the first lip service. These days, 'theory of mind' rings the bell, but how could we separate it from a 'theory of body'? The human body may be a written page, but without original entanglement with the *flesh*, we can 'write it on our belly'.

Instead of choosing between monism and dualism, I opt for maintaining the tension between the two. Body and mind cannot exist without each other; neither are they reducible to each other. They do not coincide, but there are points of contact, dynamic areas of transition or overlap, which are constantly, like ebb and flow, in motion. It is precisely in this surf that I situate the psychoanalytic body. Perhaps we can speak of the *primacy* – not of language, nor the body or of imagination without more – but of the *imagined body*. When the body speaks, it does so first of all to the imagination. Our first and last gap is our body, the abyss into which we can fall – the threat of which is palpable in the patient's dream, with the body tearing open. In this dark underground of one's own body, the first dramas take place, the raw material of our dreams, the basic contours of our whole future life, which we can conceive of as a string of *flesh-backs*. With this, we compare with Blanchot the term *écriture*, which precedes language, as a drawn line, the indentation as a trace (see Cools 2012).

These dramas are frighteningly strange: 'mind the body!', cries out, as it were, the troubled baby, who is especially watching the orifices of the body. But, these same dramas are at the same time so self-minded, so immediately belonging to his mind: mind the body!, the baby enthusiastically welcomes them; he wouldn't want to miss their hold on him for anything. The abyss not only frightens him because he may fall in but also invites him to jump in. De Cauter (1995, pp. 248–250) speaks of 'the speechless body' to which we are ultimately directed, as infantile lust (infans = not speaking, see also Chapter 11). The body, however eloquent, continues to cherish this silent, infantile dimension. Here, too, I recognize the psychoanalytic body: the body where the distinction between organism and language is precisely at stake. This combination of anxiety and attachment is precisely what makes them so fascinating. Especially as the as-yet-emerging *aktuaal pathology* demands our attention to corporeality as the cast of the most rudimentary psychic representations, it is important not to let the corporeal side of the imaginary disappear into the blind spot of our analytic reflections. It is up to psychoanalysts, together with other kinds of artists and scientists, to give space to this primal substance of the body, to stir it up, to (let it) dream.

5

From discreet whispers to public shouts

Psychoanalysis and the culture of self-disclosure

Transparency and self-disclosure

We have been living in a culture of transparency for several decades and still increasingly so (see, e.g., Vattimo 1992; Florini & Stiglitz 2007; Fung et al. 2007; Henriques 2007; Lord 2007). There has probably been no period in history when individuals share more personal things about themselves with others and find out about others than the time in which we live today. The sheer growth of communication technology alone has produced an unprecedented global explosion of data sharing (Coebergh & Cohen 2009). There are both transparency and privacy laws, disclosure obligations and privacy rules. Education, healthcare, economic, financial and business sectors, as well as government agencies themselves, are increasingly faced with the challenge of the delicate balance between openness and privacy. Some believe that transparency has long since reached its limits; others believe it cannot go far enough. Some point to the danger of the resulting excessive legalization and control mechanisms, while others emphasize that, if handled properly, even greater transparency can only enhance trust among people. The whole fuss surrounding the Wiki-Leaks illustrates how topical and wide-ranging this area of tension is.

Against the complex background of this overarching culture of transparency, I zoom in on one segment of it: self-disclosure. Self-disclosure is transparency regarding one's personal life and inner world and openness regarding one's thoughts, feelings, opinions, fantasies, desires and so on. Although for many who encourage transparency, the personal sphere is its limit, self-disclosure, in particular, has taken off. I will come back to this. I zoom in further now: with its basic rule of free association, we can also situate psychoanalysis in the 'cult of self-disclosure', provisionally abstracting from the very diverse forms it can take. We can ask whether – through its undeniable influence on Western culture to this day – it has itself helped culturally anchor this cult. Is – insofar as self-disclosure is one of the forms of transparency promotion – our culture of transparency indebted to this psychoanalytic dispositive of 'speaking out all about yourself'? And if so, how does this square with the persistent cultural unease in psychoanalysis? Or is psychoanalytic self-disclosure of an entirely different nature than the culturally stated 'basic rule'? Does culture possess its own protective mechanisms against possible

DOI: 10.4324/9781003515982-8

derailments or does it encourage them? In what follows, I attempt to illuminate the tense relationship between psychoanalysis and (post)modern Western culture from the vertex of self-disclosure.

I will discuss the phenomenon of self-disclosure first at the specifically psychoanalytic level and then at the broader cultural level and try to picture how the two forms of self-disclosure relate to each other. The degree of discretion or disclosure and the degree of free will or coercion in self-disclosure will be discussed as distinguishing criteria. Michel Foucault's cultural-historical analysis of the so-called 'incentive to discourse' will serve as link between psychoanalytic and cultural self-disclosure practices. Self-disclosure can be enforced from a dominant 'voyeuristic' pole or (seemingly) voluntarily take place from a dominant 'exhibitionistic' pole. But is the contradiction between the ruthless intrusion into privacy by a secret service like the Stasi in the former GDR and the current proliferation of self-disclosure in the Western media as absolute as it seems at first glance? How sensitive are psychoanalysis and the broader culture in which it operates to excesses in self-disclosure? In my final hypothesis, the status and handling of secrecy take on a decisive role in the form that self-disclosure takes. The difference in this status, I believe, is partly at the root of the tense relationship between psychoanalysis and culture.

Free association

Let us start with the analytic rule of free association, as stated in the privacy of the analytic room. Since Freud abandoned hypnosis and suggestion for the so-called 'free association' in the 1890s, the actual psychoanalytic method has emerged. Even before he used this designation, we see precursors of it in passages in which the patient allows himself to go wild in his speech and whose therapeutic value Freud begins to suspect (see, e.g., The Treatment of Emmy von N. in Freud & Breuer 1893/1895, pp. 484–485). In his discussion of the method of dream interpretation, he describes the technique for the first time, still without using the term 'free association':

> One tells [the patient], therefore, that the success of the analysis depends on his paying attention to everything and telling everything that arises in his mind, and that, above all, he should not allow himself to be tempted to suppress incidences, some because he considers them unimportant or sees no connection with the subject, others because they seem nonsensical to him. That his attitude toward the incursions should be completely impartial; for that it was precisely because of this criticism that he had previously failed to find the sought decipherment of the dream, compulsive imagination and the like.
>
> (Freud 1900a, p. 119)

Freud recommends that instead of thinking, the patient adopt the state of mind of the 'uncritical self-observer' to overcome resistance to the '*unwanted* thoughts' (Freud 1900a, pp. 120–121; Freud 1901, p. 14).

To my knowledge, the Rat Man (Freud 1955, p. 88) is the first patient to be explicitly presented with the method in question at the beginning of his analysis, as a main condition of treatment. Free association made its formal entry and, since 1910, has also been referred to by name as such (Freud 1910a, p. 180, 183). In his recommendations on psychoanalytic technique, Freud calls it a 'precept' to initiate treatment:

> So say everything that comes to mind. Behave like, for example, a traveler who sits at the window of a train compartment and describes to someone sitting by the aisle how the view changes before his eyes. Finally, never forget that you promised full sincerity, and never omit anything because its communication is unpleasant to you for some reason.
>
> (Freud 1913a, p. 197, see also 1923a, pp. 351–352, 1924, p. 54, 1925, pp. 107–109)

The stringency of this formulation, which sounds like a commandment, is further emphasized in the connecting footnote, where he says that the patient must indeed say everything without restriction, including the names and secrets of others. On one occasion, Freud (1913a, pp. 197–198) mentions that, to his regret, he did encounter a restriction once, namely in the analysis of a high official who could not allow himself to communicate state secrets. Free association was instituted as an efficient technique to overcome resistance to becoming conscious of repressed psychic material. It serves to uncover the 'hidden', to expose the 'most intimate secrets' of man (Freud 1910a, p. 183).

Now, more than a century later, free association in the 'classical' cure has become more than ever the core of the treatment and, not for nothing, is still called the 'basic rule', the method of working that underpins the entire analytic process. That the view of the nature of the patient's speech has changed greatly since then – one now excludes, for example, the possibility, and therefore drops the expectation, that the patient could speak 'completely impartially' – has not diminished the importance of free association. Psychoanalyses today look different in many ways than at the time of Freud, not to mention the variants of the standard method that arose later, but the basic rule remains. Free association as such is even more respected in its self-efficacy than with Freud. It is less likely to be canned with theoretical and clinical knowledge ready at the analyst's fingertips (Thys 2010, p. 158), even if the terminology concerning the purpose of an analytic process now often sounds different.

Thus, it is no longer always about 'becoming conscious of the unconscious', as in Freud, but, for example, about developing a coherent Self or developing mental representations and mentalizing (Deben-Mager & Verheugt-Pleiter 2004), getting in touch with ultimate truth O in Bion (1970), the expansion of psychic space in Ferro (2006) or 'changing the unconscious psychic processing process' (Vermote 2010, p. 240). The formulations in which the basic rule is stated today sound more inviting than imperative. To give an example, 'Try to speak freely; say as directly as possible what comes to your mind: ideas, memories, feelings, dreams. Do not prepare your sessions' (Vergote 1988, p. 36). Or Ladan (2010, p. 156): 'Try to say whatever comes to mind here, whatever it is'. Even in these modified formulations, the thrust remains unchanged: asking the patient to say, without censorship, anything that comes to mind during the sessions.

The basic rule is unchanged in the service of some form of unlocking the hidden. It, and therefore, psychoanalysis as a whole, fits – from the Greek 'know thyself' to the ontological concept of truth with Heidegger and beyond – entirely within the idea of truth or originality to be retrieved. Thus, in the wake of Freud, Klein, Lacan and Bion, each, in their way, endorsed the orientation toward truth in patient and analyst as the fundamental driving force of the analytic process (see also Chapter 6).

In the early stages of her analysis, a patient wonders anxiously during a session: 'Where is all this analysis going to take me? What if I end up with the most perverse and reprehensible person you can imagine? How will I be able to accept that?' During the few months the analysis has been running, she has already been confronted with unsuspected and, she says, not-so-nice sides of herself. It frightens her, like so many other patients. Indeed, where does the analysis take us? The specter quite often arises that one will lose familiarity with the person one is now and end up with whom one appears to be 'real' but with whom one cannot imagine feeling at home. Perhaps there is, for the time being, a strange monster lurking within us that is now safely hidden away but will soon, through the analytic process, inexorably force itself upon us and take control of us. Although many a patient, like Frankenstein (see Chapter 9), can frighten himself profusely by his incursions, most of the time, it does not go so far. But we must recognize that through a psychoanalytic cure, at least in principle, the subject can encounter himself in places he never expected. The idea that the profound self-disclosure that psychoanalysis encourages goes further than one had first estimated is not foreign to many a patient.

Moreover, without this fact of a secret place, another scene, a psychoanalytic process is inconceivable. More than any other discipline, psychoanalysis has drawn attention to the idea of a hidden inner scene. Its practice is grounded in this notion of hiddenness and its possible, though never complete, unlocking. Until further notice, this scene is still called the unconscious, although it is viewed differently in different analytic models metapsychologically and clinically.

The patient feels that through her free association, the specter of total *un*freedom may well loom, the complete imprisonment in a reprehensible specimen, which now disgusts her but from which she will no longer be able to escape. This image of free speech turning into its opposite of a paralyzing stupor can be seen as the possible excess of psychoanalytic self-disclosure. The supposed and intended beneficial effects of truthful speech do not necessarily exclude its violent and destructive power. The analyst foresees, as it were, the possible perversion of the whole analytic enterprise. This perversion is far from the aim of the analytic cure, but it nevertheless fascinates as a limit proposition to which analysis is indirectly implicated when the self-disclosure it invites loses its limits. I discuss this further in Chapter 11. Let me now place this psychoanalytic self-disclosure in a broader context.

Discreet confessions – the inspiration of Foucault

In his cultural-historical analysis of 'the incentive to discourse', Foucault (1984) focuses on self-disclosure in the field of sexuality and what role psychoanalysis has played therein. From this focus, I want to zoom out afterward to self-disclosure in the broad sense, the communication of all that goes on in one's inner world of thoughts, feelings, fantasies, desires and so on.

From the 17th century onward, Foucault argues, there would be an increasing repression of overt talk about sex. But – and this is his central question – doesn't this 'suppression hypothesis', this ban on sex, point precisely to a persistent injunction to promote sexuality as an extremely important topic of conversation? Over the last few centuries, discourse on sexuality has, on the contrary, been stirred up, although speaking about it has been carefully delineated to certain places and situations where untamed sex has the right, safely contained, to realize itself clandestinely in narrowly defined and coded types of discourse (Foucault 1984, p. 10). 'What characterizes modern societies is not that sex is doomed to remain in the shadows, but that they have set themselves the task of always talking about it and doing so by asserting it as the secret par excellence' (Foucault 1984, p. 38). This socially controlled 'transformation of sex into discourse' (Foucault 1984, p. 17) exposed a 'will to know' and set in motion a mechanism of increasing stimulation that metastasized rather than contained. Thus, with confession after the Council of Trent came an increasing extent of the 'confession of the flesh'; 'Everything must be said' (Foucault 1984, p. 23).

The imperative prescription of self-disclosure soon goes beyond violations of the laws of sexuality and extends to 'the practically limitless task of expressing oneself, of saying to oneself and another, as often as possible, everything that belongs to the play of innumerable pleasures, sensations and thoughts which, through soul and body, have some affinity with sex' (Foucault 1984, p. 24). Foucault quotes a certain P. Segneri from his *L'Instruction du pénitent* of 1695:

> Examine therefore diligently all the faculties of your soul: the memory, the mind and the will. Examine also diligently all your senses. . . . Examine further all your thoughts, words and actions. Even go so far as to examine your dreams to find out whether, in a waking state, you have not given them your assent. . . . And finally, do not think that in this matter, so thorny and perilous, there is anything trivial and light.
>
> (Foucault 1984, pp. 23–24)

But also much earlier, in the 4th–5th century AD, with someone like Cassian, a contemporary of Augustine, Foucault sees confessional practices emerging starting from 'the thoughts with their disordered and spontaneous course and their images, memories, associations and behind them hidden libidinal motives' (see Westerink 2019, p. 135).

That does sound – albeit in a very different context – very psychoanalytic. In addition to pastoral care, education, criminal justice and psychiatry, for example, became hotbeds for sexuality discourses. These are all places where Western society, which had become a 'confessing society', installed rituals from which the production of truth is expected. Holding a true discourse about oneself became, in itself, the hallmark of the individual (Foucault 1984, p. 60). 'Western man has become a confessional animal' (Foucault 1984, p. 61). The obligation to confess has become so commonplace that people have come to experience it as naturally as if the deepest secrets within ourselves demand nothing more than to be brought to light. And Foucault wonders whether the duty to conceal (of sex) is not merely an aspect of the duty to confess (Foucault 1984, p. 63). We could say that the psychoanalytic situation, more than any other, has made confessional discourses its trademark and has promoted the analysand as the confessional animal par excellence, with the analyst behind it – literally and figuratively.

Indeed, Foucault also sees psychoanalysis as a confessional procedure. Psychoanalysis illustrates how to make the rites of confession function according to the schemes of scientific regulatory systems, including by clinically codifying 'making it talk'. Similarly, free association is a means of integrating the confessional procedure into a field of scientifically acceptable observations (Foucault 1984, p. 67). Gradually, the confession refers not only to what the subject wishes to conceal but also to what is hidden from the subject itself (Foucault 1984, p. 68), which brings us to the unconscious. And through the method of interpretation, the revelation of the confession is doubled. 'The one who hears is not merely the lord who pardons, the condemning or acquitting judge, but he is the lord of truth. His function is hermeneutic' (Foucault 1984, p. 69). The ancient commandment of confession has connected with the methods of clinical listening (Foucault 1984, p. 70) and has taken on the new meaning of a commandment to remove repression (Foucault 1984, p. 128).

Foucault wonders whether, with all this evolution, the *scientia sexualis* has begun to function, at least in part, as an *ars erotica*.

Perhaps this production of truth, however intimidated it was by the scientific model, multiplied, intensified and even created its own inner lust. . . . We have invented at least one new lust: lust for the truth of lust, lust for knowing that truth, for showing it, for revealing it, for the fascination of seeing and expressing it, for captivating and capturing others through that truth, we experience lust when we communicate it in secret, track it down employing a ruse.

(Foucault 1984, p. 73)

And Foucault continues: 'the blissful feeling of being interpreted', 'the slight shudder at speaking the truth, the proliferation of secret fantasies for which one pays dearly to be allowed to whisper them to the one who understands the art of listening to them, in short, the enormous 'lust of analysis' (in the broadest sense of the word)'.

(Foucault 1984, p. 73)

Here, a brief reflection on the interesting notion of *assujettissement* or 'subjectivizing submission' introduced by Foucault in his examination of the relationship between power and lust is appropriate (I refer to Visker 2010, pp. 109–113). At play here is the simultaneity of the two meanings of 'subject': on the one hand, the subject, as self-consciousness and identity from which it can actively relate and, on the other hand, the subject, as subjected to language and other symbolic systems. The confession in which expressing oneself completely at the request of another results is not only a mere submission to a (medical or legal) authority but also results from an acceptance of the invitation to do so, from a benevolent willingness to examine and put into words the truth of oneself. The relationship is reciprocal; both participants occupy a certain position of power and both get a portion of 'lust' out of it. Master and servant need each other, to speak in terms of the Hegelian dialectic. *Assujettissement* is submission as well as subjectivation in the sense of developing, through free speech, into a person who assumes the unearthed truth. It is then truthful speech that generates a subject, rather from an active attitude and choice than from a mere passive submission to an authoritarian demand. We see this shift from an emphasis on submission to subjectivation increasingly in the psychoanalytic relationship as well. Whereas initially, with the starting of Freud, the patient submitted rather docilely to the doctor's authoritarian demand of the basic rule so that the latter could reveal and interpret the truth of the former, the emphasis has increasingly shifted to a subjectivizing spontaneous willingness on the part of the patient to examine himself while speaking and to develop an active attitude therein; the finding of truth has then become a co-creation of the analytic couple. There is then hardly any question of strict submission.

Insofar as today's culture of confession, as it has notably also acquired a place in psychoanalysis (and psychotherapy in a broad sense), is to be sought as an extension of Christian practices of confession, Foucault refers to two early Christian concepts (see Westerink 2019, pp. 63–64) that can be understood analogously to subjection and subjectivation. On the one hand, there is *exageuresis*, the commandment of permanent verbalization to reveal hidden and forbidden truths about oneself for the sake of another (subjection). On the other hand, there is the dimension of *exomologesis*, where the emphasis in confession is more on freely acquiring personal truth and establishing a personal bond with it (subjectivation). While *exageuresis* is more about relinquishing or giving away personal truth, *exomologesis* is more about appropriating or receiving and inwardly integrating it. Although resistances are at work in analytic free association and the transference relationship to the analyst plays an important role, we can ask whether the analytic practice has not largely shifted from *exageuresis* to *exomologesis*, making it more of a practice of *parrèsia*, the frank and candid witnessing of truth (see also Foucault 2011). I believe that contemporary psychoanalysis responds nicely to how Westerink (2019, p. 64) paraphrases Foucault (2011):

This parrèsia should not be understood as the expression of what constitutes the core of one's subjectivity. Nor is the expression of truth the reporting of an insight gained. This practice is more like a laboratory for creating an ethical attitude. Speaking the truth is a self-technique, a kind of exercise in the service of subject formation.

Psychoanalysis is not an 'insight-giving' therapy. In the therapeutic effect of 'getting better by truth' (Thys 2006a), insight is secondary.

In any case, the Foucaultian view shows us how the psychoanalytic method of free association did not fall out of the sky but can be assumed to be an exponent of the cultural confessional craze that was in full swing during the genesis of psychoanalysis. The importance attributed to expressing oneself as freely and in detail as possible is indeed found in the psychoanalytic method – and then, in a broader sense, than just about sexual matters, even though these were given special status from the beginning. There, too, it is about 'saying everything, and not thinking that something is trivial'. This is not the place in this cultural-historical perspective to dwell on exactly how the process of free association works and what effects are intended and achieved with it (see Chapter 11 for that). The point here is that psychoanalysis secured a place for itself in a set of socially supported practices of confession (although, of course, its origin and establishment cannot be reduced to that). Despite fitting itself into a broader socially supported practice, that psychoanalysis was nevertheless often perceived as inappropriate indicates that things are more complex. The least that can be said is that adaptation to scientific discourse is not an absolute, isolated or sufficient as a condition of social acceptance.

Importantly, Foucault situates this cult of confession in 'secret rooms', sufficiently secluded from public space. According to him, the lust we experience in it stems from the secret nature of the whispered revelations. Now – with or without lust – psychoanalytic therapy also operates precisely thanks to the seclusion of its setting. Public discretion is essential for the functioning of the analytic relationship (Van Haute 1997). Psychoanalysis does not happen in the marketplace. The basic rule applies only to the specific analytic setting. Psychoanalysis has never claimed that it is good to say everything that comes to mind outside the analytic room as well. It has never wanted to extrapolate the rule of free association to the public space. It is a therapeutic tool and its perfection is a goal to be pursued only within the uniqueness of the therapeutic framework, it is not an end in itself. But hasn't culture gradually installed its own 'basic rule'? Have not the delineated and controlled confessional zones described by Foucault burst at the seams?

The hypothesis I want to develop is that the reluctant compulsion and urge to confess described by Foucault, which was at first still nicely demarcated to specific social segments, later came to permeate and characterize the entire social system. What Foucault very presciently called a 'culture of confession' in the 1970s was only a faint foreshadowing of what was yet to come in that regard. The extent to which the eagerness to reveal the lives of others and oneself was socially installed and positively valorized was gradually skyrocketing. While psychoanalytic self-disclosure is fundamentally voluntary and discrete, forms of self-disclosure arose in addition in which that voluntary and discrete character is at the very least under pressure or which takes place without further ado in the open and/or under coercion. And whether all involved experienced equal or the same pleasure in this remains to be seen. To simplify, I distinguish here, respectively, a voyeuristic and an exhibitionistic pole. In the voyeuristic pole, the lust lies primarily with the one who extracts another's truth and makes it visible, whereas the other is rather in a position of submission (*exageuresis*). In the exhibitionist pole, lust lies primarily with the one who reveals his truth of his own accord and thus subjectivizes himself (*exomologesis*).

The lives of others (the voyeuristic pole)

Florian Henckel von Donnersmarck's 2006 German film *Das Leben der Anderen* is not coincidentally set in the Orwellian year of 1984. The Stasi, the *big brother* of the then GDR, wants to know everything; no detail must escape it and the most insignificant thing can yield highly important information. Stasi agent Wiesler, alias HGW XX/7, is assigned to eavesdrop day and night on playwright Georg Dreyman and his lover, the actress Christa-Maria Sieland. The Minister of Culture Bruno Hempt wants 'hard truths' about this intellectual, seemingly nicely in tune but who, through subtle clues that one thinks one can only perceive through a magnifying glass, is nevertheless suspected of writing subversive texts and perhaps even publishing them abroad. His apartment is thoroughly fitted with the necessary listening devices and the dutiful Wiesler, cut off from the rest of the world by headphones, begins his obsessive assignment. The situation here is not that a society tolerates or actively supports certain practices of disclosure, which flourish only in specific fields and which, incidentally, aim to promote the well-being of the subject who holds the secrets and, in this sense, harbor a therapeutic ambition, but now it is the state system itself that pursues and meticulously organizes the unveiling of all the secrets of its citizens. An important feature of the Stasi system was that the hard truths found on which suspicious individuals were caught and tried, and confessions subsequently extracted, were intended only for the Secret Service itself, even if they were to serve the public interest. Given later researchers, the archives themselves were censored. The Stasi claimed a monopoly over other people's truth.

The confessor or analyst has become an agent and a secret agent whom one has not approached himself. The subject is now not protected from overly direct and intrusive contact with the listener by the perforated hatch in the confessional or the fact that the analyst is seated out of sight behind the couch. Now, the presence as such of the eavesdropper himself is rendered invisible and unknowable. Personal secrets are extracted without the person in question knowing that he is being spied on. The secret eavesdropper has himself become a secret. Consequently, the unsuspecting bearer of the secrets does not experience the confessions as confessions, but they are all the more so for the eavesdropper: real, true confessions, after all, never happen of their own free will but are provoked by a hidden ruse, seems to be the paranoid starting point here. What Foucault still gently referred to as the 'ruse' to uncover secrets escalated in the Stasi into an unsolicited, violent intrusion. In confession or psychoanalysis, the ruse itself is not obscured (even if the one who submits to it does not have full insight into its precise efficacy) and they are, therefore, not cunning in the strict sense. The ruse par excellence completely obscures itself, which is what happens in the perverse strategies of the secret state police, for example. As is well reflected in the film, the suspect subject does know of the existence of such strategies and may try to escape from them if it has reason to suppose that it is itself the object of them. Both parties must not be inferior to each other in the paranoid content of their attitude to life, each perceiving the other as undermining its survival.

Also interesting is the relationship between the two positions regarding the place of lust. Wiesler's lust for spying on the private lives of Georg and Christa is unmistakable, albeit obviously of the serious kind. Gradually, however, he comes to discern precisely their lust, a lust that they share – sexually and otherwise – moreover, give to each other and receive from each other. In contrast, the loneliness of his own life stands out. The scene in which he receives a prostitute in his bare, impersonal apartment, who soon has to go back to her next client, is of a painfully desolate force. The monotonous emptiness of his life stands in stark contrast to the richly filled life of the spied-upon couple with their many friends and in their equally lavish home filled with art and culture. *Le plaisir c'est les autres* seems increasingly to become Wiesler's motto.

The evolution of Wiesler's attitude forms the most fascinating and central line in the film. Without detailing its course and surprising twists and turns, it boils down to the fact that Wiesler comes to sympathize with the suspicious subject. A crucial tilt occurs when he becomes visibly moved by Georg's piano playing. Unbeknownst to the latter, who by now knows he is the subject of the state investigation, Wiesler now protects him by falsifying and censoring the reports that he regularly delivers to his superior. He now has a secret of his own, both to the person whose secret should come to light and to his client, who wants to bring that secret to light. But, precisely by wanting to protect Georg and Christa, he puts them in additional danger by not passing on a plan to smuggle someone across the border, the discussion of which (deliberately done aloud by Georg and his companions to test whether they were overheard) with mention of time and border crossing. By not passing on the plan, so that no inspectors are on to it either, Georg thinks that he won't be overheard anyway, which makes his group less cautious in discussing other plans. This creates the fascinating fact that the location of the secret eventually becomes unclear. The question of what is worse: eavesdropping on someone in secret to catch them or protecting them from another secret is also still difficult to answer unequivocally.

Das Leben der Anderen presents an intriguing picture of how the pursuit of total, *involuntary* transparency is necessarily and paradoxically accompanied by the nurturing of secrets on both sides. If true confessions are never freely made and can only be discovered through intrusion and coercion, the price one pays for this is to install yet another secret. One-sidedly driven transparency further encourages concealment. The perversion of self-disclosure here has a *voyeuristic character*: one party wants to 'see everything' and the other has much to hide – at least, that is what the first party assumes. In forced self-disclosure, each privacy is cornered *by another* and a voyeuristic pole dominates. At the end of the film, when the Berlin Wall and the GDR regime have fallen, the former culture minister, looking back and reminiscing, can no longer hide his perverse pleasure when he smilingly 'confesses' to Georg his own secret: 'We knew everything'.

Of course – one might suggest – this is a dynamic that psychoanalysis is not about at all. But is it entirely separate from it? First, before returning to psychoanalysis, let us look further at the social sprawl of self-disclosure.

My life for others (the exhibitionist pole)

Safely sheltering such social excesses of surreptitiously imposed self-disclosure in supposedly totalitarian regimes, which we keep – temporally or geographically – far from our bed, in 'other people's countries', gives the illusion that we ourselves have nothing to do with the terror of all-pervading transparency. However, this illusion is quickly punctured if we take a closer look at how our own Western, supposedly free and democratic society, too, is increasingly committed to overall transparency and induces its citizens to self-disclosure in subtle and not-so-subtle ways. If we were to examine carefully how our culture is riven with all sorts of self-disclosure practices that are no longer demarcated in relatively hidden places, appropriate professional sectors or by a secret government agency but taking place *on the public scene*, we have no option but to conclude that we are living in a veritable *culture of self-disclosure* (as part of the culture of transparency). I will give some examples to which the media and the Internet lend themselves best.

If we go through radio and television programs in which one witness after another turns up to talk about himself – and this ranges from the most banal anecdotes to profound soul-searching – we notice how often the expression 'on the couch' is used. Whether the furniture refers to the setting of the psychoanalytic cure or the intimate confines of the living room, 'on the couch' has achieved the status of the formula par excellence for intimate, self-disclosing candid conversations but now on the *public* stage. Intimacy is no longer discreet; intimacy is public. In the program *De laatste show* (*The last show*) on Flemish channel TV 1, for example, Flemish writer Herman Brusselmans lies on the couch with interviewer Michiel. Natalia is allowed on the couch in *Goedele* on the same channel. The ultimate and greatest honor is, of course, if one manages to end up on the couch with Oprah. A strong example of how, while all of Flanders is watching, an illusion of private intimacy is conjured up was the recurring moment in the TV 1 program *Morgen Maandag* (*Tomorrow Monday*) from 1993, in which Mark Uytterhoeven sits down with his guest in a too-cramped seat for two and asks him or her very personal questions. In the late 2020s, Flemish television has the so-called human interest series 'The House', which lets a well-known guest 'reveal his or her soul'. RTBF has the television program *L'Indiscret* (*The Indiscrete*), where well-known figures are interviewed 'in-depth'. The combination of fame and confession does very well in the market.

A strong example of this in the written press is the inexhaustible series in the Flemish weekly *Humo,* 'The 7 Deadly Sins', in which, in true confessional style, the semi-darkness of the former confessional is exchanged for the full light of day in which a well-known media figure reveals his or – preferably – her less attractive sides. The same weekly magazine presents a similar series, 'The Wonder Years', in which famous Flemings bring a spontaneous anamnesis by bluntly recounting important experiences from their childhood, their fears and pleasures, their relations with their parents, their first sexual experience and so on. One of the many variations on the same theme I saw, for example, in the weekend magazine at the newspaper *De Standaard* of October 16, 2010, in which a series of famous Flemish people tell how they sleep (in what position, in what kind of bed, with what rituals and so on). For example, one singer says,

> Remember those blankets with tassels on? Everywhere I come across such a blanket, I pull off those tassels. And then I rub them under my nose when falling asleep. If I don't have one of those blankets or one of those ribbons separately, I can't sleep at all. A strange habit, maybe, but I just can't sleep without it. I also can't sleep on my back. I lie on my stomach, with my arms up and my head to the right side, my right leg always fully raised and my left leg extended.

Highly important bed secrets.

Production house *Woestijnvis* programs such as *Man bijt hond* (*Man bites dog*) and *In de gloria* probably owe their enormous success largely to the accurate way in which they portray ordinary people ('such as you and me') with their vulnerable, oh so human but preferably also somewhat bizarre sides. In *In the gloria,* there is the fixed fiction sketch in which Tom Van Dijck invades people's homes uninvited and catches them, not without the necessary portion of schadenfreude, in disconcerting situations that are not meant to see the light of day and in which the viewer can hardly escape the unpleasant feeling of vicarious shame.

Even an institution like the University of Antwerp announces on its site a workshop: 'Soa on the couch'; or a college like Lessius the lecture 'Met ons brein op de sofa' (Our Brain on the Couch). In the Netherlands, Radio 1 even has a program simply called *Op de sofa* (*On the Couch*), which is presented on its site as follows: 'Each episode features a well-known or unknown personality who is *analyzed* and/ or coached *live* by a well-known psychologist using psychological methods that are also of *direct use* to the listener' (my italics).

While psychoanalysis as a professional discipline has become socially marginalized and in the Netherlands, for example, health insurance no longer wants to pay for analyses, there is plenty of money available for a radio program apparently enjoyed by many that presents itself with the pre-eminent symbol of psychoanalysis: the couch. *Public 'analysis' has won out over discrete analysis.* The proto professionalization of our inner lives among the larger public initiated by psychoanalysis has now taken the reins and distanced itself from its original inspiration. The psychoanalytic setting, whose seclusion is a necessary condition for its efficacy, is giving way to all kinds of public self-disclosure practices under the motto of the ephemeral slogan 'on the couch', at least insofar as the furniture refers to the psychoanalytic situation.

Another domain in which transparency scores high is the Internet. If one of the main aspirations of culture is to bundle people into larger units, as Freud (1930, p. 495) believed, then the Internet is undoubtedly a great cultural achievement. Culture will avail itself of every means to bind members of the community together on a very large scale (Freud 1930, p. 499). We have reached this very large scale, the global, by now. All those who are present in one way or another on the Internet can no longer hide from anyone in the world – nor do they want to; on the contrary, most users want to be present, to show themselves. And with the social network *Facebook*, 'the life of others' comes even closer: constantly, we can follow what others reveal about what they do, think, want, feel and so on. The virtual contacts on social networks may often be 'shams' (Kinet 2008, p. 124), but the medium does create the powerful and performative illusion of unlimited openness. We used to have a few friends, and next to them, in the background, there was the anonymous mass. Now, the mass itself is our friend and forces itself into the foreground on the computer, which now acts as our listening device.

Another example is the phenomenon of weblogs. In the weekend magazine of *De Standaard* of March 12, 2011, Tom Heremans begins his article on women's blogs as follows:

> Long ago, it was the dream of every young man to be able to read the secret diary of the girls of his dreams. In it, he would then find the necessary clues to finally unravel the mystery of those wonderful creatures. Nowadays that is easy enough: those secret diaries are simply on the Internet, in the form of weblogs in which women let us look into the deepest recesses of their souls.

Today's *sexting*, the spreading (especially among young people) of sexually graphic messages and images on social media, is the latest outgrowth of this. The deepest caverns, not just of their souls. 'Technology itself now makes it possible to follow the trail of an entire life and find anyone anywhere, with a speed and precision that would have made a Stasi general drool', writes Timothy Garton Ash (*De Standaard*, October 10, 2010).

One might argue that the difference between the secret eavesdropping practices in the GDR and other totalitarian regimes is that all of these contemporary Western forms of self-disclosure are voluntary. It seems that the Facebook generation still attaches little importance to privacy and, therefore, could not care less about its loss or erosion. However, this is a quick and all too easy conclusion. Is not the terror emanating from this global-scale loss of what was then so sacred privacy even more comprehensive than that of the old-fashioned Stasi system? Olivier Malnuit lists, as one of the ten commandments of 'liberal communism', '*Say everything: there will be no secrets.* Endorse and practice the cult of transparency, the free flow of information. All humanity should cooperate and interact with each other' (in Žižek 2009, p. 23).

With today's social networks, this call seems to be realized. However, one consequence of global 'friendships' is also that in 2009, more than a third of companies in the United States were rejecting job applicants based on information obtained on social networks (David Kirkpatrick in *The Facebook Effect*, in Ash's cited newspaper article). And governments, too, seek for and find ways to get their hands on information about Facebook users, collecting entire servers full of data on their own. Again, Ash:

> For example, anyone – voyeurs, stalkers, thieves, terrorists – can quietly view detailed photos of your home on Google Earth and Google Street View. Your smartphone tells you where you are. Your search history on Google is an intimate portrait of your life. All of your credit history is scrutinized as a matter of course by banks and mortgage lenders. And the British and American governments have quietly arrogated to themselves the right – in the name of security – to monitor all that information, up to and including your e-mails and cell phone calls.

If we allow this state of affairs to percolate in its entirety, secret agents like Wiesler are still going to command respect and sympathy: at least they were still doing it out of an ideological conviction; now, it's only about power-seeking and profit or some personal gain.

The enthusiasm and indulgence with which social networks are used is increasingly accompanied by calls to try to recapture lost privacy. For example, in the aforementioned article, Heremans rightly asks, 'How can a diary be secret when it is available for the whole world to read on the Web?' Right, many writers keep their identity secret and use a pseudonym. And 'the anonymous blogs are the best (or at least the juiciest) because in them women throw all inhibitions overboard'. Disclosing highly personal 'secrets' is easier when these secrets are no longer tied to a personal identity. While in psychoanalytic *parrèsia*, for example, truthful speech is in the service of subjectivation, of the development into a subject, the unrestricted Internet self-disclosure, on the contrary, tends to de-subjectify, to encourage the renunciation of one's subjectivity.

However, all this does not alter the fact that, unlike what we see in, for example, *Das Leben der Anderen*, self-disclosure has taken on a different color in the contemporary West. Its voluntary nature (which, of course, does not exclude the possibility that here, too, there is a more hidden but therefore not yet underestimated 'social coercion' and whose adverse side effects, as cited previously, one is now beginning to see and regret) means that today's mediagenic self-disclosure is much more exhibitionist in nature. In the first instance, I am not covertly overheard and spied upon by a voyeuristic agency from which I want to protect and cover myself, but I am showing myself to the other. Look, *I have nothing to hide*. We see this exhibitionist trend, even in a literal sense, all the way to the art world. Think, for example, of the video work by Fleming Jan Fabre in which the artist himself performs a striptease number, or *Balloon*, Pawel Althamer's naked blow-up doll suspended 25 meters above Bruges and depicting the artist himself, or the American photographer Spencer Tunick who has succeeded on several occasions in capturing a mass of undressed extras in distinctly public locations in world cities (such as, for example, 5,000 naked people on the steps of the Opera House in Sydney or 18,000 in Mexico City, it seems that the candidates are sometimes so numerous that many have to be refused). Look and enjoy, this is my body/soul.

Of course, this process only works if there is also a voyeuristic pole to surrender to, and there is, but the starting point is different. The production of lust here is driven rather from a dominant exhibitionist pole, from the point of 'wanting to show oneself (expressing oneself, letting oneself be heard . . .)' than from the point of 'wanting to see (hear . . .) the other'. With the Stasi, there was, as it were, the autocratic and solipsistic pleasure of a voyeuristic system; now, in our Internet society, there is the collective lust in which voyeurs and exhibitionists 'amicably' join hands. This means that even transparency itself – in our culture of 'hyper-visibility' (Baudrillard 2002b, p. 78) and of 'ruthless self-confessions' (Žižek 2009, p. 60) – no longer has to hide. *There are no more secrets.* The situation now looks as if Georg knows only too well that he is being bugged; the bugging equipment, by the way, was installed with his consent and in his presence and he does not mind it at all, on the contrary. So, Wiesler does not have to be sneaky at all, and both of them each have their share of lust that is also granted to them by the other party. In any case, an important difference is that the disclosure is no longer directed to one person or agency but becomes available to all. This situation is literally applied in the Dutch Radio 1 program *Het luisterend oor* (*The Listening Ear*): 'Someone is followed for a day, not by a journalist but by a microphone attached to the body. While the microphone is slowly forgotten, the listeners listen in on his or her life'. So, these days, one can voluntarily be eavesdropped on.

With these non-coerced, voluntary but excessive forms of self-disclosure, are we back – albeit now in a public format – to its basic psychoanalytic form or not? I wonder how Foucault would have described today's discourses characterized by boundless transparency.

The cultural self-disclosure game

From the foregoing, the question arises: has our culture collectively and unrestrainedly adopted the self-disclosure pursued in psychoanalysis via the basic rule, which was already prepared by and embedded in the general knowledge striving of the Enlightenment and confessional tendencies? It seems that the basic rule of free association has evolved from the seclusion of the analytic cure into a general cultural, hypertrophied injunction to self-disclosure: show yourself! Whereas, according to Freud (1910b), the culture's hostility to psychoanalysis stemmed from the fact that psychoanalysis revealed what the culture wanted to cover up, now the culture itself has become revealing but nevertheless still and more than ever wants to cover up psychoanalysis. What about that?

My statement is that the self-disclosure resulting from the social overgrowth by the collective basic rule is very different from its analytic predecessor. I will try to make it clear that the cultural self-disclosure excess, even though it is virtually present in and consequently may have been fueled by analytic practice, leaves behind or at least deals differently with the ethics of that same psychoanalytic clinic. The cultural excess is not an extension of but an uninhibited overshoot of a psychoanalytic potential. The public scene realizes as if it were the excess, or it pretends to do so, which – as the patient from the introduction to this chapter sensed well – is inherent in but at the same time kept at bay by psychoanalysis. This makes it possible to understand, even if both are complicitly on the same stream of self-disclosure, the continuing tension and even hostility between psychoanalytic and broader cultural self-disclosure. That the culture has 'revealed' the analytic basic rule, so to speak, while at the same time, it has nevertheless raised what many believe to be the doomed psychoanalysis itself, I believe, has much to do with how one relates to the secret in both fields.

Let me first try to picture the excess of self-disclosure our culture seems to be heading for. Unbounded (self)disclosure lands us in what we can call 'the obscene'. Baudrillard (2002b, p. 16) characterizes the obscene as 'more visible than visible' and as 'excessive visibility' (Baudrillard 2002b, p. 83). Obscenity is absolute proximity, the elimination of any distance, the unfolding of any hiddenness. Hertmans (1999) illustrates this cult of the close-up using pornographic metaphors and shows that in unbounded transparency, there is precisely nothing left to see. This also applies to unbridled transparency in a broad sense: 'If everything is transparent, you can't see anything anymore'. (Coebergh & Cohen 2009, p. 51), 'The more so-called transparency is offered, the more hidden you get' (Coebergh & Cohen 2009, p. 69). The woman who completely exposes herself before the narrowed, fascinated gaze of the voyeur, up to and including her sex, which is also completely 'unfolded', ultimately shows that there is 'nothing' to see. The voyeur who excitedly sets out to let nothing, but nothing, slip from his ever-narrowing field of vision comes back à la limit from a barren journey. After all, beyond every secret, there is nothing left to unveil. Moreover, zooming in further and further takes away our view of the human (Coebergh & Cohen 2009, p. 9). It is precisely in the 'too much' human of the infinite close-up that the human is deprived of any space. The *passion* for the woman thus degenerates into the *fascination* with partial objects, where her subjectivity and humanity no longer matter. In the hyper-visibility of the obscene, every scene, every representation or imagination, every reference, every hidden meaning, illusion or hidden truth disappears (Baudrillard 2002b, pp. 76–77). All that remains is the pure appearance of an overpowering object without meaning providing context, a fascinating object. Just as in pornography, the sensual body as the source of intersubjective pleasure disappears and only pure nudity itself remains (Baudrillard 2002b, p. 83). The expansive dynamism of passion shrivels to the narrow impassivity of fascination, which threatens to dissolve any (inter) subjectivity. Through excessive projective identification (see Chapter 2) or 'forced extraversion of all that is inner' (Baudrillard 2002b, p. 104), every living subjectivity merges into an all-pervading, killing object pole (as discussed in the chapters of Part I).

An interesting illustration of this is Antonioni's 1966 film *Blow Up*. The voyeuristic fashion photographer Thomas (David Hemmings) secretly takes pictures of a loving couple in the dark park. Zooming in further and further on the black-and-white film, the grain gets coarser and coarser and, in the end, it is hard to make out anything. The only image that seems to impose itself and increasingly take control of the photographer is that of a dead body, which, however, is not found in the place in question. The film shows through the successive 'blow-ups' in the drive for revelation, as it were, the dehumanizing movement from real passionate love to the fascination for an unreal corpse, from Eros to Thanatos (see also Vande Veire 1997a).

Absolute transparency, which ultimately lands us in obscenity and a killing fascination, brings us to the 'supremacy of the object' (Baudrillard 2002a, p. 175). Unbridled transparency is lethal to the subject, which only 'disappears on the horizon of the object' (Baudrillard 2002a, p. 56, 180); just as in fascination, the subject threatens to merge into or coincide with the exclusive and imposing, all-dominant object, as we saw in the first chapter. Whereas in the materialism of the 18th century, the subject was still relegated to being a 'ghost in the machine' (De Kesel 1998; Kinet 2010), in today's fascination looms the image in which only the machine remains (see also Chapter 11). Not desire – of the subject – but seduction – by the object – gets the upper hand. This brings us back to the already mentioned dominance of exhibitionism in our culture: the most coveted and powerful position is that of the revealing, seducing object, the object into which, in turn, the voyeuristic, fascinated other wants to merge. This self-disclosure must go as far as possible, as illustrated by the increasing success of the self-disclosing well-known media figures: it is precisely from figures about whom so much is already 'known' that we want to see even more. Our eagerness in this regard is merciless: we want to see everything revealed until nothing remains of it and the 'object' in question lies completely unraveled and disintegrated in the street. We recognize this excess in the interpretation of Lady Di's death as the sad consequence of the unsparing paparazzi who chased her. The ideal of total self-disclosure ends in a destructive final act, after which the curtain falls, but not without first having 'analyzed' everything from a needle to thread in the media.

Making self-disclosure public and unlimited is accompanied by (the increasing risk of) a desubjectivation and dehumanization. As mentioned previously, this tendency goes in the opposite direction to the subjectivizing truth-telling in psychoanalysis, among others. The terror of showing and demonstrating everything acquires something monstrous. Previously (see Chapter 3), I had already described the inhuman as that zone where the human and the non-human merge into one another and are almost indistinguishable. I argued that it is precisely that inhumanity that fascinates us so much. It is precisely by extremely zooming in to a colossal close-up that the objectual becomes concentrated in a density that no longer represents anything and in which, in the absence of distance and perspective, any perception is compromised. Excessive self-disclosure, therefore, belongs in a *culture of fascination*, this pornography of the psychic that I believe we are now experiencing, a culture in which all interiority is externalized and eroded. Just as a fascinated subject is captivated by the death drive (Thys 2008a), so a culture of fascination is focused on or obsessed with its demise and death (more on this in Chapters 10 and 12). Zwart (2010, p. 13ff) speaks of the fascinating cultural phantasm of global catastrophe.

What matters to me, and where exactly the dehumanization is hidden, is that the excessive diligence with which self-disclosure is practiced today creates the ultimate illusion that everything has been revealed, or at least that this is possible in principle, and that, therefore, nothing more is or will be hidden that could still escape our gaze. In the same sense, Hertmans (1999, p. 11) calls the obscene a disappearing act: showing everything in such a way that there is nothing left to see, utter emptiness without meaning or truth. This provides a very different situation from the one Foucault analyzed in the 1970s. In Foucault's analysis, the procedures of disclosure – concealed and demarcated – paradoxically served as a dominant strategy of oppression. Disclosure and concealment were intertwined there: through demarcation into specific places in well-defined professional sectors, disclosures nevertheless remained secret. In today's self-disclosure game, however, the two are taken apart: the former commandment to self-disclosure no longer hides behind and gets its raison d'être not exactly through a prohibition that delineates it but now comes out into the open and this more and more as it also leaves formerly privileged places of speech. Now, only the naked commandment to self-disclosure remains.

We can suppose that a narcissistic omnipotence desire is at work here: the helpless subject surrendered to the world tries to regain control through quasi-identification with a fascinating object. Seduction is the weapon against lostness. The seemingly light-hearted exposure camouflages a fear of pursuit and its attendant vulnerability. All of our culture is marked by a kind of Stasi ideology, according to which everything can and must be revealed, and the extent to which it succeeds in getting its members to surrender to 'spontaneous' self-disclosure is remarkable, to say the least. The culture of transparency *does not tolerate secrets* and its members, therefore, pride themselves on *having nothing to hide*. Baudrillard (2002b, p. 84) calls this 'end of secrecy' our fatal condition. It is, of course, true, as one might object, that even today, people have all sorts of things to hide, but the point is *that it is precisely this that is being hidden*. That is exactly what citizens in a totalitarian regime delude themselves and others: 'I have nothing to hide'. One's secrets are disregarded. After all, those who have nothing to hide need not fear those who steal secrets. When this misrecognition falters or gives way for a moment, it quickly creates an uneasy feeling, which one resolves by either fixing the misrecognition or quickly revealing what is hidden. In our culture of self-disclosure, the source of uncomfortable feelings is no longer the disclosure but the concealment. Even though everyone handles it differently, there is a general social pressure to reveal oneself, with the message that shame is out of the question. After all, those with nothing to hide are wary of nothing to be ashamed of. With excessive self-disclosure, there is 'nothing' left to be ashamed of. Anyone caught trying to evade that pressure is (secretly) accused of being antisocial and 'fainthearted'. Rather than the disclosure, the concealment has become shameful.

It can be argued that the aforementioned excesses and their disastrous effects (for subjectivity) in reality do not take place at all. Everyone has nothing but fun in the pastime of self-disclosure as light entertainment; meanwhile, life goes on undisturbed. This seems to me to be precisely the reassuring *play* of our culture of self-disclosure: the culture pretends that everything is revealed and that disclosing ourselves does not meet with any resistance and need not be accompanied by any tears or pain at all. One imagines that there are no more secrets and one disregards the playful nature of exhibitionist effacement. Unlike the anxious patient, the masses delude themselves that the – alleged – self-disclosure excess has no risk in it. In my opinion, it is precisely in this disdain for or denial of the secret by our contemporary culture that the tense relationship to psychoanalysis lies. How does psychoanalysis relate to the secret?

Inflation of the secret

The patient's fear relates to the possible confrontation with herself as a monster, to the transformation into an inhuman creature as a result of an overreaching self-disclosure. Indeed, she was invited by her analyst to say anything that comes to mind without censorship. She began the analysis of her own free will, prompted by her mental suffering, in the hope of alleviating her suffering. Yet she feels the threatening possibility, by giving in to it, of ending up somewhere else entirely. It is as if she senses the excess I have tried to evoke. Virtually, this excess is always present: the horror of going so far in revealing inner secrets that *nothing* (human) remains. The analytic process can then be compared to a series of ever-deepening *blow-ups*, in which the increasingly gritty subject gradually disappears as a corpse.

Is psychoanalysis, which, after all, encourages thorough self-disclosure, aiming at the same excess as the public self-disclosure craze? That analyses have been getting longer and longer since Freud and that speech and revelation are becoming more elaborate and endless seems to indicate a runaway self-disclosure frenzy. While language and speech, the symbolic order in general, are usually seen as appeasing, domesticating and conciliatory in the face of real violence, Žižek (2009, p. 59ff.) poses with Lacan the challenging question of whether, on the contrary, true violence does not lie precisely in and is brought out by speech itself. If language eschews any code of discretion or limitation, it is heading toward an excess inherent in human desire itself. This is another reason, along with the one already described by Freud (1937a), why any analysis is basically infinite. This thoroughly human but ultimately destructive orientation toward and fascination with the 'inhuman' is what psychoanalysis shares with cultural self-disclosure tendencies.

That it nevertheless does not seem to belong in, and is often even anything but welcomed by, its own culture of self-disclosure has to do, in my view, with the aforementioned fact *that culture increasingly rejects the notion of the secret, a notion that psychoanalysis, on the other hand, cherishes more than ever.* While the public self-disclosure craze testifies to a naive pleasure in unveiling 'secrets' that lie almost on the surface, psychoanalysis is a place where – against much resistance – the pain and heaviness of self-disclosure can take place in protective discretion. In this sense, psychoanalysis, more than the broad cultural self-disclosure, still belongs to Foucault's analysis. The analysand's suffering is central, his tragedy the engine of analysis (Thys 2007, p. 61). Psychoanalysis does not focus on the easily sayable but on the (almost) unsayable, on those aspects of ourselves over which we do not simply have control (see also Chapter 11). It will, therefore, adopt a rather hesitant attitude toward the potentially sayable. In psychoanalysis, each unearthed secret – much more than that of its revelation – acquires the status of announcing innumerable other, still concealed secrets. Man, after all, is eternally pregnant with an infinite mass of secrets. He is that infinity itself, by which Bion (1965, p. 46) chose to designate the unconscious.

On the public scene, on the other hand, the notion of 'secret' has undergone enormous inflation: it has become something that can be easily and quickly grasped or, at least, it should be. Above all, it has also become something that can be bared without question and in its totality. That something would stubbornly and long-lastingly, let alone forever, resist this unveiling urge seems to have become unbearable. The public (self)disclosure shows a bulimic gluttony that leaves no time to digest anything. This gluttony and eagerness has absolute saturation as its highest goal. There is less and less room for the idea of a real secret, one that commands respect and awe and remains, by definition, unsaturated. In varying tones, the various psychoanalytic models interpret that, first, the secrets at stake in the human psyche are anything but easy to locate, let alone unravel, and, second, that we will never definitively get hold of them. For it is symptomatic of man – and it is from there that he develops his symptoms – that he is an inwardly divided being who will never coincide with himself and will, therefore, always find himself confronted with an 'other scene' that continues to both draw and elude him at the same time, despite the different forms that this scene – the unconscious – takes in the respective analytic models and schools, its notion as such recurs in all of them.

In our culture, with its terror of hyper-visibility, there is less and less room for the unconscious. Everything must be directly accessible, without detours, without reflection or delay. Psychoanalyst Bollas (2018) speaks of the phenomenon of the *transmissive self,* the subject that massively transmits all kinds of private information to the world without any reflection or analysis. In this, a pseudo-intimacy dominates, an intimacy without concealment, transparency for the sake of transparency itself. Baudrillard (2002b, p. 104), as already mentioned, speaks of the 'extraversion of all the inner', reminiscent of the excessive projective identification discussed in Chapter 2. All the inner is in the street; it loses any screening; it is *on* the screens. Everything is out in the open; nothing is left to be imagined.

There is no more room for secrets or hidden meanings. Baudrillard puts it powerfully: 'The inhumanity of this enterprise becomes visible in the abolition of everything 'human, all too human' in us: our desires, our failures, our neuroses, our dreams, our handicaps, our viruses, our frenzy, our unconscious, and even our sexuality' (Baudrillard 2002a, p. 19). Man without the unconscious means the end of psychoanalysis, as Baudrillard saw coming already in 1983 (2002b, p. 51). *After all, those who have nothing to hide cannot go looking for anything in an analysis.* Here and there, even within psychoanalysis itself, which is not immune to this social pressure either, we see signs of an increasing abandonment of the central notion of the unconscious (cf. Vermote 2010).

Many cultural sociologists point out that today's pervasive transparency, of which self-disclosure is one aspect, is a major breeding ground for equalization and uniformization. Baudrillard (2002a, pp. 22–23) talks about how culture systematically clones people into identical copies mentally and socially. The more we reveal ourselves in public, the more we want to resemble each other. We are very curious about 'other people's lives', but we don't want to be too surprised by it. What falls short of our expectations, we quickly pathologize; that, too, is an undeniable trend. This is an element of the desubjectifying effect of unlimited public exposure: it encourages uniformity and shrivels individual singularity and identity. It is to relinquish one's subjectivity and allow it to be absorbed into generalization rather than reinforce it in discrete singularization. It is choosing anonymity rather than personal identity.

Again, insofar as psychoanalysis focuses its attention on singularity and on the uniqueness of each person, it goes against the grain. Despite the inevitable virtual excess that characterizes its self-disclosure practice, and perhaps mainly because it is so aware of it, it remains focused on subjectivation. The free association aims to promote subjectivation, not normalization, uniformization or adaptation. While on the public scene, it seems to be about the pleasure of self-disclosure for the sake of self-disclosure itself, analytic self-disclosure is not an end in itself but a means of getting somewhat in touch with the hidden regions that each of us, in our own highly individual way, unavoidable carries within us. This brings us to the conclusion that the idea along the lines of Foucault that subjectivation results from truthful speech is only half the truth. Subjectivation is not only speaking out but also realizing and accepting that one can never speak out completely. Subjectivation is speaking and – as yet – remaining silent. *Assujettissement* is also submitting to that fact – namely, that the unsaid forms an endlessly shifting reservoir.

In our current accelerating culture, slow psychoanalysis remains hopelessly behind and has become obsolete. Psychoanalysis has been overtaken by the increasingly greedy excess it has itself helped to provoke. The laboriousness of speaking in secret has become overwhelmed by the easy lust of public speaking. Discreet whispers have been drowned out by public shouting. Has psychoanalysis failed to stop the virtual excess of its speaking violence, an excess that is now being thrown back in its face like a boomerang? The paradox is that the cultural self-disclosure game without borders, in reality, reveals much less than what is discreetly revealed in the analyses. Therefore, one may argue that there is no excess at all; after all, it is all just appearances. The participants in the game will, therefore, be a little troubled by the fear our patient experiences of her monstrous inner self. The point, however, seems to me that this game character as such is misunderstood and that the culture is under the illusion that it has indeed moved beyond any secret. How eagerly does she boast that all taboos have been removed? At the same time, she repeatedly enjoys having now overcome 'the last taboo'.

In that picture, of course, psychoanalysis and the unconscious do not fit. Whereas in its early days, psychoanalysis was rejected as too revealing and too perverse, now it is rejected or at least looked at obliquely for not being revealing enough. Mainly, the latter is because psychoanalysis does not conceal the fact that a man will always have something to hide and that that is precisely what makes him so human. What I think is also in play is that, according to the culture, psychoanalytic disclosure is not fast enough, not efficient enough and also not startling enough, with far too little ado. Self-disclosure should be a spectacle. Psychoanalysis fails in this respect: it is no longer spectacular enough. Psychoanalysis used to be taboo because it broke taboos; now, it is taboo because it assumes that there will always be taboos or secrets. Psychoanalysis, once branded as shameless, punctures the illusion that we will ever get past shame. In this, it joins Darwin, who called blushing the most human expression (see van der Zwaal 1988, p. 20).

It is interesting to note how, in *Das Leben der Anderen,* secret agent Wiesler ultimately chooses to keep the secret back. After recovering his shame, he and his overheard 'objects' become subjectivized again. It is as if he is paraphrasing Baudrillard (2002a, p. 61) in saying: we must make man, through all self-disclosure, even more incomprehensible, even more enigmatic.

Psychoanalysis and (the rest of) culture are both focused on self-disclosure and the unveiling of secrets. In this, they find each other and are both exponents of their common time. But at that same point, they seem alienated from each other due to polarization regarding the status given to the secret, particularly as something to be respected or overpowered. Psychoanalysis and culture, as it were, each embody one of the two attitudes that every secret inevitably evokes: preserve or abolish. Insofar as these are two sides of the same coin, they remain – possibly in altered guise – equally inevitably linked.

6

Inescapable and elusive

Identity between melancholy and megalomania

The particularity of the subject between body and other

In one of his essays that deals with imagination and similarity, the French writer and art philosopher Maurice Blanchot writes about 'the inaccessible, which one cannot get rid of, which cannot be found and which therefore cannot be avoided'. Then he says, 'The elusive is that from which one cannot escape' (Blanchot 1997b, p. 62). I approach human identity as something elusive and unattainable from which we cannot escape. I cannot avoid it, but neither can I escape it. I undeniably carry, possess or am some identity, but I never quite get hold of it. I can never describe it completely. Or should I say that I am carried or possessed by an identity? This question resembles the question raised in Chapter 4: am I or do I have a body?

I will try to show that it is precisely this characteristic feature of psychoanalysis, inspired by its practice and by philosophical anthropology, that makes room for this paradox both in its theoretical reflections and in the experience it generates or aims at in its clinical work. This troublesome paradox is not only essential but is also to be cherished. If we let it go as analysts, the uniqueness of psychoanalysis will also slip away from us. But the question also arises as to whether this paradox is not mere appearance. Is it no more than logical that something we cannot escape from must have the character of something we cannot control and, in that sense, cannot grasp? We are grasped by what we cannot grasp.

Since Freud, the status of the discipline of psychoanalysis can be understood as threefold: it is a research of the psyche, treatment and theory. These three dimensions are, of course, closely intertwined. Certainly concerning the first two, leaving aside the third for a moment, this is distinctly the case. One might even suggest that in the treatment setting, research and therapy coincide: the therapeutic effect assumes precisely the analytic setting as the research situation; the therapy is the research. Or vice versa: the research task of psychoanalysis realizes itself precisely through the therapeutic process; the research is the therapy. There is much to be said for this, but it is a bit short-sighted. Entanglement is not yet a coincidence. The very fact that research also takes place outside the clinical situation – some

DOI: 10.4324/9781003515982-9

even think it is pre-eminent – compels us to take this turn with caution. I would, therefore, put it this way: in the clinical situation, there is a tension between the research and therapeutic aspects. In their strong connection with each other, they are also at odds. We could say that the very different therapeutic applications of psychoanalysis vary, among other things, in giving weight to one aspect or the other. Sometimes, the research attitude gets all the attention and one trusts in the therapeutic effect that will result from it; sometimes, the therapeutic ambitions and results are in the foreground and the concern for what these teach research-wise is of secondary importance.

There is, of course, much to say about this, but I only briefly cite this to get to my starting point. Indeed, besides the fact that any psychoanalytic praxis, of whatever signature or in whatever variant, is always also a therapy (Dumoulin 2015), I assume that it is always also – and this, therefore, to varying degrees – a research setting and in this sense can be called 'scientific', can even invoke its rigorous scientific attitude. Psychoanalysis investigates – in its way – the human being and it is, in this sense, an anthropology, not a socio-cultural anthropology and not a philosophical or biological anthropology, even though these are all relevant areas of interface. It is a very specific, psychoanalytic anthropology; namely, it is particularly attentive to the particularity of the subject. And precisely there, in what we might call a 'subject anthropology', lies the radicality of psychoanalysis.

More specifically, the subject studied is a suffering subject, the subject who suffers from himself, the subject who offers himself from this suffering with a therapeutic question. We all suffer, but in some people, suffering takes over to such an extent that it begins to overly determine their lives. Following the 'crystal principle' formulated by Freud (1933, p. 125), according to which pathology reveals the hidden structure of the general human, only gradual differences between pathology and so-called normality are involved here. Psychoanalysis teaches us about man from its examination of pathology and, in this sense, is a 'clinical anthropology' (Van Haute & Geyskens 2002, pp. 11–12). I will return to this with the question of identity.

With the notion of the subject, we dive into our theme of identity. 'Subject' and 'subjectivity' are modern concepts (see, e.g., Bartels 1993; De Kesel 1998). The existence of subjects is relatively young, let us say since the 17th century, with Descartes, which is barely 400 years ago. Later came Spinoza, Kant, phenomenology with Husserl, Heidegger, Merleau-Ponty and Sartre, just to name a few. It is in this philosophical tradition, in which no longer only 'reality' as such but especially the subject and how it – with its consciousness – relates to that reality, is examined, it is in this tradition – in addition to that of the newly emerging psychology and neurology – that psychoanalysis also originated and developed and stands at the cradle of psychotherapy as such and of the many forms of psychotherapy that have emerged from it and which have quite often turned away from psychoanalysis up to and including turning away from it. It is only with the subject that the question of identity in the sense of particularity begins to arise.

A subject is not a 'specimen'; rather, it is more than a specimen, than a copy of a species (as in the case of animals) of which all the specimens are more alike than different from one another. People also resemble each other, yet, above all, they have their individual identity and experience of identity and it is on this idiosyncrasy of the subject, by which it distinguishes itself precisely from the other specimens, that psychoanalysis in its practice directs its focus. The reality that psychoanalysis investigates is subjective reality. Identity, then, is about precisely not being identical with all others but only with that particular subject itself: 'I am (only) identical to myself'. But that is not correct either. The subject is not even identical with itself. On the contrary, psychoanalysis shows us that the notion of identity itself has no empirical or phenomenological ground precisely where the subject is concerned. Both with the phenomenological notion of self-consciousness and with the psychoanalytic notion of the unconscious, we cannot ignore the fact that the subject has a relation to itself and is, therefore, internally divided. In the subject, where the notion of identity only gets the right to exist, even imposes itself as necessary, it is difficult to get a foothold. Psychoanalysis ventures into the swamp of subjectivity. In connection with the search for private identity, whoever feels wetness under the pavement is on the right track. After all, identity *is* also that wetness.

Before entering the swamp of identity issues, I will roughly state the outline of the territory. Human subjectivity and, thus, identity is situated between, on the one hand, the body and, on the other hand, the other or in other words, its dynamics develop from these two poles. The problem of identity, as formulated by psychoanalysis, always has links both with the body and the biological and with the other, with society. It is situated in the field of tension between the body and the other. These two poles were already discussed in Chapter 4 and Chapter 5, respectively: both the bodily drives and the relationship to the other are important sources for the development of a self. The human subject *is* that tension between the two. It is, therefore, not surprising that, within this field, various psychoanalytic approaches come to place different emphases. To put it simply, without denying the field of tension and both poles, some emphasize the biological as the starting point (psychoanalysis becomes more neuropsychoanalysis) and others move more into the field of the social (resulting in a psychoanalytically inspired social psychology). Both tendencies may have their value and are legitimate, but they increase, in my view – and this as they approach the opposites – the risk of neglecting the uniqueness of psychoanalysis, namely its radical focus on the particularity of the subject in analytic practice. Of course, there may be as much that is neurologically determined and there may be as much that is influenced by the social context, but the resultant is unique in each subject and it is this *particularity of the unique interpenetration of both poles in the subject* that analytic practice is concerned with.

Among the protagonists I will now bring up, these differences of emphasis will also emerge and, consequently, the field of tension in the subject also becomes apparent as the field of tension within psychoanalysis itself. I will evoke this field of tension based on Freud, Klein, Lacan, Bion and a few others. Afterward, I will offer some reflections on the implications for practice, the place, after all, where the question 'Who am I?' or 'What about me?' initiates the analytic process and is supposed to elucidate it.

Freud: the body-ego

In my opinion, Freud remains pre-eminently the one who does justice to the whole field of tension in his theory. As I pointed out in Chapter 4, according to Freud, the ego is primarily a bodily ego (Freud 1923b, p. 393). He means primarily the unconscious ego, which forms the basis of what we call 'ourselves'. The unconscious, the actual psychic, is primarily something bodily. The ego is derived from bodily sensations, essentially from sensations that have their source on the surface of the body, of which it is, as it were, a psychic projection. Who or what I am is primarily this body, just as in a photograph we point to a body and say, 'This is Jan' and 'That there, that is Marie'. The unconscious ego is entangled in a dialectic with the Id and the Superego and is consequently imbued with the drive. The drive, this crucial concept that is subject to neglect today, is situated by Freud in the border area between the somatic and the psychic: its source lies in the soma, but its manifestations belong to psychic representations. The personality is the battleground of the three aforementioned agencies and is thus anything but a consistent, undivided whole. The ego is not simply master of itself.

The relationships between id, ego and superego are characterized by a complex dynamic of mutual influence. The id is purely drive, unconscious and does not take into account reality. The ego would arise as a derivative of the id; however, it is not sharply distinct from the id but still tries to make the id take some account of reality and endure frustration as a function of self-preservation. As for the interpenetration of the respective agencies, the superego is the most interesting. It develops from the ego, on the one hand, through identification with the prohibitions and ideals of the parental figures, but also arises from the id: 'the ego creates its superego from the id' (Freud 1923b, p. 52). The person, the subject, is a zone of conflict between various drives among themselves, between the drives and the demands of the outside world and between the three agencies. Here, processes such as repression, disavowal and splitting play an important role.

This whole battleground does not come only from the body and the drive. With 'the demands of the outside world' and identification with the parental figures, we come to the other side of the Self. Elsewhere (Thys 2006b), I spoke of the 'bipolar ego': it comes from both outside and inside. In the personality, however, the inside and the outside are not clearly distinguishable. Thus, the superego, the unconscious counterpart of what we call the conscience, does not, as is often thought, come only from outside, from the parental and wider social commandments and prohibitions, but is co-shaped by the strict, implacable claims of the drives from the id. The outside world and the id make their demands. Sometimes, Freud calls the ego a part of the id and states that it also gives rise to the superego from the id; elsewhere, he suggests that the id and superego are parts of the ego. Later (1940a), he calls id and ego in origin one. To say only that the whole personality structure with Freud is anything but unambiguously structured and is the battleground of the never-decided entanglement of body and other.

When it comes to identity, Freud's concept of 'identification' is crucial. Usually, this involves identification with (certain traits of) a drive-connected or affectively relevant other, the 'object'. This is called 'secondary identification': identification with an object previously conceived as external. Freud describes this, for example, in mourning, where the lost object is incorporated into the Self. The shadow of the object falls on the ego. In this sense, the ego is the precipitation of the given object cathexises and contains the history of object choices (Freud 1916/1917, p. 139; 1923a, pp. 394–395). The ego is the result of grief work and is *internalized absence* (Ricoeur 1970, p. 372). A conversion takes place from having the object in front of it as object to being the object (thus losing for the ego the status of an object) (Thys 2006b, p. 158, 2008b).

However, what interests me more in the context of my approach to the subject matter is the so-called 'primary identification', a kind of primal form of any identification. In its primary form, identification does not relate to what initially presents itself as an object with which the ego subsequently identifies but 'bears a direct and spontaneous character and takes place at an earlier time than any object cathexis' (Freud 1923b, pp. 396–397). The ego is thus immediately that 'object'. Within an oral, narcissistic logic, in which dependence on what is not I is not tolerated, any distance between the ego and the object is dissolved by swallowing up the object and destroying it as object. Every secondary identification goes back partly to this primary identification and seeks to restore a more original narcissistic state (Freud 1921). Thus, the identity of the subject becomes a very ambiguous matter. As we saw, it comes from both 'inside' and 'outside', but these two realms are difficult to distinguish in themselves. The inside is 'contaminated' from the start by the outside and vice versa. I and non-I flow into each other. The external objects with which the ego 'chooses' to identify itself are perhaps those that already most closely resemble its narcissistic disposition. Ultimately, it is difficult to make out whether the shadow of the object falls on the ego or whether the shadow of the ego falls on the object (Thys 2006b, p. 161).

Ultimately, everything comes together for Freud in the view that our ultimate identity is unconscious, situated on an *andere Schauplatz* (Freud 1900, pp. 506–507, referring to Fechner). Even the ego is largely unconscious (Freud 1923b). Psychoanalysis, he argues again, perhaps referring to the conscious ego, is always directed toward the 'most ego-dystonic' to be found in the soul. The unconscious, which includes the repressed, he calls the 'internal abroad' (Freud 1933, p. 124), versus reality as the 'external abroad'. The actual psychic, especially the unconscious, is for our conscious perception of the 'external world' (Freud 1900, p. 576). The most internal of the person is thus external to it. Even the interpretation of the dream, nevertheless the *via regia* to the unconscious, collides with a boundary, with passages that cannot be elucidated. These regions Freud calls the 'navel' of the dream, the place where it is attached to the unknown, from which dream thoughts rise (Freud 1900, pp. 497–498).

Perhaps in this Freudian frame of mind, we can characterize the 'navel of the subject' as an otherwise irreducible drive constellation that forms the foundation of the house built upon it with the many rooms we collectively call our identity. Egon Schiele, for example, created 170 self-portraits: 'a self-image that bursts into a multitude of identities' (Van Der Speeten in De Standaard 10-3-2018). Or consider the heteronyms of Fernando Pessoa, under whose names his writings were scattered and who also argued with each other.

Klein: between internal object and external self

What we might call the more or less 'balanced' interpenetration in Freud between body and other, in Melanie Klein's theory, goes more out of balance and weighs to the side of the body. Her very specific approach, which underlies the later object relation theory, strongly demonstrates how psychic functioning and our entire mental inner world emerge from initial bodily sensations. It radicalizes, in a sense, Freud's body-ego. I try to clarify this briefly (and thus partially reiterate what was already discussed in Chapter 4) through some concepts: the unconscious fantasy, internal objects and the oscillation between introjection and projection (see also Thys 2015b, pp. 52–54).

The unconscious fantasy in Klein's work represents a kind of animistic 'interpretation' by the infant of bodily sensations. Painful sensations are attributed to 'evil objects' operating in the body; beneficial sensations are linked to 'benign objects'. Klein 'deepens' the Freudian body-ego into an internal battleground in which good and bad objects interact. Internal objects can also be projected fantasmatically outward, for example, into the mother's body or external objects are incorporated into one's own bodily experience. These constantly intertwining projective and introjective processes mean that the distinction between inside and outside can be very indistinct. In the experience, one's own and one's mother's body can merge into one another. What is interesting is precisely the ambiguous nature of the unconscious fantasy and the internal object.

As mentioned, Isaacs (1952) specified the concept of unconscious fantasy as the mental correlate of the drive to be distinguished from repressed representations. Unconscious fantasies precede actual symbolization in which the object is represented in absence (e.g., Klein 1959, p. 251). Strictly speaking, they are not mental representations but concretistic proto-fantasies in which the corporeal and the mental are undifferentiated in an overlapping realm of body and mind. The unconscious fantasy is a first step in what Kristeva (2001, p. 148) describes as the 'anamorphosis of the body into the mind', a distorted representation of the corporeal that does not correspond to that corporeal as such but is also indistinguishable from it. Consider the patient in Chapter 4, in whom the fear of not being able to control her emotions takes the form of the fear that substances will spill out of all bodily orifices that will stain the couch and the analyst. Emotions are like bodily substances that can bring about something in the other person. Internal objects are both imaginary and organic-sensory. In addition, internal objects – the word says it all – are internal, my own, of myself and object and, thus, not-I. For internal objects, it remains undecided whether they are foreign or owned. We find the whole of this problem in her theory of the dialectic between paranoid-schizoid and depressive position, between being and not being a separate subject – and analogously between envy and gratitude (Klein 1957). For Klein, this is both developmental and structural: psychogenetically, the proto-subject is first caught up in a paranoid-schizoid logic and evolves into a depressive position in which the other appears as a whole and separated object, but at the same time, both positions continue to structurally demand their attention throughout life.

I want to dwell for a moment on *projective identification*, a process that so typically helps define the coloring of Kleinian thought and has greatly influenced post-Kleinian theories and clinics. When Freud spoke of identification, it was always about introjective identification: the ego or subject identifies with (something of) the object and incorporates (something of) the object into itself. Projective identification works in reverse: something of the subject is fantasmatically accommodated in the object that is identified with it and this is done to place unbearable aspects of self at a distance. It is thus a defensive event, a resistance process (Klein 1946, 1955). If the subject projects malignant, destructive aspects of self into the object, this can result in fear of the vindictiveness of a pursuing and threatening object.

In many places, Klein argues that introjective and projective processes constantly go hand in hand and, each moment, the result of the two determines what the subject does or does not regard or experience as itself. Precisely because of the persistent oscillation between the two, there can be a great deal of confusion about this.

Excessive projective identification, in which the subject disposes himself to a large extent and empties into the object, can lead to states of depersonalization and self-loss. In Chapter 2, I elaborated on this in the context of fascination, as we find it in severe trauma, among others. In excessive projective identification, the object can take on an ego-status to a great extent and stand in for the subject. In order not to be totally lost, the object can become a fascinating object, demanding all attention and where the shaky and diluted subject hopes to recover its mental functioning. The distinction between self and object becomes very confusing. The object is fascinating insofar as the subject recognizes itself in it in a strange guise; it is a strange object in which the subject nevertheless recognizes itself. The identity of the subject is, as it were, outside the subject; it is buried in the object.

Just as in the primary introjective identification, as described by Freud, a potential object is immediately incorporated into the ego and thus, so to speak, does not have the chance to become a full-fledged external object, so in the excessive primary projective identification, the ego is to a large extent excorporated along with it so that the first object-in-the-making retains predominantly an ego character. What is on its way to becoming an object solidifies into a bulge or metastasis of the ego. In Klein's vision, the object can be internal to myself and the self can be external. The combination of both primal states and psychoanalysis teaches us that we never completely leave primal states behind, showing that the localization and delineation of our identity is a tricky matter and is never settled. This means we can never say that we function and act from a fixed *core identity* that we would restlessly appropriate, let alone direct ourselves, from an 'autonomous ego' as Anna Freud and ego psychology conceived it. It is against the idea of such an autonomous ego that Lacan opposed. And so we come to our third figure on whom I want to hang the psychoanalytic question of identity.

Lacan: the empty subject

Just as I said of Klein that she weighted the Freudian balance between body and other toward the body, we can say of the early and best-known Lacan that he gives, by far, the most weight to the other. Again, I limit myself to explaining some concepts that reflect Lacan's view of human identity. Jacques Lacan first describes the identity of the subject both in the framework of the so-called 'imaginary' (autre) and the 'symbolic' order (Autre). Later, the *objet a* and the fantasma are added. What Lacan opposes is the conception of the subject as a substantial thing, as something already endowed or 'filled' with an identity from within itself. Against this, he argues – and this is his well-known *subversion* of the subject, that is, of that substantialist conception of the subject (Lacan 1966d; see also Van Haute 2000) – that the subject is essentially empty and indeterminate. This emptiness is covered and, therefore, misunderstood by the inevitable covering with imaginary and symbolic confections, with imaginary and symbolic identifications (see, e.g., also Mooij 1975, 2002, pp. 111–115).

Lacan situates the emergence of the ego in the so-called 'mirror stage', which he initially described psychogenetically, but later came to function as a structural paradigm for the register of the imaginary (similar to Klein's genetic-structural positions). The ego appears the moment the child recognizes his reflection, literally in the mirror and more broadly in peers and the 'other-similar' in general. This mirror situation totalizes the previously fragmented bodily experience (*corps morcelé*). The ego thus makes its appearance through the identification with an image (imago) – hence imaginary – that simultaneously separates me from myself: the image shows me who I am, I am that image there, I am that other. The first identity construction is, in that sense, alienating: I find myself in an image with which I do not coincide, which separates me from myself. At the same time, the subject clings to that fictitious imaginary grandeur of a perfect, 'completed' identity, this illusory undivided unity that is supposed to dissolve the fragmentation and emptiness. The signifier 'I' is merely a covering of that unfathomable emptiness, giving me some grip to keep from falling into it. For the same reason, naming is so crucial; it creates an identity. Not surprisingly, the proper name, as a direct reference to 'who you are', is so sensitive. But even the proper name, as foundational as it is to identity, is, in a sense, no more than a pseudonym.

To the extent that the mirror image is also provided by a third party, prototypically first the mother: 'Look, that's you', there is an immediate impetus for symbolic identification. This places and determines the subject's identity in the network of relations to the community of others on whom it depends. It is the others who determine who I am. In this sense, symbolic situatedness circumvents the imaginary and totalitarian narcissistic identification of 'this is me'. The ego is no longer everything and it is not self-sufficient in everything, but soon becomes embedded in a meaning-making system of interrelationships in which each person's identity is shaped by the position the subject holds within it. For example, you are the son or daughter of such and such. Identification is, therefore, symbolic and, here, language and culture, in a broad sense, are given a crucial role. The imaginary 'this is me' is supplemented or even drowned out by the question 'Who am I *to the other*?' and 'What does the other desire of me?' Language and desire make their appearance simultaneously. At first glance, different from imaginary identity, symbolic identity is never fixed. The fulfillment of desire (of the other) is never achieved but keeps shifting in the necessarily never-completed dynamics of the symbolic order. But, symbolic identification constantly reminds the subject that even imaginary identification is illusory: you can never definitively, completely say who you are. The image of oneself is never finished; there always remains something that is not included in the determination of the subject. The imaginary and symbolic filling up of the empty subject never quite succeeds, just as, or because, desire never reaches an endpoint. Once you have reached an object of desire, it turns out that each time, it is not quite that and the desire directs itself again to other horizons. It keeps shifting endlessly, driven restlessly – despite itself – toward something indefinite and unattainable.

This brings us to the later Lacan, for whom, even in his theory of the symbolic-imaginary register, a residue non-integrable therein continued to impose itself. Thus, he develops his theory of the object a: a 'real' remainder that resists inclusion in the symbolic that is precisely the lack or the lost object of which the symbolic lives and which sets desire in motion and keeps it going: the object/cause of desire. It is the object that makes me desire. It is the loss and, therefore, the lack of something – and then we are back to emptiness – that constitutes me as a subject and separates me from perceived completeness. This 'basic object' is the rooting and steering of my desire, but emptiness itself is not empirically demonstrable and thus not perceptible. It does, however, color what in the observable naturally arouses my attention and desire (Mooij 2002, p. 85). The fact that one's desire and life's course repeatedly, possibly despite all the misery it brings about and without the subject himself having an explanation for it, goes in a certain direction or is always looking for the same kind of objects, makes the idea of the existence of such an 'object a' compelling, even if we cannot, therefore, point it out.

An important concept in this context is *la Chose* or the Thing: the ultimate object beyond the symbolic and beyond any signifying intersubjectivity around which desire circles (Lacan 1986). Desire is indirectly oriented toward it, but it must not be overly dominated by it or lose its distance from it, for then desire would implode and subjectivity would consequently be dissolved (see also Moyaert 1994, pp. 108–109). Approaching this 'truth of the subject' too closely would, on the contrary, cause any subject identity to dissolve into nothingness.

The global construction that shapes the subject's relationship to the object or objects a is what Lacan calls the fantasma. The fantasma indicates how the subject basally views and interacts with the world; it is the basic scenario of psychic reality. For the speaking subject, it constitutes the modality of its desire and its pleasure (Libbrecht 2008, p. 73). Concerning the identity of the subject, we see that in the development of Lacan's thought, the symbolic-imaginary and phenomenological ego loses importance in favor of a real cradle of the subject that is beyond the phenomenologically identifiable. Ultimately, in our theme, we arrive at the neologism *extimacy*: our most intimate being, the 'truth of desire', our innermost core is at once foreign to us and, in this sense, external (Schokker & Schokker 2000). Our very intimacy is inaccessible. However, it is interesting how Lacan situates the 'home base' of these objects a at the level of the orifices of the body, the 'erogenous' zones, where something can escape and be lost (e.g., feces, the voice, the gaze).

Thus, in Lacan, too, we end up back at the body, which raises the question of whether he, too – contradicting himself – does not eventually arrive at the idea of a substantial subject nucleus from which the ego unfolds. Yet it seems that with Lacan, the fundamental emptiness of the subject remains intact, whether it is imaginary or symbolic identifications that fill or cover the void or the body that delineates the voids of its openings. In some ways, it seems that the emptiness of the Lacanian subject has a status akin to the non-being of Sartrian consciousness, but this fleeting analogy deserves further investigation.

What about Bion, the last figure in the four-in-hand?

Bion: transformations of O

Wilfred Bion is, in a certain sense, to Klein what Lacan was (or wanted to be) to Freud. He deepened Kleinian thought, tried to work out what Klein was 'actually' about and lifted her to an epistemologically higher level, as it were. But in this 'return to Klein' (like Lacan's return to Freud), he also removed himself from her and developed a very own thinking that continues to exude his powerful inspiration for clinical work. It is my impression that more than Klein and also more than the late Lacan, Bion, throughout the evolution of his thinking, increasingly moved away from the crucial role of the body in the psychic (see also Chapter 4). In addition to or despite his early notion of the protomental matrix, where the physical and the psychic are undifferentiated (Bion 1961), he increasingly disconnects the psychic and mental from the sensorial, even placing it in opposition to it. 'There are no sense-data directly related to psychic quality', he says as early as 1962 (p. 53). But still, in 1974 (p. 42), he is on the same track: the sensorial and the psychic are two different spheres.

Klein was blamed, however, for paying too little attention in her theory and clinic to the role of the other in the constitution of the subject and for being too stuck in a drive-oriented intrapsychic subject model. I doubt whether this criticism was justified, but be that as it may, Bion – along with Winnicott – more than made up for it by giving the other a prominent place in the development of psychic reality. In this respect, too, the position of (the early) Bion is comparable to that of (the early) Lacan, even if his theory looks quite different. Think of concepts such as *alpha-function* forming the basis of symbolization and subjectivation, the maternal reverie helping to endure unbearable mental contents, the other as a *container* of split-off and projected self aspects and so on.

What particularly concerns us in connection with our subject as typically Bionian, however, is his concept of *O*, which he introduced in his book *Transformations* and has since then become central (Bion 1965, 1970). O stands for the ultimate truth of the subject, the unknowable origin, up to and including the 'deity'. O is the unknowable thing-in-itself, and thus, the circle is complete from Freud, who also compared the unconscious to Kant's unknowable thing-in-itself (Freud 1915d, p. 70), even though Bion prefers to speak of the infinite rather than the unconscious. All symbolization, all our psychic functioning developed by alpha function, dream thoughts, all our thinking and so on, are only of the order of the transformation of O, which leads us away from the truth of the subject. Designations such as the ego, the *mind* or the *spirit* are, therefore, no longer relevant for Bion. They do not clarify anything; on the contrary, we do not know what we are indicating with them (Bion 2005, p. 68).

We might call this – analogous to Lacan's 'subversion du sujet' – Bion's 'subversion of the subject'. Naming and thinking, however inevitable they may be psychologically, are actually lying. Therefore, the Platonist Bion suggests, we need to temper our too rapid orientation towards knowing, towards transformations in K (*Knowledge*), to which he also situates the '*waking dream thought*' related to Klein's unconscious fantasy and from intuition and faith be open to the unknowable '*formless infinite*' (Bion 1970, p. 31) that is not yet contaminated by our deceptive knowledge (see also Vermote 2011, 2013, 2015, 2018). Through this transformation into O and the K that results from it, we can get in touch with this fundamentally undifferentiated and infinite level of functioning. O we cannot know but only become. In his search for the proper identity of the subject, like Lacan with his little a, Bion with his big O also ends up in a domain beyond the phenomenologically observable. I will come back to this in connection with the therapeutic situation.

I is another

In his 'Letter from the seer' of May 15, 1871, Arthur Rimbaud wrote: '*Je est un autre*', 'I is another'. In the same phrase, Ricoeur (1990) spoke of 'soi-même comme un autre'. Doesn't this well-known phrase offer the sharpest summary of all the above? The conjugation of the verb is crucial. It does not say 'I *am* another', in which the self-experience would still be named from the usual and familiar I-position, but 'I *is* another', with the conjugation in the third person so that the I is already no longer myself here but another there, a third person singular. In the same vein, we saw in Chapter 1 that for Sartre, the I or ego is a 'thing' for consciousness. In wanting to define itself, the I has already lost itself, is already displaced and is no longer in the familiar place where it thought it was. The I is not our true identity but merely the mouthpiece of a fundamental unknown reality that lies beyond the subjective personality. That is what poetry, according to Rimbaud, must aim at: beyond the subjective qualities of the poet in a language where all sentences are dislocated. What has this to do with psychoanalysis, which, after all, goes out of its way to get in touch with our true Self *in ourselves*?

Lacan refers explicitly to Rimbaud's statement, but I think the other psycho-analytic authors would also agree with it. Freud says that the ego is largely uncon-scious and the unconscious eventually encounters an unknowable residue or origin, the so-called internal abroad, a realm where the psychic and the physical cannot be separated. We find the same in Klein: the unconscious imagination, in which the corporeal and the mental are undifferentiated, precedes any subjective symboliza-tion. But even at the level of the 'internal objects', the inner life is populated with ego-dystonic figures. In Lacan, it is the concept of 'extimacy' that best captures the paradox of human identity: our most intimate identity lies outside us. And Bion should not undercut it: O, the truth of the subject, is unknowable; all the psychic, all subjectivity consists only of deceptive transformations.

It always comes down to this: *the ego is only an echo*, an echo of something else. That other is bipolar: it deals with both an external outside and an internal outside, but each time an outside. An outside that is also inside and an inside that is also outside. In all these variants, the same fact of 'I is another' recurs. Psy-choanalysis turns the subject inside out or outside in, which is the same thing. The authors discussed use different concepts, but all four end up with the idea that our most essential, most inner being core, is out of reach, that is, outside. There-fore, psychoanalysis enters paths *beyond psychology* as it is usually understood. It comes most fully to itself as meta-psychology. If we abandon metapsychology, the specific value of psychoanalysis disappears and it is reduced to an 'ordinary' psy-chology of consciousness. Certainly, on the question of identity, the constant refer-ence – through all the differences between the respective authors – to the *andere Schauplatz* plays a crucial role. With its metapsychology, psychoanalysis is, in a certain sense, analogous to metaphysics (cf. Thys 1993). To understand psychic phenomena, in our attempts to describe the workings of the human psyche, we end up – as it turns out – each time with concepts that have to indicate 'the other', what is located beyond the phenomenologically demonstrable or experienceable, beyond the symbolic. The ego is the phenomenological designation of the intangible.

Thus, we come to the fact that our identity has two sides: the two sides also reflected in the title of this chapter: inescapable and unattainable. On the one hand, there is the elusive pole of *metapsychological* identity. Our 'proper' identity, who or what we 'really' are, always – slippery as it is – continues to elude us, does not allow itself to be pinned down, does not cease to shift. On the other hand, there is the *phenomenological*, 'psychologized', subjectivized pole of identity, by which we 'present' ourselves, make ourselves present in the world, as 'this is me'. This pole is inescapable for the subject but also for the network of intersubjective relations that constitute the world. *While the metapsychological pole of identity continues to escape us (unattainable), we do not escape the phenomenological pole (inescapable).* We cannot escape it, which is what experience itself teaches us: to live and act as being that or that person. I do experience myself as myself. Even if I feel that I am not myself but another, I still feel that I am the one, namely me, who feels that way. Even if, through the preceding reflections, I am imbued with the realization of having no ground for my actual identity, I am nevertheless the one who is imbued with it. Sartre (1988) taught that however much the ego is a thing in the world, we cannot avoid it; we cannot step out of our ego.

From Sartre (2003), we also know, as we have already seen in Chapters 1 and 3 and to which I will return later, the desire-for-being: man wants to be, to be a full-in-itself without lack. Even the most radical psychoanalytic thinkers of the human lack, such as Lacan and Bion, thematized this: human desire is involved in the Thing, the thing-in-itself or we must aim to become O because we cannot know it. Neither can help but give it a name and thus still attribute an ontological status to it, even if they keep that designation – with the indefinite minor a or major O – as empty as possible. For human beings, it is inescapable to want to eliminate intangibility if only by thinking and naming it. *Human identity is precisely the tension between these two poles.* Human identity is inevitably both unattainable and inescapable. Both poles are necessary and call each other into existence. If either one falls away, anyone, the human, comes under pressure. Precisely because we would otherwise be absorbed into nothingness as persons, we have to create an ego for ourselves and precisely because we feel that this ego never conclusively determines us, we have no choice but to think of for ourselves, ad infinitum – until death separates us completely from ourselves – a 'another' ego.

I would like to briefly illustrate the paradox or rather the unavoidable tension of the elusive-unavoidable through the paradoxical experience of *finding oneself most intensely in losing oneself.* This sounds bizarre, but at the same time, it flows quite logically from the foregoing. If we must ultimately think of our actual, intangible identity as a void, as a nothingness, as a not-anyone, then we can only experience this 'purest being' in losing ourselves. The subject finds itself when it transcends itself, for it is precisely in that thinness in which the weight of all limited determinations of itself is suspended that it can come into contact with its very self, that is, with nothing. The incessant search for his so-called 'true self' is à la limite an orientation toward a state of 'selflessness' (cf. De Kesel 2017). 'Absolute subjectivity is subjectless', says Adorno (1987) in an essay on Kafka. And Max Brod quotes Kafka in his biography as follows: 'Nothing is lacking in me except myself' (Brod 1967, p. 77).

Exactly when we passionately become absorbed in something or someone, that is, being 'outside of ourselves', disappearing for a moment, we will describe that experience afterward as a moment when we were more than ever ourselves or closest to ourselves as possible. Outside of ourselves, we enter most fully into who we are, that is, into another. I is another. It is a momentary liberation from the tyranny of our desire, of our wanting to be ourselves and of all imagination of that might be.

Blessed, but that can never last long and it is necessarily only afterward when we have already lost it, when we are back (in) ourselves, that we can appropriate that experience as such *as* experience. With Lacan (1973), we can trace this experience back to a basic experience of the proto-subject, of the nascent almost-subject that, in confrontation with the first other – and it is only through the other that one can become a subject – sees itself overwhelmed, completely 'swallowed' by the object. The first form in which the subject appears to itself is its own disappearance – in another (see Vande Veire 2015, p. 288). Here, we find ourselves again in the bizarre state of fascination described previously. My disappearance, my self-loss, is the basic nature of my identity. To find myself is to lose myself. Man arises where he leaves himself.

Pathology and truth of the subject

What is the relevance of all this for analytic practice? Following on from my reflections, I would like to make just two points. The first is about psychopathology; the second is about the weight of truth.

The whole issue of identity, of course, revolves around the narcissistic problem of 'Who am I?' Many patients contact an analyst, stimulated to do so by their suffering from themselves, with that question. It can take many forms: 'Who am I?', 'I have lost myself and want to find myself again', 'What is it with me?', 'I am at odds with myself', 'I feel that I cannot develop myself fully', 'I feel so worthless', etc. Some are anxiously curious about which aspects of themselves are still hiding and will emerge in the analytic process. Consider the patient who, in the early stages of her analysis, wonders where all the analysis will take her. Perhaps she will turn out to be a reprehensible person and she fears that, somewhere inside her, there is a monster that will take over all her doings. Yes, some suspect that their I is indeed another. The problem of identity has its own pathology, which I have already said is merely an enlargement of what is generally human. It stretches between *melancholy* – 'I am nothing', and *megalomania* – 'I am everything'. In that spectrum, there is room for fear of self-loss, depersonalization, identity diffusion, inauthenticity experiences, as well as identity delusions and so on. Now, the ambitions and clinical orientation of both patient and analyst may vary according to the identity issues present.

We can perhaps relate the identity problem to the distinction I made between the metapsychological and phenomenological identity poles. On the one hand, there is 'too little' or 'too fluid' identity: the person has no anchor points to hang his identity experience on; therefore, it lacks consistency and continuity and he is constantly 'someone else'. The 'I is another' becomes all too literal. The identity experience is tenuous and has an extremely low density that floats in the air. Or: there is too much wetness, too little pavement. On the other hand, we see rather 'too much' or a 'too fixed' identity: the person is trapped in a rigid, sterile identity within which no movement is possible. There is no room for 'I is another'. The identity experience is weighed down by an extremely high density that does not get off the ground, off the pavement. As pathology moves toward one of these two extremes, the dynamic in the tension between the two, which is peculiar to subjectivation, slackens. So – to get the dynamics moving again – at times, so to speak, the identity must be lightened, loosened, at other times weighted, strengthened. Some patients benefit more from the construction of an identity and then treatment takes on an important supporting role and is so-called 'ego-reinforcing' or 'covering', like the draining of the Zuiderzee (cf. Freud 1933a, p. 144). Others benefit more from the dismantling or deconstruction of a suffocating identity and then we get a more 'dis-covering' treatment that cuts through the pavement. I am presenting it here in a somewhat short and black-and-white way, but clinical reality has all its nuances, shades and alloys.

My second point concerns the weighty matter of the truth of the subject. The question 'Who am I?' echoes the preoccupation of 'Who am I actually, basically?' Insofar as this preoccupation becomes an important thread in treatment, the research dimension – in addition to always the therapeutic dimension, as I discussed in the introduction – begins to claim a larger share for itself. Insofar as psychoanalytic praxis is research, it is research into the private truth of the subject. All four authors discussed devote considerable attention to this aspect of treatment, which is an important element in its ethics.

Freud (1915a, pp. 440–441) strictly stated that psychoanalytic treatment is based on truthfulness and that the analyst must not be tempted by any deviation from the truth. For Klein, too, 'the desire for truth' was an important catalyst of treatment. 'I believe that a patient's co-operation has to be based on a strong determination to discover the truth about himself'. (Klein 1957, p. 232) For Lacan (1966c, see also Van Haute 1989), analytic dialogue enables the analyst to appropriate his unconscious truth in an 'original word'. He calls this the 'full' speech (*parole pleine*) as opposed to an 'empty' speech (*parole vide*), an 'improper' speech that carries away from subjective truth in stereotyped babble. 'L'analyse ne peut avoir pour but que l'avènement d'une parole vraie'. (Lacan 1966b) Even if, for Lacan, the subject and the order of truth as such continue to have a transcendental status, the analytic situation is unabatedly aimed at appropriating strange associations with which the patient at first sight has nothing to do, nevertheless recognizing them as his own (as we saw in the clinical examples in Chapter 2). And with Bion (1970) it sounds – in the same vein – that to get in touch with O, the ultimate truth of the subject, we must let go of our thinking, wanting to know and our search for connections and mentally surrender as much as possible to a kind of emptiness and be open to what arises spontaneously. Hence his recommendation, which has become a slogan: 'no memory, no desire, no understanding, no coherence'. Later, in his *Cogitations*, he says it again plain and clear: 'Psycho-analysis is a joined activity of patient and analyst to determine the truth' (Bion 1992, p. 99).

The whole truth debate is very complex and could take us very far. There are many kinds of truths, not to mention the relationship between truth and meaning. What about truth-finding if we conceive of analysis as a hermeneutical practice, which is first and foremost concerned with meaning and significance? I will not go into that now and refer to Chapter 11 for that. I can, however, endorse the view of California researcher Saks (1999) that patients should reject the hermeneutic approach to psychoanalysis insofar as the analyst's interpretations do not claim possible truth. Not the certain truth content as such of the interpretations is an evaluation criterion, but rather the aiming or assumption of a possible truth. This is in line with Heidegger's (1998, pp. 288–293) statement that even if truth cannot be proved in its necessity, we cannot but presume its existence. Even Nietzsche, for whom in his rant against all metaphysics there is no room for anything like the thing-in-itself or an actual truth – even truth is only a metaphor – confronts us with a fundamental and unavoidable self-deception: truth does not exist, but we cannot but think it and thus imagine its existence. In this sense, too, we can say that the unattainable is inescapable. Should we indeed call that 'self-deception'? In any case, it seems to me to be a human truth. This brings us back to psychoanalytic practice, which can only be effective and ethical if it at least believes in a private truth of the subject. Every patient is entitled to a believing analyst. For Bion (1970, p. 32), psychoanalysis is ultimately an *act of faith,* which he characterizes as a *scientific state of mind.*

The whole of this debate can be applied to the question of identity, linking it to the question of the 'authenticity' of the subject on which psychoanalytic therapies are nevertheless focused. For this, I refer to the illuminating review article by Hebbrecht (2014), in which authenticity is linked, among other things, to the capacity to change alienated identities, to authorize oneself and to carry and express emotional truth. Winnicott's (1960) distinction between a *true self* and a *false self* is a good illustration of this. By extension, Fonagy et al. (2006) speak of the *alien self,* which they associate with *deviating parental affect-mirroring,* which causes the child to internalize mental states of the other that remain alien to the self. This, of course, is a different alien self than what we were talking about earlier when I talked about Freud's internal abroad or Lacan's extimacy. We could distinguish here between a 'real' strange or false self à la Winnicott and Fonagy and a strange self that is not strange at all, but rather refers to the 'real' self. But also, Winnicott (1971), in the context of the true self, speaks of an *incommunicado* core, an unknowable origin of the self. For Winnicott, then, there are two strange selves, one true and one false.

As far as I am concerned, this brings us to the fundamentally paradoxical nature of identity. We find the paradox at the top with Žižek, where he says that the true authentic subject is outside himself. The subject realizes itself pre-eminently when it is no longer itself and precisely there, the subject is 'more the subject itself than the subject itself' (Vande Veire 2015, p. 241). The Flemish author Ivo Michiels describes how in his *Journal brut – Ikjes sprokkelen (gathering small egos),* his ego is seen as an infinite sum of selves, of which it is absurd to want to aggregate them. The selves are scattered from your birth, in all the streets and houses you had ever been in, in all the beds you had slept in. As you would try to piece all these selves together, only more new selves are added (Michiels 1958, pp. 22–23). All those pieces of yourself lie there, strewn, outside yourself. Perhaps this is how we can understand Pessoa's play with his heteronyms: by leaving himself (his name, which is also only a pseudonym) and breaking open its confined identity, freeing himself from it and merging into others (other names), he explored precisely the many regions that together raised something of his unbridled multiple conglomeration of forms. It is precisely in his *diaspora*, his scattering, that the subject comes into its own. Pessoa shows us a poetic version of the spectrum between melancholy and megalomania, between 'I am nothing' and 'I am everything' or at least many others. For example, he lets Álvaro de Campos, one of his heteronyms, write, 'I am nothing/I will never be anything/I can't want to be anything either/Apart from that I cherish all the dreams of the world'. Coupled with this, we can say that the subject is only truly free when it is free of itself. Does not also apply to analytic practice what was discussed earlier: to find oneself is to lose oneself? And to return to Blanchot: we can only find that untraceable if – in serendipity – we do not look too hard for it.

Ultimately, human identity is truly an uncanny matter. In his essay 'Das Unheimliche', Freud (1919) presents a comprehensive linguistic and etymological analysis of the word '*unheimlich*'. This shows that the uncanny means simultaneously familiar and strange; the familiar and its negation go hand in hand or flow into each other. Does this not also apply to the identity of the subject, which refers both to a familiar ego that carries us through life so that we have solid ground underfoot and to an underlying dimension that constantly strains its solidity? Both the pavement and the swamp? Can the Zuiderzee ever be completely drained? In his linguistic analysis, Freud gives the following description from the *Wörterbuch der Deutsche Sprache* of an experience that can be called both *heimlich* and *unheimlich*: 'a plugged well or a dried-up pond. You cannot walk across it without the constant feeling that water might suddenly reappear' (Freud 1919, p. 96).

Part III

Narrative challenges

Hopper, Levinas and the quasi-subject

The subject outside time

Edward Hopper and the freezing of subjectivity

In the 1944 painting *Morning in a City* (oil on linen, 112 x 153 cm, Williamstown, Massachusetts, The Williams College Museum of Art) by American painter Edward Hopper (1882–1967), we see a naked woman standing upright beside a bed against a bare wall. Her gaze is blank, yet focused on something, something outside the painting – in a corner of the room or outside. Through the window, we see a glimpse of an almost abstract urban environment, bathed in the morning light of a new day. The woman, however, seems to have no part in it and rather to be cut off from this – promising or ominous? – environment. Holding a towel in front of her, she shields her naked vulnerability from the penetrating sunlight. But even this pose (it can hardly be called an act) does not seem to emanate from the woman herself or be prompted by personal motives. No, she just stands there like that or was put there like that by someone. The woman is a petrified figure, staring motionless without seeing anything. Her mental functioning, or even the idea of interacting with or being part of the human world, seems solidified in an eternally still image. The woman is cut off from the outside world but equally cut off from her inner world. She seems robbed of her interiority and orphaned in a withered, petrified urban desert landscape. The woman, though central to the painting, shines in absence.

This makes her likewise cut off from a possible history, a possible passage of time, in which certain events, actions or experiences – her own and others' – are sequential and possibly meaningfully connected. In other words, a possible narrative dimension of the image is minimized or nipped in the bud. The narrative dimension is virtually abolished; the image is still only a stilled snapshot from which any narrative movement has been removed.

Insofar as the human always carries a narrative dimension, we can see this narrative atrophy as a dehumanization or dementalization. The viewer may, therefore, feel inclined to reinsert some narrative into it, thus saving the figure in the painting from total dehumanization. The notion that the woman hesitates whether or not to enter the world does not come from her but is an attempt by the viewer to bring the frozen figure to life. Let her at least hesitate, then! The image evokes all sorts of ideas about scenes that preceded or might follow this state (Renner 1990, p. 71).

DOI: 10.4324/9781003515982-11

The image suggests that the woman has just gotten up, but at the same time, she seems to have nothing to do with the bed or the room. Still, what has her night been like? Did she spend it alone or with someone else? In the latter case, has her partner, just now or in the middle of the night, already left the room or is he – out of sight – elsewhere in the room or apartment? It is a double bed (there are two pillows), but you cannot see whether one of the two pillows is slept on because the woman is standing partially in front of it. And what will follow this scene? Will the woman lift the stillness and yet proceed to action? Will she get dressed, eat breakfast, start her work or do other daily activities? Or will she remain in the grip of paralyzing fear, reveling in the nightly or morning passion or look back on it with disgust or throw herself in despair out the window or back on the bed and burst into tears? The viewer has all these questions, but they seem to be of no concern to the woman herself. We like to think that the artist is suggesting a story and inviting the viewer to construct it from one still image. The viewer wants to undo the 'dying down' (Renner 1990, p. 65) of every human mood evoked in the painting.

One might say that every visual work by any artist or within any art movement inevitably represents a momentary state that succeeds or precedes other unimagined states. In a sense, every work of art dwells in what Levinas refers to as 'the intermediate', an eternal present as an interval in time, a material fixation of duration that suspends the future forever. Thus, the tense muscles of Laocoon will never relax and the budding smile of Mona Lisa will never bud (Levinas 1988, pp. 45–55). This solidified time characteristic of art, however, is not usually a point of interest to the viewer; the sense of stalled motion does not usually impose itself on him.

In this painting by Hopper, on the other hand, more than anything else, this freezing of every movement and eventfulness is highlighted. In its absence, in its merciless suspension, human movement is made present. The spectator is addressed in his compelling need to keep the world going, to make time flow again and bring humanity back to life. The intermediate, Levinas says (Levinas 1988, p. 54), is, after all, something inhuman and monstrous.

Many of Hopper's paintings are difficult to unravel; on the contrary, they resist our spontaneous and recalcitrant tendency to discern symbolic connections, meanings and structures in everything, a tendency that they themselves encourage. What I find extraordinary about Hopper's work is that he does so precisely in a distinctly realistic design in which nothing strange or bizarre is shown. They are ordinary, everyday human scenes that are simultaneously very alienating. In that sense, I find them more powerful, confusing and confrontational than those of modernist contemporaries from the surrealist school, among others (see, e.g., Dalí, Magritte, Delvaux), who also depict the alienating and bizarre pictorially in the background or the surroundings of the figures but do not let it emerge as much from within the person himself.

In a strict sense, one cannot call Hopper a modern artist: he placed himself in the tradition of American realism and had an aversion to abstract art (Van Hove 1993). What Hopper does – within a distinctly realistic design – is to abstract or freeze the mental, the subjective and, in short, the human as such. It almost turns the very realistically depicted figures into things, into objects to be viewed, whose mental world lies, as it were, outside them. Is it perhaps this externalized, her slipping off-screen subjectivity to which the empty gaze of the woman is directed?

We see this Hopperian trademark of 'frozen subjectivity' in many of his works, especially since the 1940s. (Images of Hopper's works mentioned in this chapter are readily available on the Internet.) Paintings such as *Morning Sun* (1952) *and A Woman in the Sun* (1961) are very similar to *Morning in a City*. (Semi-)nude women in a decidedly passive pose seem to be hesitating whether or not to take the plunge into the world, which beckons but also threatens through the window through which the sunlight, almost lasciviously, penetrates. This decision, however, is out of their control; they are at its mercy as if paralyzed. But even in works where a lone female figure seems to be 'waiting' or even 'looking forward' to another, the suggestion of possible contact with the other is far from obvious. I think, for example, of *High Noon* (1949), *Cape Cod Morning* (1950) and *South Carolina Morning* (1955). Will the other ever arrive or will the women wait forever? Even in works where several figures are depicted at the same time, as in *Hotel Lobby* (1943), *Summer Evening* (1947), *Sunlight in a Cafeteria* (1958) and *People in the Sun* (1960), a possible interaction or intersubjectivity seems suspended in an irrevocable separation. They are in the same space but are not there together; they seem to have nothing to do with each other and only share their solitude.

The combination of the various groups of paintings suggests that even when the one we are waiting for or looking forward to appears, it does not result in contact but only the company of a new waiting person. They seem, again and again, Pompeian scenes in which all the figures are similarly disconnected beneath the invisible lava. All these disconnections – from oneself, from the world and others, from time and history – make it difficult for the viewer to come into contact with these unattainable creatures, to take a position towards them, let alone enter into a human relationship with them. They are, in several ways, 'eccentric' subjects, as described in Chapter 3. The viewer involuntarily tends to warm up and humanize the frozen or petrified forms. Thus, he tries to escape the fascination in which the figure in the painting is trapped. But at the same time, is it not precisely these sculpted, petrified, dehumanized figures that exert a sucking force, as if they were precisely expressing something essentially human? It seems that with his petrified figures on the edge of the human, Hopper manages to evoke precisely something fundamentally human.

These initial reflections on Hopper's work form the starting point of my approach to aesthetic contemplation, which is no more than a modest attempt to gain some insight into what happens to subjectivity during this contemplation (Thys 2013). I limit myself here to the visual arts, which does not exclude extension to other art forms. I deliberately choose Hopper because he strongly illustrates that what is valid from a certain art philosophical current is also applicable to aesthetic experience in a broader sense. It is as if Hopper, with his very specific visual language, reveals emphases that transcend his work, which we find in a broader debate about the phenomenology of aesthetic experience. More specifically, I try to draw this approach into a possible understanding of the experience of 'aesthetic pleasure'.

From what does aesthetic contemplation derive any pleasure and what exactly does that pleasure entail? In any case, is the term 'pleasure' appropriate here? If we take the dynamics of human subjectivity and the relationship to the other that is necessarily part of it as a starting point, psychoanalysis and philosophical anthropology provide a suitable frame of reference.

Art is typically human and thus presupposes 'subjectivity'. But in the contemplation of art, the subject does enter into a very special relationship with the other, that is, the work of art. Isn't subjectivity precisely under pressure there? In this typically human activity of art creation and contemplation, is not the typically human subjectivity precisely challenged? This question of exactly how art blissfully makes us teeter on the border of being human is the starting point of this chapter. The answer to it will suggest something of how art – in a specific sense – yes, can indeed save the world, again and again, from the downfall it itself evokes.

Levinas and Blanchot: the exdigenousness of art

Precisely because he places subjectivity at the center of it, we can start from some of Emmanuel Levinas's philosophical reflections on art (especially Levinas 1988 and 1990). From there, in a few rough lines, I sketch the debate that he conducts – explicitly or implicitly – with some other protagonists that put us on the track of emphases in aesthetic contemplation and enjoyment that I have in mind. Levinas adopts Heidegger's ontological distinction between existence and existent and situates within it the experience of the *il y a* or 'there is'. The 'there is' is the pure experience of being existence, separate from any existents that make up the reality of the human world; this is the world in which the subject dwells and relates to himself and the other. While for Heidegger, existence remains inseparable from existent, Levinas radicalizes their distinction by separating existence and existent in the experience of 'existence without existent' (Schulte Nordholt 1991, pp. 94–95). This 'existence without existent', in which reality withdraws and only the border experience of existence as such remains, Levinas describes, among other things, based on sleeplessness in the night: it is no longer a conscious ego that lies awake, but 'it watches' (de Boer 1988, p. 9). All that remains is the dark nothingness of existence, a nothingness that is, however, oppressively omnipresent. It is a presence one absolutely cannot avoid (Levinas 1988, p. 64). The term 'experience' hardly applies, the distinction between subject and object common in the world no longer applies and external and internal are no longer given. Any perspective is absent (Levinas 1988). The subject loses its subjectivity in the horror of being condensed to suffocation (Levinas 1988, p. 67). There is no more empty space. This primary 'relation' to existence, Levinas says, emerges in the situation of the end of the world (Levinas 1988, p. 27). The depersonalized subject is at the mercy of pure existence. The 'there is' has us totally in its grip and, therefore, we tremble before it; it is horribly, inhumanly neutral (Levinas 1988, p. 20). There is only the stillness of a silent, indefinite, absolute threat (Levinas 1988, p. 65). It tends to be a consciousness without subjectivity, an impersonal wakefulness (Levinas 1988, p. 66).

Levinas sees the 'there is' as a pre-personal, pre-worldly anonymous state that precedes subjectivation. In that border experience, any inner division of the subject – and thus the unconscious – is suspended. Subjectivation is precisely the never-ending process of deneutralizing and personalizing the pre-personal neutral 'there is'. This 'hypostasis', in which subject and world appear simultaneously, is an act of appropriation that we accomplish in saying 'I' (de Boer 1988, p. 10). In some respects, we can perhaps compare this hypostasis to what Sartre calls (as we saw in Chapter 1) the 'original negation', in which the differentiation between in-itself and for-itself ontologically constitutes itself (see Sartre 2003, p. 254). General, anonymous existence then becomes *my* existence. Through self-consciousness, the ego becomes a personal existent among the existents, against which it can distance itself or enter into an intimate relationship. Stifling density becomes 'intimate detachment' (Thys 1999). The infinite task of subjectivation challenges the subject to transition from being caught in the paralyzing grip of existence to the eventful dynamics of relating to existence. Hypostasis is to bring existence (back) into the world, to 'mentalize' existence, if you will.

Now Levinas suggests that a sense of the *il y a* also arises in the experience of art (Schulte Nordholt 1991, p. 89; Levinas 1988, p. 58ff.). For him, every (visual) art is characterized by exdigenousness or exoticism. The object is made into an image and thereby withdrawn from the world. Through depiction, the objects are again stripped of the reality in which they normally circulate and become pure, otherworldly 'things'. In this approach, Levinas leans more to Kant than to Heidegger. For Kant (1978 [originally 1790], see also De Visscher (1991, pp. 57–58), in purely aesthetic contemplation, the image is devoid of any meaning and importance, deconceptualized and demundialized. The mind towards it remains passive. Similarly, Levinas suggests that the image or the rhythm of music or poetry represents a unique situation where one cannot speak of personal consent, initiative or freedom because the subject is seized and carried away by it. Things detached from reality impose themselves on us without our assuming them; our consent turns into passive participation (Levinas 1988, p. 30). The work of art replaces the intelligible object and neutralizes a possible relation to it in the world. There is no longer a self; the anonymized subject is enchanted and absorbed by the work and consciousness is paralyzed in its own non-commitment. In aesthetic contemplation, I put myself as being-in-the-world out of play.

Heidegger also speaks of 'world loss' and 'world decay' in art and argues that works withdraw themselves from worldly relations (Heidegger 1996, pp. 31–32). But while Heidegger nonetheless conceives of art as the putting-into-existence of the truth of the existent (Heidegger 1996, p. 27, 30) and the work of art thereby remains connected to the existent, Levinas will allow the work to be absorbed into the pure existence of the *il y a* that detaches itself from the world. For him, the work of art is, by definition, exdigenous, an 'existence without existent'. The inhuman neutrality of the 'there is' that the work of art evokes leads the viewer to the strong need to deneutralize this 'there is', to bring the work of art, as we saw with Hopper, back to the world, to humanize it.

What Levinas calls the *il y a* is developed almost simultaneously by Blanchot under the term *le neutre*, which I want to translate as the 'neutrum', also in the sense of neuter, genderless. It was already apparent how Levinas, too, speaks of the image in terms of 'neutralization' of the object and our relation to it (e.g., Levinas 1988, p. 28, 44). Besides the striking similarities between what both terms cover, I would like to point out one important point of difference given what follows (see Schulte Nordholt 1991, p. 96ff.). According to Levinas, for whom as subject, as existent, we are always and inevitably already in relation to existence, the 'there is' can only be the result of an imaginary reduction: 'let us imagine that all existents: things and persons, disappear again into nothingness' (Levinas 1988, p. 63), the only thing that remains is then the fact that there is existence.

With Blanchot, on the other hand, this return of the world to naked existence, the 'neutrum', does not result from an intellectual operation but is inherent in language itself. Beyond the meaning-generating operation of words, language, because of its nature, culminates in a materialization of words, language ultimately degenerates into a materialization of sounds and letters in which the world itself remains absent (see also Chapter 11 on this subject). Language itself – and I want to extend this to the symbolic and the human world as a whole – is thus directed toward a pole that transcends and leaves it behind. This aspect of the 'neutrum' Blanchot calls *le dehors*, the 'outside'. And that brings us back to Levinas after all: once the poem is written, once the work of art is finished, it detaches itself from the artist and the world and isolates itself definitively in its materiality in 'the elusive strangeness of the exdigenous' (Levinas 1988, p. 24).

It seems that the figures in Hopper's work are involuntarily directed toward this 'outside' – indeed, outside the frame of the painting–, the pole beyond the world and the human to which man, as a symbolic being à la limite, is indirectly involved. Thus, *Morning in a City* embodies, as it were, a doubling of our theme: as a work of art, it is already exdigenous and it also depicts this exdigenousness pictorially.

As in Levinas, in Blanchot, we find the Heideggerian theme of the existence decay, the exodus from the world. Levinas says that the object in the work of art dies, decomposes and disincarnates into its reflection. Blanchot (1997b) compares the image to the corpse, the remains (see also Schulte Nordholt 1991, p. 104; Vande Veire 1997b, p. 78ff.). The gray, yellowish, bleak color of the woman's body in *Morning in a City* is not strange to this. Thus, we paradoxically arrive at visual art, this product of human creativity and emblem of beauty, as the guide par excellence to death and the downfall of the world. Aesthetic contemplation takes on an almost necrophiliac allure.

Fascination and aesthetic contemplation

Having in the preceding section briefly situated the work of art in the 'exdigenous-ness' and characterized it as the depiction of the decaying objects of the human world; we come to the question of the state of mind in which the contemplating subject finds itself when confronted with such 'horrible neutrality'. What happens on the subject's side? In other words, what kind of relationship does the subject enter into with the work of art, if we can even speak of 'relationship' in the full sense of the word? What can the sight of a painting like *Morning in a City* evoke? How do we experience its contemplation?

I would now like to characterize this condition as fascination. Without claiming that all works of art would be fascinating to the same degree for everyone at every moment, I think that what I understand by fascination and its relation to the fascinating object is closely related to the way Levinas and the other philosophers mentioned previously have described aesthetic contemplation. I think that fascination, in its general contours, can serve as a kind of prototype of what is involved in aesthetic contemplation to varying degrees and is at least one of the dimensions present, to a greater or lesser extent, in any experience of art. It is this dimension that I wish to illuminate. Despite its connection to the phenomenological theory of art outlined previously, however, we will see that the object of fascination does not correspond in all respects to Levinas's 'there is' and Blanchot's 'neutrum' and can boast a colorite all its own.

For a description of what I understand by fascination, I recapitulate briefly what was described more extensively in the chapters in the first part. In fascination in the strict sense, all power lies on the side of the object; the subject is powerless and passively at the mercy of it; it is seized by it. Thus, fascination is not a choice of the subject prompted by a strong desire; the subject does not dwell in it of its own accord. This involvement of the subject in the object is so strong that the rest of the world falls away and only the fascinating object remains. Consequently, in fascination, we are dealing with an exclusive object or, in other words, the world is reduced to that one fascinating object. For the subject, the fascinating object occupies the entire world, the entire field of perception; it cannot avoid it, literally cannot see beyond it because there is no more space outside the object. So, there is also hardly any space left for the subject itself, which is, as it were, minimized. Squeezed against the object that takes up almost all the space, the subject loses its three-dimensionality, so to speak, and is reduced to a subject-minimum. While hardly anything remains of the subject, the fascinating object is hypertrophied into a colossal close-up that threatens to swallow up the subject. The subject clings to the object; it can only distinguish itself from it with difficulty. Yet it does not coincide with it; there is no fusion between subject and object. After all, to be fascinated, there must still be a minimum of subject.

Fascination is precisely the condition of the subject reduced almost to nothing that threatens to be absorbed completely by a terrorizing objectality. Fascination is the last possibility to keep the world and the subject from disappearing altogether. This explains the extreme ambivalence that characterizes fascination and that can eventually lead the subject to a hopeless and paralyzing impasse: the subject is extremely 'attached' to the object because it embodies its last hold, but at the same time, it is extremely anxious about it because it threatens to be absorbed by it and thus to disappear altogether. This merging of the expressions of attraction and repulsion can result in an affect implosion whereby any affective differentiation is removed. In extremis, the fascinated subject is mindless, an affective 'neutrum'. Fascination is close to the powerful affect states with which it forms the rupture, from which it is the dissolution. We can, therefore, characterize fascination as the still eye of the affective storm: it is silent and unmoving there, but around it rages the – suspended – violence of the most extreme ambivalence.

With this vision of fascination in mind, let me return briefly to Hopper's *Morning in a City*. The woman in the painting seems captivated by something that the viewer cannot see; she seems paralyzed and stripped of any affectivity and mental functioning, so any tendency to act has also come to a halt. She is cut off in her subject-minimum from the rest of the world, which has been reduced to what fascinates her. In a self-conceived narrative, the viewer can assume all sorts of affects experienced by the woman before and following the scene, but in the image itself, these have imploded. More so, the painting suggests that these suspended affections are stormy rather than calmly rippling in nature, that they will bring the woman into supreme confusion and division. Hence, its oppressive and ominous atmosphere makes the painting so illustrative of fascination as the eye of the affective storm. The affective turmoil seems every moment to make the fixed image burst at the seams and break the frame of the painting.

To what extent and in what way can the work of art itself function as a fascinating object and put the viewer in a state that Hopper pictorially depicts here? As an art object, can *Morning in a City* itself be fascinating? In my description of fascination, we find a lot of Kantian and Levinasian elements. Precisely insofar as the painting or any other work of art depicts something of the world, it deprives it of its familiar place and thereby isolates it from its ordinary relations to other objects, relations that make it part of a symbolic, meaningful network. Marcel Duchamp absolutized this fact by removing not an image of it but the object itself, a so-called *objet trouvé*, for example, a urinal (*Fountain* 1917), from its familiar context: the urinal became a work of art because shown in an exhibition space, it was detached from its familiar context and use (see Thys 1998).

This 'exdigenization' and 'demundialization' are additionally reinforced in the case of the fascinating object by its exclusivity: because it is the only remaining object for the subject, all possible relations to other objects are eliminated. As a result, the colossal object also starts to lose any meaning; after all, meaning is generated only by its difference from and relationship to other objects. If we zoom in close enough on the fascinating object, making any space around it disappear, it eventually starts to represent nothing. This is nicely illustrated in Antonioni's 1966 film *Blow Up*, as we saw in Chapter 5. The subject is then fascinated by something it cannot 'bring home' but to which it is nevertheless very strongly attached. As Levinas says of the confrontation with the 'there is' and Blanchot with the 'neutrum', the fascinated subject is also depersonalized and loses its genus and subjectivity. Against the horrible neutrality of the fascinating work of art, the minimized subject is also affectively neutralized, which is marked by what Kant called a 'passive mind'. It thus appears that fascination in various ways, through the exclusive nature of the object, represents a radical form of aesthetic contemplation as described by Kant, Levinas and Blanchot and thus both confirms and underscores their approach. The exclusivity doubles, as it were, the exdigenousness that marks the work of art in any case, which also withdraws the spectator, like the contemplated object, all the more strongly from the human world and lands him in a kind of no man's land in which he loses not only himself but also gets lost in the world. He becomes a *sujet trouvé*. Insofar as works of art are characterized by exdigenousness, they lend themselves pre-eminently, albeit to varying degrees, to the status of a fascinating object.

However, this same exclusivity of the object also makes the aesthetic contemplation viewed from the point of view of fascination look different and less radical than that conceived by the philosophers of art. None of the philosophers mentioned involves the property of exclusivity in his reflections. The essential difference boils down to the fact that in the fascination with the atrophied subject, one object, one existent, remains, while Levinas approaches aesthetic contemplation from the experience of existence without existent. The distinction may again become less sharp if we understand Levinas's description of the 'there is' in the aesthetic context as a limit proposition. As mentioned, according to Levinas, it is indeed a question of an 'imaginary reduction' (Schulte Nordholt 1991, p. 97) that we, as subjects, cannot possibly experience in reality. If fascination, the confrontation with an exclusive object, already brings the subject to the edge of what can still be humanly experienced, then this problem poses itself a fortiori for the 'there is'. In fascination, we go back one step: there remains one more object, one more existent, in which the world is drawn together in extreme density and to which the subject-minimum is surrendered in (imploded) extreme ambivalence. Again, the world has already almost completely disappeared, but there is still one existent, the work of art into which I merge, so we cannot speak of a surrender to pure existence. As we have seen, in this state, the disappearance of the world and the ego threatens in any case, but this threat does not quite push through. The threat of the 'there is' becomes palpable, but that one fascinating object prevents its total downfall for the time being.

Having arrived at this state of affairs, we are left with at least two questions: How does the work of art relate to the self and in what way is some room for enjoyment conceivable in this unsavory situation?

Fascinating object and quasi-subject

An influential and ancient movement in art interpretation circles – in different variants – around the idea that a work of art always expresses in some way something of the subject that created it. The artist puts (something of) himself in the work, which then becomes the material representation of (an aspect of) his subjectivity. The Freudian view of art also fits into this. In his essay 'The Moses of Michelangelo', for example, Freud suggests that what fascinates us in a work of art can only be what the artist wanted to express in it. The psychic constellation that the artist provided as the driving force for his creation must be recalled in us. From a careful study or analysis of the work of art, as with any other facet of the soul's life, we can uncover the artist's intention. In other words, we can *interpret* the meaning and content of the work and, thus, clear up the riddle of the tremendous impression by which we are overpowered in the sight of the work of art (Freud 1914b, p. 298).

Therefore, Freud argues that in the Moses that Michelangelo so masterfully shaped, aspects of his character are also expressed (Freud 1914b, p. 320). Along the same lines, Freud had already associated Leonardo da Vinci's *Mona Lisa* and, more specifically, her enigmatic, fascinating smile with early memories of the artist's ambivalent bond with his mother (Freud 1910c, p. 251). He agrees with Marie Herzfeld's view when she says that Leonardo met himself in Mona Lisa and that it was, therefore, possible for him to put so much of his own being into the portrait (Freud 1910c, p. 252). Marcel Duchamp also suggested, along with others, that the *Mona Lisa* is, in fact, the image of Leonardo himself, to which his 'Mona Lisa with mustache and goatee' (*L.H.O.O.Q.* 1919) alludes. Perhaps that is why it was no coincidence, Darian Leader wonders, that when the *Mona Lisa* was temporarily exhibited at the Uffizi, it was in the room of self-portraits (Leader 2012, p. 162).

In this view, every work of art is something of a self-portrait and is always in some way the representation and *reflection* of (something of) the creative subject (see also Sels 2013). What the artist has put of himself into it reflects into the gaze of the art lover, who in turn can recognize something of himself in it. But can we reduce the status of the work of art, both in its process of creation and in its contemplation, to this *imaginary* approach, to this order of imagination and portrayal through which the self of the artist and the self of the art lover even come to a certain communication?

With Leader (Sels 2013, p. 37), we can argue that if the artwork were no more than a mirror, we would not need works of art. Unlike the animal, he quotes Lacan, the human subject is not completely trapped in this imaginary captivity. This is precisely why the split between the mirror image and the work of art is so crucial (Sels 2013, p. 39). Indeed, the approach from the imaginary register, in which the self enters the picture, is miles away from the previously described view of art as outwardness, in which the self, on the contrary, is compromised and threatens to escape any portrayal. In the imaginary approach, the movement of the self, not only of the artist but also of the viewer, into the work returns from the work back to the self as a mirroring. Thus, in line with Heidegger and Freud, the work of art reveals a truth of the subject and, by extension, of the human; the work of art is the carrier or mediator that expresses human reality par excellence. According to this view, the work of art thus brings man to himself as a meaning-giving ('signifying') being at home in the network of symbolic connections.

In the approach to the work of art, on the other hand, as exdigenous and, more specifically, as an object of fascination, this feedback, this reflection, is absent or at least sorely lacking. Insofar as identification takes place at all, it is 'primary', that is, it creates an object in which the subject is involved, as opposed to an identification with a pre-existing object and it falters, continues to falter at the level of the object pole (see Chapter 6). In other words, the image, the art object, does not return to the subject pole (Thys 2006b, p. 165). This view is closely in line with what Levinas characterizes as the 'radically thought' work of art, namely, a movement of the self that never returns to the self (De Visscher 1991, p. 67). In the same sense, we can say that the artist is someone who precisely does *not* complete 'the arc of sublimation' (Leader 2012, p. 109). In this view, the work of art cuts us off from the symbolic and does not belong in the imaginary but leads us to the Lacanian order of the real, the order of being beyond any representation of symbolic relations.

The angle of fascination, therefore, radically questions certain characteristics of the artwork. The self may be powerfully contained in the art object, but it becomes hardened, solidified and trapped in it. The subjective remains, as it were, entangled in the object pole; the subject, therefore, cannot 'bring it home' or return it to itself. It remains – however much it sticks to it – cut off from it, leaving barely any subjectivity left at the subject pole.

In this, the fascinating object differs fundamentally from the mirror object. In the mirror object, the subject finds itself and is *full* of it; in the fascinating object, it loses itself and is *away* from it. Of course, we know from Lacan that the mirror image also alienates, but this does not take away the fact that in the field of recognition, we are dealing with a different situation: in the mirror image, recognition alienates, in fascination, the strange obscures recognition (Thys 2006b, p. 219). The alienating effect of the mirror image does not prevent recognition: 'That image there, that's me'. In fascination, conversely, the object comes across as me insofar as I almost coincide with it and am almost completely absorbed in it, but I do not recognize myself in it. The mirror image is the other I recognize as myself; the fascinating object is myself in a strange, unrecognizable form.

While the mirror image tends toward a *doubling* of the self, the fascinating object, as we saw in Chapter 1, tends toward a *metamorphosis* of the self. Put another way, in the imaginary register, we deal with a *self-image*; in the fascination register, with a *self-thing*. In the work of art as an object of fascination, we are dealing with a kind of 'commodification' of the self, of subjectivity. Thus, we are back to the freezing of subjectivity, as seen in Hopper's work. While in the *Mona Lisa*, we can still be captivated by the enigmatic smile, in *Morning in a City*, the woman, along with her subjectivity as such, has perished any laughter. I want to situate this decay or this 'transciency' of the subject one last time in the art philosophical debate.

From the foregoing, the ambiguous character of the fascinating object emerges strongly. For the fascinated subject, it has something distinctly subjective insofar as it – albeit in a bizarre and unrecognizable guise – occupies the place of the subject, but at the same time, it is only a thing, an object. A painting or a sculpture, of course, is not a subject, yet it gives the impression of 'containing' something of it.

Now, this ambiguity corresponds remarkably well to how Dufrenne (1953), this forgotten art philosopher, characterizes the aesthetic object as a *quasi-subject*. It resembles a subject insofar as it 'expresses' something, as they say, and expressiveness is precisely subjectivity par excellence (De Visscher 1991, p. 63). This is, I think, a crucial phenomenological fact, something that everyone knows intuitively from their own experience: of a work of art, be it a painting, a piece of music, a choreography or a novel, we say that there is something 'in' it, that it 'has' something. We spontaneously attribute to it a 'depth', a 'content', which it then 'radiates'. All this contrasts a utilitarian object or an object from nature, and as soon as we think we see something 'in' it, it quickly acquires artistic connotations.

Without being a subject, the aesthetic object is in some sense 'animated' and carries a 'promise of interiority', of an inner world. Where Dufrenne speaks of the work of art as *'un pour-soi de l'en-soi'* (Dufrenne 1953, p. 197) and calls the aesthetic object a 'quasi-pour-soi' (Dufrenne 1953, p. 302), we come close to the Sartrian desire-for-being according to which the for-itself wants to become an in-itself while retaining its consciousness and psychic interiority (a for-itself-in-itself), as I discussed in Chapter 1. Then, the work of art acquires a 'divine' character insofar as, after all, only God can attain such a status (see Chapter 12). Along the same lines, Blanchot (1997b, p. 59) wonders whether the image is not always more animate than the depicted object.

But, we may ask with De Visscher (1991, p. 64), is such a quasi-subject anything other than a mere projection of myself? From this perspective, then, is the expression of the work of art anything other than a disguised self-expression putting us back into an imaginary approach? I think that despite the quasi-subjective character that the work of art acquires in the contemplation, we should at the same time not lose sight of its exdigenous nature. The combination of both makes precisely its ambiguity, quasi-subjectivity does not mean 'ordinary' subjectivity hiding as such. What is crucial, I think, is to recognize that quasi-subjectivity does not refer to personal subjectivity. It is a pre-personal, 'abstract' subjectivity that belongs to neither the artist nor the beholder. Exactly as with the fascinating object, it is not a question of the 'expressed interiority' being something of mine (or of the artist), embodying something personal. No, as a depersonalized self, it still embodies only a hint of interiority, of subjectivity as such, disconnected from a fulfillment ('personalization') with my or someone else's desires or representations. The personal is precisely suspended in aesthetic contemplation; nevertheless, the object imposes itself on me as 'something subjective'.

We see this reflected in the confusing experience of fascination: the object has something subjective to which, shriveled to subject-minimum, I would like to pull myself up and fill myself with, but at the same time, it has nothing 'of me', I can recognize nothing of myself in it. As a fascinating object, as a quasi-subject, the work of art evokes an as-yet impersonal promise of subjectivity. Involuntarily, the spectator, like the confused and distraught fascinated subject, is inclined nevertheless to attribute some animation to the thing. This ambiguous character of the aesthetic object as an 'animated thing' is strongly reminiscent of the blurring of the distinction between the psychic and the physical, which I thematized philosophically in dialogue with Sartre in Chapter 1 and psychoanalytically along the lines of Klein in Chapter 4.

But doesn't the frozen subjectivity of fascination involuntarily evoke something of a possible thawing?

Fascination and aesthetic pleasure

Paintings and other works of art are always made by human beings and their raw material, therefore, necessarily derives from the human, from the symbolic world of human subjectivity. At the same time, by its material demarcation, the work of art isolates itself precisely from the human world, silencing its movement in the intermediate. It is a metamorphosis rather than a reflection; the human becomes lost and entangled in it rather than emerge and show itself in it without further ado. This retreat makes the artwork exdigenous. Yet it intrigues, as a fascinating object and quasi-subject, it continues to harbor within it a hit of humanity that we cannot solidify, but neither can we let it drain away or evaporate. I believe that at the height of this sticky intrigue on the edge of the human, we should situate aesthetic pleasure.

In some artworks, this ambiguity between the human and the non-human, what I call the 'inhuman', is also powerfully pictorialized, as we saw with Hopper's *Morning in a City*. Any human narrative there seems stalled, solidified or frozen, yet it still leaves a distant echo of it. This standstill occurs as an implosion of the affective, which we can conceive as the core of subjectivity, and its echo is the simultaneous dying away and return of precisely the most powerful affectivity.

We also see this suspension of narrative and affect in the suspension of the still smile of Mona Lisa and especially in the frozen wrath of Michelangelo's Moses. Aptly, Freud describes how the image evokes in him the expectation that Moses is going to leap up at any moment and let his wrath run wild, but 'instead, the rock stiffened more and more, an almost strangling sacred silence emanated from it' (Freud 1914b, p. 307). According to him, what the statue shows is the stilled remnant of a movement that has taken place, an undone violence (Freud 1914b, pp. 316–317), which makes him characterize the statue in Rome's San Pietro in Vincoli as 'a moment out of the storm of passions' and 'the silence after the storm' (Freud 1914b, p. 325). This Moses is the concrete petrification of a familiar and swirling narrative from the Old Testament. All this ties closely to the fascinating object as the stilled eye amid the affective storm. Hence the contrast expressed in the image between 'apparent calm' and 'inner turmoil' (Freud 1914b, p. 308).

This impression of 'inner movement' brings us back to the 'promise of interiority' as Dufrenne attributes it to the artwork. The sculpture may be made of the hardest stone, in which there is no movement, but at the same time, it expresses an emotion so powerful that it could make the stone mass burst from within, bringing space to its suffocating density. This promise promises to revive the dying subjectivity. As long as this promise of the resurrection of subjectivity does not cancel itself out, the dying down does not finally accomplish itself; the human is not lost for good. On the fringes of the human, precisely in this perilous lingering on the edge of the abyss without falling into it, the work of art provides the bizarre pleasure of an eternal 'not yet'. The human, the subjectivity, does not disappear just yet and not yet. It is not the enjoyment of the *encore*, encore of the unquenchable desire (Lacan 1975) but of the *pas encore*, pas encore, pas encore of its imminent stillness. Hence, the almost involuntary inclination of the beholding subject to give a continuation to the narrative stalled in the work of art, to please the woman in Hopper's painting to start her day with hope, to let Mona Lisa finally laugh fully and to let Moses live out his anger then so that the course of human history can continue. The promise of interiority is the promise to save the human world at the last minute, just on the verge of its demise.

The work of art is, on the one hand, only a material thing, but as a quasi-subject, it is, on the other hand, at the same time, a source of a world, carrying a world within itself. In the demise of the world and the subject, a new world already looms in the aesthetic object. In this sense, art does nothing but constantly save the world. And how can it do that more powerfully and convincingly than simultaneously bringing the world to the brink of its existence? Rescue work is all the more exciting and its success is all the more lustful the more risky it is. The more lifeless the situation, the more intense the satisfaction if the rescue can nevertheless take place. From the 'sum of destruction', perhaps, like a phoenix, something new can yet sprout. Precisely, this both frightening and promising orpheic tension in a work of art, where downfall and rise and death and birth meet, is the most fertile ground for aesthetic pleasure.

This anxious enjoyment on the verge of self-loss, an enjoyment that we must distinguish from a comfortable 'worldly' enjoyment, is closely aligned with Lacanian *jouissance* (Lacan 2004). I adapt the phrase of Levinas (1988, p. 27) mentioned earlier as follows: the fascinating object is the first and last incarnation of the primary relation that connects us to existence. As *objet géant*, the aesthetic object is both the last remnant, the impressive corpse of a human world and the highly pregnant announcement of a world yet to be born. Every exotic aesthetic fascinating object, especially as it emerges as a colossal close-up, is a high-pregnancy memorial of the human.

And we would not be human beings if we could completely refrain from wanting to liberate works of art – and thus ourselves – from this tension and to clarify their enigma by unleashing our stubborn hermeneutic reflexes and zeal for interpretation on them, to domesticate them, far away from the abyss, to the full in our human world and to incorporate them into our familiar symbolic fabrics. This retrieval of the work of art from its exdigeneity, this maieutic of getting out of it what we think is 'in it', is also a source of pleasure. But at the same time, we equally appreciate and enjoy the fact that the works of art do not give in easily and do not simply relinquish their marginal, pregnant status. And we cherish the hope that the great impression the work made on us will not be undone by its interpretation. At best, this hope is not in vain.

8

The corpse of Polynices

The obscene and tragedy as *fascinum*

Over my and his dead body

'Disown me not, I pray, but grant me burial and due funeral rites' (Sophocles 2006, v. 1405–1410). Thus, in *Oedipus at Colonus*, Oedipus' son Polynices urges his two sisters, Antigone and Ismene, not to leave him unburied if he should die. Later, the brothers, Polynices, who returned from exile, and Eteocles, who refused to transfer power to his brother according to the agreement made, kill each other in a duel in their struggle for kingship over Thebes. Creon, their uncle and Oedipus' brother, draws power to himself and issues a ban on burying the body of Polynices, seen as an enemy and attacker of the homeland, according to the rites then in force. It seems as if Polynices had an inkling of what might happen to him with the entreaty to his sisters in *Oedipus at Colonus* (the action of which chronologically precedes that of *Antigone* but is not premiered until years after *Antigone*), which goes unmentioned in *Antigone* and to which Creon thus puts a stop. To be killed, preferably not, but that's one thing. Not to be buried – that's the worst thing that can happen and must be avoided at all costs. Antigone feels the same way and puts her own life and the entire state system at risk to fulfill Polynice's imperative request.

Like other Greek tragedies, *Antigone* has been the subject of commentaries and interpretations from different perspectives for more than 2,400 years. It has been filmed and continues to be performed as a play, whether or not edited or adapted to our times, but always with the central act of Antigone's refusal to comply with Creon's prohibition and all the calamities that ensue. There was still the 2015 creation directed by Ivo van Hove and starring Juliette Binoche.

Psychoanalysis also makes its interpretive contribution. Freud himself, unlike the over-consumed *Oedipus Rex*, only mentions it in his work in passing in an example of the technique of the joke. A performance in Berlin was criticized for lacking antique character, from which the word joke arose: *Antique? Oh nee (no)* (Freud 1905a, p. 366). In a letter to Fliess, Freud calls his daughter Anna 'meine Antigone Tochter'. She later accompanied her father in his London exile, like Antigone accompanied the blind Oedipus to Colonus (Mulder 2011, p. 10).

It is Lacan who brings up the tragedy as an illustration in the context of his ethics of psychoanalysis (Lacan 1986, pp. 285–333). As far as I can see, most

DOI: 10.4324/9781003515982-12

psychoanalytic Antigone commentaries are inspired by this Lacanian-Kantian reading (see, e.g., Baas 1992; Moyaert 1994; Van Haute 1996; Žižek 1996, 2016; De Kesel 2002, 2015). Invariably it is about how *Antigone* illustrates that human desire is directed toward a point beyond the law, toward the 'Thing', beyond any human signification. In her absolute, unstoppable resolve to bury her brother without concern for others, Antigone personifies the 'pure desire', *le désir pur*, which is ultimately a desire for death. Seen from that interpretation, the chorus is wrong when it sings in the first act, 'No one is so foolish as to desire death' (v. 220, I further rely on Schomakers' Antigone translation: see Sophocles 2015). 'Polynices not buried? Over my dead body!' echoes Antigone's mantra. The Lacanian reading revolves emphatically around the desire of the character Antigone. With this almost exclusive focus on the particular traits of Antigone's desire, the very object of that desire almost escapes attention. In the narrative of the tragedy, that object concerns the corpse, the corpse of her beloved brother Polynices. The play is about his corpse. Phenomenologically, of course, the status of the object and the nature of the affect relation to it are not separable, but this does not preclude putting either in the foreground as a starting point.

In my approach, I want to take the corpse of Polynices to focus and restore it to its rightful place, indeed bring it from under the dust as the very gravitational point of Antigone's passion and thus of the tragedy. The question then becomes: what role does the status of Polynices' corpse play in the meaning of the tragedy? And more broadly: What is the anthropological status of the corpse? Given the fact that tragedy gloriously survives the funerary perils involved in it in our Western culture, this status – at least that is my premise – must surely transcend the crucial importance of the funeral rites specifically required in ancient Greece. Even in our time, the corpse of Polynices continues to stir minds and consequently seems to refer to a timeless, transhistorical theme. This transhistorical character – given the very different funeral rites worldwide – should, of course, be limited to our own Western culture with its Greco-Roman origins (I will come back to this). From this fact, I would like to start and thus perhaps, in all modesty, add a new accent to the existing *Antigone* reading, about which Georges Steiner (1984) provided an erudite study.

We still cannot manage to bury Polynices, and his perimortem condition continues to demand our attention. We cannot simply say 'forget about it'. *Antigone* keeps us captivated and does not let go. A powerful fascination emanates from *Antigone*, so it is said. But what should we understand by such a 'fascination'? Which elements in the tragedy are so fascinating? And does this fascination also play out in the play itself? Is the corpse of Polynices a fascinating object? Can we even describe Antigone's attitude towards it as fascinated? I want to explore how the 'immortal' reception of the tragedy relates to the dynamics around which the play itself revolves.

To begin, I will look at what happens to Polynices' corpse in the play and place it against the backdrop of the delicate importance of how we generally deal with the human corpse. This handling ends up in the dialectic of showing and hiding, where the corpse presents itself as a potentially obscene object that evokes the dissolution of the human. Next, as part of my vision of fascination, I will highlight the sisters' opposing attitudes toward the object: the passion of Antigone versus the fear of Ismene affects, that Creon believes to be above. Finally, the question of how the spectator experiences the play brings me back to the initial question about the fascinating power of tragedy and how we can understand that *Antigone* – with Polynices' corpse as the core object – holds such a firm place in the canon of our culture. I see tragedy as a *fascinum*, in the sense of a symbolic form that culture employs to protect itself from the crippling, undermining and dehumanizing power of the truly fascinating. *Fascina* makes the fascinating manageable, making use of its power without completely domesticating it. Thus, *Antigone* emerges as a narrative strategy, confronting us with the margins of the human but making our relationship with it just barely bearable, with Polynices' corpse as cannon fodder.

What to do with a corpse?

Dealing with a fellow human being who has died is one of the pre-eminent areas of cultural rules and customs. How one deals with a corpse is very closely related. This fact alone makes *Antigone* a haunting illustration. This fact alone makes the confrontation with human remains an existentially and anthropologically charged matter in a general sense. A corpse cannot just lie around or be left randomly some-where. Perhaps precisely to undo the uncanny that a corpse evokes, we want to bring it home again as soon as possible, give it a 'proper' place. How disruptive it is when that is compromised, we see when corpses are somewhere they don't belong, for example, on the street in a residential neighborhood or a field in eastern Ukraine after the 2014 crash of flight MH17. To give death a place, we must at least give the dead body an appropriate location.

Man has always shown a special interest and sensitivity to the corpse of his equal. We cannot possibly imagine our death, said Freud (1915b). Only the dead body of our neighbor forces our awareness of death upon us, and the closer this neighbor, the more penetrating this awareness. Even though it always remains the dead body of another, the awareness of one's own impermanence that the con-frontation with it brings into existence, as it were, constitutes the source of human culture (Van Coillie 2004, p. 18). It is fascinating to study, compare and see how the manners of the corpse have evolved over time and in the most diverse cultures.

A study, such as Ariès' (1987), on the handling of death in our Western culture from the early Middle Ages onward is very instructive in this regard. Man is the only living being to ritually bury his dead and give them a dwelling place, and he has been for about 40,000 years. 'From then on, the cemetery – or the single grave – becomes the permanent sign of human habitation, bearing witness to an unbroken relationship between death and culture' (Ariès 2003, p. 7). Cultures can differ greatly in the meaning attributed to death, in the religious representations surrounding an 'afterlife' and in the related actions and procedures the corpse must undergo. Cultures also differ greatly in the degree to which they emphasize the con-tinuity or break between this life and the next. All that would take us too far here.

My point is that despite all these differences, the fact remains that every culture, in whatever way, pays special attention to shaping this transitional moment that death is anyway. Regardless of how one thinks about death in a particular culture or community, one cannot ignore it; one has to 'do' something with it. Dealing with the body of the deceased is part of this.

What to do with a corpse? That is the whole stakes of *Antigone*: What to do with the corpse of Polynices? On that question, not all agree. So, we can place the whole act of *Antigone* in the broader anthropological context of the immense importance of what is done with the corpse. 'Yet these are the laws to which Hades demands allegiance' (v. 519), Sophocles lets the intransigent Antigone say in her dispute with Creon. Sophocles' other tragedy, *Ajax*, also revolves – albeit in a different context – around the same theme, in this case, whether or not to bury Ajax's corpse. Menelaus and Agamemnon want to forbid it to his brother Teucer, but Odysseus exhorts them to reason and can persuade them to allow it anyway, even though their former supporter Ajax has become a traitor. The discussion surrounding the 'godless ban', which in *Ajax* is still contained and leads relatively smoothly to a reasonable solution, is taken to extremes in *Antigone* and escalates into a devastating denouement. While Odysseus' speech in *Ajax* is 'illuminating' and calms tempers, Creon's speech in *Antigone* becomes unreasonable (cf. Tindemans 1991, p. XI) and tempers are tested to the limit of what is human. Further on, I try to show that *Antigone* derives its fascinating power precisely from this. No tragedy other than *Antigone* so inexorably demonstrates that this – whether or not the ritual takes place – is a matter of life and death. What is at stake?

Among the ancient Greeks of the 5th century B.C., and certainly not among them alone, it was a matter of making the body of the deceased undergo certain operations: cleansing, oiling, dressing, ministering libations, weeping and burial (or cremation) within a certain time frame. Without all this, the soul of the dead person could not cross the Lethe and could not be admitted to the underworld. So they were concerned with the soul, that form of being human in which man lives on even after death and thus with the guarantee of continuing to live on *as a human being*. Executed criminals and enemies killed in battle were denied this right: their biological death coincided with their also symbolically ceasing to exist as human beings. Their corpses were thrown into the sea or left in open pits. Not all corpses are equally equal before the law; some even fall outside it. Those who are not buried according to prescribed rites fall outside the culture and are consequently denied as human beings.

As Polynices points out in the quote from *Oedipus at Colonus*: it is either to be buried or disowned. For Creon, Polynices was an enemy of the homeland and consequently did not deserve to be respected and buried as a human being; for Antigone, however, he was first and foremost her blood relative and irreplaceable brother. Behold immediately the incompatibility of the two qualities of Polynices around which the play further unfolds. Thus, Antigone speaks to Ismene in the prologue, 'Have you heard? Or will you not see the evil that marches from our enemies to our loved ones?' (v. 8–10) This seems to me, at least, to be the stakes: is Polynices to be seen as human or not? *To be or not to be human* – that's the question.

If we take a look at all that Polynices' corpse has to go through, we see how this ambiguity of his humanity takes shape in the play. In the prologue, Antigone informs her sister Ismene of Creon's prohibition: 'Not weeping, not burying is the [corpse] left as a delicious larder to birds foraging for food' (v. 29–31). And she immediately announces that she will not let this happen. In the first act, we hear Creon himself reiterate the prohibition: 'The decree is that the city shall not honor him with a tomb, no one may even lament for him, and his body shall be left uncovered as food for birds and dogs, yea a disgraceful sight' (v. 230–236). In a subsequent scene, one of the guards comes to report the 'disaster' that an unknown person has violated Creon's ban without leaving a trace. However, the wording in which he does this creates a great deal of confusion. First, he says, 'Someone (he has already left) *buried* the corpse with a layer of thirsty dust on the flesh and with the rituals due' (v. 245–247, my italics). And a few lines further: 'The corpse had become invisible, *not buried*, but covered with a thin layer of dust' (v. 254–256, my italics). So, it's not really buried after all. Anyway, the corpse, first destined for the vultures, is now covered and honored as human. Then, we read in the second episode, 'we [the guards] swept away all the dust that covered the corpse, we made the decomposing body completely free' (v. 408–410). Polynices, as a human being, back to square one. Next, the guard reports on how Antigone is caught covering the naked corpse again with dust and watering it with libations (v. 426–431). Polynices, included in the circuit of symbolic rituals, reappears as a human being. The guards interrupt Antigone's actions, once again undo Polynices' burial and thus human-ness, and bring Antigone to Creon.

So we see a constant oscillation between the corpse being or being deemed human and the corpse not being human. The outcome remains undecided. Is Polynices now buried or not? Consequently, is he a human being or not? We don't know. Antigone – by making his body undergo the symbolic, humanizing rituals – at least wants to turn it into a human being, but it remains unclear whether she has succeeded. Apparently, she herself is not convinced of this either; otherwise, she would not have to bury the corpse a second time after it had been bared by the guards, which comes with a distinct urgency. For his part, Creon maintains that Polynices does not deserve the human ritual, but again, it is unclear whether he effectively considers his body to have been buried after all or whether he considers Antigone's intention to do so, which is only half-heartedly translated into actions, sufficient to carry out the death sentence. Was the forbidden act committed or not? It is alluded to in several places that it was. Thus, Creon says, 'the mercenaries who committed this act' (v. 302) and, 'it is she who committed the act' (v. 384) and Antigone herself says, 'I did it' (v. 443). But, the description of the acts cited previously and their undoing indicates rather that they were confined to an impetus without taking place. 'She was burying him' (v. 384–385) and 'She was burying that man' (v. 402), says the guard. So here, the act is presented as not yet completed; it was interrupted before it was accomplished.

The act of burying the corpse is *simultaneously done and not done*: the 'done' is evident in the intransigence with which Creon seeks to punish Antigone for it; the 'not done' is expressed, for example, where at the end of the fifth episode, i.e., after Antigone has been caught and tried, the chorus implores Creon to 'erect a tomb for him who lies yonder like dirt' (v. 1101). According to Adkins and Adkins (2005), covering the corpse with three hands of earth was sufficient to admit the deceased into the underworld. Thus, the thin layer of dust would suffice. But, besides the fact that this minimalism may not have been the preferable, let alone the common practice, the fact that this bit of dust stays there is apparently also important. Otherwise, the guards would not find it worthwhile to take it away again and Antigone, as mentioned, would not want to repeat the act like a fury.

All in all, quite a few elements leave the impression that the status of Polynices' corpse remains in limbo, accompanied by complete confusion as to what is right and what is wrong, as sung in the second choral song (v. 620–623). On the one hand, there is nothing to suggest that the corpse is now sufficiently covered so as not to serve as bait for the animals; on the other hand, it is bluntly assumed that Creon's prohibition was violated. Polynices' corpse is left in an undecided state. It seems to me that precisely this unresolved tension, this simultaneity of irreconcilable modes of existence, drives the tragedy that inevitably emerges. No tragedy without quite this 'trouble with Polynices', with which Žižek (1996, pp. 44–45) refers to Hitchcock's film *The Trouble with Harry*, in which a corpse is likewise at the center of the action.

The corpse as obscenity

If we now zoom in further on this field of tension, we see that whether or not the corpse is buried is differentiated by whether or not it is *visible*. Being buried and being invisible are undoubtedly related but also do not coincide. What is buried is certainly also invisible, but conversely, what is invisible is not necessarily buried. The already mentioned decree of Creon is twofold: the corpse must be unburied as well as visible (v. 204–205). Not to be buried is insufficient; neither should it be made invisible. Hence, the guard has every reason to panic with the announcement, 'He lay invisible, not already in a grave, but covered with thin dust' (v. 254–256). The vehemence of the tempers thus appears to relate to whether or not Polynices' corpse is visible.

The oscillation between being buried or not ends up in a *dialectic of showing and hiding*. That this visibility would only matter to the vultures and dogs seems implausible to me: they will find the unburied corpse, whether it is sprinkled with a bit of sand or not. What must matter here is its visibility *to humans*. In ancient Greece, but by extension in large parts of Western culture, human remains are hidden from view as soon as decomposition is visible. Insofar as the dead body is shown or even displayed, it is a cleansed, clothed and beautifully made body. The body is displayed only when it has been made 'presentable', that is, embellished with symbolic signs that emphasize the fact that it is the body of a human being.

For the sake of completeness and nuance, I should mention here that customs vary widely around the world, of course. For example, there are the Toraja people on the Indonesian island of Sulawesi who keep the deceased embalmed in a coffin at home and only bury them one or several years later. Some communities instead give the corpse a visible place in the family home and even continue to feed it and do so until a distant state of decomposition. There are groups where the successor will lie under the corpse of the deceased chief or priest to absorb his powers and this is until when the corpse is unrecognizable and disintegrates. And in Tibet, there is the common custom of the so-called 'aerial burial': the corpse is cut up and fed to vultures in full visibility. This act is the exact opposite of avoiding at all costs that the corpse would fall prey to the vultures in classical Greece. What was and is 'normal' in Buddhist Tibet would be degrading to the Greeks. These examples may suffice to undermine the evidence that direct contact with and visible display of the corpse would always be taboo (for this theme, see Bloch & Parry 1982). In this sense, my further reflections on the obscene must also be placed in their cultural context, which constitutes precisely the symbolic: what is obscene in one culture is not necessarily so in another.

Having said this, I now concentrate further on the Greek-Western culture that is familiar to us. There, the human body is shown in its hiddenness, which is also a security secured in the wrapping of the symbolic. The ordinance of Creon thus radically goes against this as human preservation of the corpse of Polynices. On the contrary, it is degraded to mere flesh, whose human form will soon disappear. For the eyeing animals, that flesh may be a fresh supply; for humans, it is a distasteful confrontation with the malodorous degradation of the human. If the symbolic rituals are not performed firmly enough, the human too soon becomes unmasked as only a 'thin layer of dust'. Thus, we can understand the whole tension over whether or not to bury Polynices' corpse as an almost unbearable undecidability about whether that corpse is a human being or merely flesh.

The frank display of what must remain hidden brings us to *the obscene*. The obscene always has to do with exposing to the eye what, according to prevailing moral standards, should remain covered. To speak of obscenity, however, it is not enough that what is shown arouses disgust or revulsion; there must be a bodily element involved and it must also contain a pole of attraction (van Emde Boas 1966). The obscene is, therefore, less unambiguous than the abject, which designates the simply reprehensible. The pornographic lends itself pre-eminently to the obscene, but the obscene is broader than the pornographic and covers the whole terrain where corporal visibility intriguingly violates a taboo.

At the same time – and this makes the obscene something very ambiguous in its relationship to the taboo – every culture also has its niches where the obscene is flourishing and performs precisely its paradoxical cultural function. Where the obscene is intrinsically transgressive, it reveals the hypocrisy of the culture that explicitly forbids it but implicitly, blindly allows it. Consider the morally widely overtly rejected but ubiquitous pornography scene on the Internet. In this sense, the obscene – especially insofar as it can hardly be removed from the economic circuit of goods – is also culturally symptomatic. It is a kind of cultural return of the repressed, the reappearance in the public space of that which culture prefers to obscure. The obscene is that which exhausts itself in an 'excessive visibility', to quote Baudrillard (2002b, p. 83).

Insofar as Polynices' uncovered corpse shows what should humanly be hidden, it is an *obscene object*. This is what Creon – especially in Antigone's eyes – does: degrade the body of her beloved brother into an obscenity, into a surplus rotting away at the edge of the human symbolic. It is this hyper-visibility, this embarrassing loss of decorum of her hero, that she wants to undo as yet, that cannot be allowed to continue. 'She hates the overt obscenity of the decaying corpse' (Hertmans 2007, p. 120). Her act is an undoing (wanting to undo) Creon's obscene act. In this sense, her desire, often presented as monstrous and boundless because it threatens to drag the symbolic order into ruin, is aimed precisely at *restoring the boundary*, at concealing again that which too much affects the security of the symbolic. Her obsession, which extends to the (self)destructive, is at the same time and, in the first instance, inspired by a desire to repair what threatens to break down completely, to disintegrate. With the courage of despair, she tries to put a stop to the decomposition – of Polynices' human body, but more broadly of the symbolic fabric as such – at least to hide it from view. Antigone says no to Creon but wholeheartedly says yes to the symbolic law. Who is monstrous here, Antigone or Creon? The tragedy throws the question in our faces and leaves it further open.

The corpse of Polynices thus constantly balances between the personal and the impersonal, between a human subject and a desubjectified thing. As an obscene object, it lies there in full visibility in an impending dissolution, but as a subject, as the human Polynices, it has already almost decayed and disappeared from view. The indeterminacy of this irreconcilable simultaneity is strongly reflected in the concrete positioning of the corpse as a 'character' in the play. On the one hand, it is the 'core object' from which the entire tragic course emanates; on the other, it shines in the absence and has no place on the theater scene. It is *offscreen*, *offstage* or *hors-champs* (cf. Hertmans 1999, p. 122ff; 2007, pp. 161–162). The spectator does not get to see the corpse, but all the more, the horror of those who testify to having beheld it. 'The obscene is the end of every scene', says Baudrillard (Hertmans 1999, p. 84). No embarrassment on stage.

I would add that it is precisely in this non-place that the obscene object also delineates the scene, indicating at least its wings in which it resides and from which it can emerge again at any moment. Is it not precisely Polynices' corpse – at once invisible and hyper-visible – that stages the whole tragedy of *Antigone*? The obscene object may be outside the scene, but at the same time, there is no scene without the obscene object; the obscene object precisely makes the whole *Antigone* scene possible. In this sense, it is precisely the obscene object, which does not tolerate the daylight of the scene, that pre-eminently on the scene attracts all the attention to itself. The obscene, obsessive object *obscenes*.

The obscene, however, not only involves the public display of what must remain hidden but, moreover, in its pervasive visibility, shows that in the end, there is nothing left to see (cf. Hertmans 1999, see also Chapter 5). Therein lies the radicality of the obscene: visibility never has enough of itself and is propelled involuntarily. If something forbidden is shown anyway and attracts our attention, but we then turn our gaze away again and focus on something else, okay, then a taboo has been momentarily violated, but no more than that. However, when the obscene really grips and intrigues us, there is never enough to see; there is no calming saturation point. No, we want to see more and more and more, and we want to keep seeing it, again and again and from even closer. There is then a dynamic of intrusive and greedy wanting to penetrate the object. An exhibition without inhibition.

Doesn't something similar happen in *Antigone*? Antigone tries to overlay the corpse, but each time, it still reappears in the pernicious light of day. The spectator is forced to look at it again and again, even though it does not appear on stage – or precisely because it appears on stage as nothing. That, I think, is the threat that hangs over the entire play and that Antigone wants to stop at all costs: the fearful approach of the point at which it appears that there is nothing to see, that nothing remains of man, this high-level being. In all its organic concreteness, there also lies the metaphorical power of the visibly decomposing corpse of Polynices: nothing remains of it in the end. As for the effects of this unstoppable urge for revelation, reference can again be made to Antonioni's film *Blow Up*, in which zooming in further and further on the photographer's black-and-white film only results in a corpse that, in reality, is not found.

When *all* can be seen, there is *nothing* left to see. It is this eschatological truth that man is knowingly heading toward his own destruction that shows the tragedy and yet again does not – in the aforementioned oscillating dialectic of showing and hiding. 'Man was always committed to his own disappearance', we read of Blanchot (2012, p. 64). This concretizes itself in the corpse, in which the dear living 'unites with the solemn impersonality of itself' and makes 'the hitherto unknown original' appear, 'the corpse is its own image'. 'At a certain moment, the corpse is the likeness par excellence, only likeness and therefore nothing more'. 'But what does it resemble? Nothing' (Blanchot 1997b, pp. 61–62). The corpse no longer resembles the person of the deceased but becomes something pre-human and pre-personal that was always already hidden in the living individual (Vande Veire 1997b, p. 80). The corpse shows something of the thing-like pure existence dimension of the human being, the illumination of which at death is quickly covered up again by the funeral ritual. In the visibility of the disintegrating corpse, Polynices begins to merge more and more with himself and to look more and more like nothingness. This nothingness to which the hyper-visibility ends is the disappearance of every secret and of – that is, the same thing – every symbolization and imagination. Nothing is still veiled; consequently, there is nothing left to (look out for), to reveal.

The oscillation between showing and hiding also leaves the dynamic between obscenity and secrecy undecided. Neither pole gains the upper hand. On the side of obscenity, we have the clammy naked corpse that is exposed again and again; on the side of secrecy, we have the repeated attempt to cover up the corpse. The thin layer of dust, located between the actual burial and visible display, does make the difference while maintaining a reference to both poles. Just as a transparent veil simultaneously covers and highlights nudity, the mysterious and the obscene almost merge. Through this intermediate position, the core object is neither fully absorbed into the symbolic circuit nor disappears unceremoniously into the abyss of the obscene. Polynices and other dead keep returning, says Žižek (1996, p. 40) with Lacan, because they have not been buried properly, something has gone wrong in their burial, the symbolic ritual has been disturbed. Here, I think we should especially emphasize that their obstinate return has to do with an *indecisiveness* regarding the accomplishment of the required ritual. In particular, it cannot simply be said that it has not been performed. The symbolic and, therefore, the status of the corpse of Polynices is *in suspenso*. It is precisely this tension, this veiled lingering uncertainty about the past away body, that keeps our attention awake and makes the very act of performing the tragedy an endless, never-completed ritual.

The corpse in the eye of the storm

By leaving the status of Polynices' corpse in limbo, the tragedy evokes the tension between, on the one hand, the corpse clothed with all the symbolic honors that make the dead body something respectable, indeed something great and, on the other hand, the unclothed, naked corpse that in its inexorable decomposition shrivels into an insignificant nothingness, with visibility that is not to be seen. If the play ended in either of these poles – certainly in that of the all-connecting symbolic but equally in that of the dissolving into nothing real – there would be no tragedy and certainly no tragedy that survives millennia. The tragedy is *about* impending nothingness, *about* the possible disappearance of the human, but tragedy itself overcomes precisely this destruction and allows precisely this tragedy of the typically human to flourish all the more strongly. It does this precisely by not shying away from bringing this theme into the limelight. The tragedy itself can hardly be called an obscene object; rather, it reveals itself as a grandiose and impressive object that never ceases to nail the spectator to his uncomfortable chair. She does avail herself of the obscene, but the fascination that emanates from it cannot be reduced to it. *Antigone* invites us to distinguish between the obscene and the fascinating. How about that?

Certainly, in its radical form, fascination always has to do in one way or another with being seized by a colossal exclusive object that occupies the entire field of observation, which you can hardly distance yourself from and cannot avoid. The extreme attention of fascination is impersonal and sterile and no longer emanates from the subject itself. Virtually all subjective functioning is suspended, 'flattened' against the all-space-occupying object. Every affective dynamic is also frozen. Due to the lack of distance, any movement between attraction (toward the object) and repulsion (away from the object) has imploded. In the fascinated impassive, the opposites of passion (extreme attraction) and fear (extreme repulsion) have merged but virtually form the extremely ambivalent storm raging around it. Fascination is the silent eye of this suspended but threatening storm. The paradox of fascination is that the subject sacrifices its own subjectivity in order not to be completely lost by disappearing into the object. It is a suicidal attempt to maintain some semblance of itself as a subject. All this has been discussed in more detail in previous chapters. How can we understand the position of Polynices' corpse in this context? What kind of object is it?

Throughout the action in the tragedy, it is certainly not a fascinating object, but *it constantly raises the possibility that it could be.* I already called the corpse the 'core object' of the tragedy, the object around which everything revolves. The difference with a fascinating object is precisely that everything is indeed revolving around it, swirling around it and is not suspended or stationary. Tragedy is precisely the swirling storm that rages around the corpse of Polynices. The corpse is the eye of the storm, a storm, however, that is in full swing. Passion and fear are not imploded into one subject, as we saw in Chapter 1, that happens in fascination, but on the contrary, sisterly split into the figures of Antigone and Ismene.

Already in the prologue (v. 69–97), Antigone pushes off her fearful sister, resolutely severing the fear imposing itself on her as such. As a result, Antigone is all passion and goes all out without a shred of fear. Because of the consequent elimination of the affect implosion, there is no fascinated halt as the ultimate defense against self-destruction, but she heads without looking back toward her own death. Antigone: 'Then I will go to where my powers reach' (v. 91). What in fascination is a *threatening but suspended* absorption into the object becomes, in pure passion, a real disappearance in it. The relationship to the obscene taps into the power of the passionate and is the total disinhibition of it. The object continues to open itself shamelessly. In fascination, on the other hand, the object closes itself, upon which any passionate dynamism is, therefore, crushed. Fascination can never simply be passion or attraction.

The passionate disinhibition in the tragedy becomes clear when the text shows that the distinction between Antigone and Polynices is blurred in several places. Also, Antigone is still alive yet already dead. From the beginning, her death is announced and at the end, she indeed commits suicide. Polynices is unburied dead and Antigone is buried alive – a reversal that amounts to the same thing. Both are in an in-between space, between the subject/I and the non-subject/other. 'I am already dead', says Antigone, 'my soul has long since died' (v. 559–560) – insofar as 'she' is still the one speaking, her 'I' is already dead. As befits pure passion, Antigone and Polynices merge, bonding in final dissolution. Antigone buries herself, as it were, in the unburied corpse of Polynices. This is reminiscent of the unconscious fantasy Klein describes in the context of excessive projective identification, in which the projected parts of the self are 'buried' (*entombed*) in the object (Klein 1946, 1955). Whereas Klein speaks of claustrophobia in this context, Antigone involves *claustrophilia*.

However, what is important in the play is that Ismene, the personification of the split-off fear that makes her keep a safe distance from Polynices' corpse, unlike Antigone, does not leave her passionate sister alone. Even when Antigone has already been caught and brought to Creon, Ismene still tries to rescue her from her passionate self-destruction in an ultimate attempt to undo the split and join her with her anguish: 'But now that you are sailing in misery I want to be an open and exposed traveling companion to your suffering' (v. 540–541). Ismene, it seems, does not want to go through life in pure fear and forge a coalition with passion: 'If I lose you, I lose my desire for life' (v. 548). Similarly, Antigone – in the fourth episode – laments her terrible fate when she realizes there is no escape. Her wailing could be seen as an incentive to fear, yet a fear that remains too weak to temper the overpowering force of her passion at all. Antigone and Ismene both move, as it were, toward the other split-off affect pole; however, they do so without removing the split. Despite attempts toward 'the other side', they remain largely stuck in their own affect position. Neither pure passion nor pure fear are long-lived; only their joint dynamics are viable.

The chorus's repeated warnings to Antigone also mean that fear is constantly close on the heels of passion. The two affect poles spin stormily around each other, admittedly without canceling each other out, without blocking each other in absolute density *as* affect, but in such a way that a possible implosion never seems far away. Fascination lurks. Antigone, however, will not budge and will not be swayed by her sisterly opposite. She is trapped in her passion, cannot go back and is no longer accessible to anyone (see also Groot 2005, p. 35). She becomes more and more of an eccentric subject. Her insistent passion, therefore – beyond fascination – shoots through to self-destruction. Instead of colliding with the 'everything' of the impenetrable fascinating object that fills the entire space, she penetrates it and disappears into the 'nothingness' of the void in the disintegrating obscene object. The conclusion that in the play, the obscene wins out over the fascinating in this sense only applies to the figure of Antigone, whose passion – devoid of any fear – indeed reveals itself as or transforms into a desire for death. For the tragedy as a whole, however, this conclusion is premature. How does the tragedy itself fare?

The tragedy as *fascinum*

For the obscene to also become fascinating and for the dissolution of the subject not to take place at the drop of a hat fully, fear must join passion and they must implode together into a solidification of the affective as such. In the play, however, the respective affect poles with corresponding object relations remain separated and isolated from each other in the respective characters, where they fiercely rage. Besides the passion of Antigone and the fear of Ismene, there is the indifference of Creon. For a long time, he stands – under the illusion of being above all affect – indifferent to the corpse of Polynices and is miles away from any fascination, of which, after all, indifference is the counterpart. Creon undoubtedly has an interest in what happens to the corpse, but this is a functional interest to which the value of the corpse itself is only secondary. This indifference is increasingly disturbed by Antigone's irritating passion, which eventually drags him into her tragedy.

But what happens to the spectator? For him, confronted with both, it is more difficult to keep passion and fear apart. He is tossed back and forth in his identification with the various characters. In the playing out right in front of him of the constant oscillation between the two, the avoidance of a possible fascination becomes a perilous matter. That the spectator does not become paralyzed in a state of fascination is precisely the result of keeping this oscillation in motion, which has everything to do with how the play is written and constructed. The sequence of the various episodes and choral songs makes Polynices' corpse *alternately, but almost simultaneously, all and nothing.* It is everything to Antigone; it means nothing to Creon. At the same time, the capacity of the corpse – seen from both opponents' point of view – is both the cause of all misery and the possible salvation from it.

The viewer is given the back-and-forth between alternating identifications with the positions of the respective protagonists regarding Polynices' corpse. As a result, neither the corpse nor the play as a whole becomes a paralyzingly fascinating object. If the spectator were truly fascinated, there would be little left to behold and he – devoid of any distance and affectivity – could not experience the play. By keeping the oscillation in motion compositionally, neither does the spectator become absorbed – neither in passion nor in fear nor indifference. What does happen, in my opinion, is that he experiences firsthand the extreme ambivalence between fear and passion on the edge of fascination and his seat. The play overwhelms and is emotionally confusing. This balancing on the edge of the abyss without being able to get away from it, without falling into it but also without turning to stone, makes the tragedy a haunting experience of something essential that you are not well. That is what makes *Antigone* a *fascinum.*

Fascinating objects paralyze by their imposition of an all too direct involvement with the inhuman, with the limits of our subjectivity on which, precisely as human beings, we are nevertheless fundamentally involved. In this sense, fascination is degrading and destructive. *Fascina*, on the other hand, are powerful cultural products that bring us into contact with that fascination and evoke something of it, but without the observation of it absorbing or paralyzing us. *Fascina* are thus not fascinating objects themselves but protect us from their enchantment by enchanting it in turn. In this regard, Lacan gives the example of the 'evil eye', an object that distracts from and protects against what is truly evil (Lacan 1973, p. 107; Mertens 2013). A similar function had the Roman small phallus-shaped amulets worn to ward off evil. The phallic shape had not so much an erotic connotation as a magical defense function as a life symbol deployed against death and destruction (see Thys 2006b, pp. 336–337).

Without imploding affectively, the *fascinum* makes us lurch back and forth between fear and passion at a still just bearable distance from the imposing object. Impressing without imploding. *Fascina* are narrative strategies that powerfully bear witness to the fascination, almost collapsing from it themselves but thereby rising from the disaster all the more grandly. Those caught in fascination lose any narrative point of view and thus have nothing left to tell. The strongest cultural and artistic achievements are the ones that – on the edge of fascination – almost could not be realized but, at the very last minute, allowed themselves to be given a narrative form. Like a judo grip, the *fascinum* takes over the destructive power of fascination and bends it into something constructive, but without completely eliminating the fascinating, without domesticating it too much. *Fascina* are products of culture that use the power of that against which culture wants to protect itself. Precisely by balancing on the edge of the unspeakable, *fascina* have the most pronounced eloquence. No wonder that precisely such catastrophic feats can be found in our cultural canon. Besides, for example, ancient folktales that defy time (see, e.g., De Sterck 2020), Greek tragedies are also impressive illustrations of many generations of surviving narratives. I return to this theme in more detail in Chapter 10.

Similarly, we can conceive of *Antigone* as a *fascinum*. From the nothingness toward which the action in the tragedy descends, the tragedy itself erects itself and rises like the everything, like a great monument. It is precisely in the 'cultivation' of ultimate destruction, in the reporting of defeat, that the human rises most powerfully. *Antigone* is a strong example of how the grandiose and the traumatic dwell near each other and are related to each other in their evocation of the fundamentally human (cf. Mulder 2011; Thys 2014a, 2014b, see also Chapter 3). The unraveling of the human, concretized in the visible decomposition of Polynices' corpse, evokes our horror and despair, but Sophocles, as a narrative strategist, manages to resurrect this abomination that leads to nothing into an impressive testimony towering above everything else, which we still eagerly consume. From the corpse as food for the vultures to the tragedy as food for the people.

Conceiving tragedy as *fascinum* illuminates how it transforms what would otherwise be meaningless horror into an aesthetic and meaningful phenomenon, as Nietzsche (2006) already made clear to us. It is, however, an *esthétique noire*, an aesthetic without apology, without a happy ending, without answers to pressing questions and in which everything, as in *film noir*, lingers and gnaws in limbo. As a result, it becomes a horror to which we are attached, a catastrophe that obsesses (cf. De Kesel 2012b on Auschwitz), an object of horrifying delight.

As a narrative strategy, tragedy succeeds in putting us in touch with the transitional zone where the human continues to falter on its boundaries with the non-human, this fringe area where the distinction between the two is unclear. In its undecidability as to its status as a human being, Polynices' corpse is a striking example. Paraphrasing Blanchot (1980, see also van Poucke 1997, p. 176), calamity destroys almost everything by leaving everything more intact than ever. Thus, with the immortal tragedy itself, the corpse of Polynices, languishing in the tragedy, which we just can't get a decent burial, is given a monumental tomb in which the unforgettable Polynices can keep turning over to his heart's content.

9

Monstrous Frankenstein

The narrative at the last minute

As the subject is – for example, in fascination – on the edge of the human, symbolization, imagination and the formation of a narrative come into dire straits. Any narrative structure that seeks to bear witness to such a condition necessarily escapes from fascination proper. After all, a testimony implies sufficient distance from that to which it bears witness, a distance that is precisely lacking in fascination itself. Powerful testimony, however, succeeds in bringing the reader or spectator (or analyst) into contact with the border experience without succumbing to it as a subject. Kafka's 'Metamorphosis' could only become a story through the testimony of Gregor's parents and sister. Approaching fascination as closely as possible without getting caught up in it puts us in a state of extreme ambivalence, which we have seen to be the closest thing to fascination.

Thus, the most powerful narrative strategies by which culture protects itself from fascination are characterized by a fierce confrontation between passion and fear. From that confrontation, it raises in us an inkling of how catastrophic it must be to be fascinated. Such artistic testimonies transcend the creativity crippling fascination and, at the same time, testify to the narrative distress from which culture confronts the inhuman, embracing and marginalizing it at the same time. We saw this in the previous chapter through a reading of *Antigone*. In this chapter, I want to examine Shelley's *Frankenstein's Monster* as another powerful example of such a narrative, which at once illustrates the role of the excessive projective identification we discussed in Chapter 2.

In the introductory stage directions to his play *Kaspar,* Peter Handke says that Kaspar is in no way like a clown but much more like Frankenstein's monster (Handke 1972, p. 115; see also Chapter 11). Mary Shelley's *Frankenstein's Monster*, originally published in 1818, can be read and interpreted in many ways. Among other things, it lends itself to various psychoanalytic interpretations. However, I want to bring up this story from the canon of Western *fascina* only because, in my opinion, it gathers together many of the issues discussed previously and, at the same time, as befits a work of art 'of all times'. Like Kafka, Shelley offers us a less than uplifting vision of the destructive power that can emanate from fascination and related states, but at the same time, a narrative shaping of precisely that ultimate downfall of the human in its struggle with the non-human is the most hopeful response we can make in the face of it.

DOI: 10.4324/9781003515982-13

To get in touch with our hope, the things that happen to us must be hopeless to a sufficient degree; they must challenge our hope. Narrative shaping of states that make any narrative shaping impossible are real cultural victories. The narrativization of despair is the strongest weapon against it and despair is the most grateful object for narrativization. The strongest artistic achievements are those that almost could not be realized, that allowed themselves to be given a narrative form just at the last minute. In its confrontation with the limit of the human, its creator has surpassed himself, as it were, by still extracting from the destructive threat a boost of inspiration and symbolization. Herein lies the survivability of tragic stories in which the hero does not survive his own. Culture is fond of them. Quite apart from everything else, *Frankenstein* immediately offers us a strong example of the conjunction of the anabolic and the catabolic pole in fascination: precisely in the 'cultivation' of ultimate destruction that the human rises itself up most powerfully. Frankenstein and his monster do not survive, but the story endures all the more.

In *Frankenstein,* several aspects of phenomena at the edge of the human that have already been discussed emerge. First, Shelley's description of Frankenstein's creation of the monster and the preparations for it illustrates the phenomenology of fascination (see Chapter 1). The way his relationship with the monster subsequently develops throughout the novel provides material for metapsychological reflections (Chapter 2). Finally, the firm positioning of this classic in our culture makes *Frankenstein* an icon of the fundamentally anthropological status of the inhuman, on which the fascination is focused (Chapter 3). These three tracks intermingle. I am not going to unravel and explicate them too much, but let the story speak for itself as much as possible.

From idyll to horror

The first-person narrator, Victor Frankenstein, was born in Geneva or Naples. There is immediate confusion about the place of his birth and, thus, the origin of the whole drama. His childhood is described as idealized to the point of caricature. His father married a much younger woman, the daughter of a recently deceased friend. Shelley portrays their close and loving relationship as that of a protective father toward a vulnerable young woman who is almost accorded the position of a daughter. For a long time, Victor was the only child in a safe world with nothing but love and human warmth.

To give an idea of the idyllic terms in which the first-person narrator describes his childhood:

> However much [my parents] were attached to each other they seemed to be able to draw inexhaustible supplies of affection from a true mine full of love, to bestow on me. My mother's tender caresses and the smile of benevolent pleasure with which my father looked at me are my very first memories. I was their toy, their idol, and something even more wonderful – their child, their innocent, helpless being that Heaven had bestowed upon them.

(p. 33)

Sometime later, his parents take in Elizabeth, a girl of noble birth, as a foster daughter, whose mother died at birth and whose father is without a trace. She, too, was a 'being sent by Heaven'. She was 'my more than sister'. His mother had said, 'I have a nice present for my Victor' (p. 35). So, the young mother gives her son a child. Later, William and Justine, also taken from another family, follow. Victor and Elizabeth grow up as brother and sister; it will later be revealed that Elizabeth, at the mother's request, is destined to become his wife.

As the still young mother lay on her deathbed (she became fatally ill by nursing the sick Elizabeth), 'she put her hands on Elizabeth and me: 'My children', she said, 'my firmest hope of future happiness lies in the prospect of your marriage. This expectation will now be a comfort to your father. Elizabeth, my love, you must take my place with the younger children' (p. 42). There is thus an unmistakable incestuousness: the great age difference between the parents, the mother giving her son a child, the brother and sister becoming husband and wife, the sister/wife taking the mother's place. The positions between them are by no means clearly defined. The idyllic, morally idealized mood picture is actually overloaded with 'immoral' relationships, which, however, do not present themselves as such. We can effortlessly infer them from the text, yet they do not tarnish the beautiful picture; quite the contrary.

When the mother dies shortly after having arranged the marriage, Victor is 17 years old. He describes himself predominantly as an extremely studious and ambitious young man, curious, 'with an eager desire to learn' (p. 37), eager to seek out the secret laws of nature and of life, with 'a joy akin to rapture when these unfolded before me' (p. 36). He avoids the great masses and attaches himself ardently to a few, of whom his friend Henry Clerval plays a major role throughout the story.

And then, the reader gets a glimpse of the later misery into which these lofty and admirable traits will plunge him. It is about 'the passion that later ruled my fate' (p. 38) or 'the fatal impulse [to study], which led to my downfall' (p. 39). 'Full of delight' and 'possessed', he searches the books for the elixir of life. He comes to 'associate that study with evil' (p. 41), against which the spirit of good is no match. Meanwhile, as a student, he lives in another city, away from his family and withdraws more and more from the world of man while he is 'completely absorbed' (p. 51) in studying. We encounter this last element again and again and we already saw it in the discussion of the 'eccentric subject': the fascinated subject isolates himself from the world of men and withdraws from any intersubjectivity.

'To investigate the causes of life, we must first visit death. . . . I had to observe the natural decay and decay of the human body' (p. 51). Days and nights, he sits in tombs and charnel houses. 'I saw how the beautiful form of man degenerated and decayed away; I saw the decay of death succeed the blooming cheeks of life; I saw how the worm claimed the wonders of eye and brain' (p. 52). As in the two previous chapters, we again get caught up in the dissolution of the human. While so preoccupied with 'the transition from life to death and death to life', he then suddenly has a vision that reveals to him the cause of life and creation and that 'enabled [him] to bring lifeless matter to life himself'. This discovery, 'at the height of my desires, . . . was so great and overwhelming that all the steps that had led me to it were swept away, and I saw only the result' (p. 52). What that secret is that then comes to light, the reader does not find out and that is just as well: it would only lead him to his downfall, according to Victor.

Frankenstein now decides, because of 'the obstacle posed by the nullity of the parts, to make a being of gigantic size' (p. 53). Thus, we already get the picture of the puny subject versus the gigantic object. He then describes the final moments that will lead to his creation that put him in an increasing state of trance. 'Who can imagine the horrors of my furtive labor, when I tampered amid the ungodly damp of graves or tortured a living animal to animate the lifeless clay? . . . I seemed to have completely lost my soul and my feelings' (p. 54).

Unmistakably, it depicts how the 'soul' passes from the puny, poor subject to the grand object. *The thing gets a soul; the subject is desouled.* The whole process of preparation, hitherto cast in undisguised terms of an ever-elevating passion, towards the end mixes more and more with fear and disgust, but Victor cannot go back. 'Many materials I took from the cutting room and the slaughterhouse; and often my human disposition turned away from my occupation in disgust while still driven on by an ever-increasing eagerness, I saw the completion of my work approaching' (p. 55). Along with this extreme ambivalence, the object imposes itself in its increasing exclusivity while the rest of the world disappears.

> I simply could not turn my thoughts away from my pursuits, however repulsive they were in themselves, but they had taken an inexorable hold on my imagination. I wanted to postpone, as it were, everything connected with my feelings of affection until the great plan, which absorbed all the habits of my nature, would be accomplished.
>
> (p. 55)

A study that destroys the orientation toward other human beings is 'decidedly illegitimate' and 'unfit for the human spirit' (p. 55). 'I avoided my fellow men as if I were guilty of a crime' (p. 56).

A faltering split

And then it happens, 'with an eagerness bordering on agony' (p. 57), the thing, largely made of animal organic matter, comes to life, 'opens the dull, yellow eye of the creature'. 'Now that I was ready the beauty of the dream vanished and my heart was filled with breathless horror and disgust' (p. 57). Unable to bear the sight of the created being, Victor flees the room. Eventually, he does fall asleep from exhaustion and dreams:

> I thought I saw Elizabeth, blooming with health, in the streets of Ingolstadt. I embraced her, delighted and amazed; but as soon as I pressed the first kiss on her lips, they turned pale and took on the color of death, her features seemed to

change, and I thought I was holding the corpse of my dead mother in my arms; her form was wrapped in a shroud and I saw grave worms crawling in the folds of the flannel.

(p. 58)

When he then awoke from his sleep in horror, he saw

the wretched monster I had created, . . . with his eyes fixed on me. His jaws soaked apart and he muttered some unarticulated sounds, while his cheeks wrinkled with a grin. Perhaps he spoke, but I did not understand; he held out a hand, seemingly to stop me, but I fled and ran down the stairs.

(p. 58)

Frankenstein feels as if he has been caught by the monster in his incestuous dream in which life and death also merge.

As of now, Frankenstein is on the run from his creation. The more he tries to escape it, the closer the monster comes to his heels. There is no escape. Before the creation of the object, passion dominated in Frankenstein, becoming more and more intense. At the moment of creation itself, the all-consuming passion was mixed with unbearable fear and horror. Now, after the creation, fear takes over, though without the passion to give in completely. The constant attempts to escape the monster's (perceived) threats take on passionate allure. Fleeing becomes a wandering as if he no longer has a place of his own. He becomes mortally ill: now that his monster has come to life, he threatens to die himself, as if his own life has passed into that of the lifeless thing. His friend Henry Clerval helps him recover.

The main storyline in the sequel consists of successively all persons who love Victor and whom he loves being killed by the monster or, indirectly through the monster, find death: his little brother William, his foster sister Justine, who is executed on charges of murdering William, his friend Henry, up to and including his beloved and future wife Elizabeth, after which his father also dies of grief. This development is accompanied by an interesting evolution. There are gradually more indications in the text of the fact that it is not the monster in itself, as an independent and self-contained being, that causes death and destruction, but that Frankenstein himself is the actual murderer, who, as it were, has the actions performed by 'his' monster: 'almost as if he were my own vampire, my own ghost, loosed from the grave and forced to destroy everything I held dear' (p. 77), 'I, the true killer' (p. 88), 'I had been the perpetrator of irrevocable evil' (p. 92) and 'I was, though not in deed, the actual murderer' (p. 94).

The more powerless Frankenstein feels, the greater his sense of guilt becomes. He feels that he has unleashed a terrible enemy on humanity and that the imminent destruction of all that is human is his fault.

How would all men not abhor me and drive me from the earth if they knew of my wicked deeds and the crimes, which had their origin in me! . . . William,

Justine, and Henry – they all died because of the work my hands did . . . I am the murderer of all these most innocent victims; they died by my machinations.

(p. 184–185)

It becomes increasingly clear that *Frankenstein himself is the monster*. What initially appears as a strange being increasingly imposes itself as a transformation of Frankenstein; in other words, it acquires an ego-status, albeit in an inhuman guise. Hence, the title of this chapter is not about the monster *of* Frankenstein in the sense of a creature he manufactured, but about the monstrous in Frankenstein himself.

In each murder, he arrives just too late to save the victim and sees just a glimpse of the disappearing monster. So, he is always at or near the scene of the crime. The climax of this fact occurs shortly after the wedding ceremony between Victor and Elizabeth, during the wedding night on the bed where their marriage would finally be 'consummated'. However, just before the moment suprême, Frankenstein decides to 'retire' for a moment and make sure that the monster is not in the house. From an adjacent room, he then hears a scream. He finds his wife murdered on the bed.

There she lay, lifeless and motionless, thrown across the bed, her head hanging down and her pale, departed features partially hidden beneath her locks. Wherever I turn, I see the same image everywhere – her bloodless arms and limp body, which had been thrown down on the bridal bed by the murderer.

(p. 195)

Afterward, as in his dream, he embraces his wife's corpse. 'I stormed toward her and embraced her fervently' (p. 195). Here, barely concealed, a deadly sexual act is suggested and, at the same time, the incestuous climax is prevented at the last minute by . . . the monster. Thanks to the monster, Frankenstein's monstrous crime is prevented.

So, here we see that the positioning of 'the monstrous' becomes very ambiguous and both figures are still difficult to disentangle in this respect. Here, too, the monster, whose hideous form he sees for a moment through the open window, can just barely avoid him. Constantly, we recognize what we discussed in Chapter 6: the monster, which is Frankenstein himself, is as inescapable as it is elusive. It grants him an identity that does not let him go but that he cannot get hold of either.

This story element reflects well that there is no or only minimal distance between the subject and his monster. Throughout this evolution in the narrative, we recognize the excessive projective identification discussed in Chapter 2. We also see the paralysis in the undecided oscillation between identification and object, as I saw in Freudian primary identification: is the monster for Frankenstein an object or is it Frankenstein himself? It is both at the same time. We can conceive of the monster as a kind of coagulation, however swirling (after all, without that storm of fear and passion, whose very fascination is the eye, no story is possible), of an outwardly projected (part of the) self.

Frankenstein's monster is indeed a monster, a *sample* of Frankenstein. The monster is a *monster of truth* (Thys 2024), revealing a truth about Frankenstein himself. The strange object into which Frankenstein projects himself sticks to him and he cannot get rid of it. All of this evolution is accompanied by the shriveling of Frankenstein as a subject, as the source of mental functioning and an extreme increase of power to the object pole. Through excessive projective identification, Frankenstein has discharged virtually all of himself into the creature. *Frankenstein* is the story of a traumatic transcendence. 'Remember that thou hast made me more powerful than thyself', the monster says at one point to its creator (p. 100). Or, 'Thou art my creator, but I am thy master' (p. 167).

During the creation of the monster, the shrinking of the world already took shape because Frankenstein was so preoccupied with its preparations that he forgot everything else. Now, it is the monster itself that further destroys the human world, an act that goes hand in hand with descriptions of an increasingly overwhelming nature, in which the monster feels more and more at home and almost becomes part of it and against which man is increasingly powerless as a minuscule and helpless creature. This narrative line, in which the human world gradually disappears and is violently diminished, can be seen as the reversal of the process in which the subject gradually creates a world for himself, a human universe that becomes more and more differentiated and extensive.

The whole fact of the missing or at least highly pressured distance between Frankenstein and the monster does not take away from the fact that Shelley does introduce two characters, Frankenstein and the monster. Narratively, of course, this gives much more movement possibilities and creates space for the tearing whirlwind surrounding the elimination of any distance. From that storm, however, the author shows well that this distance, which keeps trying to install itself, cannot be sustained. Almost 100 years later, in 'The Metamorphosis', Kafka manages to give this fact a much more pressing shape by having the two figures converge within one guise: there is no Gregor on one side and a giant dung beetle on the other; no, they are literally in the same place. This makes the story much more oppressive, while the structure of *Frankenstein* develops much more epically through vast scenes and landscapes and is, therefore, easier to tell.

The structure of the story makes it all too clear that this is not simply a split that splits off the monstrous in the sense of the evil and subsumes it forever in a separate guise, freeing the 'good' Victor from and no longer besieged from within by the 'evil'. On the contrary, the split, as expressed in the creation of the creature, never permanently sets in. It continues to falter, as it were. The two positions remain riveted together and even become increasingly interchangeable. First, there is the idealized Victor as an innocent victim of the monstrous object, which haunts him. Gradually, the monstrous comes to lie more with Victor himself; he becomes the perpetrator of all the disaster and becomes a pursuer of the monster. In frenzied rage and revenge, he tries to capture and kill the monster.

Meanwhile, it becomes clear that the monster itself is not at all as monstrous as it initially appeared. The alleged murders turned out not to have been committed by him. The monster suffers because people shy away from him and do not want to take him in. He would so love to be human among humans. So the inhuman wants to integrate himself back into the human, so to speak, but the humans refuse to do so. When the monster, in desperation, gives up this endeavor, it asks his creator only one thing: to make for him an equally ugly and monstrous woman who can love him and with whom he can live a withdrawn life far away from humans.

Here, the monster takes on almost distinctly human traits. Through thorough projective identification, the monster thing becomes ever more subjectified. We can call it, with Žižek (2009, p. 49), a 'subjectified thing' (see also Chapter 11). This further illustrates how the inhuman is not totally alien to humans. To be intriguing or fascinating, the monstrous must contain something of the human. Frankenstein is at first inclined to accede to this righteous request, but after a long hesitation, he still refuses. Now, it is the monster's turn to feel victimized by the cruel and unapproachable Frankenstein. The relentless lust for revenge that this induces in the monster finds its climax in the murder of Elizabeth: what he himself was not granted, being able to share love with a woman, is now also taken away from Frankenstein.

The monster now has no choice but to fight Frankenstein to the death and, now, together with him, leave the human. In the end, it is no longer clear who is pursuing whom. It seems that the monster lures Frankenstein away from the human world and allows himself to be haunted by him. Here, the monster fulfills the function of a magnet, an attractive object that draws Frankenstein to itself. In the beginning, he fled the monster; now, Frankenstein goes after it to eliminate it. But eliminating the monster is eliminating himself. Both their vengeance is infinite and, certainly, in that aspect, they are barely distinguishable from each other. Periodically, the monster leaves tracks so that Frankenstein can keep following it. Eventually, they both end up in 'the eternal ice fields of the north', a world where almost everything is frozen and dies almost simultaneously. Shortly after Frankenstein succumbs, the monster leaves to commit suicide. Read: their existence is only possible thanks to the other; they cannot exist without each other.

The narrative as a monster victory

Let me dwell for a moment on how the story of Frankenstein and his monster comes to the reader illustrates how fascination on the edge of the human tends to resist any narrativization and opposes it, as it were. The actual history, the broad outlines of which I have presented previously, is framed by Shelley and carried by various narrative positions that indicate that the story has only been able to get to people with the greatest difficulty and after overcoming many obstacles. To begin with, throughout the story, there is no one other than Frankenstein himself, who-ever gets to see the monster. Thus, during the unwinding of the entire history, there are no witnesses other than the monster's creator himself.

To make it a narrative testimony in any case, Frankenstein must have told his horrific experiences in detail to at least one other person who also saw the monster himself. This indeed happens, but literally at the edge of the actual history. The book begins with a certain Walton, an English explorer, and his men trapped (literally frozen) in the northern ice sea with their boat. This Walton figure is an alter ego of Frankenstein: he, too, is a courageous and ambitious scientist who is not afraid to face the greatest dangers in the service of science. He, too, 'ventures beyond the usual paths of man' (p. 21).

At the beginning of the book, toward the end of the story, Walton hoists Frankenstein, who was chasing the monster and dying of exhaustion, from his sled aboard. This occurs several hours after he had seen the monster at a distance on a similar sled: 'On the sled was a creature that had the guise of a man, but apparently of gigantic dimensions' (p. 23). Frankenstein, this 'feral stranger' 'on the edge of his demise' is barely able to speak. After a time, his languishing body is 'animated by new life' (pp. 24–25). It seems to be about the newly created monster here: the quasi-thing becomes animated. What the reader first faces is a series of letters from Walton to his sister Margaret about his bizarre encounter with Frankenstein. After first resting a great deal and with great difficulty, Frankenstein reports on his misadventure, on what is almost impossible to tell. Walton takes notes, which Frankenstein proofreads and corrects. The whole account, the actual story, written down in this way, eventually reaches Margaret.

The end of the book is again written in the form of letters, in which Walton tells his sister how Frankenstein dies. In the final letter, we read about Walton's confrontation with the monster near Frankenstein's corpse, during which a discussion unfolds about how to judge the terrible events. Walton has learned his lesson from the story of Frankenstein: he manages to keep his ambitions from ending up in a self-destructive spiral, returns to England with his men and lets them leave service.

So, the book is structured so that the actual story is framed and propped up by the letters at the beginning and the end. Frankenstein tells it to Walton, Walton tells it to Margaret and Margaret delivers it, as it were, to Shelley, who ultimately submits it to humanity. In this way, the author seems to indicate that this cannot be a story that is simply available firsthand. This technique creates the necessary distance needed to tell and listen to a fascinating experience anyway. It is a story that draws its strength from the fact that it is about something for which there are no words, which, moreover, can barely be told by the dying hero, like a last breath, and which the witness can barely write down, let alone how those letters could have reached England from the North Pole.

Shelley reaffirms all this when, in her introduction to the 1831 edition, she tells how the whole story unwittingly sprung from her imagination, which kept her awake at night. She tried to get rid of the image of the monster, but it kept haunting her. She then tried to get rid of it by writing a short story of a few pages about it. However, her husband urged her to develop the idea in more detail. We may truly consider ourselves 'lucky' that the history of Frankenstein has come to us. This cunning and heroic narrative strategy is a true monster victory over fascination.

Part IV

On the edge of the human

10

Disaster tourism and violent transformations

Cultural guises of the inhuman

The fascinated witness and the disaster tourist

The strategies discussed in the previous section, which we see at work in visual art, theater and literature, among others, bring us into contact with the border experiences of the human. These strategies transcend the individual nature of marginal experiences and make the transition to more shared, collectively available expressions of the inhuman. They are modes of experience that culture itself produces and makes available, as it were. It is on these cultural forms of the margins of the human that I want to elaborate in this chapter, again starting from and zooming out from fascination. In Chapter 3, the inhuman was already discussed at some length; in other chapters, it was regularly referred to in passing. The inhuman is that zone of experience on the edge of the human in which the human and the non-human merge to such an extent that they are still difficult to separate and distinguish from one another. We already saw the Gregor/beetle in Kafka's 'Metamorphosis', Frankenstein's monster and Polynices corpse as strong literary illustrations of inhuman objects.

Fascination and related states put us eminently in contact with this inhuman. They constitute an essential anthropological category insofar as they represent a dimension to which man is essentially oriented. We saw this orientation through the Sartrian longing for being, the Lacanian *la Chose* and the Bionian O, among others. The engagement with the limits of the human, in other words, is 'of men' and thus transcends the peculiarities of individual boundary experiences, which they all gather in themselves. An anthropology of the inhuman in the broad sense is, of course, not detached from the totality of individual experiences; it seeks to encompass them precisely in a broader experiential context, but it nevertheless – through this encompassing – takes a certain distance from them. Concerning the individual, the question was: what happens when someone is fascinated? Or, how is the individual subject when it goes beyond itself and the experience of the self? The broader anthropological concern now sounds slightly different: What fascinates 'the' human being? This question concerns the border experience to which man is directed without already being fully in a state of self-loss. What objects or situations lend themselves to being found 'fascinating' by several or even large groups of people?

DOI: 10.4324/9781003515982-15

While in previous chapters, I have examined the very condition of fascination and self-loss, I now want to concern myself with bringing into focus objects or situations that lend themselves eminently to assume the status of fascinating objects or objects that confront us with the margins of the human. This somewhat different focus, then, concerns not so much the condition as such but rather the objects that are supposed to promote in humans the possibility of falling into that condition, objects that allow themselves to be recognized, as it were, in their distinctly fascinating, dehumanizing potential. These are objects or phenomena whose strong suction power that emanates from them can compete with the equally present enormous fear of being completely absorbed by them.

What fascinates humans 'anthropologically' are objects that – from a distance – make one sense or suspect something of what kind of experience fascination might be in a strict sense. This 'anthropological distance' implies two interrelated things.

Because this is about the relationship to that which fascinates rather than the self being stuck in the fascination, *we cannot*, first of all, *exclude any affectivity.* As soon as there is distance and the object of my attention cannot boast of an exclusive status, there is room for affect. In this context, I want to make the distinction between the fascination in which the fascinated subject himself is entangled or the 'fascination of the first degree', on the one hand, and how others can witness from a distance how someone is so fascinated without also being absorbed in the fascination himself, which I call the 'fascination of the second degree', on the other.

Again, we can take Kafka's story of metamorphosis as an example. For Gregor himself, his ego and the dung beetle are in the same place, which is how I ended Chapter 1. If we now move from the position of Gregor himself to that of the other figures surrounding the event – the external witnesses – we leave the actual fascination, which, however, so to speak, 'radiates' to the bystanders. Gregor's parents and sister undergo the event with bewilderment. They become distracted by the confusing union of Gregor and the beast. That creature in Gregor's room is indeed a dung beetle, yet it is also Gregor. They see Gregor in a creature in which they nevertheless recognize nothing of Gregor. The only thing that unites these two incompatible figures is their shared place: in Gregor's place is now a dung beetle. This dizzying back and forth between familiarity and strangeness, between recognition and unrecognizability, the human and the non-human, is no longer the actual fascination because – for the ego of parents and sister – it concerns an object at a distance. Their consciousness and ego are not in conflict with each other; not the identity of their ego but that of another is at stake. The witnesses observe a fascination that someone else, not themselves, undergoes. That is why we can speak of fascination of the second degree.

In the discussion of Sartre's phenomenology of fascination in Chapter 1, the distinction between internal and external negation was discussed. In the fascination proper, the fascination of the first degree, seen from the subject, Gregor himself, internal negation is also compromised: I, Gregor, can no longer distinguish between myself and the dung beetle; the distinction between I and not-I (the negation of I) is compromised. On the other hand, the fascination of the witness relates only to the disappearance of the external negation: I, as a third party, as an outsider, see that another, Gregor, is indistinguishable from the dung beetle. In the internal negation of the subject itself, the distinction between myself and another/something else is at stake. The external negation of the witness concerns only the distinction between two other objects which remain external to the witness.

The witness experiences no confusion regarding the position of his own ego; the distance to the other is not under pressure. The witness continues to distinguish himself from the bizarre object in which Gregor and the dung beetle coincide. For the witness, therefore, the negation or difference is less drastically affected, so the affective experience is not compromised either. Consequently, what mainly distinguishes the position of the witness from the actual fascination is the intense affective entanglement in an extreme ambivalence imploded in the actual fascination. Gregor's family members are simultaneously beset by fear, disgust and anger on the one hand and love and concern on the other: they would like to do anything for their dearest Gregor and, at the same time, they cannot suppress their disgust for that beast. The same applies to the readers of the story, who in their identification with the witnesses, the parents and the sister, also find themselves in the position of witnesses. The reader, too, thus finds himself in the fierce ambivalence storm between fear and passion.

What both positions have in common is the uncanny nature of the experience, but *das Unheimliche* of the witnesses is no longer fascination in the strict sense because their ego and consciousness remain 'faithful' to each other. The uncanny in fascination is sterile; beyond it, it is highly affectively charged. In the struggle between ego and consciousness, Kafka lets the ego win the battle. In the end, consciousness resigns itself to the new identity and says, as it were, 'Okay, I am a dung beetle; the former Gregor will not return'. Gradually, even for the family members, the beast becomes just an animal and the associations with the human Gregor disappear. With the waning of the fascination, the uncanny character withdraws from the witnesses as well. Nothing remains of the initial extreme ambivalence. In the end, the beast no longer has anything confusing. True, it is a strange beast and one remembers that it used to be Gregor, but that was before; it is no longer Gregor. One has already said goodbye to Gregor; now the beast itself can die and the story can end (as happened to Frankenstein and the monster).

Thus, when we feel fascinated in this more common sense of the word, for example, as a reader, in witnessing a work of art or in literally witnessing a traumatic event that someone else undergoes, our spirits can run very high, to the point of extreme ambivalence: that which fascinates or intrigues us evokes both strong attraction and an equally intense repulsion. Or we may experience a strong attraction at first, which we shy away from in the next moment for fear of becoming too absorbed in it. What fascinates us is precisely the imminent fusion of the human (Gregor) and the non-human (a dung beetle). When I ask myself what fascinates people par excellence, it inevitably involves a highly affectively charged relationship toward things whose common feature is that we see human affectivity and familiar human functioning or the human figure as such disappearing from it. The possibility of cutting off the subject from any affective and mental functioning is something that can precisely evoke very strong affect, especially if this possibility arises in situations that we, as witnesses, perceive precisely as highly affectively charged. In this sense, the fascination that emanates, for example, from Pasolini's film *Salo or the 120 Days of Sodom* is due in large part to the fact that the most horrible atrocities are carried out and endured imperturbably, without any affective emotion (cf. Vande Veire 2005).

What fascinates man, we might say, concerns matters that 'transcend' any affect, that defies any imagination and meaning. It is about things that confuse man emotionally and throw him off balance, but from which he nevertheless cannot simply detach himself; they stick to him.

A second consequence of anthropological distance is that it is now a fascination *that we can share with others*. Unlike the 'eccentric subject' of fascination proper, which is isolated in its subject-minimum from every other subject, an anthropology involves multiple subjects who share the same fascination. Fascinating power, by definition, transcends the individual and is recognizable by many. Phenomenologically-psychologically, any conceivable object (such as a bathroom or a root) qualifies in principle to be fascinating to a given individual at a given moment, but anthropologically, the question shifts to what fascinates people in common.

Both factors, affectivity and commonality, are intertwined: sharing something with others implies affect in itself and, conversely, affect is inconceivable without a relationship to the other. The confusing affects of attraction and repulsion are shared by the witnesses of Gregor's metamorphosis. Gregor's parents and sister are by no means isolated in this; they can exchange their feelings and discuss what steps would be best taken among themselves and so on.

Analogously, readers of the story can share their reading experiences. By extension, this applies in principle to any experience of a cultural product made available collectively. But with Gregor himself, who seems to lack any human affect, all contact is lost. The difference in position between being caught up in the actual fascination and witnessing is clear. A dung beetle has nothing fascinating in itself and the idea of seeing oneself turned into a dung beetle will not seem recognizable to anyone, but everyone will agree that seeing someone else turned into a dung beetle is fascinating. It is about the difference between being fascinated completely isolated and mentally disengaged by a subject undergoing trauma (fascination in the narrow sense) and being fascinated (in a broader sense) by someone watching another undergo the trauma. An anthropology of fascination is about human beings as *fascinated witnesses*.

What man then finds so fascinating, I referred to in Chapter 3 as the inhuman. The fascinated man bears witness to things that appear to him to be inhuman, who bears witness to situations which, according to him, take place at the edge of what he can still call human. I have distinguished the inhuman from the non-human. Unlike the non-human, which by definition does not belong to the human, I conceive of the inhuman as typical of human beings. We do associate the term 'inhuman' with bestiality. But even that bestiality is typically human. Animals are not beastly. We do not avert our gaze from incomprehension or indignation at horrific scenes such as we sometimes see among animals (nature documentaries in which animals attack, tear and devour each other are very popular, by the way). We as humans may be shocked by what animals can do to each other, but at the same time, we find such cruel scenes normal and understand them as entirely in line with their animal nature. Animals also cannot become 'inanimalistic'. Animals are animals. Animals plainly belong to the non-human. Only man witnesses states that he cannot or hardly can still call human but which he must nevertheless attribute to human beings and which he cannot, therefore, call non-human.

This possibility of the inhuman is not an accidental afterthought or curiosity but belongs essentially to the human. It is inherent in human beings that they can see themselves or others dwell at the edge of what is human and can see the foundations of what makes them human slipping away. Concerning the inhuman, we are intrigued by situations that strip man of his humanity, that he can no longer integrate into the human but is not radically distinct from it. Nothing is more human than the inhuman and than the fascination evoked by the inhuman.

To avoid misunderstandings, I would like to emphasize, as an extension of the foregoing, that by the inhuman, I am not unreservedly referring to all kinds of atrocities of which man is capable and which we readily designate with the condemning qualification 'inhuman'. The cruelty and endless horror that we see circulating among humans we must – unfortunately – label as 'just' human or call it excesses of the aggression inherent in man. This 'all too human' does not affect the human; on the contrary, it is an exuberant magnification of it that makes it come apart at the seams and – stripped of any affect, as we saw previously – shamelessly exhibits it.

My association of the inhuman with violence does not – or does not necessarily – concern a moral connotation regarding behavior to be repudiated. It can be that, too, and the reprehensible certainly lends itself to it, but it is not essential to the inhuman. More specifically, the aspect of violence concerns how the intrusion of the non-human affects and transforms the familiar contours of the human, in that sense, 'violates' the human. Excessive, thoroughly human violence is fascinating not in itself but by the reference it makes to this ultimate violence that can undermine the human as such. Insofar as the senseless, excessive atrocities of man also indeed raise the image of the destruction of the human and humanity, they lend themselves eminently to an almost unbearable fascination.

The inhuman does not leave us indifferent; on the contrary, it grips us with horror, exuding a sinister attraction. The inhuman reveals itself preeminently in situations that are accompanied in the witness by an ambivalence so strong that it almost paralyzes him. Situations in which the destruction of the human being imposes itself as a possibility without actually realizing it upset him considerably. Insofar as these same situations do not let him go and demand his utmost attention, the witness is a *disaster tourist*. Thus, all of humanity is, as it were, in the 'watch-file' and the silenced contemplation of the inhuman is a welcome respite from its hurried drive.

One might ask whether the general fascination with the inhuman does not go back to a kind of 'primal memory' of a state in which one's humanity was still anything but self-evident and did not yet allow itself to be radically distinguished from the non-human, a memory, in other words, of the foundation of every possible experience. This must be a remembrance beyond all memory. Can we not think here of the *Hilflosigkeit* in Freud's work, the complete powerlessness and helplessness experienced by every child? (See, e.g., Freud 1950, p. 344; 1926d, pp. 263–264.) I will return to it in Chapter 12.

Thus, all sorts of distortions of the human figure lend themselves eminently to fascinating objects, such as mythological figures that are both human and animal, zombies or all sorts of monsters. Or, in reality, the unimaginable horror of war, genocide, murderous terror, but also, for example, severe disabilities and mutilations, dementia, extreme criminality and eccentric perversions, hermaphroditism and so on. Or consider the endless abortion and euthanasia debate: is this already a human being or is this still a human being? These are all states that force the question, 'Is this a human being?' And the answer each time is: yes, this is a human being, but a human being who finds himself at the limit of the familiar human and – we might add – precisely because of that, exposes his humanity or the possibility of it par excellence.

Guises of the inhuman

So the inhuman, on the edge of the human, is the human insofar as it cannot be sharply distinguished from the non-human. Now, that which I call the inhuman can take the most diverse forms. Far from wanting to be exhaustive, I give an overview of several possible manifestations in what follows. They can collectively form the raw material of what could be an anthropology of the inhuman. I believe that their fascinating power increases as they, first, involve violence and, second, relate to the human figure itself. The most fascinating forms we find in situations where both factors are jointly present to a strong degree, namely where the human figure is violated and transformed drastically, but without destroying the familiar human form completely.

But let's not get ahead of ourselves. There are also many milder regions, to which the characterization 'inhuman' barely applies, but which nevertheless already reveal or evoke something of a transitional zone between the human and the non-human that is difficult to grasp. I am trying to structure this somewhat thematically, but the various categories undoubtedly overlap. Characteristics of fascination that have already been discussed earlier, such as the grandeur of the fascinating object, its sudden and unexpected appearance, the absence of a context or the complete powerlessness of the fascinated subject, will again come up in varying degrees.

Between nature and culture

The first group concerns finds of prehistoric objects that depict or appear to depict the human figure. Indeed, it is often not clear whether the stone objects were simply shaped that way by natural erosion or whether they were nevertheless purposefully worked by human hands to give the stone a human form. This confusion raises the intriguing question: is it a purely natural object that happens to look somewhat human-like or is it nevertheless a cultural product and thus an expression of symbolization and representation? I give an example of both possible answers.

In 1925, in Makapansgat, a cave in South Africa, a small stone was found among bones of the Australopithecus Africanus, which lived there some three million years ago. Through the openings in the stone – eyes, nose, mouth – one cannot help but see an uncanny resemblance to a human face. However, research showed that it is not a manufactured object but also that the stone was not in its natural habitat. The hypothesis is that the stone was brought from elsewhere and was kept in the camp as a 'symbol' of the human face and perhaps given a ritual function. The Makapansgat stone would then possibly be the earliest example of symbolic thinking (Dart 1974).

An example of the reverse is Israel's so-called 'Venus of Berekhat Ram'. At first glance, a crude, ordinary pebble turns out on closer inspection to be a man-made small sculpture of a female figure. A microscopic examination revealed the original stone already looked somewhat like a female and the sculptor reinforced this by adding grooves around the neck and along the arms. With an age of 250,000 to 280,000 years (Homo Erectus), this is one of the oldest known figurative engravings in the world and can be situated at the cradle of human symbolization (D'Errico & Nowell 2000). There are many other examples, including more recent objects from prehistoric times, in which the distinction between nature and culture is not straightforward and causes confusion.

Another group of objects, already much closer to our time, which do not concern the human figure itself but were made by man without clearly demarcating themselves as such from their natural environment, brings us to the architecture of antiquity. Here, too, we are dealing with objects that find themselves in a zone between what is given by nature and what is created by human culture as a transformation of the natural given. I think a striking example of this is the Egyptian pyramids of Dasjur of King Snofroe. The fascination of these gigantic structures is aroused by the fact that, although it is clear that they are man-made constructions and therefore products of culture, at the same time, they give the impression of being, as it were, merely 'bulges' of the natural material in which they are located. They are almost one with their natural environment of sand and stone, have, among other things, the same color and therefore hardly separate themselves as objects from other objects. This makes them much more fascinating, for example, than the famous pyramids of Giza, which are excessively surrounded by fences (literally demarcated), recent auxiliary buildings, spotlights and speakers (for the sound and light show), houses and traffic noise.

The same fascination can emanate from archaeological remains in general insofar as they seem, as it were, to be reabsorbed by and almost already merging with 'mother earth', with the natural substance from which they were constructed. An additional feature of the pyramids that informs their fascinating power is their overwhelming grandeur. They thus materialize in all concreteness that a fascinating object is always gigantic, at least larger than one would expect, precisely because, in my fascination, it occupies my entire field of observation, even if it is only a silly root or dung beetle. These are forms of something human yet, at the same time, present themselves as still lying almost completely sunk in a non-human mode of being. They are already separated from it but, at the same time, refer to it so obtrusively that the distinction could disappear at any moment. Here, we can think back to a still very tentative installation of negation in the world so there is no clear differentiation between distinguished objects, with the result that objectality tends to manifest itself as exclusive.

Another example is the rock temples in Jordan's Petra: with unimaginable violence, man has literally cut into the indifferent nature here and yet this cultural achievement remains part of that nature. From a certain distance, one moment one sees 'only' huge rock formations and the next moment something else looms up, which one then quickly loses sight of again, which reappears immediately afterward and so on. These are objects in which the traces left behind by man are still just visible, about to disappear, in which the human element is as good as erased but remains unmistakably present.

Let me give one last example. Some southern Tuscan towns (such as Pittigliano, Bagnoregio and Sorano) rise almost literally out of the rocks, especially if one sees them from some distance below. The gray rock of the natural rock formations, perpendicular to the surrounding hills, at a certain height suddenly turns out to be part of the facade of a house, almost imperceptibly the extension of the smooth rock wall below. A few more meters higher, it is clear: a few square, wood-rimmed holes in the stone – windows, we call them – indicate that these are human-built houses. The curious thing, however – and this is precisely what makes such structures so fascinating – is that the transition from the purely natural to the human is not localizable. At one height, the stone formation is clearly a rock; at another height it is unmistakably a house, but the transition or demarcation between them cannot be pinpointed. It is an in-between space made up of the same matter and structure as the two dimensions, the space of which we cannot say whether it is still rock or already house, whether it is still nature or already culture, whether it is human or not. We are amazed when we see from a distance a whole collection of such alienating formations – a village or a city we call it – in which the natural and the human merge elusively. The human and the non-human invade and affect each other in a way that confuses us. The fascinated tourist suddenly discovers in a natural landscape a form that betrays a human contribution, which at the same time does not belong and yet is part of it.

The fascination of cultures

Not surprisingly, man's focus on his limits and downfall manifests itself in all kinds of cultural phenomena. Cultures are, as it were, themselves fascinated by what might bring them to the limits of their survival and undermine them. Like a subject, a culture or community can be traumatized and only with difficulty get past certain traumatizing events in its history that continue to fascinate it, as it were. As I described traumatized individuals who return again and again to the scene of the crime to recover their mental capacity, some cultures remain preoccupied for long periods with disruptive fault lines that continue to define their functioning. It seems a cultural necessity to keep in sight the fascinating object that made the culture see eye to eye with itself while threatening its survival and not to neutralize the supremacy that emanated from it into a purely historical fact.

Often, these are dictatorships, as in Cambodia, Chile or Peru, for example, where entire populations were decimated and which still keep the country in question captivated decades later, dividing it, as it were, into a camp of passion and a camp of fear. A recent example is the genocide in Rwanda in 1994, whose 'cultural recovery' is still in full swing. In the almost untold chunky stories of persons in psychoanalytic consulting rooms and elsewhere who fled the Rwandan or other horror, the individual and the collective trauma come together poignantly. One young woman from Rwanda testified, among other things, how she saw dogs on the streets munching on debris from human corpses, as Polynices unburied, and babies sucking on their dead mother's breasts. 'This is nothing to tell living people, this is something for the dead', she added (Thys 2007, pp. 56–57).

Our own most familiar fascinating object is, of course, Hitler and Nazism. It is an object that Europe cannot let go of. We must keep remembering it lest it be repeated, it is said. This seems to suggest that if we are not sufficiently alert, we do indeed risk forgetting the inhumanity of our own culture. However, I wonder if the preoccupation with Hitler and all that he stands for is not primarily an illustration of being fascinated by an object that passionately and anxiously confronts culture with the margins of its own identity, which, like a fascinated subject, it is naturally inclined to project into an object that, at the same time, however, cannot simply be externalized. Our concern not to forget Hitler, in my view, must obscure the painful fact that we *cannot* forget him. The flourishing disaster tourism in various Nazi extermination camps is a strong illustration of this. The demarcated exhibition and strictly regulated viewing of the horror that should not see the light of day is, without doubt, an economic success formula. It is cynical to see how hard people still work in Auschwitz, as if the slogan *Arbeit macht frei*, which still adorns the entrance gate there, still wants to invoke its validity (see Chapter 3). The same fascination emanates from what Pol Pot's Red Khmer did in Cambodia. There, too, just outside Phnom Pen, you can visit an impressive and poignant memorial site, with large parking and many ticket offices and audio guides in several languages. All go there!

Another example of how cultures are fascinated by what can undermine them is incest (and, by extension, child sexual abuse). The incest taboo is considered one of the fundamental pillars of the cultural as such. In previous chapters, we saw how much trouble transgression entails directly or in the next generations and simultaneously the fascination that emanates from it. Think about Antigone, the daughter of Oedipus, and several incestuous elements in the story of Frankenstein. Just as a subject may fall into a state of fascination while undergoing incest, so culture as a 'witness' may be fascinated by the phenomenon of incest within its own ranks. Just as incest threatens the functioning as a human subject of those who undergo it, so the phenomenon of incest threatens the functioning of culture as a whole. At the same time, incest is of all times and all places and manifests itself as a universal 'inhuman' phenomenon from which one cannot get rid and cannot turn a blind eye. Cultures have to do something with incest. To prevent it from tainting all its members, some communities try to 'segregate' incest by imposing, in opposition to the general prohibition, a circumscribed incest injunction on the king as a supreme representative, who must marry his elder sister or his mother and where the incest may or may not also be physically performed. By generously canning the extreme transgression exactly limits transgression on a large scale: no one can and should surpass the king in this.

Another area in which cultural fascination asserts itself is confrontation between different cultures. We prefer to place the source of the threat to our own culture outside, but all the rhetoric about enemy evil cannot hide the fact that wanting to emphasize the difference between one's own culture, one's values and achievements and the other culture or community must obscure the recognition of mutual equality or the threat thereof. Just as we have seen, the subject is fascinated by an object pole that barely presents itself as an object-other and cultures are fascinated by the other culture that comes too close, to which the 'subject culture' fears it can barely differentiate itself. Proximity is then quickly experienced as an intimidating intimacy. Cultures constantly undertake actions to profile their own identity and they often go to great lengths to inflate even the smallest differences into real beacons of their individuality. Freud (1930, pp. 138–139) speaks in this connection of the 'narcissism of small differences': it is precisely when the differences with the other culture become too small and the narcissistic demarcation of our own identity is threatened that we begin to inflate the differences. In times such as ours of large-scale migrations and the mutual penetration of different cultures, this issue is never far away. In psychoanalytic practice, we also see how people struggle with this collective identity problem on an individual, 'intrapsychic' scale (see Gomperts 2006b, 2008).

Subject culture, concerning object culture, sometimes exhibits a pronounced ambivalence between exoticism and xenophobia (Thys 1998), a kind of passion and fear on a cultural scale. On the one hand, the strangeness of the other culture is glorified; on the other, it is reviled and labeled as dangerous. A symptom of the latter is the 'defensive pathologizing' of all the weirdness that the culturally different brings to our own familiar culture: 'unfamiliar is unhealthy' (Thys 2009). Consider, for example, the boom in tourism to Muslim countries that goes hand in hand with racist reflexes and conflicts with Muslims at home. In the tricky process of European unification, too, we see the two movements: while the respective states – in varying degrees of enthusiasm – commit themselves to unity, all sorts of regions are suddenly on their hind legs to highlight their individuality. Tendencies toward healing and division are calling and repelling each other. On a broader scale, too, we see that the world is becoming smaller and smaller and the perception of mutual distance is compromised as a result. The immense spaciousness of a *monde désert* shrivels up to my backyard, whose fence is increasingly flattened. All sorts of scapegoating and projective mechanisms are at play here.

For example, I think we can say that George Bush and the United States were fascinated by Saddam Hussein and Iraq and vice versa. Saddam was, for Bush (and by extension, the Western world), the personification of evil and inhuman, just as Bush personified for Saddam and his entourage the Western devil. Who would have the greatest imperialist ambitions or who would jeopardize world peace the most? The other is portrayed as inhuman, but as soon as the 'high-minded human culture' engages with it, confusion increases over the locus of the inhuman and the initial struggle between good and evil seems to degenerate into a struggle with itself. The whole problem of the tension between the strange and the familiar, which has already been raised several times, could be revisited here from a cultural and ethnic perspective.

Let me give one more striking example in which the factor of the inhuman in cultural fascination is evident. Certain Indian peoples on the North American Northwest Coast, particularly the Kwakiutl, regularly perform a four-day hamatsa ceremony (Root 1998). The Canadian folktale 'The Great Cannibal of the End of the World' recounts how the hamatsa ritual originated (see De Sterck 2020, pp. 24–27). According to myth, from the northern end of the world, a cannibal monster descends to their area screaming to capture men to turn them into cannibals as well, to make them desire to eat human flesh. In doing so, the monster is accompanied by terrible bird monsters with huge beaks and wide-open nostrils to smell human flesh even better. In the ceremony, the men must confront this starving cannibal spirit. They are sent into the forest, chased, swallowed and consumed by the monster. The men's return from the forest shows that they have not really been 'consumed' by this cannibalism; they have not disappeared into it, as it were, in an all-consuming identification, but it is precisely through their contact with it that they can be all the more firmly incorporated into human culture. This ceremony seems to want to indicate that by testing the limits of the human and confronting the non-human, at the risk of one's own life, man can only truly become human.

During the colonization of what was then British Colombia, missionaries and other colonial authorities found these ceremonies suspect. They believed that the hamatsa ceremony was 'real', that what was, in reality, a theatrical representation of (victory over) cannibalism was a covert ritual in which people were actually eaten. Consequently, between 1884 and 1951, such ceremonies were prohibited by law and the colonists confiscated the masks and other attributes used in them (they ended up in museums and markets and inspired European surrealists). The ritual objects were stripped of their spiritual charge by the colonists, transformed into mere 'art objects' and surrounded by an artistic and scientific Western discourse. Anthropologists and art lovers even believed they were thus 'saving' the hamatsa objects. Root interprets the accusation by the Kwakiutl settlers of cannibalism as a projection. When we see on what a massive scale cultural objects were deprived and 'consumed' by the West, the question arises: Who consumed whom? In other words, who was the real cannibal? This strikes me as a poignant example of the interplay of passion and fear in cultural fascination. Fearing that the supposedly inhuman (in this case cannibalism), which nevertheless intrigues us immensely, would infect and destroy us, we try to eliminate it in the other, but precisely in this rescue operation, it focuses all the more on ourselves. The situation described here is also an example of how we try to domesticate that which fascinates, impassions and frightens us to include it in a context familiar to us, to 'colonize' it.

Psychological and corporal deformations

Another domain that fascinates us collectively is all sorts of phenomena in which *the human figure* has been distorted or affected, both in its behavioral and psychological functioning and in its concrete physical manifestation. The inhumanity here consists in the fact that the familiar human figure has been unmistakably transformed into something that appears strange but in which the human remains just as clearly shone through. The example I frequently referred to is the dung beetle trying to get dressed to go to work.

An interesting variation on Kafka's story is David Cronenberg's film *The Fly* (1986), in which Seth Brundle (played by Jeff Goldblum), a somewhat unworldly scientist who wouldn't hurt a fly, subjects himself to teleportation while not noticing that a fly has gotten into the cabin. Afterward, the genetic material appears to be fused and, slowly but surely, Seth starts to feel and behave like a fly, for example, loosening solid food by first vomiting it down with a caustic enzyme. His genetic and gradual morphological metamorphosis makes him more aggressive and superhumanly strong. As with Kafka's Gregor, we also see a gradual shriveling of the external world and a withdrawal of the human from the character himself, who at the same time becomes more violent. His collaborator and mistress Veronica becomes fascinated: she becomes afraid of him but also continues to love him. This fascination lasts as long as the human and the non-human cannot be disentangled and ends as soon as the insect has overgrown all that is human. Things get even more interesting when Veronica turns out to be pregnant, from a love-making just after the merger when Seth still looked quite ordinary. She panics at the thought of an insect monster growing in her body (there is the nightmare that she gives birth in pain to a giant writhing larva), while Seth assumes it is a human fetus. So, here again, the confusion and mixing between the human and the non-human is at play. The pregnancy provides a powerful metaphor for the 'incorporation' of the fascinating object, which she wants to evacuate via abortion, which Seth, however, tries to prevent her from doing.

To add to the previous paragraph, we also find the confrontation with 'strange beings' who are nevertheless human beings in the experiences of explorers, anthropologists and settlers who first encountered a particular population. Devisch (2017) writes penetratingly about the confusing, uncanny effects of first encounters with a foreign culture. This may involve the human figure itself (a different skin color, strange attitudes or habits, living closer to nature) or its dressing and trappings. Not infrequently, in those pioneering times, discussions sprang up about whether or not the people in question were made up of 'real' people. The whole phenomenon of the trade in African slaves *and* its denouncing might not have been possible without this twilight zone at the time between the human and the non-human, even if we can no longer grasp it now. For what we experience as inhuman always contains a dimension of strangeness and newness, something that we cannot fit into our familiar world (though, as we saw, without being totally alien to it). As soon as the newness and surprise are removed and it is integrated, it loses its initial fascinating content. Fascination thus constantly shifts to new unknowns.

As we discussed in the phenomenology of individual fascination, this ambiguity of being simultaneously oneself and yet also someone or something else is also a central element in the use of masks, a universal human phenomenon. Regardless of all kinds of possible interpretations within the framework of the culture or religion in question, we see the use of masks recurring in almost all cultures. Apparently, it is a deeply rooted human hobby to transform oneself into a strange creature, not hiding the fact that it is a disguise. Even in our own carnivals, we like to transform ourselves into someone else, another human being, as well as into non-human, often animal, forms. By strictly delineating such carnivalesque disguises in time and place and linking them to certain collective manifestations, the culture seems to want to make manageable a general tendency to become absorbed in the impending fusion with an object with an ego-status.

People are fascinated by deviations and distortions of the familiar human figure in its concrete physicality. As fairground rides, such as the 'elephant man' (see David Lynch's film *The Elephant Man*, 1980), they used to enjoy success. But, even today, we are anxiously drawn to exceptional morphological variants of the inhuman in the sense I assign this term. Some examples, which are also of great scientific interest and are covered in TV documentaries with high ratings, include Siamese twins (in which the physical demarcation of the individual is trampled upon) and Cockayne syndrome (a disease in which children stop growing at a very young age and grow old at a breakneck speed, evoking the bizarre image of children who are very old, thus calling into question the connection between physical appearance and age). Hermaphroditism and the currently increasingly prominent transgender issue, in which the familiar demarcation between the sexes is blurred, also attract fascination (whether or not combined with moral rejection). Flashy mutilations in which entire limbs are missing, for example, can also capture our gaze. We find a combination of the last two categories in the castration theme, which may particularly fascinate psychoanalysts but which can undoubtedly be found – in various forms of amputations – in numerous dreams and fantasies of unsuspecting patients.

Another example is the pharaoh mummies in the Egyptian Museum in Cairo, whose special, almost magical atmosphere is enhanced by the fact that they are laid out in a separate room for which a separate entrance ticket is required. It is forbidden to speak there as if to avoid waking the great pharaohs from their millennia-long sleep. Looking at the almost black leather shriveled remains of Ramses II, the question arises: is that a person or an object? Is it neither or does it have something of both? It is a human being reduced to its objecthood, yet it is not a mere object either. It is skillfully fabricated and remains transformed, as it were, into things but at the same time, without doubt, containing man himself. And yet, something that has looked so recognizably like a human being for 3,500 years could not be more human after all.

For example, in a completely different context, there is the fascinating moment when, in the film *Alien* (Scott 1979), one of the crew of the spaceship suddenly turns out to be a robot. We see this at the moment when his body is cut in half in a fight, revealing the non-human inside; this, however, while the human upper half of the body continues to function (move, speak) for a while. The human and the non-human come together in one form here. The confusion is compounded by the fact that the non-human interior, consisting of a uniform whitish slime and not of, for example, mutually distinguishable metal parts, nevertheless retains an organic character.

Similarly, we are fascinated by transformations in our psychic functioning. All manner of bizarre psychotic images, in which the subject imagines himself to be someone or something else, provide perhaps the strongest illustrations here. Insanity is something we prefer to keep at bay, a distance that is, however, directly proportional to the covert interest with which we undo it. In the same vein is the alienating impression that autistic children or the demented elderly can make on us. Other states in which 'normal' mental functioning or behavior is affected visibly also interest us in an almost lurid way. I am thinking, for example, of extreme criminality and moral decay, violent transgressions and eccentric perversions. What recurs in many films based on this theme is the fact that in the most disgusting and immoral figures at certain moments still very general human traits that are incompatible with them or they are anyway, come forward.

The fascinating segment par excellence of our psychic life is, of course, the world of dreams, an area in which we are all experience experts. In our dreams, we produce the most bizarre scenes where the human is constantly at risk and is the object of the most impossible and surrealistic combinations and transformations (see also Chapter 4). While we can call some dreams truly fascinating objects that completely capture the dreamer, at the same time, they already constitute a first narrative transposition of what is fascinating. Insofar as we can assume an intersubjective factor in the creation of any dream narrative, the dream work in fascination is compromised because of the absence of any alterity and, therefore, intersubjectivity. All that fascination might allow is static dream tableaux without even narrative elaboration. In Chapter 11, I elaborate on the tension between incoherent dream elements and a coherent narrative.

Always, in all examples, these are forms in which the human as such is not questioned, but nevertheless undermines the obviousness of the human figure. Fascination with the inhuman concerns the disruption of the unwavering. We inevitably experience this dislocation as a form of violence, as an assault on the supposedly safe security that our human mode of being gives us. The violence that transforms and tarnishes the human body worldwide can count on our fascination. Scenes of war, torture, mutilation and self-mutilation, blind terror, family tragedies, as well as spectacular traffic accidents or risky surgical operations in which the body (especially when it comes to the brain) is altered from the inside, we cannot fail to see. Here, man shows himself to be a disaster tourist, pure and simple. The more terrible the violence, the more convincingly it fascinates us. Fascination relates to the catastrophic.

Thus, we end up back at the close connection between fascination and trauma. Just as the subject undergoing trauma can fall into a state of fascination, we, as witnesses, are fascinated by these same traumatic situations. We are fascinated by the utter powerlessness, helplessness and submissiveness in the face of an objectality that is so overpowering and exclusive that it crushes and minimizes the previously supposedly self-powerful subject, barely leaving room for a guaranteed humanity. This non-human object pole that sucks up human subjectivity while transforming it into an 'inhuman' form is the fascinating object. *What fascinates us always refers to a form of violence that compromises our humanity.* Fascination, therefore, has a privileged relationship to the tragic.

To be or not to be human

I have already spoken of an anabolic and a catabolic pole of fascination. Even in an anthropology of fascination of the second degree, this tension between the emergence and decay of the human constitutes an essential aspect. We can always approach the previous examples in two directions: from the non-human to the human or from the human to the non-human. Both vectors meet, as it were, at a midpoint, where their distinction (almost) disappears or at least loses its importance. What matters is that the non-human always confronts us with the limits of our existence, which, for us humans, is always being human. We are at a point where the distinction between existing and non-existing, between existing-in-itself and existing-for-itself, blurs. Fascination is being paralyzed in the boundary movement from nothing to something or from something to nothing. Therefore, fascination always refers to one's origin and/or one's end. What ultimately fascinates us is the violence that accompanies these movements. It is the violence of conception and death. In conception, two poles merge into one. The male element, the sperm cell, penetrates the female, the egg cell. The erotic violence of the sex act refers to that same 'primal leap' or origin. Death marks the beginning of the disintegration of that unity again, but at the same time, it heralds another fusion, that of the individual body with the matter that surrounds it. Human subjectivity finds itself between the two, 'between mother and earth' (Thys 2000). Just as the sex act refers to the origin, so destructive violence and deadly diseases and traumas refer to the end.

All forms of fascination occur in one way or another in the transitional zone on both borders, where the subject is in its emergence or its decay, where it is about to become a human being or cease to be a human being. As an extension of all the previous examples, conception/birth and death are the literal prototypes of this. Again, these are situations in which precisely the distinction between the human and the non-human falters and in that faltering, becomes rigid. One may wonder whether embryos and the dying, from their still or already minuscule subjectivity, are distinctly susceptible to being fascinated by, to feeling immersed in and barely distinguished from the rising or setting world. Preeminently, these too are confusing bodily forms and moments when the purely bodily/organic does not yet or already not allow itself to be connected with the psychic or mental, in short, the human. The confusion between the psychic and the physical has already been discussed several times.

The problem is that the boundary between the two modes of being cannot be pointed out unambiguously and there lies precisely the breeding ground for possible fascinations of culture as witness. From when, from how many weeks, is an embryo or a fetus a human being? From conception is a clear position, which, however, is shifting on the question of abortion. Until what week is an abortion 'justified'? In an embryo, human contours already present themselves, but we cannot yet speak fully of a human form. Yet it is indeed a human being-in-the-making, a form of life that we cannot, therefore, separate from the human. Is the 'product' of a spontaneous abortion already a person? Is the non-viable, premature child given a name? A similar problem arises in the transition zone from life to death. At that boundary, too, the generally applicable prohibition against killing another human being applies in the first instance, but equally, we try to indicate a boundary from which the subject is already more dead than alive so that the killing cannot be called 'killing' but 'euthanasia'. Someone who is brain-dead or has been living a vegetative, comatose life for years is not yet dead, but is he still human? Based on what criteria can someone who was human all his life be said to no longer be human? For that matter, is a person, after undisputed death, no longer human? (See van Reusel 1999, p. 105.) As we saw in Chapter 8, Blanchot suggests that the person as a corpse is most himself, reduced to his core, namely nothing (personal).

Abortion and euthanasia are interventions that are extremely fascinating to man and which are, in the first instance, active interventions to get out of the grip of a fascination with the looming or dying human being. Here, a long quotation from van Reusel's study (1999, pp. 37–38) fits:

The embryo reminds us of our origin, the dead body confronts us with our destiny. Embryo, brain-dead, dying, newborn: they remind us how the human being is always close to another reality that is foreign and threatening and that does not allow itself to be integrated into our constructions of meaning and projects. They illustrate how human being always dwells in the environment of non-being. . . .

The defenselessness of the brain-dead body springs from the fact that it is in a border situation; similarly, the embryo is on the border between the human and the non-human. Both are within our reach, but are also close to a reality that is not yet or no longer ours.

We can see the prenatal beginnings of life as a metaphor for the humanizing transcendence in which the separation into an individual human life announces itself; the dying or newly dead at the end of life as a metaphor for the dehumanizing transcendence where individual humanity is about to disappear again. The fascination evoked by these boundary situations of the human shows how difficult it is – and it looks like it will become increasingly difficult – for man to submit to natural givens. Powerless nullity in the face of an indifferent, non-human overwhelming objectality is hard to bear. In the case of life termination at the beginning and end, this unbearable powerlessness produces endless and heated ethical and ideological debates that can only result in arbitrary demarcations. This problem brings us to the question of what cultural resources human beings have at their disposal to make their fascination with 'crimes against humanity' manageable.

Cultural strategies

Insofar as the orientation toward the limits of the human is fundamentally human, we must conclude that the violence that inevitably accompanies this orientation can never be definitively overcome. This fact constitutes an indelible challenge to culture. It must constantly try to keep its two sides in balance: the 'border violence' must be recognized, given its right to exist and be able to express itself in one way or another, but at the same time, it must shape that violence in such a way that it does not become totally destructive to the collectively human. It must be simultaneously permitted and contained. In other words, can man cultivate the inhuman and bring it into culture? What strategies does culture have at its disposal to keep this ever-precarious balance from tipping in either direction?

In his *Civilization and its Discontents*, Freud (1930) gave a metapsychological analysis of the unresolvable conflict between drive and culture. In the same vein, we can suggest in an anthropological sense that culture as such embraces the field of tension between the cultural expressions of the human orientation towards the inhuman on the one hand and the protection strategies of that same culture against dehumanization on the other. Culture *is* that field of tension. Culture cannot conjure away the inhuman, but it can perhaps take care not to be bewitched by it. We cannot ignore the inhuman and our fascination with it, but we must 'use' it to keep ourselves from being destroyed by it. Culture is like a judo grip, in which it uses and adopts the violent force of the other to overpower this other with it.

Thus, culture is forced to take on the power of fascination. Instead of allowing itself to be engulfed by it, it tries to take it in its grip 'in a controlled manner'. Therefore, to defend themselves against fascination and the violence raging around it, man has no choice but to visualize the fascinating object itself for this purpose but in a delineated and tempered form. Later, with the help of some illustrations, I give an impression of possible cultural attempts to protect us from fascination, paradoxically precisely by 'offering' the objects that lend themselves to it.

Domesticating rituals

Again, the already mentioned hamatsa ceremony at the Kwakiutl can serve as an illustration. To protect itself from the overgrowth of possible cannibalism, which would destroy the cultural and social system, the community proceeds to 'tame' that same cannibalism by botching it within a clearly defined ritual without actually realizing it. To contain subversive individual fascinations, the community goes about canning the fascinating object supra-individually and keeping it at bay individually, as it were, by making it collectively accessible and 'symbolizing' it in that sense. That which could undo the cultural achievements is promoted to the object of a veritable festival of culture that precisely strengthens social bonds. Cannibalism is thus 'celebrated' in its various meanings simultaneously: honored and revered, unleashed and indulged in and domesticated in an established ceremony. By analogy, we can understand our carnival rituals as a controlled and circumscribed domestication of forces that otherwise threaten to undermine the community.

Without venturing into too far-reaching anthropological interpretations, here I would also like to mention all kinds of sacrificial rituals that are supposed to symbolically propitiate the deity by offering him food. Plant and animal food serves as a substitute for the human flesh that the god originally demanded. The god on whom the survival of the culture depended originally allowed himself to be pleased only if a member of that same culture was presented to him. Moyaert (1994, p. 134) writes:

> In line with the awe-inspiring, fascinating Other, to which one submits and is subjected, always appears the 'phantasmatic figure of a monster' for whom no sacrifice . . . is enough and who seems to be at peace only with the destruction of the subject.

Human sacrifice, however, we find inhuman; sacrificing a sheep or some rice makes us escape the inhuman: we renounce the radical sacrifice and replace it with an imitation or staging of it (Moyaert 1994, p. 135). An escalation of the inhuman is thus symbolically constrained. A well-known Old Testament example is Abraham escaping the fascination with the limitless omnipotence and demandingness of Jaweh by sacrificing a lamb instead of his beloved son Isaac. Moreover, as in Islam, for example, the slaughtering of the sacrificial animal is, in turn, subject to fixed rules.

The god or supreme power is thus supposed to protect the community from evil, but at the same time, it turns out that evil emanates from this same omnipotent agency if it is not sufficiently served at its beck and call. The divine lends itself ideally to the capricious nature of a fascinating object, as I outlined earlier: our existence depends on it and, at the same time, it can destroy us. It is at once the origin and the end of my humanity. It underlies my existence but, at the same time, keeps reminding me incredulously of my nullity. As an exclusively fascinating object, it is, on the one hand, my only foothold and, on the other, has complete control over me.

This 'religious fascination' is poignantly described by Otto (2002), where he analyzes the relationship with *Das Heilige*. The sacred, which for him is the essence of every religion, represents both the good and the demonic, which unites itself as a kind of 'contrast harmony'. It is a *'mysterium tremendum ac fascinans'*. Here, we recognize the extreme ambivalence of simultaneous fearful shudder and passionate attraction. I already related fascination to the catastrophic. Otto's definition of the sacred is a clear example of the reduction of the fascinating to the extremely attractive, which is placed in opposition to the extremely repulsive or *tremendum*, while I let implode the tension between the two in fascination itself. In addition, Otto conceives of the sacred as the totally other, while in my analysis, the fascinating object cannot be the absolutely other because of its ego-status. Nonetheless, in his phenomenological description of the experience of the sacred, the extreme ambivalence of losing all distance in the face of and being engulfed by the monstrous object that I fear and to which I surrender is unusually expressed. Religion thus emerges as perhaps the most powerful tool at the disposal of culture to protect man from fascination without depriving him of it. Religion offers mankind a fascinating object that is 'subjected' to cultural rules in such a way that it simultaneously protects man from the actual, destructive fascination. Another vision in which the connection between the divine and the violent is central and phenomena related to fascination are given a place, but whose discussion would take us too far here, is that of René Girard (see, e.g., Girard 1994).

Other means made available by culture for protection against fascination are all sorts of initiation and healing rituals that symbolically bring the participant to the edge of the human, which is often accompanied by animal transformations, to emerge all the stronger as a human being and take his place in the social order. Curious but consistent with this is that many such rituals take place at the edge of the community, the village or in the forest. In quite a few communities, the shaman leading the ritual is also himself a 'fringe figure' who figures on the margins of society. As Western witnesses, we are fascinated by such bizarre-looking rituals, but primarily, the subject himself of the culture in question who undergoes the ritual enters a state of 'possession' that closely resembles how I described fascination. Depending on the myth or narrative structure on which the ritual is based, the subject undergoes a metamorphosis into animal or natural forms, concretized by a wide variety of attributes. The participant discards the human, as it were, and identifies with non-human modes of being.

Such rituals, directed according to strict rules, erode sharp demarcations and promote transitional states between the internal and the external, between self and non-self, between life and death, between emergence and disintegration, between lust and dislike, between the human and the non-human (see Devisch 2006). The community plays a game between fusion and separation. A similar blurring of demarcations between categories that precisely underpin human culture is sometimes found in the use of fetishes (see Devisch 2003). Also, in its Freudian interpretation, the – sexual – fetish refers to the ambiguity of gender difference (Freud 1927). Lacan (1994, p. 160) calls the fetish a fascinating object.

Each time, culture provides objects that invite the subject who is already, through illness or other states, in danger of falling victim to a slippage of the human to confront the non-human but in a socially orchestrated and secured manner. Not surprisingly, many such rituals are organized precisely in the universal transitional zones that a human life typically passes through: birth, puberty and death. These are the three zones par excellence where bodily transformations manifest themselves. All cultures have birth and death rituals that translate the transition from the non-human to the human and vice versa into clearly agreed-upon markers. Consider, for example, Christian baptism: only when the new child is baptized does it also become a human child. Certainly, it used to be a matter of getting there quickly. If the infant died before it was baptized, there was also no afterlife guaranteed and it could not be buried in a Christian manner. A similar meaning has the 'holy sacraments' administered to the dying, which even today is often mentioned on death certificates to indicate, as it were, that the person in question died 'as a human being'. In addition, every culture has its rites of passage at puberty that accentuate the difference between the sexes, as if not sure if nature, unafraid of any confusion, would adequately perform this task. Rituals are usually embedded in collective narratives in which man is historically situated in an order that transcends him. Thus, each culture, each in its own way, possesses creation and apocalyptic stories of the origin and demise of the human.

My earlier reference to the use of fetishes brings us to another tactic the culture employs to protect its members from destructive fascinations: the employment of objects to distract and fascinate the 'evil eye' as fascinating objects themselves. Not infrequently, (fragments of) mirrors are incorporated into these objects. A curious example of this is the Roman *fascina*: small phallus-shaped amulets worn to ward off evil. Immediately, the question arises as to what the phallus has to do with the fascina. Importantly, these phallic objects had not an erotic but a magical defense function. They must be placed in the worldwide phallic cult of fertility. From Japan and India to Africa, Europe and Central America, the phallus, the erect penis, is a symbol of the life-giver and is associated with the creative god of the universe. He is revered and worshipped, carried in processions in colossal size and adorned with flowers and topped with milk, walled in in more modest proportions to protect houses and worn around the neck as small amulets. Only in the latter capacity was it called *fascinum* by the Romans. In all other functions, they called the isolated phallus *mutinus* or *tutunus* (see Dulaure 1974, p. 102). So, I think caution should be exercised in equating phallus with *fascinum*, as Mattelaer (2000, p. 28) tends to do. That the *fascina* were phalluses, I believe, refers not so much to the particular fascinum of the phallus but to the fact that at that time, the phallus flourished as a symbol of fertility and life and as such, is the antithesis of 'evil' that sows death and destruction. Amulets (like some fetishes) serve to control evil, which can be understood as a potentially fascinating object that threatens to destroy the human by fascinating it in turn. An amulet fights the fascinating with its own weapons by bringing it into a state of fascination and this by diverting its 'attention', bundling it (the original meaning of the Latin *fascinare*) to the opposing force of the good and creating life. So here again, we see how culture uses the power of that against which it wants to protect itself.

In a broader sense, we could say that all the mentioned means by which culture arms itself against fascination are *fascina*: fascinating objects to control the fascinating, to enchant it. I call them 'narrative strategies' because, in various ways, they capture the exclusive, fascinating object in a story in a narrative context that can be both linguistic and visual, taking it out of its isolation and causing it to lose destructive power. One integrates it into a field of meaning while being careful that it does not yet overgrow that field and contaminate it in its entirety, as we saw in the chapters of Part III. Hence, the importance of the seemingly random formal elements that are invariably part of rituals. Rituals must include well-defined actions and no others. They must be accompanied by those specific statements or formulas from which one cannot deviate. Indeed, as soon as the form of the rituals becomes looser, the danger looms that they escape our control and the way lies open for all possible transformations. The protective power of ritual is then eroded and fascination, in turn, threatens to overtake it and take over again.

A narrative strategy to which I have already referred and which, more than the others, escapes cultural interference, is the manifest dream narrative, the dream as we can remember it. We can conceive of the unconscious dream processes as one of the most personal and basic forms of the fascinating. They are very basic and singular manifestations on the edge of the symbolic where the collective culture has little to say. In each case, they are surprising, difficult-to-integrate images of a reality unattainable for our conscious daydream representations. During dreaming, the dreamer is completely captivated by the dream images, which he, as it were, coincides with and cannot avoid. The dreamer *is* the dream – in all its strangeness. In his study of the imaginary, Sartre argues that the dream is nothing other than the consciousness that is suddenly completely seized by an 'imagination'. He, therefore, characterizes the dream as a fascination, an enchantment to which the dreamer is helplessly at the mercy of and completely cut off from the world (Sartre 1986, pp. 235–237). At the same time, the dream is a very singular impetus to a narrative, which only allows itself to be shared with the other in the second instance. Only in the second instance does culture begin to interfere and leave its mark in the way it interprets and deals with dreams. The bizarre and uncontrollable are thus embedded in a common frame of meaning and subjected to collectively supported narrative structures.

We see a powerful example of this among the Warlpiri in Australia (Dussart 2000; Poirier 2005). They interpret a dream as a message from the ancestors to the whole group of relatives, as a testimony to a common cosmological connection (*dreaming*). The dream is immediately told and interacts with the dreams of the other sleepers in the same room. Afterward, it is included in the process of ritual chants, dances and paintings. Thus, the dream is completely taken over by the cultural community and little remains of singular psychic processes as we know them (see Thys 2009, p. 257). At the same time, these and other taming procedures will never definitively succeed. We will continue to produce the most bizarre dreams so that the cultural processes of the meaning assignment will also tirelessly exert their hermeneutic labor.

These narrative strategies constitute a weapon against the fascinating that gags us and deprives us of any linguisticity. As we saw, fascination, which brings the subject to the edge of his subjectivity, is the most powerful attack against linguistics and signification. Conversely, language – and the symbolic in a broad sense – is the strongest defense against this attack. Narrative strategies are a defense belt necessary for culture against 'de-lingualism', which would herald a degeneration of the human and thus of culture. The word of God may have become flesh, but the human word must ensure that that flesh remains human and does not merge into a purely natural, organic mode of being. Especially in bodily transitional stages, where the flesh does not yet have or lose its familiar form, words offer powerful support to safeguard the human. In initiation rituals at puberty, for example, '[culture] provides language to rediscover the changing flesh, . . . clothe it with meaning and firmly frame it' (De Sterck 1998, p. 109). Girls who underwent the menstrual ritual among the Navajo Indians say it was the words that had changed them from girl to woman (De Sterck 1998, p. 108).

Just as a traumatized individual needs to come up with a story, for example, in psychoanalytic psychotherapy, to free herself from the mind-numbing fascination, so too does every culture need stories to protect herself from her downfall, stories that she makes available to her members. It does so with insistence or even imposes the stories. Conversely, we can say that even psychoanalytic practice, where patients can unfold their stories, itself constitutes a story in our culture. The psychoanalytic theory and tradition since Freud has imposed a powerful narrative entity on Western culture, which, like a *fascinum,* was and still is always the object of extreme ambivalences, of passion on the one hand and disgust on the other. Like all powerful rites, psychoanalysis allows the subject to come to his inhuman side and scare himself the socks off with his unconscious monsters, in which he must recognize himself in disguised form with much resistance. Through his free-associative but, by a strict framework, guarded and supported speech, the patient can be helped to somewhat humanize these sacred monsters and integrate them into the story of his life history and give them context. Like all Western and non-Western cultural practices, this highly personal, individual psychoanalytic process is underpinned by and is only possible thanks to a collective support base, a supra-individual discourse from which – even if one should not make it explicit in all its aspects to the 'initiandus' – it derives its meaning and effect.

Art between canon and innovation

Fascina, we saw, derive their power from and find their inspiration in that from which they are supposed to protect man. We might, by extension, *conceive of all culture as one great, monstrous fascinum*. The most powerful narrative strategies are by no means alien to some fascinating operation either. The narratives that preserve human beings from destructive fascinations par excellence have something fascinating themselves because they evoke something of the inhuman they seek to curb. They can only curb it *if* they evoke it – in derivative and bundled ways. The most 'much-talked-about' stories are those that take in the fascinating itself rather than ignore it or give the false appearance of overcoming it too easily. Precisely, the most powerful narrative strategies help us escape the core fascination by offering a milder, manageable form. In the previous chapters, I worked out some examples of this.

Albeit very slowly, narrative strategies evolve along with the culture they are part of. They shift constantly because, over time, they become saturated in their fascination as the novelty wears off. What was uncanny a hundred years ago, we now find bland. The once impressive *fascinum* may lose its erectile potency; only a weak decoction remains of the respectable phallus. Culture is thus compelled to be ever ready to seek new forms or to vary sufficiently within existing forms to continue to seduce its members with domesticated fascinating objects. This necessity has, at the same time, something threatening for the conservative culture, which is reluctant to relinquish its fixed forms precisely so as not to outsource its protection against fascination. As in fascination itself, a ceaseless tension between attracting and repelling forces plays out in a culture's attitude toward its own products.

On the one hand, there are stories that survive such shifts anyway. They constitute, as it were, the canon of the most powerful narrative weapons against destructive fascination. A canon is a collection of texts, customs and symbolic forms in the broadest sense that have such cultural value that the culture believes they should be passed on to posterity. Indeed, often, these narratives naturally transcend successive generations. They are narrative strategies that, across generational shifts, preserve their capacity to aggregate fascinations collectively. *Antigone* and *Frankenstein* are illustrations of this. Other examples in our culture include other classical Greek myths and tragedies such as *Medea* and *Oedipus Rex*, Ovid's *Metamorphoses*, several Bible stories, some of Shakespeare's tragedies, folk fairy tales, vampire stories, as well as figures such as Robinson Crusoe and Kaspar Hauser. *Robinson Crusoe* by Daniel Defoe (1995, originally 1719) is a romanticized story in which a civilized Englishman leaves the human behind, as it were, on a seemingly uninhabited island only to choose it again all the more resolutely afterward. He, too, has to deal with cannibals. The Robinson motif continues to haunt us and even invades our private space through television series of the same name. In *Kaspar Hauser*, discussed further in Chapter 11, we see the human gradually emerging into a bizarre creature that at first glance looks little human but that we cannot count as another species either. Here, then, the opposite path is taken in comparison to

Kafka's Gregor. Inimitably, these great stories – and anyone can probably think of others – testify to man's commitment to his limits and how the human is constantly besieged. These same stories, from the *Metamorphoses* to *Frankenstein*, are suffused with the metamorphosis or transformation motif and form a gallery of forms of the inhuman.

In contrast, on the other hand, is the speed with which successive stories or representations of the inhuman succeed each other nowadays. For several decades, we have been overwhelmed with horror films in movie theaters and on the ever-expanding television screens. One monster is not yet cold or another is already warming up. We are currently experiencing an endless relay of the inhuman. It is gradually becoming difficult to think of a monstrous transformation that has not yet been made into a movie. The fleeting monsters of today are not long-lived. They barely materialize into a fascinating object worthy of the name. Our contemporary, accelerated culture, feverishly searching for something to dwell on, seems to yearn for a little paralysis in the unstoppable excitement, which, at the same time, it does not seem to be able or dare to shut down out of a fearful premonition that any impassivity will smother it in a real fascination. Therefore, we increasingly shy away from declaring our new monsters sacred yet.

Is culture losing the battle against fascination? Certain current trends seem to indicate that the distinction between the *fascinum* as a protective cultural product and the fascinating object it is supposed to protect against is blurring. Are the penetrating, fascinating objects themselves now engulfing narrative strategies? The overly penetrating fascination of naked violence threatens to render them barren. While fiction was supposed to protect us from unmanageable reality, sometimes the distinction between reality and fiction is still far off. What we get on our plate these days is called *faction, reality TV* or *docu-soap*. The ultimate Western example is the so-called *snuff movies*, in which abuse, rape and murder – or yes, cannibalism – really take place, with *Cannibal Holocaust* from 1980 by Umbero Lenzi as the prototype. I say 'would' because this film genre, even if its existence seems plausible, is also dubious because, in a style midway between documentary and feature film, it seeks precisely to blur the distinction between imagination and reality and confuse the viewer. In this sense, it surpasses the hamatsa ceremony at the Kwakiutl.

These fascinating phenomena, I believe, are symptoms of a *weakening symbolic potential* and a *narrowing field of imagination*. The narrative transforms itself into a fascinating object instead of keeping the fascinating object at a distance. The narrative, 'designed' to enable an indirect and suggestive relationship toward the inhuman, escapes it less and less itself. Hence, any subsequent attempt to can the impending fascination is immediately fled again because the attempt is still barely distinguishable from a truly fascinating object. The result is that the cultural compulsion to control runs faster and faster past itself.

Other creations in contemporary visual art can fortunately temper this rather pessimistic outlook. They succeed in capturing eschatological cultural trends in artistically high-quality products. These are creations that make the fascinating presentable, 'stilling' it without eliminating it, and thus perhaps carrying a future canon content within them. I think, for example, of the figures of painters such as Francis Bacon, Lucian Freud or Marlene Dumas. Photographer Loretta Lux's images manage to lend an elusive strangeness to the static portraits of children, which simultaneously charm and repel. Are they children of flesh and blood or are they dolls after all? In their everyday, almost colorless defenselessness, humanity reigns supreme, while something undeniably inhuman creeps in, but one cannot put one's finger on it. Or take the pale pink flesh-colored paintings and sculptures of Berlinde De Bruyckere, in which the human figure seems to disappear and appear at the same time. On the edge of the sayable and the imaginable, between figure and flesh, they evoke something of the 'extreme regions of the human' (cf. Mengoni 2014). As transformed figures whose almost unstoppable materiality of the body expresses emotional truth, they also refer to the traumatic (cf. Carrion-Murayari 2014, see also Alloa 2014). I am thinking, for example, of her watercolor series 'Sewn Together' from 2000. All of these artists know how to present the tension between flesh and soul, subject and thing, in haunting aesthetic ways.

Man can never definitively cultivate the inhuman because then he would lose his inhuman side, and this is a side that is essentially human. It would, therefore, be self-destructive to want to distance oneself from it absolutely. Meanwhile, it seems that in his efforts to integrate the inhuman, which cannot help but insist, man is swallowing up that inhuman to such an extent that he is finding it increasingly difficult to digest. Currently, therefore, it is vomited out full of disgust delightfully. And so we are back to the Sartrian *nausée*. Beneath the slimy lumps of postmodernist vomit, the great stories of yesteryear threaten to suffocate and lose their symbolic fragrance. But the latter resist. The contemporary revival of Greek tragedy, for example, is a signal of this (see, e.g., Vanden Berghe 2004). Even Shakespearean dramas are diligently adapted, transposed and dramatized to our times. Or take the way Berlinde De Bruyckere is inspired by Lucas Cranach so that a visual language from half a millennium ago continues to contribute to hers.

Thus, the struggle continues between, on the one hand, a 'canonical' pole in which culture wishes to see its historical identity consolidated in a canon and, on the other hand, a pole of constant renewal in which this consolidation is relentlessly suspended. Nowadays, the canon idea has also entered political territory and is in danger of being placed in the service of a conservationist idea of identity. It is about the tension between a static, solidified versus a dynamic, fluid vision of identity. Think of the metaphor of the pavement and the swamp that I used – inspired by A.F.Th. van der Heijden – in Chapter 6 on identity issues. It is indeed a struggle in which the new and the permanent relieve and repel each other or penetrate and overlap. What now belongs to the canon was once very innovative. I hypothesize that precisely those cultural products that most powerfully evoke the extremes of cultural identity and subvert its calmed down, dormant evidence with fascinating metamorphoses of the human are most likely to transcend transient currents and become stayers, stayers in their innovative potential.

Meanwhile, humanity is experiencing an unprecedented development that can hardly keep up with itself. More than ever, this development enables it to destroy itself. It seems to me that it is not inconceivable that man may fall prey to how he wants to protect himself from being involved at his limits. Individual fascination bears the risk of undermining our mental and creative faculties, but at the same time, the emptying of these faculties can create a promising space for new creative horizons. The precarious balance between the two tendencies may never be definitively settled. We should not underestimate the role that the collective creative power of culture plays in it. The tension between the cultural defense against fascination on the one hand and the infiltration of the fascinating into these means of culture on the other is inherent in the culture as such. A culture can never arrivistically rest on its laurels and, if it wants to keep itself and its function alive, it must remain cautious. The possibility of cultural self-destruction never seems to me to be absolutely absent and is, therefore, of all times, which does not exclude the fact that some periods are more marked by it than others. For example, Nietzsche – and he will not have been the first – stated as early as 140 years ago, 'We live in a time whose culture is in danger of being ruined by the means of culture' (Nietzsche 2000 [1886], p. 252). The question remains whether the cultural creative potential will be able to escape being drawn ever closer to that by which it must be inspired. Will humanity be like Frankenstein, this modern Prometheus, who, in his greatest creation, chases his own downfall?

After this broad cultural and anthropological fanning out of the subject matter, in the next chapter, we return to the cultural ritual called psychoanalysis, which – inspired in part by some artistic and philosophical voices – lands us on the margins of language and meaning.

11

From Charcot to Chaplin

On the infantile, the traumatic and the grotesque

Quest for sense

Knowing or not knowing the meaning of a word, say the word 'barg', may or may not play an important role in one's sense of happiness or in a sense that life has meaning despite everything. At least, that is how it happened to Winnie in Samuel Beckett's play *Happy Days* (1962). The main character, Winnie, who is buried up to her waist in the first act and up to her neck in the second, tries to make the best of her absurd existence while babbling. At one point, when she finds out what the word 'barg' means, an intensely blissful expression appears on her face. 'This really is a happy day', she exclaims. Her appetite for meaning has been satisfied – however briefly. That day can't be ruined; she can get on with the daily senseless routine for a while.

Between 1934 and 1935, Beckett was under analysis by the well-known English psychoanalyst Wilfred Bion, an analysis that has been the subject of much ink (see, e.g., Anzieu 1989; Miller 2013). According to Bion (1965), *meaning*, significance, is not a logical but a psychological necessity. It is only from a psychological urgency that something like meaning persists. Only secondarily, as an effect of this insistence, does something like a logical order emerge from which we try to rationally understand and order the meaning already at work. Meaning-making is a fundamentally narcissistic function, which makes its undermining enormously threatening. Winnie, like several characters in other Beckett plays, constantly balances on the edge of that undermining and we, therefore, understand her deep sense of happiness at the revelation of a new meaning, even if it is only a silly word. It is typical of Beckett to carry that fact through to the absurd. The strength and specificity of Beckett's theatrical text consist in the convergence of the two notions 'sense' and 'meaning': life gets sense through the linguistic assignment of meaning. In an impenetrable but unmistakable way, the experience of meaning – and thus language or symbolization in a broad sense – generates the experience of sense, even if the ground of the meaning so experienced remains as such equally obscure.

Far from wanting to underestimate our attachment to meaning, my starting point is that the notion of sense thrives best where it is not up for grabs or even in danger of disappearing. Sense gives pleasure insofar as we are surprised by it; we did

DOI: 10.4324/9781003515982-16

not expect it and it seems far-fetched, but at the same time, it takes us by surprise. Sense needs non-obviousness. What is interesting in this context is the distinction between senselessness and nonsense – not nonsense, but senselessness is the antithesis of sense. Kamagurka's cartoons under the motto 'it smells like nonsense here' actually teem with – albeit intangible – sense. The smell of sense is all the more satisfying the more it appears unexpectedly in what, at first glance, presents itself as bizarre or banal nonsense. Nonsense is an unexpected announcement of sense; however, without being able to grasp it, an unsuspected suspicion of meaning throws us off guard and into confusion. In this sense, sense is a kind of transition between complete senselessness and full sensefulness. It is not for nothing that Deleuze begins his *Logique du sens* with an analysis of the barren 'nonsense' of Carroll's *The Adventures of Alice in Wonderland* (Deleuze 1990).

How is this dynamic at work in the adventures of psychoanalysis? Beginning with the early Freud, still under the impression of Charcot, isn't psychoanalysis most innovative in its surprisingly finding or assigning meaning in or to phenomena that initially present themselves as nonsensical? Freud's innovative way of interpreting and thus assigning meaning to dreams is a powerful illustration of this. His sense of smell was undoubtedly well-developed. For Freud, the phenomena that present themselves as nonsensical or bizarre constitute the challenge to explore possible sense, to explore meaning. Especially interesting in this regard are the passages in his *Traumdeutung* on absurd dreams. According to Freud, the absurdity of the dream content is only appearance and disappears when one delves into the meaning of the dream (Freud 1900, p. 409). Using several examples, he shows that the dream is made absurd by the dreamer from unconscious motives (p. 416). Dream thoughts are never absurd, more so: *the dream is often most profound where it appears most idiotic* (p. 425, my italics). Exactly where it smells of nonsense can the most sense be detected. Nonsense is promoted to privileged sense-bearer. This is reminiscent of how also Deleuze understands sense and nonsense to be intrinsically linked; he calls nonsense the opposite of the absence of sense (Deleuze 1990, p. 80, 83).

In its relentless search for meaning and sense, psychoanalysis has come a long way as hermeneutic theory and practice since Freud – in various guises. As Deleuze puts it, 'psychoanalysis is the psychoanalysis of sense' (Deleuze 1990, p. 105). Think also, for example, of the way Klein makes the baby ascribe meaning to the earliest bodily sensations, of Lacan's meaning-making symbolic order, Bion's theory of thought and so on. The common thread throughout all these variants is the central role of language and speech (and thus the relationship to the other), but also how that role is intertwined with the link between meaning and the sensual. Together, all these approaches form the track of the orientation toward meaning and sense, the track of so-called 'subjectivation' along which the order of 'the personal' or the ego is formed. This is the track of *hermeneutism* in the broad sense of the word: the whole order of understanding, interpreting, representing, explaining, making sense of, creating and expressing meaning, all this always in function of making 'truth' emerge. By extension, the whole dynamic of historicization and narrativity unfolds: to a large extent, the analytic process is an unfolding of the personal history of life and the interest in it and the analyst's investigative attitude to it constitute a major motor in that process.

But there is also the other track, the track in which the tracing of meaning and sense and the focus on the personal, on symbolization and thought, are abandoned. It is the dimension of what appears naturally, not subjectively intentionally, without concern for possible meaning. I call this the track of *automatism*, of 'desubjectivation' if you will, where the subject, on the contrary, becomes detached from the personal and his ego and surrenders to what speaks out of him without being able to appropriate it. It is the track on which the psychoanalytic practice of free association and free-floating attention leans, about which more later.

Together, both tracks form the dubious guise of psychoanalysis: while the former is the way of hermeneutics, the latter goes away from hermeneutics. Usually, and at best, both tracks correct each other's excesses and keep each other somewhat under control. I now focus further on the second track and try to think it through in its radical essence without banishing the other track from my mind, without forgetting that in an analytic process, as in life itself, we cannot help but be oriented toward meaning and sense. This focus implies a critical questioning of the idea that truth presents itself pre-eminently as a coherent narrative: the more coherence, the more truth. No, here the question rather arises as to whether we do not sell our thoughts short if we want to order them (too quickly) (cf. Geiger 2019, p. 316). As in a psychoanalytic process, is there not always a relative balance and a dynamic tension between order and coherence on the one hand and chaos and fragmentation on the other (see also Chapter 12)?

In this second track of surrendering to automatism, we recognize the Bionian track of 'get rid of memory, desire, understanding and coherence' (Bion 1970, p. 43, 46), which are 'inevitable but worthless' ((Bion 1970, p. 32), or of the Lacanian 'gardez-vous de comprendre' (Lacan 1971, p. 23). Even if we harbor the Bionian and the Lacanian slogan and the free association and the floaty neutral attention, does it not nevertheless and fundamentally – as with Winnie – remain difficult to let go of our eager orientation toward finding meaning? Can't our zealous tracing of meaning and wanting to abolish the 'attacks *on* linking' (Bion 1959) nevertheless derail and degenerate into a terror of attacks *of* linking instead of leaving room for nonsense, for the bizarre, for phenomena disconnected from any context? What about psychoanalysts' quest for sense and happy days in the routine of their daily work?

Insofar as signification refers to representation, symbolization and thought and thus to language, it is also about the tension between language and languagelessness. It is then about states in which access to linguistics is at least under pressure or, in a precarious state, states on the edge of the human. The infantile and the traumatic then seem to me to be two privileged entry points, somewhat in line with what Haverhals (2018, 2020) and Guiot (2018) call the 'order of the archaic'. We then touch on the domain of pure presence, where experiences are not bound by representations and remain resistant to symbolization, as Van Camp (2020) elaborates in his examination of affect. With this background, my thoughts unfold around a kind of phenomenology of free association. What is free association really if we think through this strange activity to its extremes, *ad absurdum*, as Beckett does? I believe that in free association, the two tracks of hermeneutism and automatism go hand in hand.

In light of these issues, I would now like to outline four tableaux. What do Kaspar Hauser, Frankenstein's monster, Charcot's patients and Chaplin have in common? All of them are worth seeing as artists of a kind of grotesque choreography on the edge of language that precedes or already transcends any narrative. They are all *unterwegs zur Sprache*, to speak with Heidegger.

Grotesque choreographies on the edge of language and meaning

Kaspar from the well-known history of *Kaspar Hauser*, the 16-year-old neglected young man who turned up in Nuremberg in 1828 (see von Feuerbach 1990), had lumbering motor skills, did not know how to walk properly and beyond a few fragments of words he could not speak. During periods, he suffered from epilepsy and catalepsy. Some regarded him as an idiot or savage; others believed he was of royal descent. After a time when Kaspar began to dream, he first thought that dreams were real events. The inner world of the mind was long alien to him. This 'child of Europe' inspired several theatrical and film adaptations. There is the well-known 1974 film adaptation by Werner Herzog under the title *Jeder für sich und Gott gegen alle*. I remember an impressive 1978 performance of *Kaspar*, Peter Handke's 1967 play, starring the legendary Julien Schoenaerts, directed by Walter Tillemans.

In the introduction (Handke 1972, p. 115), Handke writes that the play could also have been called 'Speech Torture'. This reminds me of Agamben's (2019, p. 117) statement that the tool of torture in Kafka's story 'In the Penal Colony' is, in reality, language: the torture tool writes, carves into his flesh, the law that the condemned person broke. Language is injury. Indeed, in the performance of *Kaspar* with Schoenaerts, it is staged how Kaspar is relentlessly forced to speak by anonymous voices echoing from everywhere, as it were 'from the current of voice which comes from above' (Deleuze 1990, p. 266). The whole play shows the painful process in which Kaspar comes to speak and experience meaning, in which sense and nonsense of language run in front of each other. Once you are fully absorbed in language, speaking may be a blessing, but the road leading up to it is sometimes suffering and literally trial and error because Kaspar must also learn to walk properly. Word fragments become words; word sequences become sentences. Speaking or, rather, producing sounds, precedes meaning. At first, sentences can mean anything. One of Kaspar's first 'normal sentences' sounds like this: 'Before, when I was away, I never had so much pain in my head, and one did not torment me as much as now since I am here' (Handke 1972, p. 134). But some time later, 'Formerly plagued with sentences, now I cannot get enough of sentences. Formerly beset by words, now I can string letters together' (Handke 1972, p. 169). And at the end, 'I have been brought to speak. I have been placed in reality' (Handke 1972, p. 196).

While speaking can be torture at first, losing it afterward becomes truly torment- ing. In his stage directions, Handke calls Kaspar's way of walking mechanical and artificial, a constant alternation of different ways of walking. When he describes how Kaspar, for example, throws one leg high in the air and drags the other labori- ously behind him (Handke 1972, p. 119), I involuntarily think of the 1970 skit *The Ministry Of Silly Walks* from Monty Python's Flying Circus. A *Kasperle*, by the way, is a marionette, a puppet. But, Handke says, Kaspar in no way resembles a clown; he is much more like Frankenstein's monster (Handke 1972, p. 115).

Frankenstein's monster, already discussed at length in Chapter 9, is a creation of Mary Shelley from 1817, so roughly from the same period as *Kaspar Hauser* (Shelley 1994). In the novel, the monster is a creation of the scholar Victor Frank- enstein. A monster or sample is a leading example, a specimen that demonstrates what similar cases look like. Frankenstein wanted to make a man and made a mon- ster in his own image, just as God created man in His image. In both cases, the result is corresponding, even though both saw for a moment that it was good. The Latin *monstrum* means a not well-endowed living being, a monstrosity, a grotesque creature that threatens the social and moral human order. And this creature, too, however gigantic, appears as an infantile being who cannot really speak, can only emit a few strange sounds and cannot really walk. He, too, like Kaspar Hauser, moves woodenly and stiffly as if the joints were not yet lubricated. Frankenstein's monster is a directionless giant toddler, large in stature and small in spirit, whose subsequent history does not exactly run smoothly either. Behold man, that gro- tesque monstrosity.

Shelley's novel presents a creature on the edge of the human and of language and shows that precisely such a monster provides a sample of the human as such. The idea is that even man himself is not without pain and effort and never quite emerges as a programmed automaton, grotesque in his grandiloquence. The inhu- man is not alien to man but inherently part of it. An example of this age-old fact is Ian McEwan's novel *Machines Like Me*, in which the most advanced robots, indistinguishable in their outward appearance from real people, are attributed to unbearable existential pain. '[They will] hold up a mirror to us. In it, we will see a familiar monster through the new eyes we ourselves have designed' (McEwan 2019, p. 208).

In his juxtaposition of the concept of drive in Freud, Deleuze and Guattari, we read in Moyaert: 'Robotic processes dwell at the heart of our existence, and, profoundly, the life of a robot is the life the mind looks forward to' (Moyaert 2019, p. 98). Does this echo Sartre's 'divine' in-itself-for-itself toward which the desire-for-being is directed? Žižek (2009, p. 49) calls Frankenstein's monster a 'subjectified thing', a thing but a thing with subjectivity, which is also reminiscent of the artwork as a 'quasi-subject' from Chapter 7. Insofar as we conceive of the fascinating object as the self in a strange guise, an 'I-thing', this characterization of 'subjectified thing' applies there as well.

To some extent, we also find this crazy choreography or, in this case, chorea-graphy – to move on to my third tableau – in the 19th-century iconography of *hysteria*, more specifically in the patients that the French neurologist Jean-Martin Charcot performed at the la Salpêtrière clinic in Paris. In the short text 'Notes on Gesture', included in the interesting volume *Infancy and History. The Destruction of Experience*, Agamben (2007b), refers to 'la démarche de Charcot'. He does so in line with an 1886 reflection on *Etudes cliniques et physiologiques sur la marche* by Charcot's colleague in the Salpêtrière, Gilles de la Tourette. Each time, it is about how, in locomotion, the muscles seem to dance in an uncontrolled way, independent of any motor purpose. The quote Agamben gives from *Leçons du mardi* by Charcot could just as well be about Handke's Kaspar, but also involuntarily evokes images of certain choreographies by Pina Bausch. 'Hysteria never looked so good' is the title of an article on her work (Gotman 2007, see also Krtolica 2018).

I take some snippets from Charcot's quote:

> There he is, with his body bent forward and the legs held stiffly together and balancing on his toes; they glide across the floor, propelling himself by a kind of muscular twitching. . . . He could fall head over heels at any moment, but it seems impossible to stop of his own will. Usually, he needs to hold on to someone else near him. It is *as if he were an automaton propelled by a spring*, and in these rigid movements forward, rather convulsions, nothing resembles smooth walking.
>
> (in Agamben 2007b, pp. 150–151, my italics)

Also, in Charcot's hysterical patients, an automatically functioning motor activity is in the foreground, accompanied – as in the previous tableaux – by a total or partial mutism or the absence of normal language. Each time, we see a hushed and mechanical physicality up to and including a catastrophic catalepsy. In his early texts, Freud (1888), whom Charcot regarded as his teacher, speaks in the same breath of astasia and abasia (the inability to stand and walk) and the well-known aphasia (inability to speak). How Charcot describes hysteria is later implicated in phenomenological psychiatry to psychotic and, more specifically, schizophrenic symptoms, where it deals with robotic and marionette-like lumbering movements and tension between flowing and interrupting (see, e.g., Moyaert 2019). My broader perspective raises the question of whether we cannot ascribe a broader anthropological status to these phenomena, whose manifestations in specific pathologies are merely particularizations.

Agamben's reference to Charcot occurs in the context of a reflection on movement and gesture in silent film, where between successive 'moving images' (and here he refers to Deleuze, I'll come back to it) a crippling *ligatio* must be overcome, lifted each time, resulting in a short fluid movement and its interruption each time. This brings me to my fourth and final tableau, from Charcot to Charlot.

Charlie Chaplin – along with his contemporaries Buster Keaton and Harold Lloyd – is one of the iconic figures of comic silent cinema. Like no other, he knew how to portray and hyperbolically corporatize the *mouvement automatique*, detaching it from motor or psychological purposes. We see this in his typical *silly walk*, which is more of a toddler-like dancing hopping and always a nearly tripping over his feet than an effective stepping, more of a swiftly oscillating between being paralyzed and momentarily regaining motion than a smooth walking.

In the legendary factory scene in his 1936 masterpiece *Modern Times,* we see him using his two wrenches to continue the same automatic movement from the factory belt as he walks down the street, not sparing the voluptuous bosom of a passing lady. In the wonderful scene of the so-called 'Nonsense Song' in the same film, in which he has to entertain the audience in a dance bar while singing, he literally loses his lyrics, which were written on his cuff. In an extending movement of both arms, the cuffs fly away and with them, the language that was supposed to support and give meaning to his motor skills. Unforgettable is how he pulls himself out of that dejected loss of language: he begins to emit rhythmic sounds that, while in resonance with the music, almost form a melody, are mostly stuck in a childish gibberish to tremendous comic effect. Mechanical motoring is now accompanied by an equally mechanical production of sounds, on the edge of language, on the edge of meaning. The audience is delirious, the performer is endearingly relieved and sturdily recovers.

This is a beautiful moment of wavering between meaning and sound (Agamben 2019, p. 25), where language leans closer to the purely rhythmic and musical, as in poetry or the early language development of the child, than to a mature subjectivized language overloaded with meaning. It is an autonomous automaticity that is not (yet, no longer) bound or constrained by particular representations. It is more of the order of motor, including linguistics, than of symbolization. It is the zone where language and sound are not opposed to each other but coincide and hop together – language *as* sound. It is language as a shaky, precarious impetus to symbolization that skims along the boundaries of the 'unimaginable presence', as Van Camp (2020, p. 113) characterizes the musical.

In a letter from Freud to Max Schiller dated March 26, 1931, we read how he admired Chaplin and missed a possible meeting with him in Vienna in the nick of time. He understood his portrayal of the poor, helpless wanderer with nowhere to go as an artistic expression of Chaplin's own poverty-stricken childhood, which he had never processed (see Holowchak 2012). I find Adorno's additional interpretation in his already cited text on Chaplin more interesting. There, too, Chaplin is a victim, but more specifically, an 'undestroyable' victim: his abrupt, quick-witted agility is rather reminiscent of 'a predator ready to leap'. He *seeks* victims, pounces on them and tears them apart. Adorno shows himself to be almost a Kleinian when he suggests that the clown Chaplin projects his own violence onto the other through which he establishes in himself an innocence that then gives him more power than any other power (Adorno 2012, p. 84). This brings us again closer to the drama of Frankenstein's monster, in which we likewise see a simultaneity of violence and victim. Insofar as the monster is a projection of the violence of Frankenstein himself, the monster ultimately returns this projection to the sender and becomes a violent victim who wanders helplessly.

With Chaplin, we are all the way to the infantile and the traumatic, as well as the grotesque and the comic. Agamben (Adorno 2012, p. 156) points out that in *being-in-language* there is essentially always a *gesture* of a *non-making of sense in language*. There is always a *gag* in the different meanings of the word: a joke or wit, but also something in the mouth that prevents speaking. In this context, he speaks of the essential mutism inherent in language. *Being-in-language* itself is an incurable speech defect.

In each of the four tableaux, we see a motor automatism, an uncontrolled and inefficient (forward) movement of the body, each time accompanied by a quasi-mutism or a random emitting of (mis)sounds. Moving and speaking are equally rigid. As Handke shows with Kaspar, there is a speaking, or rather a production of sound, that precedes meaning or, as with Chaplin, a speaking that turns into gibberish and is detached from the preceding meaning. Then sounds or words can mean anything, so they mean nothing (in particular). Like the faltering locomotion, speaking is an automatic occurrence, largely an imitation of others. We can thus transfer the crazy walking and moving to speaking from motor to verbal automatism. We end up in *The Ministry of Silly Talks*.

The figures in the tableaux are all described as 'small-minded'. There is little mental functioning, little thought activity or reflection. They just do or babble on autopilot, possibly following what they hear and see in others. Echopraxy and echolalia of the highest order, with lots of echoes and little ego. We find ourselves on the border of the representational, where even language is only a hollow echo. We can also situate this transitional state in the zone of dysincarnation discussed in Chapter 4, between flesh and soul, between organic motoring and symbolization.

In his 'Formulations regarding the two principles in mental functioning', a short text to which Bion likes to refer, Freud calls thinking, which develops from representation and imagination, a suspension of motor discharge and action (Freud 1911, p. 335). In the figures I sketched previously, this suspension is suspended: little remains of thinking; motor activity, including that of speech, again has the reins. Automatism of movement takes over from thoughtfulness; nonsense wins over reflection. Now, I want to connect two considerations to that fact. First, with this proposition, are we not entering the realm of the infantile as well as the traumatic? And secondly, is it not this same domain of small-minded nonsense into which a consistently implemented free association ultimately ends? Let us now turn to the psychoanalytic situation, from the silent film to the speaking patient, albeit quite often loss for words or stumbling over his words.

The infantile and the traumatic

The Latin 'infans' means 'non-speaking', but Freud uses 'the infantile' in the broader and common sense and it covers with him the whole area of the early infantile, the 'infantile organization' (Freud 1905b, p. 74), such as his theory of infantile sexuality and the sexual theories of the infans themselves. The latter can easily be called bizarre and comical. He continued to emphasize the important role of 'infantilism' in the etiology of neurosis (Freud 1906, p. 234), with its magical thinking and defective sense of reality. Elsewhere, he speaks of 'psychic infantilism' in this context (Freud 1912, p. 513). Even if Freud uses the term in a broader sense, this does not take away from the fact that the characteristics of the original infantilism combined occur with a still defective use of language, which recurs in the Charcotian/early Freudian view of hysteria even among otherwise eloquent adults.

With the psychoanalytic 'primacy of the child' (Geyskens & Van Haute 2003), infantilism thus conceived remains a fundamental anthropological and clinical category, the category in particular in which representationalism or symbolization is still shaky and has not yet gained a foothold. To the possible objection that these infantile fantasies involve a great deal of imagination and thus representation, we should note that these – little hindered by reality checks – go their own automatic way. I associate this with the image of the toddler whose unimpeded movements, trivial sounds and magical thoughts go in all directions, the born specialist in *silly walks and talks*. The grotesque figures evoked in the four tableaux are actually grown children, adults in whom infantile choreography is staged as if in an automatism.

Besides the infantile, the traumatic is also a fundamental pillar in psychoanalytic thought. I cannot do justice to traumatism in all its complexity here nor elaborate on the metapsychological and etiological link between infantilism and traumatism. My only consideration is whether the phenomenology of severe trauma is broadly similar to the picture of infantilism outlined.

In his examination of the traumatic neurosis, Freud argues that an unprepared and drastic breakthrough of the stimulus defense brings about a gigantic counter-cathexis 'in favor of which all other psychic systems are impoverished so that an extensive paralysis or lowering of the remaining psychic functioning is the result' (Freud 1920, p. 187ff, see also Chapter 3).

We could speak of a shriveling and stiffening of subjectivity. Many trauma victims testify to a depersonalization state. Their functioning has often become mechanistic; they still feel little control over their actions. They are stunned, their ability to speak is thoroughly impaired and they seem to have dropped out of the verbal. Severely traumatized persons may feel psychologically dead and reduced to meaningless physicality. There is the well-known *freezing*, reminiscent of hysterical catalepsy. They can't say anything anymore and have little left in the automatic mechanics they have become. Only raw reality remains and hardly any imagination is left. A powerful example of such a state on the verge of the human is found in

Agamben's evocation of the so-called *Muselmänner* in the German concentration camps: living, speechless and will-less corpses, monstrous biological machines, moving mechanically and functioning only when someone else operates the buttons (Agamben 2018).

In Manuscript K, in his correspondence with Fliess, Freud speaks of '*border representation*', a concept that subsequently disappeared from his writings. It is a representation that hardly deserves that name, specifically an undistorted piece of traumatic reality belonging to the conscious ego that is accompanied by a psychic void (Freud 1985, pp. 298–299). 'Border representation' remains an interesting concept precisely because it indicates the borderland or margin of the representational, the representational that has not yet been acquired or is already in danger of losing its 'suppleness'. It is the whole domain of the 'primitive mental states' as it also took shape in the Bionian impairment of alpha-function up to the Phonagyan mental process disorders. These characterizations also lean toward dysincarnation.

In short, the traumatized subject – taking as its prototype the traumatic and war neuroses with their motor and psychic disorders of which Freud (1920) writes – is akin to an infantile being on the verge of language or mental and motor functioning as such. The infantile and the traumatic share, as it were, a similar phenomenology. A patient told me that as a somewhat older child, she was laughed at because she walked so crazily, like a somewhat limping chicken, and could not keep up with the other children walking. This was when she had been sexually abused by an authority figure in her familiar environment for many years, from the age of five. She didn't feel her legs and feet properly; she wasn't in her lower body. And then, in her searching speech, she found the right description: 'I actually walked like a toddler who can't walk properly yet'. The infantile and the traumatic are both located beyond language and are both characterized by a 'verbal dystrophy', by a language impaired in its symbolic potential.

But, of course, they differ fundamentally in terms of which side of it they are on. In this respect, they are even each other's antipodes. The infantile precedes, the traumatic follows and is a decay of language and subjectivation. One is pre and the other is post. In this sense, we can call the infantile 'anabolic': it refers to the emergence, the construction, the acquisition of speech and meaning. The traumatic, on the other hand, is more likely to be characterized as 'catabolic': it refers to the fading away, the breakdown and loss of speech and all that is associated with it in terms of mental functioning. The traumatic, at least when it occurs to some degree, is in some way always a relapse into something infantile, as we see in the case of the aforementioned patient, while, of course, the infantile as such is not necessarily traumatic. Freud, as mentioned, also assigned infantilism an important role in the etiology of neurosis in general. But whereas in neurosis, the infantile plays out in a hidden way and must be sought and decoded between the scenes, in trauma, the 'infantile automatism' shows itself on stage in all its undisguised awkwardness; nothing is left to decode. Loss of language and loss of decorum do not infrequently go together in this process. As I suggested in connection with Kaspar, while the acquisition of language can be torture, the loss of it is truly tormenting. The infantile is the emergence, the traumatic is the decay of the human. Language dwells in between emergence and decay.

I am tempted to say that, in Chaplin, we see a coming together of or an oscillation between the two. There language constantly dwells in a precarious state, a state of being both almost and almost no more unable to speak, both acquiring and losing. We can see the motor form of this in his typical, almost tripping-over his feet walk, which makes a run for the illusion of a firmly stepping subject heading straight for his goal. I will return to this later, in connection with the comic and the tragic.

While the infantile is usually characterized negatively as not being able to speak, Agamben elevates the infantile to the essentially human, namely, the infantile as *the ability to* speak. Precisely because man has within him the ability to speak but must learn to do so and because speaking is not a natural given from the beginning, he is human (Agamben 2007a, p. 63). Human speech is only possible through the infantile. The infantile, on the edge of the human, is precisely what makes man.

The (non)sense of free association

From this latter consideration, let us consider the free association to which patients are invited in their psychoanalysis. With the basic rule of free association, the analyst invites the patient to express everything that comes into his or her mind without exception, that is, without judgment, consideration or censorship (see also Chapter 5). If we look at the basic rule in depth and think it through in all its radicality, does it not culminate in the production of nonsense? Insofar as nonsense is the carrier par excellence of meaning, this should not be a problem, on the contrary.

While Wittgenstein's seventh proposition in his *Tractatus logico-philosophicus* reads that about which one cannot speak, one must remain silent (Wittgenstein 1998), we expect our patients to speak about precisely that, the as yet unspeakable. The basic analytic rule formulated since Freud (see, e.g., Freud 1900, pp. 119–121; 1901, pp. 13–14; 1904, pp. 323–324) explicitly asks the patient not to think, not to organize his speech logically into a coherent whole, not to produce beautiful fluent sentences and not to show off in the use of understandable language. The question is precisely to leave out all that usual language and let 'it' speak, to 'simply' say what comes in, to let the language take its course and to let go of the focus on what one would like to say. Actually, the patient is invited – in the first moment – to be absent-minded, to get lost (automatism), but to have – in a second moment – an attentive and uncritical, nonjudgmental self-observation (hermeneutism) for the thought sprinkles that thus appear improvisationally, unintentionally and to one's own surprise.

The constant alternation of these two moments or modes – absent-mindedly letting everything flow and attentively dwelling on it – is reminiscent of the choreography of Charcot's patients, Kaspar Hauser and Monty Python's *silly walks*: an unrestrained aimless movement, followed each time by its suspension or a brief standstill (ligatio), only to go at it again and so on. In other words, are we not asking the patient to initially allow an *automatism in speech* to take its course, analogous to the motor automatism we saw in the four tableaux, an automatism we recognized in both the infantile and the traumatic? As if the patient is asked – à la limite – to drain his thinking and give his motor drain verbal free rein. 'Just say anything, it doesn't matter what exactly and, above all, don't worry about what the saying might mean'.

Free association can return the infantile lust for words without concern for the demands of communication and meaning (Freud 1905a; see also Geyskens 2007). More so especially the unintentional, worthless, seemingly incomprehensible, bizarre incursions are welcomed. The more free association eliminates meaning-generating encoding processes, the more it makes a psychotic impression, as Moyaert (2019, p. 82) points out. *Precisely what appears as nonsensical turns out to be especially valuable* (Freud 1923a, p. 352). So let the nonsense come. Here, we recognize what has already been discussed in connection with the dream interpretation: the nonsensical is the sense-bearer par excellence. Profundity loves nonsense. In his short text on Chaplin, Adorno, echoing Benjamin, says that profundity is sick to death of profound subjects and prefers to focus on something that has no intention behind it and does not by itself offer meanings and perhaps even tends toward the banal and obtuse (Adorno 2012, p. 83). Thus, psychoanalysis prefers to signify the insignificant.

Here, contrary to what one might expect based on his view, just cited, it is better to keep quiet about that about which there is nothing meaningful to say; we can make Wittgenstein connect. Indeed, he also says that precisely the things about which there is nothing meaningful to say are the things that life is all about. Precisely, the things that fall outside meaningful language are the things that make or appear to make a human life valuable. Where Wittgenstein then refers to things like religion, music and poetry, psychoanalysis has in mind the unconscious, which, incidentally, it does not consider alien to those domains. The only meaningful propositions, he adds, are those of the natural sciences, but these, in turn, tell us little about what really matters in a human life. Even more: 'The unspeakable perhaps provides the background, against which that which I can put into words does acquire meaning' (in Eilenberger 2018). So here again: the unspeakable, which produces only nonsense, is the meaningful par excellence, which – paradoxically – we can approach only as we manage to let go of the orientation to the order of meaning and sense. This is precisely the challenge of free association. The things about which we can say anything anyway, even if it takes effort to overcome the shame or other painful emotions with which expressing them is associated, are, of course, also important and, for that matter, difficult to avoid and perhaps also necessary as a (detour) way to arrive at truly free association, but those 'psychologically relevant' things are not the actual focus of the basic rule. I mean that the basic rule does not aim at any particular substantive object, i.e., including nonsense, but merely speech as such.

Here echoes the rhetorical question posed by Deleuze in *Difference and Repetition*, in which we should merely substitute writing for speaking:

What else should we write about but things we do not know or do not know well? . . . We write only at the limit of our knowledge, at the boundary that separates our knowledge from our ignorance, where the former merges into the latter.

(in Breuer 2018, p. 468)

Analogously, Wittgenstein spoke of the urge to storm against the limits of language, an urge he could only appreciate and would not ridicule at any price (in Eilenberger 2018, p. 383).

It reminds me – remembering the psychoanalytic importance of the infantile – of what the Swedish writer Per Olov Enquist writes in one of his novels, 'Who can tell what it was like to be a child? No one. Yet you have to try. What else could you do?' (Enquist 2004, p. 85). Only psychoanalysis will discourage that 'trying': the infantile nonsense will come by itself if you don't care too much about what comes out of your mouth.

The analytical setting and the basic rule par excellence facilitate this coming into contact with the limits of language, even if it does not always run smoothly because of the also constantly present 'hermeneutic urge' to always place everything in a meaningful context, such as the secondary elaboration in dream formation. It is precisely in *the hectic between hermeneutism and automatism* that the analytical process can come into its own. It is a frenetic, often inelegant choreography in which the automatic coming into motion, the spontaneous incursion and its cessation, the self-observation, alternate, a mixture of distraction and sagacity. In between these two moments of free association, a *ligatio* must be overcome each time, as mentioned previously concerning motor automatism and moving images. A verbal choreography unfolds, where *walk* and *talk* dance around each other and tend to coincide, which can bring the patient into contact with the infantile and traumatic undercurrent of the pre- or proto-historical and -individualized.

Analytic speech is a shaky hopping and stumbling; patients become Kaspar Hauser or Charlie Chaplin or do full justice to Charcot's hysterics. To associate freely is to 'jump from heel to branch', as patients almost apologetically name their rambling speech. 'Jump on, jump on', I sometimes say. The choreography of free association interprets a truth without a story, a truth not yet masked or cleaned up by a narrative. It is an automatic, asymptotic movement that makes one experience the substratum of the symptomatic. It is an open, both nonsensical and meaningful speech that escapes narrative, just as – conversely – Beckett, for example, writes stories that escape meaning or an unshakable truth. Beckett's characters often babble on and on; they become detached from a language that talks away from essence (cf. Teeuwen 2019).

An example of such paradoxical hectic is how the analyst, in his focus on the 'creation of meaning' (the trace of hermeneutism), is particularly charmed to and intrigued by a spontaneous, startling image in himself or the patient, something 'entirely new' and linked to nothing else and thus meaningless that pops up as if by itself (the trace of automatism) (see, e.g., Busch 2018, p. 583). We saw this in the two clinical vignettes from Chapter 2: the bathroom tableau and the black monster suddenly appeared out of nowhere and seemed devoid of any meaning or context. Here again, we see that it is precisely in what we cannot bring home that we suspect the *Heimat* of meaning.

The preferential treatment toward nonsense, in which we think we are so open and in which we think we are so detached from our search for meaning, betrays a persistent underlying quest for sense. Surely, we can hardly separate automatism from hermeneutism. And conversely, our orientation toward hermeneutics itself acts as an automatism over which we have no control. If there is or appears to be no meaning, we will construct it, as a book title like *Unrepresented States of Mind and the Construction of Meaning* aptly illustrates (Levine et al. 2013). Automatism and hermeneutism come together completely in a caption to a 2013 work by artist Rinus Van de Velde: 'Yes, we are individuals with a personal history, *machines with a particular wiring that generate meanings*' (my italics).

The infantile non-ability to speak is then not or not exclusively a condition chronologically preceding and disconnected from the verbal, from the accomplished subject of symbolization or thought, but chronically feeding and inspiring the verbal, the shaping mold or container that carries and enables any content. Our eloquent speaking is imbued with a creeping mutism. The unsaid is the inspiration of the soul. It is only through the unspeakable behind or underneath through what we do put into words acquires meaning. It is precisely running up against the limits of language that generates meaning. Fluent meaning is not separate from the faltering 'nonsense of the unspeakable'; on the contrary, the latter is the breeding ground of the former. No 'mature' hermeneutism without 'infantile' automatism or – referring to Freud's 'two principles' – no thinking without motoring.

The paradoxical invitation of psychoanalysis is an invitation to learn to speak again – like the infants – and to do so by letting go of acquired and rigid speech, by denying ourselves the saying, through a desubjectivizing discharging of language, by getting in touch with the rigid and stranded basic rhythm of every subjectivation and thus making it flow again. This whole line of thought implies the idea that precisely in surrendering to automatism, we recover a kind of freedom that had been cornered in an all-too-hermetic hermeneutism. In line with Wittgenstein's 'therapeutic' program, the analyst, like the philosopher, must go to the very beginning of speech (cf. Eilenberger 2018, p. 277). Where language ends, 'the fabric of speech' begins, says Agamben (2019, p. 19), 'fabric' in the sense of food for thought or for learning. '*To language dust thou shalt return*' could be a psychoanalytic adage (see Blanchot in Chapter 7 on the 'materialization of language').

This brings me to what Maldiney, following on from Merleau-Ponty's phenomenological approach to Cézanne, says about *le moment pathique*: a kind of first presence (présence) to the world before any representation and any thematization. It concerns then not the what but the how: a tone, a style, an affective color, a certain rhythm peculiar to the way we experience our encounter with things (see Janvier 2019, p. 171). It is about an infantile pre-narrative being there *already* or a traumatic post-narrative being there *still*, in both cases, a being-outside story.

My question is whether this dimension, this dynamics of being, is not also contained in speech (as in everything), enclosed under and between the words and whether a thoroughgoing free association cannot unlock it to some extent. Is it not the automatism of free association par excellence that can bring us into contact with that rhythmicity and free it somewhat from the gravity of subjectivity weighing on it? Alongside the 'what' of personal history that lends itself to a hermeneutic approach, there then also (again) comes room for the 'how' on which this 'what' is grafted and on which hermeneutism has no hold and which we must simply let be there and not besiege with our interpretations. This pre- or proto-subjective experiential space, I believe, is always larger than the hermeneutic space; the latter will never completely overlap the former. The effect of an analytic process is never entirely reducible to what has been hermeneutically grasped. The grasped transcends the understood.

The psychic automatism and the grotesque

In his analysis of cinema, Deleuze (I follow Huygens 2009), inspired in part by Bergson, speaks of the automatic production of movement, the continuous succession of moving images. This continuous flow of images leaves no time for contemplation. This automatic movement brings us into contact with organic-psychic automatisms that underlie our thinking and occur before the linguistic level. The film is preverbal and prelinguistic. Huygens quotes Deleuze from his *Cinéma–2. L'image-temps*: 'Automatic movement gives rise in us to a *spiritual automaton*, which in turn responds to movement' (my italics). Another quote: 'What cinema brings out is not the power of thought, but its impotence, and thought has never known any other problem'. It is only through the subsequent montage of successive images that something like a coherent story and narrative continuity emerges. Deleuze illustrates the importance of automatic movement and its secondary editing in cinematic language with films by Buster Keaton, among others.

This casual reference to Deleuze is interesting insofar as Freud also compares the spontaneous, automatic incursions into free association to moving images that slide by before the patient's mind's eye while sitting in a train compartment (Freud 1913a, p. 197). And, of course, there is the imagery of dreams, whose individual, disparate images are stitched together into a meaningful narrative, forged into a whole only in secondary processing or 'montage' (cf. Freud 1900, p. 438) and only then – for example, during an analytic session – become speaking images. In the introductory chapter of his *Traumdeutung*, Freud refers to Dugas saying, 'Dans le rêve l'esprit est un *automate spirituel*' (Freud 1900, p. 78, my italics). In the same chapter, we read that Maury compared dream images to the abrupt aimless movements of the St. Vitus dance (chorea minor, chorea of Sydenham) (Freud 1900, p. 79). Does not a consistently implemented free association, where contemplation and intentional montage are discouraged, run into a *speaking spiritual automaton*, a verbal sint-vitus dance? Let us not forget that St. Vitus, that 4th-century Sicilian, was one of the holy helpers invoked to cure certain diseases, preferably nervous disorders.

In his 'Studies on Hysteria', Freud refers to Janet's 1889 *L'automatisme psychologique* (Freud & Breuer 1893/1895, p. 444). In a sense analogous to Charcot's neurological automatisms, the concept of the 'psychic automatism' to explain the *grande attaque*, he thereafter uses only in connection with the comic and the joke (Freud 1905a). Exposure to psychic automatism, says Freud, belongs to the technique of the comic and brings us back to the infantile. In the joke, thinking becomes infantile again. The comic effect relies on the exposure of the infantile, monotonous psychic automatism behind the richness and apparent freedom of psychic achievement (Freud 1905a, p. 517).

Infantilism and automatism are almost equated. Infantile 'thinking' is analogous to the motor automatism of Kaspar Hauser and company. I emphasize that this is indeed an analogy to and not an equation with pure motor automatism. Even if automatism, as we saw in infantilism and traumatism, also expresses itself motorically, it remains in my phenomenology of de-representation to be a *psychic* or *spiritual* automatism. Not only locomotion but also 'thinking' in the form of boundary representations is automatic *as if* it were pure movement automatism. Thus, psychic automatism is not mere materialism like Julien Offray de La Mettrie's 'l'homme machine' (1978), according to whom even the mind operates according to mere physical laws.

Freud (1905a, pp. 522, 534–537) refers to Henri Bergson's rich study *Le rire*, the first edition of which dates from the same year as the *Traumdeutung*. Already Bergson (1920) associated the comic with 'la mécanisation de la vie', which he too reduces to its 'infantile roots'. In this mechanization or automation, the living is relegated to the inanimate, to a mechanism stripped of the personal and subjectified affective. The person is reduced to impersonal, mechanistic gestures, disconnected from the rest of the personality. 'The attitudes, gestures and movements of the human body are laughable to the same extent in which this body reminds us of a simple mechanism' (Bergson 1920, p. 30). The comic comes from the fact that the living body stiffens into a machine (Bergson 1920, p. 50). In the case of speech, Bergson then refers to the automatically working 'speaking machine' (Bergson 1920, p. 56).

He makes the interesting distinction between actions and gestures in this context: 'The action is willed, – at least consciously. The gesture escapes us, – it is mechanical' (Bergson 1920, p. 144). Even in an analytic process, however much we give ourselves, it is the gesture that counts. In line with this distinction, he develops his pointed reflection on the difference between the comic and the tragic, between the comedy or farce and the tragedy or drama. The comic, as in infantilism, focuses on the impersonal, beyond the individualized; therefore, it can hop and jump and make nonsense; it is directed upward. The tragic, of which traumatism can be called the excess, on the other hand, is weighed down by an excess of highly personal suffering, by an overloaded, damaged individuality; therefore, it drags itself along languidly and ponderously; it is directed downward.

In my opinion, however, in both cases, in both comic infantilism and tragic traumatism, the personal or subjective, the 'thinking' and the meaningful are suspended and mechanization or automation comes to the fore. The 'impotence of thought', which acquires anthropological status with Deleuze, comes into extra focus in both cases. It is precisely this 'de-representation' that the infantile and the traumatic – in addition to their external differences – have in common. In this, I differ from Bergson, who reserves the *mécanisation de la vie* exclusively for the comic. The difference is that the suspension in infantilism is experienced as a virtuous release of any personal weight and, therefore, the movement is light and hopping, whereas the suspension in traumatism is experienced as a painful loss and, therefore, the movement is dragging and heavy. In infantilism, the mechanism is movable and well-lubricated; in traumatism, the mechanism falters and is rusty and rigid.

Automatism is not always to be laughed at, as Frankenstein's monster illustrates. That is why traumatic automatism – more than infantile automatism – shows an uncanny character. Previously, the uncanny has been discussed in several chapters as the confusion between the strange and the familiar. Another aspect of the uncanny, also discussed in Freud's essay on that subject (Freud 1919), is the confusion between the living and the dead. In a mechanization of functioning, in which the subject becomes more like an automaton, a clear distinction between something living and something dead or insubstantial is compromised. The ponderous and cumbersome locomotion of Frankenstein's monster is – more than Chaplin's comic and lively hobbling – on the side of death and, therefore, leans more to the uncanny, where (death) fear is never far away.

That 'the body gains predominance over the soul' (Bergson 1920, p. 53) thus not only applies to the comic, but we also see it in severe trauma. The comic may be 'that side of man by which he resembles a thing' (Bergson 1920, p. 87, also p. 58), but also trauma shows a tendency to thingification of the subject (see Chapter 3). In both cases, the gesture (automatism) takes over from the act (hermeneutism) and the analytic process, as we saw, is characterized by the hecticness between the two. The difference is that the infans experience lust for – anabolic, promising – nonsense, while the traumatized subject suffers from – catabolic, perspective-less – meaninglessness.

Let us return for a moment to the scene of Chaplin losing his lines with his shirt cuffs flying away. It is easy to see from the successive images how, in the first moment, this loss of language is dramatic, causes him to panic and threatens to halt the movement, but then, in a second moment, he begins to babble meaninglessly and simultaneously returns to movement, with a childlike hopping cadence and a delightful smile on the face. The playful infantilism rescues him from desperate traumatization and brings back movement to an automatism from which all life threatens to flow away. The tragicomic is the intertwining or transition between the two and it is the field where the two meet intimately. In a different way than Kafka, Chaplin also shows that there is a comic side to helplessness.

In the foregoing, I characterized the phenomena discussed as 'grotesque' and spoke of grotesque choreography. But what should we understand by *the grotesque*? Some authors, such as the German literary scholar Kayser (1981), make the grotesque lean more toward the uncanny. In others, such as Russian philosopher Bakhtin (2009), it is more akin to the burlesque. I cannot elaborate on a thorough analysis of the grotesque here. But it seems that the grotesque in itself harbors a tension between the two poles, between the frightening to the point of creepy strangeness on the one hand and the crazy extravagant strangeness on the other, between Frankenstein's monster and Charlie Chaplin. Perhaps – to put it in terms of the foregoing – the grotesque results from an disinhibited infantilization that, to some extent, makes the tragic or traumatic transcend itself.

It is akin to the tragicomic insofar as the grotesque also negates the tragic by giving it a comic twist. But the grotesque is more: it represents both the absurd, the ludicrous, extravagant, wondrous, adventurous and highly pregnant of a bizarre promise of meaning. The grotesque is a kind of hyperbolic simultaneity of the ludicrous and the terrifying. As in the so-called 'Kafkaesque', the gruesome mixes with the hilarious (see De Visscher 2011, p. 74).

I see it this way for the time being: insofar as the frighteningly confusing prevails, the grotesque tends more toward the uncanny (as in traumatic automatism), the more the exaggeration and the absurdity come to the forefront, the more it acquires something burlesque (as in infantile automatism). In another novel, Per Olov Enquist, referring to Hieronymus Bosch and through the character of a mad actor, describes it as follows: 'As the romantic idea is a mirror of our deepest hopes, so the grotesque is a mirror of the truth about ourselves' (Enquist 2002, pp. 120–121). This 'truth about ourselves' is then dispossessed of the self and takes on the guise of nonsense that we cannot or do not easily grasp hermeneutically. This slippery truth expresses itself in 'a language common to the clown and the children, devoid of meaning' (Adorno 2012, p. 84). The grotesque makes the tragic rebound and light up from its weighty impassivity and makes it dance again or – like a speaking machine – jump from heel to branch. Hopefully, psychoanalysis can be such a 'lighting up' full of truthful nonsense.

12

The subject as ruin

Back to the desire-for-being

The *event manager*

In his book on the philosophy of the *event,* Slovenian philosopher Žižek (2015) describes – along the lines of *l'événement* by Badiou (1988) – an event as something that happens suddenly, seemingly out of nowhere, overwhelms us and does not fit into or conform to the usual reality or the familiar way we experience the world and ourselves. Because we cannot connect it to other familiar representations, the event arouses surprise or dismay. I mentioned in the introductory chapter Spinoza's conception of bewilderment as the state in which we are so astonished by what suddenly appears that it stuns us and prevents us from averting the threat it poses. Now, Spinoza (1979, pp. 172, 184–185) defines astonishment as imagining a thing in such a way that we remain fascinated by it because this particular representation has no connection with other representations. We are so held by the entirely new thing that we are unable to move on to anything else in our contemplation. When astonishment is brought about by an object we fear, we speak of 'dismay'. Spinoza's definition of amazement/dismay at the edge of the imaginable leans remarkably closely to my description of fascination.

An event erodes the existing frameworks, deprives us of any grip and undermines the symbolic structures that underpin our lives as human beings. In Heidegger, *Ereignis* represents a new, groundbreaking revelation of being, the emergence of a new world, but it is also an abyss, as he elaborates in his philosophy of art, among others. It is both a promising revelation and a threatening abyss. An event is at once destructive – to the old familiar – and revelatory – to the new yet unknown. Also in Badiou, we can read that the event shakes the familiar world, but at the same time, it can rework it and create a new one (Bistoen 2024, pp. 111–112). Downfall and revelation, injury and wonder run into each other and are difficult to distinguish. Thereby, the relative predominance of either may vary. In the first case, the event aligns more with the frightening or *uncanny*; in the second, it leans more toward the *sublime*. In both, there is an element of shuddering, of 'a giddiness of the soul', which in the uncanny tends more toward a frightening regression and in the sublime toward a self-transcending progression (cf. Von der Thüsen 1997).

DOI: 10.4324/9781003515982-17

In both cases, however, they are destabilizing and disorienting events. The premiere of Beethoven's fifth symphony or the appearance of the Beatles' first LP are events: they turn the entire existing music scene, their niche of the symbolic, upside down, the familiar values falter and everything must be reconsidered. These events are disruptive in terms of existing structures but, at the same time, more promising in terms of new unforeseen developments. Newton's gravity, Darwin's theory of evolution and Freud's dream interpretation are all scientific events that shake the prevailing structures of knowledge to their foundations and generate a fundamental new turn in thinking.

But also, the rise in the 1930s of Hitler and Nazism constituted a true event, which, for many in Germany at the time, heralded a welcome transformation of the world order, but which ultimately meant for many more people a devastating, incompatible loss of humanity as such. For the Nazis humanizing, for the millions of victims dehumanizing, for both camps, it was, in any case, an event, the destabilizing swell of which, incidentally, has still not calmed down. We can assign a similar status to the piercing, literally out of the blue, of the WTC towers in New York in 2001, an impact whose terror still engulfs us.

Thus, mankind as a whole, or large parts of it, witness collective events that occupy it and from which it must collectively recover and try to fit them into the continuation of its history. Similarly, on an individual scale, there are both destructive events, as we saw with trauma, and revelatory ones, for example, with the infantile language explosion, events with which the person must work through trial and error. Events take place on a socio-political or cultural scale, as well as on the most personal level. Events in their purest form are things that disrupt existing symbolic structures, as such, that thoroughly shake up the world or our view of it, disorient us mentally or even threaten to disable us. Therefore, as I pointed out in the introductory chapter, they generate experiences in which presence prevails over representation. They belong to the order of what Musil (1996, see Chapter 3) calls 'crimes': acts that shake the symbolic order to its foundations. Events do violence to the human and force man to become a veritable *event manager*, to find ways to deal with them and limit the damage.

This book dealt with various forms and aspects of such events. They intrigue us, they suck us in, but when they get too close, fear takes over. They are sensational in the sense that they give us an intense thrill that adds to the vibrations of life – precisely in its being threatened. Disaster tourism and pushing dangerous limits are examples of this. Consequently, disaster tourism is always 'edge tourism'. *Sensationalism* is not strange to anyone, albeit that it can never be sustained for long and we must return in time to the tranquility of the obvious and predictable – until it becomes bogged down in boredom and dullness again and we are urgently in need of a new, exciting 'event' that puts things at risk. We look for something to get a 'kick' out of it (De Cauter 1995). In extremis, this leads to the state of fascination, in which both movements of attraction and repulsion block each other and lock the subject in a paralyzing impasse. But even this impasse, which for as long as it lasts seems to cripple every prospect for the future and threatens to undermine the functioning of the subject, can give rise to unexpected new creations that emerge from the quasi-nothingness of the languishing subject and shake off the old lost. Just as we know about *writer's block* for the monstrous white sheet, upon which, despite total despair, a creative boost can still – and even stronger than before – follow, so by extension, we can speak of how a mental *lockdown* still opens up to unexpected new horizons of the imagination.

We also discussed a variety of phenomena and modes of experience that escape this paralysis but are close to it. They are always peripheral phenomena, phenomena on the edge of the symbolic, on the edge of meaning and integration capacity, on the margin of language and narrativization, on the border of the imaginable. Fundamental distinctions falter, such as between I and the other, between the psychic and the physical, between man and thing, between meaning and meaninglessness, between the symbolic and raw reality and so on. In short, phenomena that somehow strain the typically human as such and blur the familiar distinctions between the human and the non-human.

Existence and extinction

We saw that this edge of the human, both collectively and personally, is not incidental but constitutes an essential dimension in human existence. Whether we call it demise by diabolical evil or elevation to divine higher spheres, man has always been involved in the escape from the 'ordinary human', in a pole of a non-human mode of being, an involvement that in certain circumstances lands him in a zone of the inhuman, the disorienting transition between the human and the non-human. *The involvement in our extinction is inherent in our existence.* With all previous chapters in mind, I want to recapitulatively frame this fact of a phenomenology of this *'eschatology of the subject'* in a philosophical-anthropological concluding reflection. To this end, I pick up the thread again of Sartrian desire-for-being.

I discussed it in Chapters 1 and 3: Sartrian phenomenology understands man as consciousness, as a for-itself that is not(thing) itself and therefore, to 'be' consciousness, cannot but be involved in the things in the world, which are in-itself, that is, without consciousness and therefore without any notion of alterity or negation simply coincide with itself. The in-itself is simply what it is and pure being as such can only be attributed to the in-itself. Consciousness, and in its wake perception, imagination and representation, attribution of meaning, in short, the 'psychic' of the ego, orientates or moves willingly and unwillingly in the direction of the being-in-itself in which every 'inner' division is dissolved. This involvement is what Sartre calls the desire-for-being. Human-reality, says Sartre, is desire-for-being-in-itself. Being-for-itself is lack-of-being; the being that lacks the for-itself is the in-itself (Sartre 2003, p. 696). The term 'desire-for-being' is somewhat misleading because, of course, no one wants to be a thing without more. Indeed, *'human-reality cannot reach the in-itself without being lost as for-itself'* (Sartre 2003, p. 160, my italics). If he were to become truly in-itself, man would disappear. Man as for-itself does not want to merge without more into a non-human in-itself. No, Sartre keeps repeating, man wants to become in-itself-for-itself. Surely, as in-itself, he does not want to reveal his consciousness. As consciousness, man 'wants' to have the impenetrability and infinite density of the in-itself (Sartre 2003, p. 697), but at the same time to be able to attribute to it an ego, a psyche. Now, this cannot be done unless one is God. God can say, 'I am who am'; he can coincide with himself without more and still be able to say, more specifically, 'I'. Therefore, Sartre argues that the fundamental project of human-reality is to be God (Sartre 2003). 'Man is in a fundamental sense desire to be God' (Sartre 2003, p. 698). That is, the consciousness turned substance, the God-man (Sartre 2003, p. 708). This desire for God is the ideal of desire-for-being.

We see this tragic theme not only in Prometheus to Frankenstein and in the other direction in Kafka's 'Metamorphosis', but also already in the all-consuming endeavor to create an *Übermensch*. Tragic is this every time because the too-dense approach to its realization inevitably implies the threat of the downfall of being human. The focus on the ultimate realization of the subject automatically evokes its end. We saw how this whole dynamic in the paralyzing impasse of fascination crashes to its limit.

But we also saw this desire-for-being operating in various milder guises. I refer back to the problem of identity from the chapters of Part II. Man is, as it were, doomed to strive for a fixed identity, to be able to say once and for all 'this is me' (I am who am) without it being possible to get a pin of alterity in between. The fact that this, of course, never succeeds does not alter the fact that this striving goes on tirelessly or rather is so thanks to the fact that it never succeeds. Or one cherishes the illusion that it does succeed – until it fails, resulting in the necessary disillusionment and frustration – and renewed attempts. Dictators, but also lesser 'gods', believe they must impose such a conviction of identity on an entire people: 'This is us' (we are who are). The dictator acts as a fascinating object insofar as he presents the people with the misconceived illusion of clumping together in a one-piece identity, without vulnerable seams or joints and being able to leave any division behind.

Not coincidentally, fascism and fascination have etymologically the same Latin root, '*fascio*', meaning bundle or union of equals, the reduction of the world to one exclusive identity and everything else must go. It is a totalitarianism – of an object, an idea, an ideology – that eliminates all thought. The rock-solid belief in a final and fixed identity undermines thought and meaning, which are by definition fluid and mobile and, in their dynamics, always refer to the other.

The striving for identity as a desire-for-being is so deeply human and, therefore, characteristic of man, but its excesses are no less subversive for that same man. If the desire-for-being is too rash, if it does not keep itself under control, it is destructive of man and man must use all his remaining strength to recover. Does not the whole history of man demonstrate how he repeatedly ends up on the losing end, dragging himself from one distress to another rescue? Exhausted but tireless, he continues – like a modern Sisyphus – to endure. And again and again, we come to the – albeit always provisional – conclusion that we are only human after all, only to forget it again and again. Man's passion, says Sartre, is the inverse of Christ's:

because man perishes as man, God wants to be born (Sartre 2003, p. 753). Man wants to be God-like and God takes on a human form.

Remnant-of-being and death drive

The extinction referred to previously, which is so peculiar to our existence, actually concerns the personal, the subjective, the 'self' – in Sartrian terms, roughly speaking, the fore-itself and the ego. In the peripheral phenomena discussed, it is always the self or subjectivity and thus the symbolic that comes into play. And if we ask ourselves why we are so fascinated by selflessness, as, for example, De Kesel (2017) does in his examination of mysticism, I think the Sartrian desire-for-being offers an interesting anthropological perspective on a possible answer. The pursuit of selflessness is an extension of or even inherent in that fundamental desire-for-being. A thing-in-itself has no self and insofar as man as consciousness or for-itself is oriented toward the in-itself, his self, his I-ness, is also at stake.

In Sartre's view, as we saw in Chapter 1, the for-itself is a decompression of the in-itself. But he adds that in it, however, the in-itself is not 'used up'. The in-itself remains in the for-itself as it were after-effects and thus present as a *memory-of-being* (Sartre 2003, p. 153). This *remnant-of-being*, this closed core as a kind of fold in the absolute openness of consciousness, gives rise to nostalgic outbursts as if it were about a former paradisiacal unity to which we long to return. However, we should not understand memory-of-being as an engagement with something from the past that arouses consciousness. Rather, according to Breeur (2002, p. 188), it is more about an opacity from which consciousness flees precisely by choosing a self to ward off the remnant of being. It is a flight from an *excess-of-being* that, however, clings so tightly to what I am that I never break free of it and to which I remain attracted forever.

Analogously, we conceive – inspired by Agamben, among others – the infantile and preverbal in Chapter 11 not as a mode of existence that simply historically precedes and is subsequently cut off from the symbolic but as an inexhaustible breeding ground for the verbal and symbolic, a residue that – precisely because it is encapsulated in the symbolic – can continue to exert its efficacy (the real or in-itself cannot generate anything human). We flee from it (which would not be necessary if we were already cut off from it) for fear of falling out of the symbolic, but at the same time, we cherish it as the support of the symbolic.

All in all, the status of the memory-of-being in Sartre seems to me very ambiguous. On the one hand, he says that the desire-for-being cannot be a desire for a simple *return* to the in-itself because the for-itself does not want to give up itself and strives to become in-itself-for-itself (Sartre 2003, p. 697). The flight-from-being brings us to the fear-of-being that I discussed in Chapter 3 in the context of fascination and trauma. But that does not take away, on the other hand, that Sartre's use of the term 'remnant-of-being' as something that remains and to which the desire-for-being is directed at least opens the way to the idea of a possible 'return' to a (prehistoric, pre-personal) originality.

Can we not conceive of the remnant-of-being, such as the Lacanian real or the Thing or Bion's O, as the inevitable idea or thought construction of the most essential core of our identity that, despite ourselves, inspires and directs our desire? We can hardly leave behind the idea of a core identity or core ego as an (intangible) substance. Even if it is no more than a 'construct', something we invent ourselves, it is a construct that seems both inevitable and highly performative: it does have its consequences in terms of how we view ourselves and are in life. A fixed identity may be an illusion, as we saw in Chapter 6, but 'identity thinking' is a persistent reality. It is a conception of the unthinkable or impossible, *a representation of the unimaginable*. This representation leans toward what Freud called 'boundary representation' (see Chapter 11), or an 'edge representation', a representation over and at the edge of our human world of imagination.

Thus, we end up with the paradox that our desire for selflessness coincides with the orientation toward our most intimate self, a self that is a thing, *an in-itself yet also a self*. Conversely, our directedness toward the realization of our essential person culminates precisely in a depersonalization, the undermining of the self or it would do so if we did not timely recoil from an excess-of-being. On the way to that being, the subject may end up in a state *on the edge of* it and thus be under the illusion of approaching his so-called 'true self' or already experiencing something of it. Or an all-consuming 'event' caps the subject, as we saw in fascination and trauma, in a state that, even though self-destructive, nevertheless evokes something of the being for which desire is striving and thereby, in a bizarre way, also attracts us. The zone where the whole movement toward being, where the subject can only fully realize itself in its disappearance, halts or curdles, is precisely the edge of the human, the inhuman. It is the zone where *res cogitans* and *res extensa* largely overlap or permeate each other, their distinction about to disappear.

This twilight zone of the inhuman is the closest possible approach to self-realization as in-itself and, thus, the most extreme expression of essentially human striving. Consequently, the most intense experiences cannot be expressed in any other way than experiences in which we both found and lost ourselves more than ever, in which the most personal and the impersonal merge. We find ourselves simultaneously on the edge and in the middle of the human. The edge *is* the middle. To speak with Agamben (2016, p. 36), it is the area where the marginal and the core of the human are intertwined. That interiority takes us beyond ourselves.

The Freudian *death drive,* understood as the tendency of living, organic matter to pass into a lifeless, inorganic state (Freud 1920), is – applied to man – perhaps to be understood as the runaway desire-for-being, which does not stop and shoots over the edge. Insofar as the unrestrained and uninterested drive 'in-itself' does not allow itself to be bound, restrained or slowed down by demands of reality, the excitement of the drives of life or the interests of the ego, it results in destroying the self from within. We see such destruction of the self, for example, in some forms of psychosis. '*The goal of all life is death,* and going back into the past: *the lifeless was there before the living'* (Freud 1920, p. 196, italics by Freud). The death drive represents the tendency in life toward a return to that previous state of the lifeless.

As in Sartre, Freud also includes the term 'return', even though here, too, we must understand it not in a linear timeline but as an inherent dimension of existence. The death drive in Freud is not an end result of life; death does not appear only with the corpse. No, death is, from the beginning, a force that is part of life. Death is there from the beginning (cf. Moyaert 2014, pp. 17ff., 78–79). This is reminiscent of Blanchot's reflections on the corpse, with which he verges on the phenomenal (see also Chapter 8). The corpse shows the utter impersonality that has always been there in the individual. The corpse is the appearance of the hitherto unknown 'original'. It is its mere thing-like *being, something pre-human that belongs to the core of the human* (see Blanchot 1997b; Vande Veire 1997b). The corpse is also the *raw material* of the human being. We could also formulate it this way: it is an in-itself that has always been part of, or better, has always been hidden behind the for-itself of the living person, a remnant-of-being that only appears in full daylight with the corpse. Thus, we can conceive of this terminus of the death drive as an in-itself, beyond the for-itself, beyond any self.

The peripheral phenomena we discussed in this book are then states in which, just before reaching the terminus of self-destruction, the movement of the deadly desire-for-being freezes and becomes one and all inertia. As a result of a kind of inner emergency brake, the for-itself that does not want to give up after all, the raging train is brought to a halt at the last moment. It is the psychic, the subjective, that comes to a halt (cf. Thys 2008a). The imminent disappearance at that point of the distinction between the – almost but not quite left behind – living and the – almost but not quite reached – lifeless we saw illustrated in the *Unheimliche* (cf. Freud 1919, p. 106), which is akin to the fascinating and is a manifestation of the twilight zone of the inhuman. We encountered the uncanny uncertainty about whether something is alive or inanimate in previous chapters with automata and robots.

In a Sartrian way, we could say that uncertainty concerns the distinction between in-itself and for-itself. These are the states in which language and meaning fall away, the moments of speechlessness and meaninglessness, where the representational threatens to implode into pure presence. These are always palpable and therefore frightening or at least confusing approaches, threats, but not fully realized, attractions not accomplished. The self-discharge – as in excessive projective identification from Chapter 2 – is excessive but not total.

Like a *deus ex machina*, as in Greek tragedy, the complete catastrophe is averted after all, but without its existential threat disappearing altogether. The machinic god, the god as an automaton, prevents – at a moment when things are already terribly bad – the worst, averts the total destruction but at the same time makes its threat felt extra. In terms of the eleventh chapter, the endless openness of the for-itself congeals into an automatism that already evokes something of the in-itself without, however, leaving behind any hermeneutics. A small-minded *ghost* in a grand machine, as we saw in the context of psychic automatism. Beyond its menacing character, however, this subject-minimum is equally the moment when out of the void, thanks to the void, a new creative eruption can take place, albeit perhaps another tragedy. Think of the hopping little child who eagerly approaches language and unsuspectingly enters the world of imagination, not yet aware of the limits it will encounter. Sometimes, we can still give the horror of transformation into pure automata, as Bergson demonstrated, a grotesque or comic twist. Laughing at the gods is salvation; the ancient Greeks, with their anthropomorphisms of the inhabitants of Olympus, were masters at that, too. Nothing is more human than the gods. In good Greek fashion, even now, the gods themselves are again seen as automatons, as in the 2018 exhibition *Autopia* by Bart Ramakers and Ben Stimulé. Thus, man and God, in their similar guise as automatons, come closer to each other.

It is precisely in the extremes of imagination that man exhausts himself – for example, in literature, film, visual art, science and religion – to seek and challenge the edge of the human and of the self. The evocation of excess, probing of the limits of the self, is a successful genre. Analogous to how psychopathology shows a magnification of the generally human, as psychoanalysis teaches us, the attraction of excess shows the generally human and underlying orientation toward self-destruction in all its glory. This glory, however, is at the same time more akin to *past* glory. It is the paradoxical glory of the – almost unfolding – transience. Think, for example, of the wax figures of Berlinde De Bruyckere, to which I already referred in Chapter 10: they are creatures in which we seem to recognize human figures, in which the human seems to emerge hesitantly and at the same time is almost about to disappear again. Precisely in their capacity as peripheral figures, bizarrely combining their near disintegration with an unmistakable solidity, they evoke something of the essentially human. They endure in their tottering. That essence is of the order of destructibility, best expressed in the zones of creation and decay. That's what makes the wax quasi-humans so fascinating, much more fascinating than if they had reached full maturity.

When we speak of 'the essential', we are also referring to the so-called 'true'. With the expression 'the true nature' of someone, we refer to his actual, essential being, which is always of the order of the hidden, of what does not simply reveal itself. It refers to who someone is 'basically'. What shows itself as such may also be true in the ordinary sense of the word but does not have that status of 'the true'. Heidegger characterized truth as that which is extracted from hiddenness (Heidegger 1998, p. 284). In this sense, truth initially always takes the form of something strange that appears unexpectedly, which we do not immediately recognize but still have to acknowledge, such as the appearance in psychoanalytic therapy of an unconscious truth. Such unknowable truth is akin to the *Unheimliche* as 'that which should have remained secret, in the hidden and yet emerged', as Freud, referring to Schelling, says (Freud 1919, p. 97, see also p. 114). It is an *event*.

Truth, therefore, does not immediately allow itself to fit into the familiar and the known. Truth is – yes, like the unconscious – inappropriate. It always sounds like a foreign language, to quote Portocarero (1989, p. 149). Precisely because it is so true, the revelation of the truth is accompanied by a moment of alienation or desubjectivation, in which the subject momentarily disowns itself. It is stripped, stripped of its symbolic foundations. A moment or phase of 'aphanisis of the symbolic function', as Baudrillard (2002a, p. 51) calls it, occurs. Afterward, at best, the subject will regain itself, gather itself together, pick up the thread of self and possibly give the new element a place in the collage of the familiar narrative of the regained self.

The subject as ruin

The self is ultimately also a narrative itself, a construction resulting from the combination of bodily-driven facts and social interactions with the environment. This construction, on the one hand – albeit with snags – usually forms one whole anyway, but on the other hand, it is in danger of disintegrating precisely in moments of confrontation with truth. Precisely, the experiences of truth, on the edge of the self, show the fragility of the self as a whole. That whole, that beautifully coherent and consistent-looking narrative of the self, is an illusion. On the frayed edge, in the inhuman, the fragments that the self continually tries to glue together into a whole show themselves, just as the manifest dream narrative brings together and assembles the loose dream thoughts. This gathering or assembly – and this is precisely the connecting and meaning-generating symbolization – always remains precarious and never reaches a final stability. When chunks fall, as in trauma, war or a psychotic breakdown, the seemingly beautiful whole collapses and we see again how things really are. Then, the ruin baffles us. I say 'again' because the debris is older than the whole, as Freud argued that the inanimate is older than the living.

What results from the catastrophic revelation is the visibility or palpability of the debris, but not the ruin of the subject. The post-catastrophe debris merely makes visible the long-standing, original debris. Everything begins with the ruin, had already begun with the pieces not yet made into a whole and sewn or bricked together. The afterward erected beautiful building, the assembled man, is only a secondary construction or amalgamation of the fragments. Truth is not a beautiful whole, not a streamlined narrative. Truth is always shattering, revealing the crumbled. Think of Bion's 'no coherence'. The pieces remain and are stronger than the whole. The pieces remain, even as they disintegrate. More precisely, in their disintegration, they reveal themselves as the pieces they are.

The true nature of the subject – although mostly invisible – is a ruin, a heap of fragments whose accumulation or crisscrossing evokes a possible earlier or later whole. The ruin of the subject automatically evokes the image of the reunion of the fragments, of the undoing of *the diaspora of the subject*. The whole and the parts are at odds and evoke each other: the parts tend toward healing and the whole tends toward division. The subject never gets rid of its diasporic dimension: it remains a collection of 'partial self-objects' (fragments) that belong together but never produce a seamless whole. The appearance of this true nature can give rise to restoration and monument conservation, where psychoanalysis and psychotherapy have a role to play.

The ruined subject is like an imaginative archaeological site, a corpse. Were the WTC towers not the most impressive WTC towers in their collapse on 9/11? And didn't the glory of Syria's Palmyra, City of a Thousand Pillars, stand out most in its destruction in 2015–2016? In decay, glory reveals itself. In destruction, the essential(s) reveals itself. We saw in Chapter 8 how precisely in her (self)destruction the figure of Antigone is transformed into a grand and impressive appearance. In her dying, she is born. Downfall and revelation, disappearance and apparition, merge.

In his essay 'Constructions in Analysis', Freud (1937b) uses the metaphor of archaeology to describe the psychoanalytic work aimed at getting in touch with unconscious truth. There, too, most of it is hidden from view and is 'in the ground'. Almost 60 years later, psychoanalyst Bion says in his Sâo Paolo seminars: 'When we observe a patient, we actually see a living archaeological specimen of an ancient civilization' (Bion 1994, p. 151). Thus, we are back to the order of the archaic mentioned in Chapter 11, the prehistoric and pre-personal inspiration of every representation and meaning that continues to inspire all of life and whose unfathomable 'primordial memory' we carry with us. We can speak of a 'paleontology of the mind'. The archaic or prerepresentative concerns the so-called 'real unconscious', not the unconscious of repression, whose very symbolism is overloaded with meaning. It leans toward Sartrian remembering-of-being and remnant-of-being.

In the clinical examples in Chapter 2, we saw how the confrontation with a painful truth about oneself can be experienced by the patient as self-destructive and send him into a turbulent storm against which he defends himself with all his might by freezing every psychic dynamic. This truth is threatening because it is (still) meaningless but anything but insignificant. The patient recognizes something of himself that is nevertheless, at the same time totally new, something strange that poses itself as something familiar. The subjective truth glories, like a true metamorphosis, and the subject closes in a mental *lockdown*. But from that moment, there is also room for the dawn of change, for a *creatio ex ruina*. Only reluctantly can the new material that this event throws before it be integrated and inserted into the narrative of the self and consequently take on meaning.

Bion speaks of *catastrophic change* in this context. Any substantial change in a social structure, a group or a patient in psychoanalysis is accompanied by a violent and subversive reversal that cannot initially be *contained*. 'Catastrophic', Bion calls (as he was whispering Badiou), is 'an event producing a subversion of the order or system of things; it is catastrophic in the sense that it is sudden and violent in an almost physical way' (Bion 1965, p. 8). The distinction between the psychic and the purely physical becomes – again – blurred. At the devastating revelation of an aspect of its true nature, the gloriously battered, dissolving subject – like a Polynices – lies shattered, no longer able to hide its fundamental division. It would like to crawl – back – into the ground of shame and be buried honorably. In the containing confines of a grave, it can still hold itself together a little.

Heidegger says somewhere that man himself is a catastrophe, and this is because he turns away from his being. After all, he denies what is most peculiar to him, in particular, the strangeness that lies within him and the abyss of his finitude (see De Schutter 2014, p. 10). But does not this 'turning away' from one's being also belong precisely to the being of man? Incidentally, insofar as the Greek *katastrophè* (verb: *katastrephein*) means turning, reversing, in addition to destroying, and we understand reversing to mean 'to leave no stone unturned' – to employ the analogy with archaeology once again – it is also about investigating, discovering. In this, we want to get to the bottom of things.

In this book, I wanted to show that the catastrophic edge of the human at the abyss of our finitude disgusts, impresses, intrigues and attracts us, full of fear from the indestructible desire-for-being that we are. That which can only catch us unexpectedly, like an 'overwhelming-of-being', evokes something of what we are so expectantly focused on. Therefore, the threat it poses is, at the same time, intriguing. Thus, at the end of this book about the unimaginable, we have arrived at our own death as the ultimate of the unimaginable, the ultimate catastrophe, where our corporeal remains, our remnant-of-being, reveal themselves and lie in state. Precisely because it is unimaginable, but, at the same time, we know that it is there, yes, throughout our entire lives and that we can expect it with certainty (in this sense, 'expectant'), we as frontier seekers are also inevitably focused on it. Our own death is the most fascinating event of human life, on the edge of it and in the middle of it.

Bibliography

(Of the editions in original Dutch and those I consulted in Dutch translation, the Dutch titles – of articles, books and journals – are listed, supplemented by their English translation in square brackets).

Adkins, L. & Adkins, R.A. (2005). *Handbook to life in ancient Greece*. New York: Facts.

Adorno, T. (1955). *Kulturkritik und Gesellschaft. Prismen*. Berlin: Suhrkamp Verlag.

Adorno, T. (1987). Aantekeningen bij Kafka [Notes on Kafka]. In: W. Benjamin, M. Blanchot, M. Robert, & J. Starobinski (eds.), *Proces-verbaal van Franz Kafka* [*Proceedings of Franz Kafka*] (pp. 52–84). Nijmegen: Sun.

Adorno, T. (2012). Tweemaal Chaplin [Twice Chaplin]. In: *Zonder richtlijn. Parva aesthetica* [*Without a directive. Parva aesthetica*] (pp. 82–86) (transl. M. Wildschut). Amsterdam: Octavo.

Agamben, G. (2007a). Infancy and history: An essay on the destruction of experience. In: *Infancy and history: An essay on the destruction of experience* (transl. L. Heron) (pp. 13–72). London: Verso.

Agamben, G. (2007b). Notes on gesture. In: *Infancy and history: The destruction of experience* (transl. L. Heron) (pp. 147–156). London: Verso.

Agamben, G. (2016). *Avontuur* [*Adventure*] (transl. W. Hemelrijk). Amsterdam: Sjibbolet.

Agamben, G. (2018). *Wat overblijft van Auschwitz. De getuige en het archief* [*What remains of Auschwitz: The witness and the archive*] (Homo sacer III) (transl. W. Hemelrijk). Hilversum: Verbum.

Agamben, G. (2019). *Idee van proza* [*Idea of prose*] (transl. I. van der Burg). Amsterdam: Boom.

Alloa, E. (2014). Het lichaam verbinden [Connecting the body]. In: A. Mengoni, E. Alloa, G. Carrion-Murayari, J.M. Coetzee, C. Lamarche, A. Mengoni, & P. Van Cauteren (eds.), *Berlinde De Bruyckere* (pp. 201–213). Brussels: Mercatorfonds.

Ansarmet, F. & Magistretti, P. (2007). *Biology of freedom: Neural plasticity, experience and the unconscious*. New York: Other Press.

Anzieu, D. (1974). *Le Moi-peau*. Paris: Dunod.

Anzieu, D. (1989). Becket and Bion. *International Review of Psycho-Analysis*, *16*, pp. 163–168.

Ariès, P. (1987). *Het uur van onze dood. Duizend jaar sterven, begraven, rouwen en gedenken* [*The hour of our death: A thousand years of dying, burial, mourning and remembrance*]. Amsterdam: Elsevier.

Ariès, P. (2003). *Het beeld van de dood* [*The image of death*]. Nijmegen: Sun.

Ash, T.G. (2010). Privacy? Niks privacy! [Privacy? Nothing privacy!]. *The Standaard*, October 10, p. 46.

Aulagnier, P. (1981). Du langage pictural au langage de l'interprète. *Topique: Revue freudienne*, *26*, pp. 29–54.

Baas, B. (1992). *Le désir pur. Parcours philosophiques dans les parages de J. Lacan*. Louvain: Peeters.

Badiou, A. (1988). *L'Être et l'Événement*. Paris: Le Seuil.

Baeyens, F. (2004). *De ongrijpbaarheid der dingen. Over de vervlechting van taal en waarneming bij M Merleau-Ponty* [*The intangibility of things: On the intertwining of language and perception in M. Merleau-Ponty*]. Louvain: University Press.

Bakhtin, M. (2009). *Rabelais and his world*. Bloomington: Indiana University Press.

Bartels, J. (1993). *De geschiedenis van het subject. Decartes, Spinoza, Kant* [*The history of the subject: Descartes, Spinoza, Kant*]. Kampen: Kok Agora.

Baudrillard, J. (2002a). *De vitale illusie* [*The vital illusion*] (transl. M. Doude van Troostwijk). Kampen: Klement.

Baudrillard, J. (2002b). *De fatale strategieën* [*The fatal strategies*] (transl. M. Nio & K. Vollemans). Amsterdam: Thousand & One.

Bazan, A. (2010). Betekenaars in hersenweefsel. Bijdrage tot een fysiologie van het onbewuste [Signifiers in brain tissue: Contribution to a physiology of the unconscious]. In: M. Kinet & A. Bazan (eds.), *Psychoanalyse en neurowetenschap. De geest in de machine* [*Psychoanalysis and neuroscience: The ghost in the machine*] (pp. 29–57). Antwerp: Garant.

Beckett, S. (1962). *Gelukkige dagen. Een toneelstuk in twee bedrijven* [*Happy days: A play in two acts*] (transl. J. Van Velde). Amsterdam: De Bezige Bij.

Bergson, H. (1920). *Het lachen. Studie over de betekenis van het komische* [*Laughter: Study on the meaning of the comic*] (transl. A. Moresco). Amsterdam: E.M. Querido.

Bion, W.R. (1956). Development of schizophrenic thought. In: *Second thoughts: Selected papers on psycho-analysis* (pp. 36–42). London: Maresfield Library.

Bion, W.R. (1957). Differentiation of the psychotic from the non-psychotic personalities. In: *Second thoughts: Selected papers on psych-analysis* (pp. 43–64). London: Maresfield Library.

Bion, W.R. (1958). On hallucination. In: *Second thoughts: Selected papers on psycho-analysis* (pp. 65–85). London: Maresfield Library.

Bion, W.R. (1959). Attacks on linking. In: *Second thoughts: Selected papers on psycho-analysis* (pp. 93–109). London: Maresfield Library.

Bion, W.R. (1961). *Experiences in groups and other papers*. London: Tavistock Publications.

Bion, W.R. (1962). *Learning from experience*. London: Maresfield Library.

Bion, W.R. (1965). *Transformations*. London: Maresfield Library.

Bion, W.R. (1970). *Attention & interpretation*. London: Maresfield Library.

Bion, W.R. (1974). *Brazilian lectures*. Río de Janeiro: Imago Editora.

Bion, W.R. (1977). *Two papers: The grid and caesura*. London: Karnac.

Bion, W.R. (1981). *A memoire of the future*. London: Karnac Books.

Bion, W.R. (1987). Four papers. In: *Clinical seminars and other works* (pp. 293–331). London: Karnac Books.

Bion, W.R. (1992). *Cogitations*. London: Karnac Books.

Bion, W.R. (1994). *Clinical seminars and other work*. London: Karnac Books.

Bion, W.R. (2005). *The Italian seminars*. London: Karnac Books.

Bistoen, G. (2024). Traumaherstel zonder methodisch houvast [Trauma recovery without methodical support]. In W. Kusters (ed.), *Trauma en waarheid: Als taal tekortschiet* [*Trauma and truth: When language fails*] (pp. 99–117). Leusden: ISVW Editors.

Blanchot, M. (1969). Le rapport du troisième genre. In: *L'Entretien infini* (pp. 94–105). Paris: Gallimard.

Blanchot, M. (1971). *Le livre à venir. Coll. 'Idées'*. Paris: Gallimard.

Blanchot, M. (1980). *L'Ecriture du désastre*. Paris: Gallimard.

Blanchot, M. (1997a). Het Buiten, de Nacht [The outside, the night]. In: A. Schulte Nordholt, L. ten Kate, & F. Vande Veire (eds.), *Het wakende woord. Literatuur, ethiek en politiek bij Maurice Blanchot* [*The waking word: Literature, ethics and politics in Maurice Blanchot*] (transl. P.I. Huigsloot) (pp. 47–56). Nijmegen: Sun.

Blanchot, M. (1997b). De twee versies van het denkbeeldige [The two versions of the imaginary]. In: A. Schulte Nordholt, L. ten Kate, & F. Vande Veire (eds.), *Het wakende woord. Literatuur, ethiek en politiek bij Maurice Blanchot* [*The waking word: Literature, ethics and politics in Maurice Blanchot*] (transl. P.I. Hoogsluit & J.J. Oskamp) (pp. 7–68). Nijmegen: Sun.

Blanchot, M. (2012). Atheïsme en schriftuur. Humanisme als schreeuw [Atheism and scripture: Humanism as a cry] (transl. L. ten Kate). In: A. Cools (ed.), *De stem en het schrift. Drie opstellen over de esthetishe distantie in de vertelling, het humanisme en de boekcultuur* [*The voice and writing: Three essays on aesthetic distance in narrative, humanism and the future of book culture*] (pp. 35–65). Zoetermeer: Klement.

Bloch, M. & Parry, J. (eds.). (1982). *Death and the regeneration of life*. Cambridge: Cambridge University Press.

Bollas, C. (2018). *Meaning and melancholia: Life in the stage of bewilderment*. London: Routledge.

Breeur, R. (2002). *Vrijheid en bewustzijn. Essays over Decartes, Bergson en Sartre* [*Freedom and consciousness: Essays on Descartes, Bergson and Sartre*]. Louvain: Peeters.

Breeur, R. (2018). Zoek het verschil. Gilles Deleuze over de differentie [Find the difference: Gilles Deleuze on difference]. *Tijdschrift voor Filosofie* [*Journal of Philosophy*], *80*, pp. 467–488.

Brod, M. (1967). *Franz Kafka – Een biografie* [*Franz Kafka: A biography*]. Amsterdam: De Arbeiderspers.

Busch, F. (2018). Searching for the analyst's reveries. *International Journal of Psychoanalysis*, *99*, pp. 569–589.

Cambien, J. (1988). Fantasie in het werk van Melanie Klein [Fantasy in the work of Melanie Klein]. *Tijdschrift voor Psychotherapie* [*Journal of Psychotherapy*], *14*, pp. 258–268.

Carrion-Murayari, G. (2014). Pijn een vorm geven [Shaping pain]. In: A. Mengoni, E. Alloa, G. Carrion-Murayari, J.M. Coetzee, C. Lamarche, A. Mengoni, & P. Van Cauteren (eds.), *Berlinde De Bruyckere* (pp. 141–148). Brussels: Mercatorfonds.

Coebergh, P.H. & Cohen, E. (2009). *Grenzen aan transparantie* [*Limits to transparency*]. Amsterdam: Business Contact.

Cools, A. (2012). Inleiding [Introduction]. In: A. Cools (ed.), *De stem en het schrift. Drie opstellen over de esthetishe distantie in de vertelling, het humanisme en de toekomst van de boekcultuur* [*The voice and writing: Three essays on aesthetic distance in narrative, humanism and the future of book culture*] (pp. 7–19). Zoetermeer: Klement/Pelckmans.

Dart, R. (1974). The waterworn Australopithecine pebble of many faces from Makapansgat. *South African Journal of Science*, *70*, p. 167.

De Boer, T. (1988). Voorwoord [Preface]. In: E. Levinas (ed.), *Van het zijn naar de zijnde* [*From existing to existence*] (pp. 7–14). Baarn: Ambo.

De Cauter, L. (1995). *Archeologie van de kick. Verhalen over moderniteit en ervaring* [*Archaeology of kick: Stories of modernity and experience*]. Amsterdam: De Balie.

De Kesel, M. (1998). *Wij modernen: Essays over subject en moderniteit* [*We moderns: Essays on subject & modernity*]. Louvain: Peeters.

De Kesel, M. (2002). *Eros en ethiek. Een lectuur van Jaques Lacans Seminarie VII* [*Eros & Ethics: A reading of Jacques Lacan's Séminaire VII*]. Louvain: Acco.

De Kesel, M. (2012a). *Žižek*. Amsterdam: Boom.

De Kesel, M. (2012b). *Auschwitz mon amour. Over Shoah, fictie en liefde* [*Auschwitz mon amour: On Shoah, fiction and love*]. Amsterdam: Boom.

De Kesel, M. (2015). De ethiek van een mooi nee. Lacans interpretatie van Antigone [The ethics of a beautiful no. Lacan's interpretation of Antigone]. In: M. De Kesel & B. Schomakers (eds.), *De schoonheid van het nee: Essays over Antigone* [*The beauty of the no. Essays on Antigone*]. Amsterdam: Sjibbolet.

De Kesel, M. (2017). *Zelfloos. De mystieke afgrond van het moderne Ik* [*Selfless: The mystical abyss of the modern I*]. Utrecht: Kok.

De La Mettrie, J.O. (1978). *De mens een machine* [*Man a machine*] (transl. H.W. Bakx). Amsterdam: Boom.

De Preester, H. & Slatman, J. (2010). Lichamelijke integriteit. Lichaamsmodel, lichaamsbeeld en identificatie [Bodily integrity: Body model, body image and identification]. In: M. Kinet & A. Bazan (eds.), *Psychoanalyse en neurowetenschap. De geest in de machine* [*Psychoanalysis and neuroscience: The ghost in the machine*] (pp. 189–214). Antwerp: Garant.

De Schutter, D. (2014). *Het catastrofale. Essay over de eindigheid* [*The catastrophic: Essay on finitude*]. Zoetermeer: Klement.

De Sterck, M. (1998). En het woord werd vlees. Inwijdingsrituelen en -verhalen [And the word became flesh: Initiation rites and stories]. In: N. Vliegen & P. Meurs (eds.), *Het voorjaarsontwaken. De adolescentie in psychodynamische theorie en therapie* [*The spring awakening: Adolescence in psychodynamic theory and therapy*] (pp. 99–114). Louvain: Garant.

De Sterck, M. (2020). *Demonen. Volksverhalen* [*Demons: Folk tales*]. Kalmthout: Polis.

De Visscher, J. (1991). Levinas: Esthetica, expressie en kunst [Levinas: Aesthetics, expression and art]. In: H. Bleijendaal, J. Goud, & E. van Hove (eds.), *Emmanuel Levinas over psyche, kunst en moraal* [*Emmanuel Levinas on psyche, art and morality*] (pp. 57–71). Baarn: Ambo.

De Visscher, J. (2011). *Het groteske. Verschijningvormen en betekenissen van menselijke excentriciteit* [*The grotesque: Appearances and meanings of human eccentricity*]. Zoetermeer: Klement/Pelckmans.

Deben-Mager, M. & Verheugt-Pleiter, A. (2004). Enkele toepassingen van de gehechtheidstheorie op de psychoanalytische praktijk [Some applications of attachment theory to psychoanalytic practice]. *Tijdschrift voor Psychoanalyse* [*Journal of Psychoanalysis*], *10*, pp. 18–30.

Defoe, D. (1995). *Robinson crusoe*. Stansted: Wordsworth Editions.

Deleuze, G. (1990). *The logic of sense* (transl. M. Lester). London: Bloomsbury.

D'Errico, F. & Nowell, A. (2000). A new look at the Berekhat Ram figurine: Implications for the origin of symbolism. *Cambridge Archaeological Journal*, *10*, pp. 123–167.

Descartes, R. (2002). *Over de methode* [*On the method*] (transl. T. Verbeeck). Amsterdam: Boom.

Devisch, R. (2003). Maleficent fetishes and the sensual order of the uncanny in southwest Congo. In: B. Kapferer (ed.), *Beyond rationalism: Rethinking magic, witchcraft and sorcery* (pp. 175–197). New York: Berghahn.

Devisch, R. (2006). Feeling and borderlinking in Yaka healing arts. In: R. Littlewood (ed.), *On knowing and not knowing in the anthropologies of medicine*. London: University College of London Press.

Devisch, R. (2017). *Body and affect in the intercultural encounter*. Bamenda: Langaa Research and Publishing Common Initiative Group.

Diamond, N. (2013). *Between skins: The body in psychoanalysis – Contemporary developments*. Malden: John Wiley & Sons.

Dolto, F. (1984). *L'image inconsciente du corps*. Paris: Seuil.

Dufrenne, M. (1953). *Phénoménologie de l'expérience esthétique (deux tomes)*. Paris: Presses universitaires de France.

Dulaure, J. (1974). *Les divinités génératrices*. Verviers: Marabout.

Dumoulin, C. (2015). *De psychoanalyse, een therapie?* [*Psychoanalysis, a therapy?*]. Ghent: Idesça.

Dussart, F. (2000). *The politics of ritual in an aboriginal settlement: Kinship, gender and the currency of knowledge*. Wahington: Smithsonian Institution Press.

Eilenberger, W. (2018). *Het tijdperk van de tovenaars. Het grote decennium van de filosofie, 1919–1929* [*The age of wizards: The great decade of philosophy, 1919–1929*] (transl. W. Hansen). Amsterdam: De Bezige Bij.

Enquist, P.O. (2002). *De vijfde winter van de magnetiseur* [*The fifth winter of the magnetizer*] (transl. C. Polet). Amsterdam: Ambo.

Enquist, P.O. (2004). *Kapitein nemo's bibliotheek* [*Captain Nemo's library*] (transl. C. Polet). Amsterdam: Ambo.

Ferrari, A. (2004). *From the eclipse of the body to the down of thought.* London: Free Association Books.

Ferro, A. (2006). *Mind works: Technique and creativity in psychoanalysis.* Hove: Routledge.

Feuth, T. (2020). *Kafka is dood* [*Kafka is dead*]. Amsterdam: De Arbeiderspers.

Florini, A. & Stiglitz, J.E. (2007). *The right to know: Transparency for an open world.* New York: Columbia University Press.

Fonagy, P., Jurist, E.L., & Gergely, G. (2006). *Affect regulation, mentalization, and the development of the self.* London: Karnac.

Foucault, M. (1984). *De wil tot weten. Geschiedenis van de seksualiteit I* [*The will to know: History of sexuality I*] (transl. J. Holierhoek). Nijmegen: Sun.

Foucault, M. (2011). *De moed tot waarheid* [*The courage of truth*] (transl I. van der Burg). Amsterdam: Boom.

Freud, S. (1888). Hysteria. *Works, 1*, pp. 46–64.

Freud, S. (1900). The dream interpretation. *Works, 2*, pp. 22–582.

Freud, S. (1901). On the dream. *Works, 3*, pp. 11–54.

Freud, S. (1904). Freud's psychoanalytic method. *Works, 3*, pp. 21–326.

Freud, S. (1905a). The joke and its relation to the unconscious. *Works, 3*, pp. 346–556.

Freud, S. (1905b). Three essays on the theory of sexuality. *Works, 4*, pp. 15–116.

Freud, S. (1905c). Fragment from the analysis of a case of hysteria ['Dora']. *Works, 4*, pp. 124–225.

Freud, S. (1906). The role of sexuality in the etiology of neuroses. *Works, 4*, pp. 228–236.

Freud, S. (1910a). On psychoanalysis: Five lectures. *Works, 5*, pp. 157–199.

Freud, S. (1910b). The future chances of psychoanalytic therapy. *Works, 5*, pp. 278–287.

Freud, S. (1910c). A childhood memory of Leonardo da Vinci. *Works, 5*, pp. 206–275.

Freud, S. (1910d). The psychogenic visual disturbance according to psychoanalytic standpoint. *Works, 5*, pp. 313–319.

Freud, S. (1911). Formulations on the two principles in mental functioning. *Works, 5*, pp. 332–339.

Freud, S. (1912). Masturbation. Medical clinic and guide. *Works, 5*, pp. 506–515.

Freud, S. (1913a). Further recommendations on the technique of psychoanalysis (I) on beginning the treatment. *Works, 6*, pp. 186–205.

Freud, S. (1913b). The interest in psychoanalysis. *Works, 6*, pp. 256–279.

Freud, S. (1914a). Introducing narcissism. *Works, 6*, pp. 329–355.

Freud, S. (1914b). Michelangelo's Moses. *Works, 6*, pp. 297–325.

Freud, S. (1915a). Further recommendations on the technique of psychoanalysis (III): Observations on transference love. *Works, 6*, pp. 436–447.

Freud, S. (1915b). Reflections on war and death. *Works, 6*, pp. 450–473.

Freud, S. (1915c). Instincts and there vicissitudes. *Works, 7*, pp. 23–44.

Freud, S. (1915d). The unconscious. *Works, 7*, pp. 65–112.

Freud, S. (1916/1917). Mourning and melancholy. *Works, 7*, pp. 133–148.

Freud, S. (1919). The uncanny. *Works, 8*, pp. 92–125.

Freud, S. (1920). Beyond the pleasure principle. *Works, 8*, pp. 165–218.

Freud, S. (1921). Mass psychology and analysis of the ego. *Works, 8*, pp. 227–292.

Freud, S. (1923a). 'Psychoanalysis' and 'Libido theory'. *Works, 8*, pp. 349–370.

Freud, S. (1923b). The ego and the id. *Works, 8*, pp. 380–420.

Freud, S. (1924). A short account of psychoanalysis. *Works, 9*, pp. 50–67.

Freud, S. (1925). Self-portrait. *Works, 9*, pp. 78–134.

Freud, S. (1926). Inhibition, symptom and anxiety. *Works, 9*, pp. 196–271.

Freud, S. (1927). Fetishism. *Works, 9*, pp. 419–424.

Freud, S. (1930). Civilization and its discontents. *Works*, *9*, pp. 461–532.

Freud, S. (1933). Lectures introduction to psychoanalysis: New series. *Works*, *10*, pp. 79–232.

Freud, S. (1937a). Analysis terminable and interminable. *Works*, *10*, pp. 270–305.

Freud, S. (1937b). Constructions in analysis. *Works*, *10*, pp. 308–319.

Freud, S. (1940a). Outlines of psychoanalysis. *Works*, *10*, pp. 446–503.

Freud, S. (1940b). Some elementary lessons in psychoanalysis. *Works*, *10*, pp. 506–511.

Freud, S. (1950 [1895]). Design of a scientific psychology. *Works*, *1*, pp. 322–407.

Freud, S. (1955 [1907–1908]). Original notes on the 'Rat Man'. *Works*, *4*, pp. 88–152.

Freud, S. (1985 [1887–1904]). Manuscripts A-N (from correspondence with Wilhelm Fliess). *Works*, *1*, pp. 248–307.

Freud, S. (2006). *Werken* (11 delen) [*Works* (11 volumes)]. Edited by W. Oranje. Amsterdam: Boom.

Freud, S. & Breuer, J. (1893/1895). Studies on hysteria. *Works*, *1*, pp. 438–702.

Fung, A., Graham, M., & Weil, D. (2007). *Full disclosure: The perils and promise of transparency*. Cambridge: Cambridge University Press.

Garnett, D. (1967 [1922]). *Mijn vos, mijn vrouw . . . [My fox, my wife . . .]*. Amsterdam: Van Ditmar.

Geiger, A. (2019). *Onder de Drachenwand [Under the Drachenwand]* (transl. W. Hansen). Amsterdam: De Bezige Bij.

Geldhof, A. (2014). *De namen van het genot. Lacan over jouissance en psychose [The names of pleasure. Lacan on jouissance and psychosis]*. Louvain: Acco.

Geyskens, T. (2007). Tussen fallische façade en discrete euforie – Freud over voorlust in Drei Abhandlungen en Der Witz [Between phallic façade and discrete euphoria: Freud on forepleasure in Drei Abhandlungen and Der Witz]. In: P. Vanden Berghe (ed.), *De gedoemde mens? Psychoanalyse, tragedie en tragiek [The doomed man? Psychoanalysis, tragedy and tragic]* (pp. 95–110). Antwerp: Garant.

Geyskens, T. & Van Haute, P. (2003). *Van doodsdrift tot hechtingstheorie. Het primaat van het kind bij Freud, Klein en Hermann [From death drive to attachment theory: The primacy of the child with Freud, Klein & Hermann]*. Amsterdam: Boom.

Girard, R. (1994). *God en geweld: Over de oorsprong van mens en cultuur [God and violence: On the origins of man and culture]* (transl. M. Perquy). Tielt: Lannoo.

Gomperts, W. (2006a). Herkenning en verschil. Vijf jaar psychoanalytische therapie bij migranten en vluchtelingen [Recognition and difference: Five years of psychoanalytic therapy with migrants and refugees]. In: W. Gomperts & G. Veen (eds.), *Migratie in psychoanalyse: Over psychoanalytische behandelingen van migranten en vluchtelingen [Migration in psychoanalysis: On psychoanalytic treatments of migrants and refugees]* (pp. 30–52). Assen: Van Gorcum.

Gomperts, W. (2006b). De intrapsychische samenleving [The intrapsychic society]. *Tijdschrift voor Psychoanalyse [Journal of Psychoanalysis]*, *12*, pp. 117–125.

Gomperts, W. (2008). De verdubbeling van de wereld. Weerstand in de therapie bij tweedegeneratie migratiegerelateerde identiteitsproblematiek [Doubling the world: Resistance in therapy in second-generation migration-related identity problems]. *Tijdschrift voor Psychoanalyse [Journal of Psychoanalysis]*, *14*, pp. 83–96.

Gotman, K. (2007). Hysteria never looked so good. *Performing Arts Journal*, *29*, pp. 66–73.

Groot, G. (2005). Ramkoers: Antigone tegenover Kreon [Collision course: Antigone versus Kreon]. In: P. Vanden Berghe, W. Lemmens, & J. Taels (eds.), *Tragisch. Over tragedie en ethiek in de 21ste eeuw [Tragic: On tragedy and ethics in the 21st century]* (pp. 17–41). Budel: Damon.

Guiot, S. (2018). Oor hebben voor het archaïsche in de kliniek van de neurose [Having an ear for the archaic in the clinic of neurosis]. *Belgische school voor psychoanalyse: 2018/2019 [Belgian school of psychoanalysis: 2018/2019]*, pp. 176–196.

Handke, P. (1972). Kaspar. In: *Theater I* (transl. K. Muller) (pp. 111–198). Utrecht: Bruna and Zn.

Haverhals, B. (2018). Een inleiding tot het archaïsche [An introduction to the archaic]. *Belgische School voor Psychoanalyse: 2018/2019* [*Belgian School of Psychoanalysis: 2018/2019*], pp. 156–175.

Haverhals, B. (2020). Tussen chaos en orde: de dynamiek van het archaïsche [Between chaos and order: The dynamics of the archaic]. *Tijdschrift voor Psychoanalyse & haar toepassingen* [*Journal of Psychoanalysis & Its Applications*], *26*, pp. 32–42.

Hebbrecht, M. (2010). *De droom. Verkenning van een grensgebied* [*The dream: Exploration of a borderland*]. Utrecht: De Tijdstroom.

Hebbrecht, M. (2014). Authenticiteit: Een psychoanalytische benadering [Authenticity: A psychoanalytic approach]. *Tijdschrift voor Psychotherapie* [*Journal of Psychotherapy*], *40*, pp. 184–196.

Heidegger, M. (1996). *De oorsprong van het kunstwerk* [*The origin of the work of art*] (transl. M. Wildschut & C. Bremmers). Amsterdam: Boom.

Heidegger, M. (1998). *Zijn en tijd* [*Being and time*] (transl. M. Wildschut). Nijmegen: Sun/Kritak.

Henriques, A. (2007). *Corporate truth: The limits to transparency*. London: Earthscan Publications Ltd.

Hertmans, S. (1999). *Het bedenkelijke. Over het obscene in de cultuur* [*The questionable: On the obscene in culture*]. Amsterdam: Boom.

Hertmans, S. (2000). *Mind the gap*. Amsterdam: Meulenhoff.

Hertmans, S. (2007). *Het zwijgen van de tragedie. Essays* [*The silence of tragedy: Essays*]. Amsterdam: De Bezige Bij.

Hinshelwood, R.D. (1991). *A dictionnary of Kleinian thought*. London: Free Association Books.

Holowchak, M.A. (2012). When Freud (almost) met Chaplin: The science behind Freuds' especially simple, transparent case. *Perspectives on Science, 20*, pp. 44–74.

Hurvich, M. (2003). The place of annihilation anxieties in psychoanalytic theory. *Journal of American Psychoanalysis Association, 51*, pp. 579–616.

Husserl, E. (1952 [1912]). *Ideeën zu einer reinen phänomenologie und phänomenolgischen philosophie, Zweites Buch*. The Hague: Martinus Nijhoff.

Huygens, I. (2009). Cinema. In: E. Romein, M. Schuilenburg, & S. van Tuinen (eds.), *Deleuze compendium* (pp. 313–327). Amsterdam: Boom.

Isaacs, S. (1952). The nature and function of phantasia. In: M. Klein, P.H. Melanie, & S. Isaacs (eds.), *Developments in psycho-analysis*. London: Hogarth Press.

Janvier, A. (2019). Voire une première fois, ou expérimenter sa proper *naissance*. Herzog, Kaspar Hauser, Deleuze. *Journal of Philosophy, 81*, pp. 151–182.

Juranville, A. (2000). *Figures de la possession. Actualité psychanalytique du démoniaque*. Grenoble: Presses Universitaires de Grenoble.

Kafka, F. (1980 [1915]). De gedaanteverwisseling [The metamorphosis]. In: *Verzameld Werk* [*Collected works*] (pp. 676–720). Amsterdam: Querido.

Kant, I. (1978 [1790]). *Over schoonheid. Ontledingsleer van het schone* [*On beauty: Decomposition theory of beauty*] (transl. J. De Visscher). Amsterdam: Boom.

Kayser, W. (1981). *The Grotesque in art and literature*. New York: Columbia University Press.

Kinet, M. (2008). *De wetenschap van de liefde en de kunst van de computeranalyse. Essays* [*The science of love and the art of computer analysis: Essays*]. Antwerp: Garant.

Kinet, M. (2010). Van neuronen en neurosen. fMRI van de ziel [On neurons and neuroses: fMRI of the soul]. In: M. Kinet & A. Bazan (eds.), *Psychoanalyse en neurowetenschap. De geest in de machine* [*Psychoanalysis and neuroscience: The ghost in the machine*] (pp. 79–110). Antwerp: Garant.

Klein, M. (1927). Criminal tendencies in normal children. In: *Love, guilt and reparation and other works 1921–1945* (pp. 170–185). London: Virago.

Klein, M. (1936). Weaning. In: *Love, guilt, reparation and other works 1921–1945* (pp. 290–305). London: Virago.

Klein, M. (1945). The oedipus complex in the light of early anxieties. In: *Love, guilt, reparation and other works 1921–1945* (pp. 370–419). London: Virago.

Klein, M. (1946). Notes on some schizoid mechanisms. In: *Envy and gratitude and other works 1946–1963* (pp. 1–24). London: Virago.

Klein, M. (1948). On the theory of anxiety and guilt. In: *Envy and gratitude and other works 1946–1963* (pp. 25–42). London: Virago.

Klein, M. (1952). Some theoretical conclusions regarding the emotional life of the Infant. In: *Envy and gratitude and other works 1946–1963* (pp. 61–93). London: Virago.

Klein, M. (1955). On identification. In: *Envy and gratitude and other works 1946–1963* (pp. 141–175). London: Virago.

Klein, M. (1957). Envy and gratitude. In: *Envy and gratitude and other works 1946–1963* (pp. 176–235). London: Virago.

Klein, M. (1958). On the development of mental functioning. In: *Envy and gratitude and other works 1946–1963* (pp. 236–246). London: Virago.

Klein, M. (1959). Our adult world and its roots in infancy. In: *Envy and gratitude and other works 1946–1963* (pp. 247–263). London: Virago.

Klein, M. (1963). On the sense of loneliness. In: *Envy and gratitude and other works 1946–1963* (pp. 300–313). London: Virago.

Kohut, H. (1971). *The analysis of the self.* New York: International Universities Press.

Kristeva, J. (2001). *Melanie Klein.* New York: Columbia University Press.

Krtolica, M. (2018). *The embodiment of the unconscious, hysteria, surrealism, and tanztheater.* Temple University Libraries.

Lacan, J. (1966a). Le stade du miroir comme formateur de la fonction du Je. In: *Écrits* (pp. 93–100). Paris: Éditions du Seuil.

Lacan, J. (1966b). Fonction et champ de la parole et du langage en psychanalyse. In: *Écrits* (pp. 237–322). Paris: Éditions du Seuil.

Lacan, J. (1966c). Variantes de la cure-type. In: *Écrits* (pp. 323–362). Paris: Éditions du Seuil.

Lacan, J. (1966d). Subversion du sujet et dialectique du désir dans l'inconscient freudien. In: *Écrits* (pp. 793–827). Paris: Éditions du Seuil.

Lacan, J. (1971). Situation de la psychanalyse et formation de psychanalyste en 1956. In: *Écrits II* (pp. 9–40). Paris: Éditions du Seuil.

Lacan, J. (1973). *Le Séminaire Livre XI: Les quatres concepts fondamentaux de la psychanalyse.* Paris: Éditions du Seuil.

Lacan, J. (1975). *Le Séminaire Livre XX: Encore.* Paris: Éditions du Seuil.

Lacan, J. (1978). *Le Séminaire Livre II: Le Moi dans la théorie de Freud et dans la technique de la psychanalyse.* Paris: Éditions du Seuil.

Lacan, J. (1985). Conférence à Geneva sur le symptôme. *Le Bloc-Notes de la Psychanalyse*, pp. 5–23.

Lacan, J. (1986). *Le Séminaire. Livre VII: L'éthique de la psychanalyse.* Paris: Éditions du Seuil.

Lacan, J. (1994). *Le Séminaire. Livre IV: La relation d'objet.* Paris: Éditions du Seuil.

Lacan, J. (2001). Joyce le Symptôme. In: *Autres Écrits* (pp. 565–570). Paris: Éditions du Seuil.

Lacan, J. (2004). *Le Séminaire, Livre X, L'angoisse.* Paris: Éditions du Seuil.

Ladan, A. (2010). *Het vanzelfzwijgende. Over psychoanalyse, desillusie en dood* [*The self-effacing: On psychoanalysis, disillusionment and death*]. Amsterdam: Boom.

Leader, D. (2012). *De Mona Lisa stelen. Wat kunst ons doet maar niet laat zien* [*Stealing the Mona Lisa: What art does but doesn't show us*] (transl. P. Van Bortel & H. Bloemen). Kalmthout: Pelckmans/Klement.

Levi, P. (2007). *Is dit een mens* [*Is this a human being*] (transl. F. De Matteis-Vogels). Amsterdam: Meulenhoff.

Levinas, E. (1988). *Van het zijn naar de zijnde* [*From being to the beings*] (transl. A. Kalshoven). Baarn: Ambo.

Levinas, E. (1990). *De werkelijkheid en haar schaduw* [*Reality and its shadow*] (transl. J. De Visscher). Kampen: Kok Agora.

Levine, H., Reed, G., & Scarfone, D. (eds.). (2013). *Unrepresented states and the construction of meaning*. London: Karnac.

Levine, P.A. (2007). *De tijger ontwaakt. Traumabehandeling met lichaamsgerichte therapie* [*The tiger awakens: Trauma treatment with body-oriented therapy*]. Haarlem: Gottmer Publishing Group.

Leysen, M. (2013). De eclips van het lichaam. Het neobioniaanse model Van Ferrari [The eclipse of the body. Ferrari's neo-Bionian model]. *Tijdschrift voor Psychoanalyse* [*Journal of Psychoanalysis*], *19*, pp. 155–166.

Libbrecht, K. (2001). Body. In: H. Glowinski, Z.M. Marks, & S. Murphy (eds.), *A compendium of lacanian terms* (pp. 33–37). London: Free Association Books.

Libbrecht, K. (2008). Fantasma. In: H. Stroeken (ed.), *Psychoanalytisch woordenboek* [*Psychoanalytic dictionary*] (p. 73). Amsterdam: Boom.

López-Corvo, R.E. (2003). *The dictionary of the work of W.R. Bion*. London: Karnac.

Lord, K.M. (2007). *The perils and promise of global transparency: Why the information revolution may not lead to security, democracy or peace*. New York: State University of New York Press.

Lyotard, J.-F. (2013). Anima minima. *Tijdschrift voor Filosofie* [*Journal of Philosophy*], anniversary issue, pp. 197–209.

Lysy, A. (2009). Het raadsel van het lichaam [The riddle of the body]. *iNWiT 5*, pp. 191–199.

Mattelaer, J. (2000). *De fallus in kunst en cultuur* [*The phallus in art and culture*]. Kortrijk: Groeninghe.

McEwan, I. (2019). *Machines zoals ik* [*Machines like me*] (transl. R. Verhoef). Amsterdam: De Harmonie.

Meltzer, D. (1981). The Kleinian expansion of Freudian metapsychology. *International Journal of Psycho-Analysis*, *62*, pp. 177–185.

Meltzer, D. (1983). *Dream-life*. Perth: Clunie.

Mengoni, A. (2014). Herinneringen aan het onvoorstelbare: schuld vereffenen, de leegte een teken geven [Remembering the unimaginable: settling debt, giving the void a sign]. In: A. Mengoni, E. Alloa, G. Carrion-Murayari, J.M. Coetzee, C. Lamarche, A. Mengoni, & P. Van Cauteren (eds.), *Berlinde De Bruyckere* (pp. 57–67). Brussels: Mercatorfonds.

Merleau-Ponty, M. (1993). *Le visible et l'invisible, suivi de notes de travail*. Paris: Gallimard.

Merleau-Ponty, M. (1997). *Fenomenologie van de waarneming* [*Phenomenology of perception*] (transl. R. Vlasblom & D. Tiemersma). Amsterdam: Ambo.

Mertens, E. (2013). Fascinatie en hypochondrie. Blik op de Wolvenman [Fascination and hypochondria: View on the Wolfman]. *sKRIPta*, *24*, pp. 45–63.

Michiels, I. (1958). *Journal brut: Ikjes sprokkelen* [*Journal brut: Gathering little I's*]. Antwerp: Development.

Miller, I. (2013). *Beckett and Bion: The (im)patient voice in psychotherapy and literature*. London: Karnac.

Miller, J.-A. (2009). Lacaniaanse biologie en lichaamsevenement [Lacanian biology and body event] (transl. H. Van Hoorde). In: *iNWiT 5*, pp. 41–140.

Modell, A. (1993). *The private self*. Cambridge: Harvard University Press.

Mooij, A. (1975). *Taal en verlangen. Lacans theorie van de psychoanalyse* [*Language and desire: Lacan's theory of psychoanalysis*]. Meppel: Boom.

Mooij, A. (2002). *Psychoanalytisch gedachtegoed. Een modern perspectief* [*Psychoanalytic thinking: A modern perspective*]. Amsterdam: Boom.

Moyaert, P. (1994). *Ethiek en sublimatie. Over de ethiek van de psychoanalyse van Jacques Lacan* [*Ethics and sublimation: On Jacques Lacan's The ethics of psychoanalysis*]. Nijmegen: Sun.

Moyaert, P. (2012). Seksualiteit is niet te integreren. Hoe Freud over de 'conditio humana' nadenkt [Sexuality cannot be integrated. How Freud thinks about the 'conditio humana']. *Filosofie* [*Philosophy*], *22*, pp. 2–14.

Moyaert, P. (2014). *Opboksen tegen het inerte. De doodsdrift bij Freud* [*Standing up to the inert: The death drive in Freud*]. Nijmegen: Vantilt.

Moyaert, P. (2019). *Hoe schizofrenie zich redt. Deleuze en Guattari in discussie met de psychoanalyse* [*How schizophrenia saves itself: Deleuze and Guattari in discussion with psychoanalysis*]. Nijmegen: Vantilt.

Mulder, E. (2011). *De Sirenen zwegen. Psychoanalyse, mythe en kunst* [*The Sirens were silent: Psychoanalysis, myth and art*]. Amsterdam: Sjibbolet.

Musil, R. (1996). *De man zonder eigenschappen* [*The man without qualities*]. Amsterdam: Meulenhoff.

Nicolai, N. (1997). Geen woorden maar daden: Over het schuldige lichaam [Not words but deeds: On the guilty body]. In: A. Ladan (ed.), *Ons vege lijf: Psychoanalytische visies* [*Our weak body: Psychoanalytic visions*] (pp. 84–100). Amsterdam: Boom.

Nietzsche, F. (1992). *Herwaardering van alle waarden* [*Revaluation of all values*]. Meppel: Boom.

Nietzsche, F. (2000). *Menselijk, al te menselijk. Een boek voor vrije geesten* [*Human, all too human: A book for free spirits*]. Amsterdam: De Arbeiderspers.

Nietzsche, F. (2006). *De geboorte van de tragedie* [*The birth of tragedy*]. Amsterdam: De Arbeiderspers.

Oegema, J. (2003). *Een vreemd geluk. De publieke religie rond Auschwitz* [*A strange happiness: Public religion around Auschwitz*]. Amsterdam: Balans.

Ogden, P., Minton, K., & Pain, C. (2006). *Trauma and the body: A sensorimotor approach to psychotherapy*. New York: W.W. Norton & Company

Ogden, T. (1994). *Subjects of analysis*. Northvale: Aronson.

Otto, R. (2002). *Het heilige. Een beschouwing over het irrationele in de idee van het goddelijke en de verhouding ervan tot het rationele* [*The sacred: A consideration of the irrational in the idea of the divine and its relation to the rational*]. Amsterdam: The Apple Blossom Press.

Poirier, S. (2005). *A world of relationships: Itineraries, dreams, and events in the Australian Western Desert*. Toronto: University of Toronto Press.

Portocarero, H. (1989). *De goudzoeksters. Een fotoroman* [*The gold diggers: A picture novel*]. Antwerp: Manteau.

Ramachandran, V.S. & Blakeslee, S. (1999). *Phantoms in the brain*. London: Fourth Estate.

Renner, R.G. (1990). *Edward Hopper 1882–1967: Transformations of the real*. Hedel: Librero.

Ricoeur, P. (1970). *Freud and philosophy: An essay on interpretation*. New Haven: Yale University Press.

Ricoeur, P. (1990). *Soi-même comme un autre*. Paris: Editions du Seuil.

Root, D. (1998). *Cannibal culture: Art, appropriation and the commodification of difference*. Toronto: Westview Press.

Rudden, M.G. (2011). The 'secret cocoon': Fantasies about the private self in the absence of consensual reality. *International Journal of Psychoanalysis*, *92*, pp. 359–376.

Sacks, O. (2000). *De man die zijn vrouw voor een hoed hield* [*The man who mistook his wife for a hat*]. Amsterdam: Meulenhoff.

Saks, E.R. (1999). *Interpreting interpretation: The limits of hermeneutic psychoanalysis*. New Haven: Yale University Press.

Sartre, J.-P. (1981). *Magie en emotie. Schets van een theorie van de gemoedsbewegingen* [*Magic and emotion: Sketch of a theory of the emotions*] (transl. M.L. Tas & H.L. Bouman). Amsterdam: Boom.

Sartre, J.-P. (1986). *Het imaginaire. Fenomenologische psychologie van de verbeelding* [*The imaginary: Phenomenological psychology of the imagination*] (transl. J.H. Mulder-Van Haaster & A.J. Kerkhof). Meppel: Boom.

Sartre, J.-P. (1988). *Het Ik is een ding. Schets ener fenomenologische beschrijving* [*The transcendence of the ego: Sketch of a phenomenological description*] (transl. F. Montens & L. Fretz). Meppel: Boom.

Sartre, J.-P. (1999). *Walging* [*Nausea*] (transl. M. Kaas). Amsterdam: Singel Pockets.

Sartre, J.-P. (2003). *Het zijn en het niet. Proeve van een fenomenologische ontologie* [*Being and nothingness: Prove of a phenomenological ontology*] (transl. F. de Haan). Rotterdam: Lemniscaat.

Schokker, J. & Schokker, T. (2000). *Extimiteit. Jacques Lacans terugkeer naar Freud* [*Extimacy: Jacques Lacan's return to Freud*]. Amsterdam: Boom.

Schulte Nordholt, A. (1991). De kunstervaring en het 'il y a': Levinas en Blanchot [The art experience and the 'il y a': Levinas and Blanchot]. In: H. Bleijendaal, J. Goud & E. van Hove (eds.), *Emmanuel Levinas over psyche, kunst en moraal* [*Emmanuel Levinas on psyche, art and morality*] (pp. 89–107). Baarn: Ambo.

Schulte Nordholt, A. (1997). Het schuwe denken: Inleiding [Timid thinking: Introduction]. In: A. Schulte Nordholt, L. ten Kate, & F. Vande Veire (eds.), *Het wakende woord. Literatuur, ethiek en politiek bij Maurice Blanchot* [*The waking word: Literature, ethics and politics in Maurice Blanchot*] (pp. 11–43). Nijmegen: Sun.

Schulte Nordholt, A. (2012). De narratieve stem en het discours van de moderniteit [The narrative voice and the discourse of modernity]. In: A. Cools (ed.), *De stem en het schrift. Drie opstellen over de esthetische distantie in de vertelling, het humanisme en de toekomst van de boekcultuur* [*The voice and writing: Three essays on aesthetic distance in narrative, humanism and the future of book culture*] (pp. 87–104). Zoetermeer: Klement.

Sels, N. (2013). De artistieke ontdubbeling. Over het kunstwerk als locus van zelfcreatie en -destructie [The artistic de-duplication: On the artwork as locus of self-creation and destruction]. In: M. Kinet, M. De Kesel & S. Houppermans (eds.), *For your pleasure? Psychoanalyse en esthetisch genot* [*For your pleasure? Psychoanalysis and aesthetic enjoyment*] (pp. 15–31). Antwerp: Garant.

Shelley, M. (1994). *Het monster van Frankenstein* [*Frankenstein's monster*] (transl. E. High). S.l.: Contact.

Slatman, J. (2007). Grenzen aan het vreemde [Limits to the strange]. *Wijsgerig perspectief* [*Philosophical Perspective*], *47*, pp. 6–16.

Sophocles. (2006). *The oedipus trilogy* (transl. F. Storr). London: Echo Library.

Sophocles. (2015). *Antigone* (transl. B. Schomakers). Zoetermeer: Klement.

Spillius, E. & O'Shaughnessy, E. (eds.). (2012). *Projective identification: The fate of a concept*. London: Routledge.

Spinoza, B. (1979). *Ethica* [*Ethics*] (transl. and annotation N. Van Suchtelen). Amsterdam: Wereldbibliotheek.

Steiner, G. (1984). *Antigones: The antigone myth in western literature, arts and thought*. Oxford: Oxford University Press.

Steiner, J. (1993). *Psychic retreats: Pathological organizations in psychotic, neurotic and borderline patients*. London: Routledge.

Stern, D. (1993). L'Enveloppe prénarrative: Vers une unité fondamentale d'expérience permettant d'explorer la réalité psychique du bébé. *Journal de la psychanalyse de l'enfant*, *14*, pp. 13–65.

Symington, J. & Symington, N. (1996). *The clinical thinking of Wilfred Bion*. London: Routledge.

Teeuwen, L. (2019). Ontsnapt aan het verhaal [Escaped from the story]. *De Standaard*, November 22, pp. L8–L9.

Thys, M. (1993). Van mimesis tot deconstructie. Het metafysisch statuut van de psychoanalytische duiding [From mimesis to deconstruction: The metaphysical status of psychoanalytic interpretation]. *Psychoanalyse* [*Psychoanalysis*], *9*, pp. 179–200.

Thys, M. (1995a). Het fascinerende object: een poging tot analyse [The fascinating object: An attempt at analysis]. *Tijdschrift voor Psychoanalyse* [*Journal of Psychoanalysis*], *1*, pp. 23–35.

Thys, M. (1995b). De fascinatie voor incest [The fascination with incest]. In: M. Thys & R. Vermote (eds.), *Trauma en taboe: Psychoanalytische beschouwingen over incest* [*Trauma and taboo: Psychoanalytic reflections on incest*] (pp. 85–116). Louvain: Garant.

Thys, M. (1998). Het 'sujet trouvé'. Interpreteren en subjectiviteit [The 'sujet trouvé': Interpretation and subjectivity]. *Psychoanalyse* [*Psychoanalysis*], *12*, pp. 153–167.

Thys, M. (1999). De intieme afstandelijkheid van het subject [The intimate detachment of the subject]. *Tijdschrift voor Psychoanalyse* [*Journal of Psychoanalysis*], *5*, pp. 5–15.

Thys, M. (2000). Tussen moeder en aarde. Verlating en dood in de psychoanalyse [Between mother and earth: Abandonment and death in psychoanalysis]. In: A. Boerwinkel & W. Heuves (eds.), *De kunst van het verliezen. Over verlating en verlatenheid* [*The art of losing: On abandonment and desolation*] (pp. 53–68). Amsterdam: Boom.

Thys, M. (2006a). Beter worden van waarheid [Getting better from truth]. *Tijdschrift voor Psychoanalyse* [*Journal of Psychoanalysis*], *12*, pp. 68–74.

Thys, M. (2006b). *Fascinatie. Een fenomenologisch-psychoanalytische verkenning van het onmenselijke* [*Fascination: A phenomenological-psychoanalytic exploration of the inhuman*]. Amsterdam: Boom.

Thys, M. (2007). De analytische sofa: een procrustesbed? Over het tragische subject in psychoanalyse [The analytic sofa: A bed of Procrustes? On the tragic subject in psychoanalysis]. In: P. Vanden Berghe (ed.), *De gedoemde mens? Psychoanalyse, tragedie en tragiek* [*The doomed human being? Psychoanalysis, tragedy and tragedy*] (pp. 53–70). Antwerp: Garant.

Thys, M. (2008a). De gestilde psyche: Over fascinatie, trauma en doodsdrift [The stilled psyche: On fascination, trauma and death drive]. *Tijdschrift voor Psychoanalyse* [*Journal of Psychoanalysis*], *14*, pp. 5–17.

Thys, M. (2008b). Fenomenologie van de fascinatie. Een dialoog met Sartre [Phenomenology of fascination: A dialogue with Sartre]. *Tijdschrift voor Filosofie* [*Journal of Philosophy*], *70*, pp. 339–371.

Thys, M. (2009). Psyche en cultuur. Transculturele psychoanalyse tussen pathologisering en culturalisering [Psyche and culture: Transcultural psychoanalysis between pathologizing and culturalizing]. In: M. Thys & W. Gomperts (eds.), *Vergezichten. Over transculturele psychoanalyse* [*Vistas: On transcultural psychoanalysis*] (pp. 249–295). Antwerp: Garant.

Thys, M. (2010). Psychoanalyse als klinische fenomenologie [Psychoanalysis as clinical phenomenology]. *Tijdschrift voor Psychoanalyse* [*Journal of Psychoanalysis*], *16*, pp. 149–162.

Thys, M. (2013). Het kunstwerk als fascinerend object [The work of art as a fascinating object]. In: M. Kinet, M. De Kesel, & S. Houppermans (eds.), *For your pleasure? Psychoanalyse over esthetisch genot* [*For your pleasure? Psychoanalysis on aesthetic enjoyment*] (pp. 141–165). Antwerp: Garant.

Thys, M. (2014a). De fascinatie voor trauma. Over het onmenselijke en het zijnsverlangen in de psychoanalyse [The fascination with trauma: On the inhuman and the desire-for-being in psychoanalysis]. *Tijdschrift voor Pychoanalyse* [*Journal of Psychoanalysis*], *20*, pp. 4–16.

Thys, M. (2014b). Ik is een ding. Over de fascinatie voor trauma [I is a thing: On the fascination with trauma]. In: L. Philippe & M. Hebbrecht (eds.), *Van verdringen tot vergeten. Een psychoanalytische herwerking van het geheugen* [*From repressing to forgetting: A psychoanalytic reworking of memory*] (pp. 193–209). Antwerp: Garant.

Thys, M. (2015a). Projectieve identificatie tussen doodsdrift en intersubjectiviteit. Een conceptuele kritiek [Projective identification between death drive and intersubjectivity:

A conceptual critique]. *Tijdschrift voor Psychoanalyse* [*Journal of Psychoanalysis*], *21*, pp. 83–97.

Thys, M. (2015b). Dysincarnatie. Over het psychoanalytische lichaam [Dysincarnation: On the psychoanalytic body]. In: M. Kinet, K. Vuylsteke Vanfleteren, & S. Houppermans (eds.), *Als het lichaam spreekt* [*When the body speaks*] (pp. 45–69). Antwerp: Garant.

Thys, M. (2017). On fascination and fear of annihilation. *International Journal of Psychoanalysis*, *98*, pp. 633–655.

Thys, M. (2024). Waarheidsmonsters: Over desubjectivering in trauma en catastrofale verandering [Monsters of truth: On desubjectivation in trauma and catastrophic change]. In W. Kusters (ed.), *Trauma en waarheid: Als taal tekortschiet* [*Trauma and truth: When language fails*] (pp. 69–88). Leusden: ISVW Editers.

Tindemans, K. (1991). Het risico en de rede. Ajax en Antigone [Risk and reason: Ajax and Antigone]. In: *Sophocles, Ajax/Antigone* (pp. VII–XIII). Amsterdam: International Theatre & Film Books.

Tustin, F. (1980). Autistic objects. *International Revue of Psychoanalysis*, *7*, pp. 27–40.

Van Camp, J. (2020). Het affect [The affect]. *Belgische school voor psychoanalyse* [*Belgian school of psychoanalysis*], 2020/2021, pp. 104–145.

Van Coillie, F. (2004). *De ongenode gast. Zes psychoanalytische essays over het verlangen en de dood* [*The uninvited guest: Six psychoanalytic essays on desire and death*]. Amsterdam: Boom.

Van de Vijver, G. (2010). Begrenzing en kritiek. Over de mogelijkheid van een verhouding tussen psychoanalyse en (neuro)wetenschap [Limitation and critique: On the possibility of a relationship between psychoanalysis and (neuro)science]. In: M. Kinet & A. Bazan (eds.), *Psychoanalyse en neurowetenschap. De geest in de machine* [*Psychoanalysis and neuroscience: The ghost in the machine*] (pp. 215–228). Antwerp: Garant.

Van Der Speeten, G. (2018). Een kort maar (heel) heftig leven [A short but (very) intense life]. *De Standaard*, March 10.

Van der Zwaal, P. (1988). Verzwijgen en bekennen: de oorsprong van twee houdingen [Silence and confession: The origins of two attitudes]. In P.J.G. Mettrop, M.L. van Thiel, & E.M. Wiersema (eds.), *Schuld en schaamte. Psychoanalytische opstellen* [*Guilt and shame: Psychoanalytic essays*] (pp. 15–30). Meppel: Boom.

Van Emde Boas, C. (1966). *Obseniteit en pornografie anno 1966* [*Obscenity and pornography anno 1966*]. NVSH: The Hague.

Van Gael, M. (2012). Betekenaars van vlees en bloed. Psychodynamische perspectieven op begrijpen en behandelen van zelfverwondend gedrag [Signifiers of flesh and blood: Psychodynamic perspectives on understanding and treating self-injurious behavior]. In: M. Kinet (ed.), *Zelfverwonding. Psychodynamiek en psychotherapie* [*Self-injury: Psychodynamics and psychotherapy*] (pp. 33–55). Antwerp: Garant.

Van Haute, P. (1989). *Psychoanalyse en filosofie. Het imaginaire en het symbolische in het werk van Jacques Lacan* [*Psychoanalysis and philosophy: The imaginary and the symbolic in the work of Jacques Lacan*]. Louvain: Peeters.

Van Haute, P. (1996). Dood en sublimatie in Lacans interpretatie van Antigone [Death and sublimation in Lacan's interpretation of Antigone]. In: N. Kok & K. Nuijten (eds.), *In dialoog met Lacan. Psychoanalytische, filosofische en literatuurtheoretische beschouwingen* [*In dialogue with Lacan: Psychoanalytic, philosophical and literary-theoretical reflections*] (pp. 121–140). Amsterdam: Boom.

Van Haute, P. (1997). De psychoanalyticus en zijn beroepsgeheim [The psychoanalyst and his professional secrecy]. *Tijdschrift voor psychoanalyse* [*Journal of Psychoanalysis*], *3*, pp. 22–29.

Van Haute, P. (2000). *Tegen de aanpassing. Lacans 'ondermijning' van het subject* [*Against adaptation: Lacan's 'subversion' of the subject*]. Nijmegen: Sun.

Van Haute, P. (2005). Lacan leest Klein: Symbolisering en de ontwikkeling van het Ik [Lacan reads Klein: Symbolization and the development of the ego]. In: M. Kinet & R. Vermote (eds.), *Mentalisatie* [*Mentalization*] (pp. 55–67). Antwerp: Garant.

Van Haute, P. & Geyskens, T. (2002). *Het primaat van de seksualiteit bij Freud, Ferenczi en Laplanche* [*The primacy of sexuality with Freud, Ferenczi and Laplanche*]. Nijmegen: Sun.

Van Hove, J. (1993). Klassieke schilder van modern Amerika. Hopper-tentoonstelling mist topstukken [Classic painter of modern America: Hopper exhibition in Brussels lacks masterpieces]. *De Standaard*, February 27.

Van Poucke, D. (1997). Waken bij de afwezigheid van betekenis. Over Blanchots oerscène en de vernedering van het vergeten [Waking up to the absence of meaning: On Blanchot's primal scene and the humiliation of forgetting]. In: A. Schulte Nordholt, L. ten Kate, & F. Vande Veire (eds.), *Het wakende woord. Literatuur, ethiek en politiek bij Maurice Blanchot* [*The waking word: Literature, ethics and politics in Maurice Blanchot*] (pp. 163–183). Nijmegen: Sun.

Van Reusel, W. (1999). *Leven of dood. Over moeilijke grenzen* [*Life or death: On difficult boundaries*]. Louvain: Davidsfonds.

Vande Veire, F. (1997a). Fotografie tussen verveling en fascinatie. Over Antonioni's Blow up [Photography between boredom and fascination: On Antonioni's Blow up]. In: *De geplooide voorstelling. Essays over kunst* [*The pleated representation: Essays on art*] (pp. 15–22). Brussels: Y. Gevaert.

Vande Veire, F. (1997b). De imaginaire bevreemding [The imaginary alienation]. In: A. Schulte Nordholt, L. ten Kate, & F. Vande Veire (eds.), *Het wakende woord. Literatuur, ethiek en politiek bij Maurice Blanchot* [*The waking word: Literature, ethics and politics with Maurice Blanchot*] (pp. 69–88). Nijmegen: Sun.

Vande Veire, F. (2005). *Neem en eet, dit is je lichaam. Fascinatie en intimidatie in de hedendaagse cultuur* [*Take and eat, this is your body: Fascination and intimidation in contemporary culture*]. Amsterdam: Sun.

Vande Veire, F. (2015). Tussen blinde fascinatie en vrijheid. Het mensbeeld van Slavoj Žižek [*Between blind fascination and freedom: The image of man of Slavoj Žižek*]. Nijmegen: Vantilt.

Vanden Berghe, P. (2004). Psychoanalyse en toneel. Freud en de tragische existentie [Psychoanalysis and drama: Freud and tragic existence]. In: A. De Block & P. Moyaert (eds.), *Oneigenlijk gebruik. De psychoanalyse voorbij haar grenzen* [*Inappropriate use: Psychoanalysis beyond its limits*] (pp. 68–86). Kapellen: Pelckmans.

Vanheule, S. (2013). *Psychose Anders bekeken. Over het werk van Jacques Lacan* [*Psychosis viewed differently: On the work of Jacques Lacan*]. Tielt: Lannoo Campus.

Vattimo, G. (1992). *De transparante samenleving* [*The transparent society*]. Amsterdam: Boom.

Vergote, A. (1988). Genezen door het woord? [Healing through the word?] In: A. Vergote & P. Moyaert (eds.), *Psychoanalyse. De mens en zijn lotgevallen* [*Psychoanalysis: Man and his fate*] (pp. 35–51). Kapellen: DNB/publisher Pelckmans.

Verhaeghe, P. (2010). Geestdrift voor het brein [Spirit for the brain]. In: M. Kinet & A. Bazan (eds.), *Psychoanalyse en neurowetenschap. De geest in de machine* [*Psychoanalysis and neuroscience: The ghost in the machine*] (pp. 59–77). Antwerp: Garant.

Vermote, R. (2010). De irrationele dimensie van de psychoanalyse [The irrational dimension of psychoanalysis]. *Tijdschrift voor Psychoanalyse* [*Journal of Psychoanalysis*], *16*, pp. 239–247.

Vermote, R. (2011). On the value of the 'late Bion' to analytic theory and practice. *International Journal of Psychoanalysis*, *92*, pp. 1089–1098.

Vermote, R. (2013). An undifferentiated zone of psychic functioning. *Bulletin of the European Federation of Psychoanalysis*, *13*, pp. 16–27.

Vermote, R. (2015). Een geïntegreerd psychoanalytisch model in het licht van enkele neurowetenschappelijke bevindingenl [An integrated psychoanalytic model in light of some neuroscientific findings]. *Tijdschrift voor Psychoanalyse* [*Journal of Psychoanalysis*], *21*, pp. 3–12.

Vermote, R. (2018). *Reading Bion*. London: Taylor & Francis.

Visker, R. (2005). *Vreemd gaan en vreemd blijven. Filosofie van de multiculturaliteit* [*Cheating and staying strange: Philosophy of multiculturalism*]. Amsterdam: Sun.

Visker, R. (2010). *Michel Foucault. Genealogie als kritiek* [*Michel Foucault: Genealogy as criticism*]. Nijmegen: Vantilt.

Von der Thüsen, J. (1997). *Het verlangen naar huivering. Over het sublieme, het wrede en het unheimliche* [*The desire for shuddering: On the sublime, the cruel and the uncanny*]. Amsterdam: Querido.

Von Feuerbach, A.R. (1990). Kaspar Hauser. Voorbeeld van een misdaad, gepleegd tegen de geestesvermogens of het zieleleven van een mens [Kaspar Hauser: Example of a crime committed against the mental faculties or soul life of a human being]. In: A.R. von Feuerbach, G.F. Daumer, & O. Von Pirch (eds.), *Kaspar hauser. Kind van Europa. Zijn leven, zijn opvoeding zoals waargenomen en beschreven door vier tijdgenoten* [*Kaspar Hauser. Child of Europe: His life, his upbringing as observed and described by four contemporaries*] (pp. 11–81). Amsterdam: Candide.

Westerink, H. (2019). *De lichamen en hun lusten. In het spoor van Foucaults Geschiedenis van de seksualiteit* [*Bodies and their lusts: In the wake of Foucault's History of sexuality*]. Nijmegen: Vantilt.

Winnicott, D.W. (1951). Transitional objects and transitional phenomena. In: D.W. Winnicott (ed.), *Collected papers: Through paediatrics to psycho-analysis*. London: Tavistock Publications.

Winnicott, D.W. (1960). Ego distortions in terms of true and false self. In: *The maturational processes and the facilitating environment* (pp. 140–152). New York: International Universities Press.

Winnicott, D.W. (1971). Playing: A theoretical statement. In: D.W. Winnicott (ed.), *Playing and reality* (pp. 44–61). London: Penguin Books.

Wittgenstein, L. (1998). *Tractatus logico-philosophicus* (transl. W.F. Hermans). Amsterdam: Athenaeum, Polak & van Gennep.

Zempleni, A. (1984). Possession et sacrifice. *Le Temps de la réflexion*, 5, p. 325.

Zempleni, A. (1985). Du dedans aux dehors: transformation de la possession-maladie en possession rituelle. *International Journal of Psychology*, 20, pp. 663–679.

Žižek, S. (1996). *Schuins beziend. Jacques Lacan geïntroduceerd vanuit de populaire cultuur* [*Looking awry: An introduction to Jacques Lacan through popular culture*]. Amsterdam: Boom.

Žižek, S. (2009). *Geweld. Zes zijdelingse bespiegelingen* [*Violence: Six sideways reflections*]. Amsterdam: Boom.

Žižek, S. (2015). *Event. Filosofie van de gebeurtenis* [*Event: Philosophy in transit*]. Amsterdam: Boom.

Žižek, S. (2016). *Antigone*. London: Bloomsbury.

Zwart, H. (2010). *De waarheid op de wand. Psychoanalyse van het weten* [*Truth on the wall: Psychoanalysis of knowing*]. Nijmegen: Vantilt.

Register of persons

Adkins, L. 138
Adkins, R. 138
Adorno, T. 61, 112, 191–192, 196, 202
Agamben, G. 188, 190–192, 194–195, 198, 207–208
Alloa, E. 183
Althamer, P. 92
Ansarmet, F. 74
Antonioni, M. 94, 126, 141
Anzieu, D. 68, 74, 185
Ariès, P. 135
Ash, T.G. 90–91
Augustine 82
Aulagnier, P. 73

Baas, B. 134
Bacon, F. 183
Badiou, A. 203, 212
Baeyens, F. 75
Bakhtin, M. 202
Bartels, J. 101
Baudrillard, J. 23, 92–95, 97–99, 140, 211
Bausch, P. 190
Bazan, A. 74
Beckett, S. 185, 188, 197
Bergson, H. 7, 199–201, 210
Bion, W. 2, 32–33, 39, 42–43, 46, 48, 54, 67, 70, 71–73, 75, 80–81, 97, 102, 109–112, 114–115, 159, 185–187, 192, 208, 211–212
Blakeslee, S. 76
Blanchot, M. 51, 62, 67, 74, 77, 100, 116, 122, 124–127, 130, 141, 146, 174, 198, 209
Bloch, M. 139
Bosch, H. 202
Breeur, R. 197, 207

For Product Safety Concerns and Information please contact our EU
representative GPSR@taylorandfrancis.com
Taylor & Francis Verlag GmbH, Kaufingerstraße 24, 80331 München, Germany

www.ingramcontent.com/pod-product-compliance
Lightning Source LLC
Chambersburg PA
CBHW050350270326
41926CB00016B/3679